Barcode in Back

W9-CZY-034

Staffing
the Contemporary
Organization

Staffing the Contemporary Organization

A GUIDE TO PLANNING, RECRUITING, AND SELECTING FOR HUMAN RESOURCE PROFESSIONALS

Third Edition

Donald L. Caruth, Gail D. Caruth, and Stephanie S. Pane

Westport, Connecticut
London

Library of Congress Cataloging-in-Publication Data

Caruth, Donald L.
  Staffing the contemporary organization : a guide to planning, recruiting, and selecting for human
  resource professionals / Donald L. Caruth, Gail D. Caruth, and Stephanie S. Pane. – 3rd ed.
    p. cm.
  Includes bibliographical references and index.
  ISBN 978–0–313–35614–8 (alk. paper) — ISBN 978–0–313–35670–4 ((pbk.) : alk. paper)
1. Personnel management. 2. Manpower planning. 3. Employees—Recruiting. 4. Employee
selection. I. Caruth, Gail D., 1954– II. Pane, Stephanie S., 1976– III. Title.
HF5549.C296   2009
658.3—dc22   2008032612

British Library Cataloguing in Publication Data is available.

Library of Congress Catalog Card Number: 2008032612
ISBN: 978–0–313–35614–8
      978–0–313–35670–4 (pbk.)

First published in 2009

Praeger Publishers, 88 Post Road West, Westport, CT 06881
An imprint of Greenwood Publishing Group, Inc.
www.praeger.com

Printed in the United States of America

The paper used in this book complies with the
Permanent Paper Standard issued by the National
Information Standards Organization (Z39.48-1984).

10 9 8 7 6 5 4 3 2 1

Dedications

To my coauthor, my consulting partner, my friend, my wife. . .
thanks for all you are.

DLC

To all of my former employers and consulting clients, past and present.
Thanks for the opportunities you have given me to learn and grow.
Thanks for all that you have taught me.

GDC

Thanks to my husband and family for supporting me in all that I do.

SSP

Contents

Contents

Figures and Tables

FIGURES

TABLES

Preface

Staffing any organization today is a challenging, complex endeavor. If anything, staffing is even more complex and challenging than when the first edition of this book appeared. Economic changes, demographic shifts, increased multiculturalism, heightened global competition, offshoring, outsourcing, organizational restructuring, expanded legislation, and a host of other factors suggest that staffing will be even more challenging in the years to come. As organizations enter a new millennium, it is readily apparent that the acquisition and utilization of human resources is as vital to continued organizational success as the advanced technology required to produce needed products and provide required services. Indeed, technology alone is insufficient since effective use of it depends upon people—the right kinds of people, in the right numbers, performing the right jobs, at the right times. Whether in the past, present, or future, it is *people*—the catalytic resource of any enterprise—that have, do, and will determine institutional success.

The uniqueness of this book is the integration of topics that are usually the subjects of separate treatment: human resource planning, legal aspects of staffing, recruiting, selecting, performance appraisal, career development, and so forth. It is our belief that the entire range of activities associated with planning for, obtaining, utilizing, and developing human resources must be viewed as an integrated system called *staffing*. We believe that unless staffing is conceived of as a system, or perhaps more accurately as a major subsystem of the entire human resource management process, activities performed in one area of staffing may negate activities performed in another area. While there are other books that purport to deal with staffing in general, we have found none that takes the encompassing systems view that we present to our readers.

This book is written as a working reference for human resource professionals, operating managers, educators, students, and others seeking practical guidance on staffing policies, procedures, techniques, problems, and issues. This book is based not only on thorough research, but also on our combined years of experience as managers, consultants, observers, students, and teachers of human resource management. Our main thrust is practicality—what has worked or will work for organizations—not obtuse scholarship.

This book also is written generically so that it can be used by practitioners in all institutions, from profit making to nonprofit, from manufacturing to service. It is also intended to be used as a text or supplement for college and university courses in human research management and staffing. Indeed, the first two editions of this book were used by a number of colleges and universities.

Many significant changes have occurred in human resource management since the first edition of this book appeared. These changes have further underscored the importance of staffing. First, new federal and state legislation has made human resource management more legalistic and complex. Additional legislation, such as the Employment Non-Discrimination Act, which would extend Title VII discrimination protection to gays and lesbians, looms on the horizon. There is a developing movement by some states to prohibit state-sponsored affirmative action programs. States are also altering their minimum wage laws, thereby making federal law in this area less important.

Second, additional decisions by the Supreme Court and the Circuit Courts have shed further light on the interpretations of various statutes. For example, *Gratz v. Bollinger* and *Ledbetter v. Goodyear Tire & Rubber Company* have given us a clearer understanding of the courts' position on affirmative action and discrimination charge filing deadline requirements, respectively.

Third, concerned with potential employer liability associated with providing references on former employees, many states have passed, and others are considering, reference-checking laws to exempt employers from liability when they provide reference information in good faith. These laws will make it easier for employers to obtain more and higher quality information about potential employees than is the case today.

Fourth, no one could have anticipated when the first edition of this book was published the plethora of employment law tort cases being filed today. Their burgeoning numbers are cause for concern that they possibly represent the new frontier in employment litigation.

Fifth, the strong and steady economic growth in the 1990s, which produced the lowest unemployment rate in over a decade, has been followed by a period of economic uncertainty. Rising fuel and food costs, job losses, outsourcing, and offshoring have generated a great deal of concern for the future of our economy. This uncertainty will have repercussions for human resource management in general and staffing in particular.

Sixth, global competition has necessitated downsizing, reengineering, rightsizing, fine-tuning, and other efforts to turn domestic corporations into leaner, more focused organizations. Additions to staff are increasingly made through the use of temporary workers or independent contractors rather than permanent employees because it is more cost effective to add staff in this manner.

Seventh, technology has had its effect on staffing, too. Through such devices as Internet recruiting, video conferencing interviews, computerized testing, and telephone interviews, even simple applications of technology have affected the manner in which staffing is accomplished. Moreover, the widespread use of technology across industry lines has intensified the competition for technically skilled individuals. In fact, technical recruiters are today some of the highest paid and most sought after of all human resource professionals.

Finally, in their quest for effective, efficient organizational management, corporations are increasingly holding the human resource management function accountable for producing results. Where human resource management cannot produce the desired results at reasonable cost, personnel functions are being outsourced or subcontracted to outside firms that can perform these services on a cost-effective basis. The emerging view seems to suggest that human resource management is coming to be viewed as a profit center that must justify its existence. Obviously, human resource management must be increasingly concerned with evaluating its performance and demonstrating its effectiveness to management.

All of the aforementioned developments and changes serve to reinforce the central theme of this book—that staffing is a complex endeavor that must be viewed as a system, a system affected by developments both inside and outside the organization itself. Staffing, it seems reasonable to state, has increased in importance since the first edition of this book was published. We expect its importance to grow even more in the years to come.

Any work such as this one depends upon the assistance, encouragement, cooperation, learning opportunities provided by, and inspiration of many people. While it is impossible to acknowledge everyone who, over the years, has had a hand in influencing us, teaching us, and shaping our thinking about human resources, we would especially like to express our appreciation to all of our students, colleagues, clients, and employers for the many human resource management challenges and experiences they have provided us.

A special debt of gratitude is owed to Mark Patton, who diligently researched hard-to-find sources, offered needed insights, and was available to share jelly beans and cookies when the going got tough. Special thanks also go to Cindy Summers for her hard work in researching various topics. Thanks also to Kayla Hanzelka for her contributions on employment interviewing.

We are also deeply indebted to our editor at Praeger Publishers, Jeff Olson, who saw the value in a third edition of *Staffing* and had the confidence to let us do it. Thanks, Jeff!

1

Staffing: An Overview

Broadly defined, staffing is the process of determining human resource needs in an organization and securing sufficient quantities of qualified people to fill those needs. Staffing is not, however, as simplistic an activity as that definition seems to imply. Staffing is actually a complex endeavor involving a number of diverse tasks, ranging from job analysis to performance appraisal, from employment interviewing to career development, from hiring to termination. Moreover, to execute properly the tasks of staffing, organizational members charged with this responsibility must be knowledgeable of the legal, psychological, and environmental contexts within which staffing occurs. The tasks that must be performed, coupled with the contexts in which they must be accomplished, make staffing a difficult and challenging activity in contemporary organizations.

The objective of the staffing process is to ensure that an organization continuously has the right quality and quantity of employees in the right place at the right time to perform successfully the work of the institution. As with the definition, the objective of staffing also appears to be simplistic, but achieving it effectively is no easy matter. The diverse tasks involved must be integrated with each other to create a process that runs smoothly and operates in a timely fashion, and these tasks must be coordinated harmoniously with the environments and contexts in which they take place.

Combining the broad definition of staffing with its objectives, we can now define staffing more specifically as the process through which an organization ensures that it has, on a continuous basis, the proper number of employees with the appropriate skills in the right jobs at the right times to achieve the organization's objectives.

Except in small organizations that do not have a human resource department, the responsibility for staffing is usually shared by line managers and human resource specialists. Human resource professionals develop programs to recruit qualified workers, but operating managers make the final decisions on hiring. Staffing specialists create the administrative procedures for such activities as promotions, demotions, transfers, layoffs, and the like, but line managers determine which employees will be promoted, demoted, and so on. Human resource professionals design the performance appraisal system, but line managers actually evaluate workers. Consequently, staffing is best viewed as a joint activity wherein human resource specialists contribute their knowledge, expertise, and counsel and line managers make the final decisions. Both groups must work together in coordinated fashion to ensure that the objective of staffing is fulfilled.

Effective staffing plays a crucial role in the short-run as well as the long-term performance, growth, vitality, and success of contemporary organizations. Indeed, it is only through effective staffing that any institution—regardless of size, industry, scope, or objectives—can remain viable.

IMPORTANCE OF STAFFING

The activities performed in the staffing process are important to enterprises of all types and sizes because of the relationship these tasks have to an organization's goals, the direct costs incurred, the indirect costs experienced, the organizational impacts created, and the legal aspects involved.

Organizational Goals

The most carefully formulated plans, the most logical organization structure, the most sophisticated marketing programs, and the most advanced automated manufacturing systems will not, of themselves, ensure an institution's success. Plans, structures, programs, and systems are not self-actuating; they can only be implemented, maintained, and realized through people. It is people—the most crucial of resources—that serve as the catalyst, the activating and energizing force, making possible the utilization of all other resources and enabling an organization to achieve its goals. Without qualified human resources available in the right numbers, at the right place, and at the right time, organizational goals and objectives will not be reached. Even in a completely computerized manufacturing plant, it is people who press the buttons, program the computers, and make the critical decisions. It is people who wait on customers, answer telephones, and solicit new accounts in a highly computerized service enterprise. Despite the most highly sophisticated electronic technology, it is still *people* who accomplish objectives. Increasingly today, the degree of success that any institution enjoys is directly dependent upon the caliber of human resources provided through the staffing process. Only by effective staffing can an organization expect to fulfill its mission and achieve its goals.

Direct Costs

Direct staffing costs encompass such items as salaries of staffing specialists, office and equipment, employment advertising, employment agency fees, tests, physical examinations, relocation expenses, etc. While it is difficult to ascertain with any degree of certainty the actual amount of out-of-pocket expenditures directly associated with the staffing process for the average company, one can easily surmise that they are not insignificant.

An indication of direct costs related to staffing can be inferred from an extensive survey performed by the Bureau of National Affairs in 2007.[1] According to this survey, budgets for the human resource departments in surveyed companies represent a median of 1.2 percent of an organization's total operating cost, or a median cost of $1,056 per worker. While these figures include all human resource management department expenses and not just staffing costs, it would seem safe to assume that the portion of expenses directly attributable to performance of staffing activities is substantial.

To put it very simply, staffing costs represent a sizable outlay for many organizations. Consequently, it is important that staffing activities be performed as effectively as possible to ensure that the organization is deriving maximum benefit from its direct expenditures in this area.

Indirect Costs

The staffing process also involves a number of "hidden" or indirect costs. Included in this category are such things as the following: (1) the time operating managers spend interviewing prospective employees, conducting performance appraisals, making promotion or termination decisions, documenting staffing actions, and so forth; (2) the time supervisors or employees spend training new workers or orienting new hires to the workplace; (3) the amount of productivity lost by new employees while they are in the process of learning to perform jobs; and (4) the amount of scrap or wasted materials resulting from new employees' mistakes while still learning a job. Because costs of this nature are buried in normal operating budgets, they are often overlooked as staffing-related expenses. Nevertheless, they are as real as the direct costs. Little work, unfortunately, has been done to determine just how much indirect cost may be associated with the staffing process. We can, however, assume from their nature that indirect staffing expenditures are considerable.

Organizational Impacts

Performance of the staffing function affects the overall organization in many ways. Some of the obvious organizational impacts include morale, employee turnover, productivity, customer service, community relations, employee relations, and corporate image. If staffing is performed effectively, morale will tend to be high, turnover will tend to be low, and productivity will tend to be above average. If staffing is done ineffectively, customer service will tend to suffer, community relations may be affected negatively, corporate image could be tarnished, and employee relations may be poor. Thus, it is extremely important that staffing activities be performed in such a manner as to increase positive impacts on an organization and ameliorate negative impacts.

Legal Aspects

While all phases of human resource management have become increasingly legalistic in recent years, staffing is the one area that has been most affected. The overwhelming majority of federal employment legislation enacted and court decisions rendered since the beginning of the modern civil rights era has been directed to various parts of the staffing process. Laws and regulations have imposed new requirements on staffing activities. The potential liabilities for violations of the law have increased significantly. Staffing can no longer simply concern itself with securing the right number and quality of employees to perform the work of the organization, but must carry out its tasks in conformance with a plethora of statutory guidelines. Procedures, practices, and policies must conform to the law or the organization runs the risk of investigations or legal actions.

Employees, so it seems, are increasingly willing to file suits against their employers. In 2007, for example, federal discrimination claims filed against private sector employers rose by 9 percent over the previous year. This was the largest annual increase in claims filed since the early 1990s.[2]

In the event that legal action is brought against a company, the costs involved can be substantial; for example, in 2004 Home Depot paid $5.5 million to settle a discrimination suit in Colorado.[3] In 2008 Abercrombie and Fitch settled a class action discrimination suit for $40 million and also agreed to implement new policies and programs to promote diversity.[4] Also in 2008 Lockheed Martin agreed to pay an African American employee $2.5 million to settle a discrimination suit filed against the company by EEOC.[5] The same year Morgan Stanley offered to settle a racial bias class action claim for $16 million.[6] As these cases indicate, legal costs of mistakes in staffing can be very expensive.

In summary, the importance of effective staffing should not be underestimated. It is critical to the success of the organization; the direct and indirect costs are substantial; the organizational impacts are real; and the legal ramifications are potentially great.

STAFFING AND THE HUMAN RESOURCE MANAGEMENT SYSTEM

The human resource management system in an organization comprises all those processes, activities, and tasks concerned with the acquisition, utilization, development, and rewarding of people in the workplace. Broadly speaking, all managers in a company are human resource managers because they have direct

Figure 1.1
Human Resource Management System

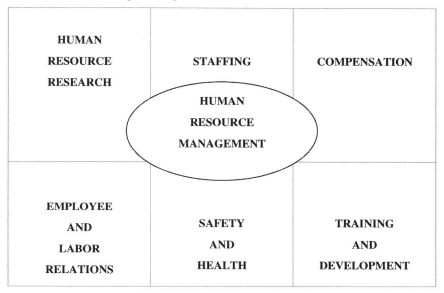

responsibility for people. The individual specifically designated as human resource manager is, in reality, the coordinator of the human resource management system, providing advice, expertise, and assistance to other organizational managers. While the human resource manager has responsibility for proper functioning of the system, it is operating managers who implement and use it.

The human resource management system is composed of six major subsystems or processes as shown in Figure 1.1. Staffing is the process that sets the other processes in motion; staffing also influences and in turn is influenced by the other five processes. The relationship between the other five parts of the human resource management system and staffing is described in the following paragraphs.

Compensation

Compensation consists of all of the rewards—tangible and intangible, monetary and nonmonetary—that an organization provides its employees in exchange for the work they perform. This definition suggests that compensation is more than just pay, and indeed it is. The three components of compensation are direct monetary rewards (wages and salaries), indirect financial payments (benefits and services), and psychological satisfactions (status, recognition, good working conditions, meaningful work, and so forth).

The compensation program a firm develops exerts a major influence on staffing. An inequitable compensation program may make constant recruiting necessary because employees leave the organization to take higher paying jobs elsewhere. Moreover, a poor compensation plan may increase the difficulty of finding sufficient numbers of qualified workers. On the other hand, an equitable compensation scheme can facilitate recruiting and increase the likelihood of hiring and retaining well-qualified employees.

How does staffing affect the compensation system? Primarily, it is through the employees it brings into the firm. If employees are consistently hired at the upper ends of the pay scales, the compensation plan may have to be changed frequently to maintain internal equity and external competitiveness. If employees are consistently hired at the lower ends of the pay scales, the compensation plan will have to be altered less frequently.

Training and Development

Training and development are concerned with improving the productivity of individuals, groups, and the entire organization. Training normally involves the imparting of skills that help workers to perform their present jobs better. Development is concerned with assisting employees to realize their full potential. These two efforts begin when an individual joins an organization and continue throughout the person's tenure with the firm.

Training and development have a significant impact on staffing. A company that has gained a reputation for providing excellent training and development may find it easier to attract and retain qualified employees. Turnover also may be reduced because workers are reluctant to leave an organization that provides the needed knowledge, skills, and learning opportunities for attaining personal goals. Additionally, productivity is typically enhanced because employees are better able to perform their current jobs and to assume positions of higher responsibility when these positions become available.

Safety and Health

Safety and health include those things an organization does to protect employees from on-the-job injuries or work-related illnesses and to promote the general physical and mental well-being of employees, respectively. While progressive companies have long been concerned with these factors, federal legislation, local regulations, and the development of a health-conscious attitude on the part of the general public have heightened the interest of organizations in safety and health issues.

How does safety and health relate to staffing? Different organizations, obviously, project different images in this area. Some merely adhere to the minimum standards regarding safety and health while others respond vigorously to these concerns. The image that an institution projects and the reputation it has earned can either help or hinder the staffing process. A reputation for being concerned about safety and health issues facilitates staffing efforts; a reputation for lack of concern increases the difficulty of finding sufficient numbers of qualified employees to carry out the work of the company.

Employee and Labor Relations

Employee and labor relations are concerned with the following: (1) the way a company manages its work force, and (2) how it interacts with its union, if it has one.

Vitally important to every employee is the concept of fairness in the employment relationship. Although fairness may not mean the same thing to each individual, every employee is concerned, generally speaking, with equity in the workplace. In matters of discipline, promotion, demotion, layoff, termination, and pay, employees tend to value equity, fairness, and consistency of treatment very highly. Certainly, the reputation a firm has in employee relations either facilitates or hinders the staffing process. How management deals with its employees soon becomes public knowledge that either enhances or tarnishes the company's image and consequently affects staffing.

The term "labor relations" refers specifically to the organization's interactions with its union-represented employees. Again, it is the reputation or image in this area that impacts the staffing process positively or negatively.

Human Resource Research

Human resource research is that human resource management function concerned with the gathering, analyzing, and interpreting of data relating to an organization's human resources. It permeates all of the other processes in the human resource management system.

Human resource research provides information that may be used to improve the staffing process. Data on the types of employees who have proven to be the most successful with the organization, turnover ratios, employee attitudes, accident frequencies, and productivity are often of assistance in recruiting, selecting, promoting, and planning staffing needs. Information gathered through research may be used to change staffing practices, revise procedures, or develop new policies in an effort to increase the effectiveness of staffing.

Obviously, all parts of the human resource management system must be integrated so that they do, in fact, function as a system. Staffing is affected by everything else that occurs in human resource management and, through the people it brings into the organization, staffing affects all other human resource processes. Actions taken in staffing must be carefully thought through to assess their actual or potential impact on other areas of effectively managing people in the workplace.

THE STAFFING PROCESS

Although staffing is closely related to other human resource management functions, it can be viewed for purposes of analysis and study as a separate process with its own activities and objectives. The basic components of staffing are shown in Figure 1.2. Each of these components is briefly described below.

Job Analysis and Design

The activities associated with ascertaining the duties of a job and determining the skills required to perform those duties are referred to as job analysis. Inasmuch as every process within the human resource management system utilizes and relies upon the information provided by job analysis, this activity can be considered to be the most fundamental of all human resource tasks and tools.

Job design is primarily concerned with how the work to be performed in an organization should be divided into pieces or "chunks" that can be handled by individual employees. Once work is analyzed to find out what has to be done and the kinds of skills required to do it, job design takes over and determines the manner in which specific tasks may be accomplished most effectively.

Job analysis answers the questions of "what specific duties must be performed?" and "what human qualifications are needed to perform these duties?" Job design answers the question of how the work can best be performed. Chapter 5 discusses job analysis and design in detail.

Human Resource Planning

Determining the number of employees that an organization will need in the future and the kinds of skills those employees must possess is the task of human resource planning. Before many of the other staffing activities can be undertaken, human resource planning must be successfully completed. Chapter 6 explores this crucial topic.

Recruiting

Recruiting consists of those activities undertaken to encourage sufficient numbers of qualified people to apply for employment with an organization. Its primary purpose is to ensure that there is an adequate supply or pool of applicants available at the appropriate time. Recruiting is the subject of Chapter 7.

Selecting

Choosing the applicant best qualified for a particular position is the goal of selecting. Some basic considerations in selecting are presented in Chapter 8. Because of their actual or potential importance in the selection of employees,

Figure 1.2
The Staffing System

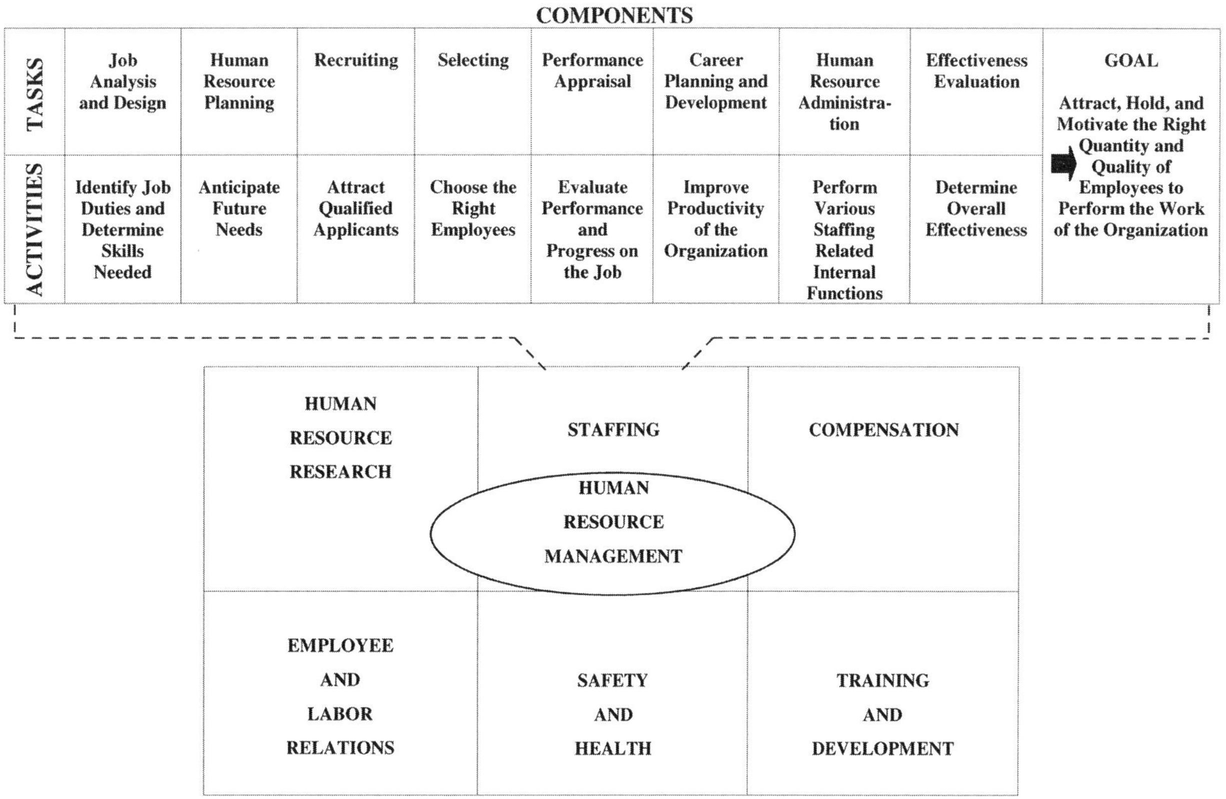

COMPONENTS

TASKS	Job Analysis and Design	Human Resource Planning	Recruiting	Selecting	Performance Appraisal	Career Planning and Development	Human Resource Administration	Effectiveness Evaluation	GOAL
ACTIVITIES	Identify Job Duties and Determine Skills Needed	Anticipate Future Needs	Attract Qualified Applicants	Choose the Right Employees	Evaluate Performance and Progress on the Job	Improve Productivity of the Organization	Perform Various Staffing Related Internal Functions	Determine Overall Effectiveness	Attract, Hold, and Motivate the Right Quantity and Quality of Employees to Perform the Work of the Organization

HUMAN RESOURCE RESEARCH	STAFFING	COMPENSATION
	HUMAN RESOURCE MANAGEMENT	
EMPLOYEE AND LABOR RELATIONS	SAFETY AND HEALTH	TRAINING AND DEVELOPMENT

employment tests are examined in Chapter 9. Interviewing, the most widely used selection tool and the most imperfectly utilized selection device, is discussed in Chapter 10.

Performance Appraisal

Performance appraisal is essentially concerned with determining how well employees are carrying out their assigned duties and responsibilities. It is also frequently used as a mechanism for identifying candidates for promotion or pay increases. Performance appraisal is an integral part of the staffing process for two reasons. First, it is the means by which employees are most often promoted to positions of higher responsibility. Second, it provides feedback information that can be used to evaluate the effectiveness of recruitment and selection activities, approaches, and procedures. Performance appraisal is explored in depth in Chapter 11.

Career Planning and Development

Career planning and development is a formalized approach taken by an organization to ensure that people with the proper qualifications and experience are available when needed. Its emphasis is on meshing the career aspirations of current employees with the future human resource needs of the company. This topic is the subject of Chapter 12.

Staffing Administration

This portion of the staffing process involves handling a multitude of administrative details that begin when an employee is hired and continue throughout his or her tenure with the organization. Among the activities included here are promotions, demotions, transfers, resignations, terminations, retirements, layoffs, and the like. Staffing administration is covered in Chapter 13.

Evaluation of Staffing Effectiveness

Does the staffing process do what it is supposed to do? How well are the various activities carried out? Is staffing performed in a cost-effective manner? These are the kinds of questions that evaluation seeks to answer. The evaluation of staffing is discussed in Chapter 14.

Interrelationships within Staffing

Referring once again to Figure 1.2, we can see that each of the components of the staffing process is related to successful accomplishment of the primary objective of staffing. Job analysis is the most basic component because of its direct impact on every other aspect of staffing. Human resource planning is dependent upon job analysis, but it is also affected by the activities that occur in performance appraisal, career planning and development, and staffing administration. These activities determine the numbers and kinds of employees who are available for movement within the organization. Human resource planning forms the basis for recruiting additional employees, thus setting the recruiting activity in motion. Recruiting sets the selecting component in motion. The employees a firm hires then affect performance appraisal, career planning and development, and staffing administration. Evaluation of the effectiveness of staffing is affected by all activities performed in each of the other staffing processes. In short, anything that is done in any of the staffing components has an effect on what is done and how well it is done in all the other staffing system components. Consequently, staffing must be viewed as an integrated process if it is to be accomplished effectively. Policies, procedures, programs, and practices used in any particular component of the staffing system cannot be developed or implemented without carefully examining their potential impact on each of the other areas of staffing.

THE ENVIRONMENTAL CONTEXT OF STAFFING

The entire human resource management system, especially staffing, is affected by a series of external and internal environmental forces. The external environment consists of those factors that affect a firm's human resource system from outside the boundaries of the organization. Major external forces include the legal system, the economy, the work force and labor market, competitors, customers, technology, unions, and society at large. The internal environment consists of those factors within the organization itself that affect the human resource system: the mission and objectives of the organization, corporate policies, organizational climate, management philosophy, and other functional areas within the company such as marketing and finance. Figure 1.3 depicts the various external and internal environmental forces.

The basic staffing tasks of an organization remain essentially the same no matter what impact is exerted by the external or internal environment. However, the manner in which these tasks are performed may be altered substantially by what occurs in either or both environments. The ways in which the various environmental forces affect staffing are briefly examined below.

External Factors

Contemporary organizations are increasingly subject to and influenced by forces operating outside the organization. To a great extent, the way an institution does business and conducts its internal affairs is shaped or even determined, in large measure, by outside influences. Staffing, in particular, is affected by such environmental factors.

Figure 1.3
Environmental Context of Staffing

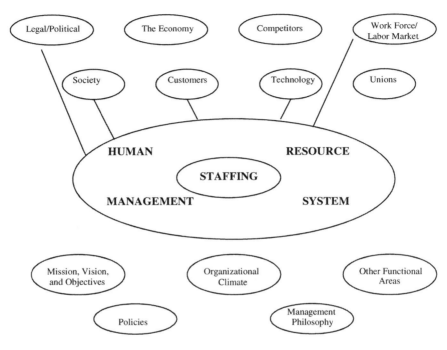

The Legal System. The external force that has had—and will continue to have—the greatest effect on staffing is the legal system. Procedures must conform to legally imposed guidelines; policies must reflect the spirit as well as the letter of the law; practices must meet statutory standards; and treatment of employees must be free of tortious acts. The legal system has dramatically altered the staffing process over the past several decades and will undoubtedly continue to do so. While the basic objective of staffing remains the same—securing sufficient numbers of qualified people at the right time—this objective must now be accomplished in accordance with a number of externally imposed requirements established by statutory as well as the application of common law to the employment situation. Staffing specialists must continuously be alert to the possibility of the passage of new legislation. For example, the Employment Non-Discrimination in Employment Act (ENDA), which would extend Title VII protections to gays and lesbians, passed the U.S. House of Representatives in late 2007.[7] Will this Act pass the Senate, and if it does pass, will it be signed into law or vetoed by the President? These are the kinds of legal happenings with which staffing specialists must deal.

Further compounding the effect of various laws and regulations is the increased willingness of employees or would-be employees to sue organizations over alleged violations of employment rights. The courts, too, seem more inclined to look with favor upon the claims of employees as evidenced by the number of cases won by employees and the amounts of settlements that firms have been ordered to pay. The result is that those involved in staffing must be fully cognizant of the legal system—federal, state, and local—and the impact developments in this area are having on the performance of staffing functions.

Economy. The economic health of the country has a direct bearing on the accomplishment of staffing tasks. In times of vigorous economic growth as firms expand, competition for qualified employees intensifies and staffing activities are directly affected. For example, job analysis and human resource planning tend to become more important as new jobs are added and plans must be made for future job increases. Recruitment efforts are accelerated in the quest for qualified applicants. Selection becomes more difficult because of the wider range of employment opportunities open to applicants. Career planning, with its traditional emphasis on upward mobility in the organization, assumes greater importance as a means of attracting, holding, and motivating workers. Human resource administration activities increase as more employees are hired, are promoted, are transferred, or leave the organization.

In times of poor economic health, staffing is also directly impacted. Job analysis and human resource planning activities slow down. Recruitment efforts decrease because of the greater number of job applicants available. Selection is improved—at least potentially—due to the availability of a larger pool of applicants from which to choose. Career planning loses some of its emphasis. Layoffs, retirements, and transfers increase the workload for human resource administration.

In short, the state of the economy tends to increase or decrease the level or intensity of staffing activities as well as change the priority or importance attached to these activities.

Work Force/Labor Market. The work force consists of the total number of non-institutionalized individuals, 16 years of age and over, who are employed or who are unemployed but actively seeking employment. It represents the total number of individuals potentially available to all employers within this country. The work force also encompasses the mix of skills available as well as other factors of importance to employers.

The work force is dynamic, changing in numbers and characteristics over time. As these changes occur, they affect the staffing process. Aggregate shortages of skills make it more difficult to attract and hold sufficient numbers of employees to perform the work of the organization. Surpluses simplify this task. A scarcity of qualified younger workers alters recruitment, selection, and career planning. An abundance of qualified older workers necessitates changes in staffing practices, policies, and philosophies. As will be seen in Chapter 12, anticipating shifts in the work force is one of the tasks of human resource planning. Organizations that fail to recognize and plan for changes in work force demographics will find their staffing activities rendered more difficult.

The labor market, defined very simply, is that geographical area—local, regional, national, or international—from which an employer usually recruits workers. It is a subset of the work force where supply of and demand for individuals with specific skills interact; consequently, it is of critical importance to an employer. For example, if the demand for particular skills is high relative to supply in a given labor market, an intensive recruiting effort may be required. Conversely, if supply exceeds demand, less vigorous recruiting tactics may suffice. Since labor market conditions change frequently (much more rapidly, in fact, than does the work force), it is necessary to stay abreast of these changes to ensure continued effectiveness of the staffing process.

Competitors. Unless an organization monopolizes the market it serves, it will be forced to compete for sales with other institutions offering similar products or services. Likewise, unless an organization is the only user of particular skills in its labor market, it will be forced to compete with other firms for the talent needed to produce its goods or services. The degree of competition extant in the labor market influences the way staffing is conducted. Intensive competition for workers results in a rigorous approach to staffing; moderate competition produces a much less intensive approach. Moreover, the actions that competing labor market institutions take often suggest that a particular employer modify its staffing practices in order to remain competitive in the skills marketplace.

Customers. The people who actually use a firm's products or services are a vital part of the external environment. An organization has the task of ensuring that its employment practices do not antagonize members of the market it serves. In some instances consumers have boycotted the products of organizations that paid substandard wages or failed to employ adequate numbers of minority workers. To satisfy the perceptions of customers relative to its employment practices, an organization may have to revise its staffing practices.

Since customers are constantly demanding high-quality products and service excellence, organizations must continually strive to employ workers who can provide these kinds of products and service levels. Product or service quality is directly related to the skills and qualifications of the institution's employees. Sales and accounts may be lost or gained depending upon the quality of a firm's employees. Thus, customers exert pressure on an organization and affect its staffing practices.

Technology. Technology refers to the processes by which an organization converts inputs into goods and services. Computers, automation, and information processing have drastically changed the conversion processes in most enterprises over the past two decades and will alter these processes even more in the future. Masses of unskilled or semiskilled workers have been replaced by fewer highly skilled workers who develop and monitor highly sophisticated automated systems. New skills are needed today to meet the demands of new technology. These skills are typically in short supply, and it is often difficult to recruit sufficient numbers of qualified individuals for the jobs that are available. Competition in high-technology jobs is intense and employee turnover is usually high. Staffing practices, as a result, have to be changed to ensure that an organization has and will continue to have the right kinds of people available when they are needed.

Unions. Unions occupy the anomalous position of being both an external force as well as an internal force. They are perhaps best viewed, however, as an external force because they are a third party in their dealings with a company.

The manner in which staffing is conducted differs markedly in union and nonunion firms. In a few heavily unionized industries, for example, recruiting and selecting is performed by the union itself rather than the company. Staffing administration, too, is often dramatically altered when a company has a union: seniority is of paramount importance for promotions; layoff procedures are rigidly specified; "bumping" or job regression rights are defined; terminations are more difficult. Also affected is performance appraisal—many labor agreements preclude its use altogether.

Although effective staffing is still of great importance in a unionized environment, procedures, practices, and policies may be quite different from those in a nonunionized firm and exert a dominant influence on the way staffing is accomplished.

Society. Members of society, too, exert considerable influence on the staffing process in a company. The public at large is no longer content to accept without question the actions of institutions. People have found that changes in organizational practices can be made through the pressure of their voices and votes. This influence of society on employment practices is evidenced by the number of regulatory statutes—federal, state, and local—passed in the past 20 years.

The image a firm conveys to the general public can greatly influence the effectiveness of staffing. A reputation for fairness and integrity in dealing with employees can result in more and better qualified applicants seeking employment with a firm. Likewise, a firm that produces safe, fairly priced products of reasonable quality may attract more employees more easily than other firms.

Society generally expects an organization to be a good corporate citizen. To the extent that an institution fulfills this expectation, staffing activities may be facilitated.

The external environment places a great deal of pressure on staffing professionals. There are expectations and demands to be satisfied; there are requirements to be met; there are challenges to be faced. It is important that the pressures brought by external forces be recognized clearly and that staffing be carried out in such a manner as to meet these external demands, pressures, requirements, challenges, and expectations in a positive fashion.

Internal Environment

The internal organizational environment has considerable influence on the way in which staffing is accomplished in an enterprise. As indicated in Figure 1.3, significant internal factors include mission and objectives, policies, organizational climate, management philosophy, and the other functional areas in the organization.

Mission, Vision, and Objectives. Mission refers to an organization's overall reason for existence, its general purpose as an entity. Vision refers to what the organization hopes to become in the future. Objectives are specific results to be achieved within a designated period of time. Mission, vision, and objectives define what an organization does, how it goes about doing it, and how it sees itself changing over time. They provide direction for an enterprise and thus influence and shape all other institutional activities.

Two very simplified examples will illustrate how mission, vision, and objectives relate to staffing. Company A has the goal of being a leader in its industry with respect to technological advances. Growth, its vision for the future, is expected to occur through the pioneering of new highly sophisticated products and processes. Company B, on the other hand, has the goal of conservative growth with little risk taking. Its vision for the future is limited. Only after another company's products have proven themselves in the marketplace will Company B commit itself to producing similar products.

In Company A, the firm will need a creative environment that encourages new ideas. Highly skilled, imaginative workers will have to be recruited and selected to bring about the desired technological advancements the company desires, both now and in the future. On the other hand, the basic staffing tasks remain the same in Company B, but the objectives and vision of the firm dictate that the tasks be altered considerably. A different kind of work force will need to be recruited and selected. Highly creative individuals are not essential to achieving Company B's goals and vision.

As these simple examples illustrate, overall company mission, vision, and objectives can and do influence the staffing process.

Policies. A policy is a general statement that guides thinking in decision making. Organizational policies establish parameters that assist managers and employees in the accomplishment of their jobs. Policies set the tone for what is done in a company as well as the manner in which it is done.

In a large organization policies are established for every area of operations— marketing, finance, accounting, production, engineering—but frequently the greatest number of policies relate to human resource management. Human resource policies reflect the tone of other corporate policy statements and set forth the kinds of actions to be taken relative to people. A company's policies say a great deal about the importance or lack of importance attached to staffing. For example, a promotion from within policy underscores an organization's commitment to preparing its present employees for advancement. Absence of such a policy suggests a lack of concern for employee advancement. In either case, policy or lack of policy influences the emphasis given to staffing activities.

Organizational Climate. The psychological atmosphere prevailing in a company is referred to as its organizational climate. An infinite number of possible climates exist. At one extreme is a negative, closed, and threatening climate. At the other extreme is a positive, open, and nurturing climate. The prevalent psychological atmosphere in an enterprise has a direct relationship to employee motivation, work quality, turnover, and absenteeism. A positive climate enhances motivation, improves work quality, decreases turnover, and reduces absenteeism. A negative climate has the opposite effect. In general, a positive climate makes the task of staffing easier while a negative climate makes it more difficult.

Management Philosophy. The prevailing values of management—often referred to as corporate culture—affect everyone and everything in an organization. The way management feels about people and the actions it takes regarding them speak much more loudly than platitudinous pronouncements and pompous sounding policies. Values, philosophy, and culture influence staffing and how it is carried out. Management beliefs and actions that suggest a genuine interest in and concern for employees and their welfare have a positive impact on staffing. Managerial beliefs and actions that suggest lack of interest and concern for employees have a deleterious effect.

Other Functional Areas. Marketing, finance, production, and all other functional areas in an organization have an effect on the staffing process. For example, if the work performed in the manufacturing arena is boring, dirty, or dangerous, staffing specialists may be forced to recruit continuously to ensure that manufacturing has sufficient numbers of qualified people because turnover is likely to be quite high. Or, if the product or service of the firm is difficult to sell, constant recruiting may be necessary to keep the marketing function at full strength. Conversely, if the work performed in finance is challenging and exciting, employee turnover is likely to be low and there may be a ready pool of qualified applicants to fill any vacancies that do occur. Thus, the actual work that is performed in a company, the way it is performed, and the conditions under which it is performed may greatly influence, positively or negatively, the work of staffing.

The internal environment shapes and molds the way staffing is accomplished in a firm; it influences the importance that is attached to each staffing task; it determines to a large extent the effectiveness with which staffing will be performed.

NOTES

1. Joshua Joseph, Bernice L. Eberhart, David J. Group, and Robert Combs, *HR Department Benchmarks and Analysis 2007* (Washington, DC: BNA, Inc., 2007), 51 and 43.

2. "Bias Cases by Workers Increase 9%," *The Wall Street Journal,* March 6, 2008, D.6.

3. The U.S. Equal Employment Opportunity Commission, "Home Depot to Pay $5.5 Million to Resolve Class Discrimination Lawsuit in Colorado," http://www.eeoc.gov/press/8-25-04.html

4. "Abercrombie and Fitch Settles $40 Million Discrimination Suit," http://yellowworld.org/civil_rights/280.html

5. Kris Maher, "Lockheed Settles Racial-Discrimination Suit," *The Wall Street Journal* (Eastern edition), New York, January 3, 2008, A.4.

6. "Morgan Stanley to Settle Bias Claims," *The Wall Street Journal* (Eastern edition), New York, Feb. 11, 2008, C.4.

7. "House Approves Ban on Job Bias Against Gays," *The Dallas Morning News,* November 8, 2007, 1 and 2A.

2

Staffing Legislation and Regulation

As mentioned in the previous chapter, one of the most important external forces affecting an organization's staffing policies and practices is the legal system. Virtually every phase of staffing—from recruitment to selection, from compensation to termination, from performance appraisal to promotion—is covered in some fashion by federal legislation, Executive Orders, or federal administrative regulations. In addition, state and local laws often impact staffing. And increasingly today, various common law provisions are being applied to different aspects of staffing. The result is a plethora of legal complexities with which human resource professionals must deal. This chapter examines the most prominent federal regulations and common law applications affecting staffing.

FEDERAL LEGISLATION

Prior to the 1930s, organizations, with few exceptions, enjoyed wide latitude in employment practices and employee relations. With the coming of the New Deal under President Franklin Roosevelt, specific, but still limited, rights of workers began to receive protection under federal legislation. The civil rights movement of the 1960s ushered in a whole new age of federal protection for employees and job applicants and produced a dramatic revision of staffing practices and employee relations. The late 1980s and the early 1990s saw a resurgence in federal legislation relating to staffing. Described below in chronological order are the statutes that have made staffing the legalistic challenge that it is today.

Post–Civil War Statutes

After the Civil War Congress enacted a series of civil rights statutes to advance the goals of the recently enacted Thirteenth, Fourteenth, and Fifteenth

Amendments to the Constitution. (The Thirteenth Amendment abolished involuntary servitude; the Fourteenth Amendment guaranteed equal protection under the law for all citizens; and the Fifteenth Amendment established the right of black males to vote—women would have to wait until 1920 and the ratification of the Twentieth Amendment before they were granted the right to vote.) Four of these statutes are now codified in 42 U.S.C. Sections 1981, 1983, and 1985. Of particular interest because they are still used in civil rights lawsuits are the Civil Rights Acts of 1866 and 1871.

The Civil Rights Act of 1866, based on the Thirteenth Amendment, is the oldest piece of federal legislation affecting staffing. Specifically, this Act provides that all citizens have the same right "as enjoyed by white citizens . . . to inherit, purchase, . . . hold, and convey . . . property," and that "all persons . . . shall have the same right to make and enforce contracts . . . as enjoyed by white citizens." As interpreted by the courts, employment as well as membership in a union is a contractual arrangement. Thus, if a black is denied employment, promotion, union membership, or any other employment advantages or opportunities because of his or her race, the courts have held that the right to make a contract has been violated. Whites and Hispanics are also now covered by this Act if they are discriminated against on the basis of race. Until 1968 it was assumed that the Act was applicable only when action by a state or state agency and not by private parties was involved. The Supreme Court overruled this assumption and broadened the interpretation of the Act to cover *all* contractual arrangements. Interestingly, the Civil Rights Act of 1866 has no statute of limitations attached to it.[1]

The Civil Rights Act of 1871 is based on the Fourteenth Amendment, which guarantees all citizens the right to equal protection under the law. Originally referred to as the "Ku Klux Klan Act," the Civil Rights Act of 1871 makes it illegal for two or more persons to conspire to deprive any person or class of persons of the right of equal protection under the law. It has been held by the federal courts that where two or more officials of a corporation, the employer and its employees, or two or more employees have conspired among themselves to deny equal rights to a person or persons on the basis of race, a violation of this statute has occurred. The Act applies to private enterprises and parties as well as states and local governments. While the Act has no effective statute of limitations, filing limitations provided for in Title VII of the Civil Rights Act of 1964 or by those expressed in state tortious conspiracies are normally adhered to.[2]

National Labor Relations Act of 1935

Commonly known as the Wagner Act in recognition of its Senate sponsor, Robert Wagner of New York, this legislation gives employees the right to form unions and requires employers to recognize unions of employees and to bargain with them in good faith relative to wages, hours of work, and other terms and conditions of employment. As specified in the Act, "Employees shall have the right to self-organization, to form, join, or assist labor organizations, to bargain collectively through representatives of their own choosing, and to engage in other concerted activities, for the purpose of collective bargaining or other mutual aid or protection." The rights given to employees are protected against interference by employers. Specifically, employers are prohibited from the following: (1) interfering with, restraining, or coercing employees in their exercise of the right to form unions; (2) dominating a union or interfering in the affairs of a union; (3) discriminating against employees in regard to hiring, job tenure, or any condition of employment for the purpose of encouraging or discouraging union membership; (4) discriminating against or terminating an employee who has filed an unfair labor charge or has given testimony under the Act; and (5) refusing to bargain in good faith with the chosen representatives of employees.[3]

The Act created the National Labor Relations Board, which has the responsibility for conducting elections to determine if employees wish to be represented by a union, determining which of two competing unions will be certified as the bargaining agent for a group of employees, preventing unfair labor practices in the area of unionization activities, and investigating reported claims of unfair labor practices.

Social Security Act of 1935, as Amended

This Act created the Social Security Administration and established the existing system of old age, survivors, disability, and unemployment compensation insurance.[4] Employees and employers share equally the cost of old age, survivors, and disability insurance—those items that are commonly described as "Social Security." Employers pay the full cost of unemployment insurance, the funding of which is accomplished through a payroll tax. Unemployment benefits are paid through state agencies in each of the 50 states. The Act also created a minimum period of 26 weeks of unemployment compensation for employees who meet the qualifications for such compensation.

Fair Labor Standards Act of 1938, as Amended

Popularly known as the Wage and Hour Act, the Fair Labor Standards Act of 1938 (FLSA) established a minimum wage for the vast majority of workers in the private sector.[5] The original minimum wage was set at 25 cents per hour in 1938. By September 1997 it had increased to $5.15 per hour. In 2007, Congress raised the minimum wage to $5.85 per hour, with an increase to $6.55 set for July 2008, and another increase to $7.25 set for 2009. The Act also established the standard workweek of 40 hours. Workers covered by this statute are divided into two categories: exempt and nonexempt. Nonexempt workers must be compensated at a rate of one and one-half times their regular hourly rate of pay for hours worked in excess of 40 during a given workweek. A workweek is defined as a recurring period of 168 hours or seven consecutive 24-hour periods. The workweek does not have to conform to the calendar week, and it may begin at any

hour of the day. Exempt employees—managers, administrators, and profes
sionals, for example—are excluded from the overtime pay requirement. Additionally, the Act set the minimum working age for covered employment at 16;
if the work is hazardous, the minimum working age is 18.[6] Some jobs that are
considered hazardous are manufacturing of explosives, mining, meatpacking or
processing, roofing, excavating, and driving a motor vehicle.[7]

Labor-Management Relations Act of 1947

This statute, an amendment to the National Labor Relations Act of 1935, was
enacted with the express intent of restoring a balance of power between unions
and management.[8] Usually referred to as the Taft-Hartley Act, it altered union-
management relations as follows: (1) by protecting the right of employees to
refrain from as well as engage in union activity; (2) by prohibiting the closed
shop (an arrangement that required all workers to be union members at the time
they were hired); (3) by narrowing the freedom of the bargaining parties to
authorize the union shop (under a union shop arrangement the employer is free
to hire anyone it chooses, but all new workers must join the union within 30 days
or they will be terminated); (4) by granting the employer greater freedom of
speech when faced with an attempt to unionize workers; (5) by granting management the right to refuse to recognize or bargain with unions of supervisory personnel; (6) by giving employees the right to initiate decertification proceedings
should they no longer desire to be represented by a union; (7) by providing for
government intervention to halt strikes for an 80-day "cooling off" period where
such strikes would create a "national emergency" detrimental to the welfare of
the country; and (8) by giving states the power to enact so-called "right-to-
work" laws precluding the union shop arrangement.

A significant feature of the Labor-Management Relations Act was that it
extended the concept of unfair labor practices to unions. Previously, such practices had been limited to management alone. Under the Act specific unfair labor
practices on the part of unions consist of the following: (1) restraining or coercing
employees in the exercise of their collective bargaining rights, (2) causing an
employer to discriminate in any fashion against an employee in order to encourage or discourage union membership, (3) refusing to bargain in good faith with
an employer, (4) engaging in certain types of strikes or boycotts, (5) requiring
employees to pay initiation fees or dues that are excessive or discriminatory,
and (6) requiring an employer to pay for services not performed by workers,
i.e., featherbedding.

The Act also created the Federal Mediation and Conciliation Service and
assigned it the responsibility for assisting employers and unions in negotiating
new contracts when the parties have reached an impasse in negotiations and
for maintaining a panel of qualified arbitrators to settle union-management
grievances.

Equal Pay Act of 1963, as Amended

This Act is an amendment to the Fair Labor Standards Act of 1938 and covers the same employers as FLSA.[9] The statute makes it illegal for an employer to discriminate in pay on the basis of sex where jobs require equal skill, effort, and responsibility and are performed under similar working conditions. Pay differentials between sexes are permitted when such differences are based on seniority systems, merit systems, production-related pay plans (wage incentives), or factors other than sex. Premium pay differentials for working undesirable shifts are also allowed. In 1972 the Act was amended to cover employees in executive, administrative, professional, and outside sales positions as well as employees in most state and local governments, hospitals, and schools. Over the years, the Act has become less significant because a violation of the Equal Pay Act is also a violation of Title VII of the Civil Rights Act of 1964, a broader and more powerful statute.

Title VII of the Civil Rights Act of 1964, as Amended

The one statute that has had the greatest impact on human resource management is Title VII of the Civil Rights Act of 1964, as amended.[10] Under Title VII it is illegal for an employer to discriminate in hiring, firing, promoting, compensating, or in terms, conditions, or privileges of employment on the basis of race, color, sex, religion, or national origin.

Title VII covers employers engaged in or affecting interstate commerce who have 15 or more employees for each working day in each of 20 calendar weeks in the current or preceding calendar year. Also included in the definition of employers are state and local governments, schools, colleges, unions, and private employment agencies that procure employees for an employer having 15 or more employees.

Three notable exceptions to discrimination as defined by Title VII are *bona fide* occupational qualifications (BFOQs), seniority and merit systems, and testing and educational requirements. According to the Act, it is not

an unlawful employment practice for an employer to hire and employ employees . . . on the basis of his religion, sex, or national origin in those certain instances where religion, sex, or national origin is a *bona fide* occupational qualification reasonably necessary to the normal operation of the particular business or enterprise.

Thus, for example, religious institutions such as churches or synagogues may legally refuse to hire individuals whose religious persuasion is different from that of the hiring institution. Likewise, a maximum-security correctional institution housing only male inmates may decline to hire females as security guards. The concept of bona fide occupational qualification was designed to be narrowly, not broadly, interpreted and has been so construed by the courts in a number of cases. The burden of proving the necessity for a BFOQ rests entirely on the employer.

The second exception to discrimination under Title VII is a bona fide seniority system such as the kind normally contained in a union contract. Differences in employment conditions among workers are permitted "provided that such differences are not the result of an intention to discriminate because of race, color, religion, sex, or national origin." Even though a bona fide seniority system has a disparate or adverse impact on those individuals protected by Title VII, the system can only be invalidated by evidence that the actual motive of the parties to the agreement was to discriminate.

In the matter of testing and educational requirements, Title VII states that it is not

an unlawful employment practice for an employer to give and to act upon the results of any professionally developed ability test provided that such test, its administration, or action upon the results is not designed, intended or used to discriminate because of race, color, religion, sex, or national origin.

Any employment testing and educational requirements must be job related, and the burden of proof is on the employer to show that a demonstrable relationship exists between actual job performance and the test or educational requirement.

Other exceptions to Title VII include illegal immigrants (noncitizens are not protected from discrimination since they are not citizens; however, they are protected from discrimination based on their national origin) and members of the communist party. Gays and lesbians also are not protected under Title VII. The courts have consistently ruled that where the term "sex" is used in any federal statute that term refers to biological gender and not to sexual preference.

The Civil Rights Act of 1964 also created the Equal Employment Opportunity Commission (EEOC) and assigned enforcement of Title VII to it. The EEOC consists of five presidentially appointed members and is empowered to investigate, conciliate, and litigate charges of discrimination arising under provisions of Title VII. Additionally, the Commission has the responsibility of issuing procedural regulations and interpretations of Title VII and the other statutes it enforces. The most significant regulation issued by EEOC is the *Uniform Guidelines on Employee Selection Procedures*. This regulation will be discussed in Chapter 4.

When a charge is filed under Title VII, EEOC investigates the evidence to determine if there is a possible violation of the statute. Where there is a state or local agency similar to EEOC that meets EEOC standards, the complaint is first referred to that agency. In the event that the complaint is deferred to a state or local agency, the deferral agency has at least 60 days of exclusive jurisdiction over the charge. After 60 days, or if the deferral agency has terminated its proceedings or waived jurisdiction, the EEOC assumes jurisdiction over the complaint. Title VII requires deferral to a state or local agency where one exists, and if EEOC fails to defer, it may lose not only its jurisdiction over the charge but also its ability to conduct an investigation.

If EEOC finds no probable cause for a case after its investigation or otherwise ends its involvement, the agency then notifies the complainant that he or she has the right to pursue the case in federal court on his or her own. Title VII contains no right of individual action until all administrative procedures have been exhausted; therefore, an individual can bring private action against an organization only after receipt of a right to sue letter. If EEOC's investigation finds that there is probable cause for a discrimination charge, the first attempt at settlement will be through mediation—a negotiated arrangement between the complainant, the employer, and EEOC that is satisfactory to all parties and adequately compensates the victim or victims of discrimination and meets the standards set by EEOC. Although EEOC is relying increasingly on mediation to resolve discrimination charges, the complainant is not obligated to resort to mediation unless he or she desires to do so.

Failing to achieve a settlement by mediation, EEOC next has the option to file suit in federal district court against the employer in question. Whether EEOC will pursue litigation itself is usually contingent upon five factors: (1) the number of people affected by the alleged practice, (2) the amount of monetary settlement involved, (3) the number of other discrimination charges brought against the employer, (4) the type of charge involved, and (5) the opportunity to establish legal principle or precedent in discriminatory matters. Because litigation involves the commitment of considerable resources, EEOC's court actions are generally limited to important cases that are likely to be favorable to the agency and have a far-reaching impact on employment practices. In other words, EEOC is not likely to pursue court action on its own.

Under Title VII, charges may be filed by any of the EEOC commissioners, any aggrieved person, or anyone acting on behalf of an aggrieved person, for example, an attorney. The time limit for filing charges is 180 days after the occurrence of the alleged discriminatory act. If the complainant is first required to file the charge with a state or local agency, the time limit for filing with EEOC is extended to 300 days.

Title VII also prohibits retaliation against employees who have opposed an allegedly illegal employment practice. Anyone who testifies, assists, or participates in discriminatory proceedings is also protected.

Age Discrimination in Employment Act of 1967, as Amended

The Age Discrimination in Employment Act of 1967 (ADEA) protects individuals 40 years old and over from discrimination by employers in matters of hiring, job retention, job privileges, and other terms and conditions of employment.[11] Covered under ADEA are employers with 20 or more employees for 20 or more calendar weeks (either in the current or in the preceding calendar year), unions with 25 or more members, employment agencies, and federal, state, or local governments.

A 1986 amendment to ADEA prohibits mandatory retirement of most private sector employees at age 70; however, high-level executives may be retired at age 65 if they are entitled to immediate, nonforfeitable pensions or deferred compensation of at least $27,000 annually. A 1978 amendment had previously eliminated the maximum retirement age of 70 for federal employees.

An exception to the provisions of the Act provides that age may be used as a bona fide occupational qualification in those instances where age is reasonably necessary for business operations or safety factors,[12] for example, actors and actresses required for youthful roles, persons employed to advertise or promote the sale of products designed for youthful consumers, or intercity bus drivers. Age is also a bona fide occupational qualification where federal statutory or regulatory requirements impose a compulsory age limitation as in the case of the Federal Aviation Agency requirement that sets a ceiling of age 65 for commercial airline pilots.

ADEA differs from Title VII in that it provides for trial by jury and there is a possible criminal aspect to an age discrimination charge. Trial by jury has significant implications for employers inasmuch as jurors may have greater sympathy for older persons who allegedly have been discriminated against. The punitive aspect of an age discrimination lawsuit means that an employee may receive more than lost wages if discrimination is proven. (Juries tend to perceive corporations, especially large ones, as "deep pockets" and may not hesitate to award large settlements to an older aggrieved employee.)

Rehabilitation Act of 1973, as Amended

This statute covers government contractors, subcontractors, or organizations receiving federal monies in excess of $2,500.[13] Individuals are considered handicapped or disabled if they have a physical or mental impairment that substantially limits one or more major life activities, have a record of such impairment, or are regarded as having such an impairment. Only physical or mental impairments are covered by the Act. Disadvantages arising from environmental, cultural, or economic factors are not covered. Clearly protected, however, are such diseases and conditions as epilepsy, cancer, cardiovascular disorders, blindness, deafness, mental retardation, emotional disorders, and dyslexia. Under certain circumstances, alcoholism and narcotics addiction are also protected. Recovering alcoholics and addicts, for example, are protected, whereas current users are not.

The Rehabilitation Act is administered by the Office of Federal Contract Compliance Programs. OFCCP has the responsibility to investigate and attempt to settle (normally through conciliation where possible, but through litigation if necessary) complaints of discrimination. There is no private right of action under the Act; consequently, the complainant must file a complaint with OFCCP within 180 days of the alleged discriminatory act, at which time OFCCP assumes responsibility for all further action.

There are two primary levels of the Act. All contractors or subcontractors exceeding the $2,500 base are required to post notices that they agree to take affirmative action (that is, positive steps over and above normal practices) to recruit, employ, and promote qualified disabled individuals. If the contract or subcontract exceeds $50,000, or if the contractor has 50 or more employees, the employer must prepare a written affirmative action plan for review by OFCCP.

Vietnam Era Veterans Readjustment Assistance Act of 1974

This Act, administered by the Department of Labor, covers disabled and other veterans of the Vietnam era.[14] It relates only to government contractors or subcontractors having contracts with the federal government of $10,000 or more. Under the provisions of this statute a contractor is precluded from discriminating against any employee or applicant for employment because he or she is a disabled or other veteran of the Vietnam era. The contractor must take affirmative action to employ, promote, and avoid discrimination against covered individuals in all areas of employment practices. Honorably discharged veterans and other veterans of the Vietnam era who served more than 180 days on active duty between August 5, 1964, and May 7, 1975, are covered. Disabled veterans are defined as those individuals with a compensable disability rated at 30 percent or more by the Veterans Administration. Also included in the Act's coverage are those persons whose discharge or release from active duty was for a disability incurred or aggravated in the line of duty. In addition, the person must have separated from the military service within 48 months prior to the alleged violation.

A major provision of the Act is that covered organizations must list virtually all job openings with the local state employment office. These listings must be provided concurrently with the utilization of other recruiting sources. Organizations with 50 or more employees that have received contracts for over $50,000 must maintain an affirmative action plan. Because of the affirmative action requirement, contractors must provide a schedule for review of all physical and mental job qualifications. This requirement is intended to ensure that all job specifications are actually job related.

Pregnancy Discrimination Act of 1978

Passed as an amendment to Title VII of the Civil Rights Act of 1964, as amended, the Pregnancy Discrimination Act prohibits discrimination in employment based on pregnancy, childbirth, or related medical condition such as abortion.[15] The basic premise of the Act is that women affected by pregnancy or related conditions must be treated the same as other applicants and employees not so affected but similar in their ability or inability to work. A pregnant woman or one affected by a related condition is therefore protected from being refused a job, denied a promotion, or being fired merely because she is pregnant, has recently delivered, or has had an abortion. An employer generally cannot cause a woman to take a leave of absence as long as she, under the advice of her physician, is able to work. Likewise, the employer cannot require a woman who has delivered to remain off work for a set period of time after the delivery. If other employees on disability leave are entitled to return to their jobs when they are able to work again, the same right must be granted to women who have been unable to work because of pregnancy and subsequent delivery.

In the benefits area—health insurance, sick leave, and disability coverage—the same principle applies. A woman unable to work for pregnancy-related reasons is entitled to disability benefits or sick leave on the same basis as employees unable to work for other medical reasons. Also, any health insurance provided must cover expenses for pregnancy-related conditions on the same basis as expenses for other medical conditions. Pregnancy, in other words, is a disability and must be treated in the same fashion as other disabilities. However, health insurance for expenses arising from abortion is not required except where the life of the mother would have been endangered if the fetus were carried to term or where medical complications have arisen from an abortion.

The net effect of the pregnancy discrimination amendments to Title VII has been to raise the cost of employee benefit plans and possibly penalize employers who have vigorously pursued affirmative action plans to increase their numbers of female employees.

Immigration Reform and Control Act of 1986

Extremely sweeping in scope, the Immigration Reform and Control Act of 1986 (IRCA) applies to every employer (even those with only one part-time employee) and to every employee (full-time, part-time, temporary, or seasonal) in the United States. It was enacted in an effort to regulate the increasing flow of undocumented workers (illegal immigrants) into the United States and to protect legal immigrants from discrimination.

Employers must require *all* new hires to complete a Form I-9 and provide documentation establishing both identity and authorization to work legally in the United States. The Form I-9 lists the various documents or combination of documents accepted as proof of identity and work authorization. Documents that establish both identity and employment eligibility include: U.S. passport, Certificate of U.S. Citizenship, Certificate of Naturalization, an unexpired foreign passport with attached Employment Authorization, and Alien Registration Card with photograph. Documents used to establish identity only are the following: a state-issued driver's license or a state-issued ID card with a photograph, or information, including name, sex, date of birth, height, weight, and color of eyes; U.S. military card; or other similar documents. Documents that establish employment eligibility only are original Social Security Number Card; a birth certificate issued by a state, county, or municipal authority bearing a seal or other certification; and an unexpired Immigration and Naturalization Service Employment Authorization. Any document establishing identity may be combined with any document establishing employment eligibility to satisfy the Form I-9 requirements. Employers are not required to validate the authenticity of documents applicants may furnish.

Employers must retain Form I-9 for three years from the date of the employee's hiring or for one year after the employee's termination, whichever is longer. I-9s must be maintained separate and apart from the normal personnel files of employees.

Failure to comply with IRCA requirements may result in penalties ranging from a minimum of $100 for failure to document a worker's identity and eligibility to $10,000 for multiple offenses of hiring illegal aliens. An employer may also be subject to rehire and back pay for any worker who is the victim of illegal discrimination. An employer who is found guilty of consistently hiring illegal aliens is subject to imprisonment of up to six months and a $3,000 fine for each worker hired. In a 1989 South Carolina case, the government imposed a fine of $580,000 against a pillow manufacturing company and a federal grand jury indicted its owners and nine managers on charges of recruiting and hiring 117 illegal aliens. The maximum prison terms carried by these charges are 653 years, plus fines of $5.1 million.[16]

Employers having 4 to 14 employees may not discriminate on the basis of citizenship or national origin. Employers with 15 employees, as previously discussed, are already prohibited from national origin discrimination under Title VII. However, an employer may give preference to an applicant who is a U.S. citizen over a noncitizen where the two applicants are equally qualified.

Worker Adjustment and Retraining Notification Act of 1988

The Worker Adjustment and Retraining Notification Act of 1988 (WARN) requires covered employers to give employees, their representatives (if employees are unionized), state dislocated worker units, and local government officials a 60-calendar day notice of plant closings or mass layoffs. The purpose of WARN is to provide workers and their families time to adjust to the loss of employment, obtain other jobs, or enter job retraining programs. An additional purpose is to allow state agencies that deal with dislocated workers an opportunity to provide prompt assistance to displaced workers.

An employer is subject to the provisions of this Act if it employs 100 or more employees, excluding part-time workers, or if it employs 100 or more employees who work an aggregate total of at least 4,000 hours per week, excluding overtime. Under WARN, an employer is defined as a business enterprise, company, firm, or business consisting of one or more employment sites under common ownership or control. Nonprofit organizations are considered employers, but federal, state, and local governments are not.[17]

A plant closing is defined as the permanent or temporary shutdown of a single site of employment, or one or more facilities or operating units within a single site of employment if the shutdown results in an employment loss at the single site of employment during any 30-day period for 50 or more employees, excluding part-time employees. A mass layoff must meet two conditions for this Act's notification requirement to apply:

it must be a reduction in force that is not a plant closing and the reduction in force must result in an employment loss at a single employment site that affects at least 50 full-time employees who comprise at least 33% of the full-time work force or involves a minimum of 500 full-time employees.

There are several exceptions to the 60-calendar day notice requirement. If the plant closing was caused by a natural disaster, there is obviously no notice requirement. The closing of a temporary facility or completion of a project where employees were hired with an understanding that their employment was temporary requires no advance notification. Problems caused by strikes, lockouts, or permanent replacement of economic strikers are not subject to the notification requirement. Nor does the notification requirement apply if the employer is, reasonably and in good faith, forced to shut down the plant more quickly to obtain needed capital or business, or if the closing was caused by unanticipated business circumstances.[18]

Any employer who does not furnish appropriate notice of a plant closing or mass layoff is liable in a civil action for one day's back pay for each affected employee for each day of violation up to 60 days, plus the value of medical expenses and other benefits paid directly to affected employees and the value of all actual payments made to third parties on behalf of affected employees. Employers are also subject to fines of up to $500 per day payable to the appropriate local government if the employer does not continue to pay benefits as required.[19]

Employee Polygraph Protection Act of 1988

Once used in American industry as a screening device, the polygraph test was the subject of a study by the Congressional Office of Technology in 1983. According to this study, the Office found scientific evidence to indicate that the polygraph was not valid for employment screening purposes. Accuracy rates for polygraph testing were estimated to range from 50 percent to 90 percent.[20] Moreover, the results of polygraph tests have never been accepted in courtrooms as evidence of guilt or innocence—a situation casting further doubt on the efficacy of polygraph testing as valid and reliable measures.

A polygraph measures three physiological indicators: rate and depth of respiration, cardiovascular activity, and perspiration. Inaccuracies in polygraph results, including a number of false positives, led to passage of the Employee Polygraph Protection Act of 1988, thus effectively putting an end to polygraph use as a screening and selection device and greatly restricting its use in other employment areas.[21]

The Act precludes an employer from the following: (1) directly or indirectly suggesting, requesting, or causing an employee to submit to a polygraph or any other similar test; (2) using, accepting, referring to, or inquiring about the results of any polygraph test of any job applicant or current employee; or (3) discharging, disciplining, discriminating against, denying employment, denying promotion, or threatening to take adverse action against any current employee or job applicant who refuses to take a polygraph test, or who fails such a test.[22]

Certain employers are exempt from these regulations, *viz,* private employers whose primary business is to provide security services, employers involved in the manufacture, distribution, or dispensing of controlled substances, and federal, state, and local governments.[23] Polygraph tests may also be administered to current employees in private industry under the following conditions: the test is given in conjunction with an ongoing investigation of an economic loss, the employee(s) had access to the property in question, the employer has reasonable suspicion that the employee(s) was involved, and the employee(s) is provided a statement of the economic loss and the basis for the employer's suspicion. The results of the test may be used to discharge an employee(s) only if the employer has additional evidence of the guilt of the employee(s).[24]

Violations of the Polygraph Act are subject to fines as high as $10,000 per violation as well as reinstatement, employment, promotion, and back pay and benefits to the adversely affected employee. The Act is administered by the Department of Labor through its Wage and Hour Division.

Americans with Disabilities Act of 1990

The Americans with Disabilities Act of 1990 (ADA) became effective in July 1992 and originally covered employers with 25 or more employees. Since 1994 it has applied to employers with 15 or more employees, the same as Title VII.

The Act defines a disability as follows: (1) a physical or mental impairment that substantially limits one or more of the major life activities of an individual such as walking, talking, seeing, hearing, or learning; (2) a record of such an impairment; or (3) an assumption by the employer that the individual has such a disability.

Various obligations are imposed on employers under this legislation: (1) employers cannot deny an individual a job if the individual is qualified and can perform the essential functions of the job, with or without reasonable accommodation; (2) the employer must make reasonable accommodation for a qualified individual to perform the job unless to do so would result in undue hardship for the employer; (3) employers are not required to lower performance standards to accommodate an individual if the standards are job related and uniformly applied to all employees; (4) selection criteria that screen out or tend to screen out applicants on the basis of disability must be job related and consistent with business necessity; (5) any tests or procedures used to evaluate qualifications must reflect the skills and abilities of those individuals rather than impairments in sensory, manual, or speaking skills, unless such skills are job related skills that the tests or procedures are designed to assess; (6) preemployment physicals after a conditional offer of employment is extended are permissible only if all employees are subject to them; (7) medical information on employees must be kept separate from other personal information; and (8) employers cannot make inquiries about an applicant's past workers' compensation claims or disabilities in general.

Employers may continue to use drug and alcohol tests, either on a preemployment or random basis, inasmuch as these tests are not considered to be medical examinations. Recovering drug and alcohol abusers are protected on the basis of disability. Current drug abusers are not and may be terminated. Alcoholics, however, are protected and must be given the choice to seek rehabilitation or face termination.

One of the greatest impacts of ADA on the staffing function has been in the areas of job analysis and job descriptions. Employers must now carefully analyze jobs to ascertain essential job functions and marginal job functions and clearly identify these items on job descriptions.

Civil Rights Act of 1991

During its 1988–1989 term, the Supreme Court rendered six employment discrimination decisions of such magnitude that a Congressional response was provoked.[25] The result was passage of the Civil Rights Act of 1991, a statute some have described as "the most sweeping amendment to employment discrimination regulation since Title VII." [26] The House of Representatives report accompanying the bill identified two primary purposes of the Act: (1) "to respond to recent Supreme Court decisions by restoring the civil rights protections that were dramatically limited by those decisions" and (2) "to strengthen existing protections and remedies available under federal civil rights laws to provide more effective deterrence and adequate compensation for victims of discrimination."

The Act amended the following five statutes: (1) Civil Rights Act of 1866; (2) Title VII of the Civil Rights Act of 1964, as amended; (3) Age Discrimination in Employment Act of 1967, as amended; (4) Rehabilitation Act of 1973; and (5) Americans with Disabilities Act of 1990. The key provisions of the Act are described below.

Monetary Damages and Jury Trials. Individuals who consider themselves to be victims of intentional discrimination predicated on race, gender (including sexual harassment), religion, or disability can seek compensatory damages for pain and suffering and punitive damages as well. These damages are available only from private sector employers and are not applicable to adverse impact cases. Alleged victims of intentional discrimination are provided the right to demand a jury trial. The amount of damages that can be awarded depend upon the size of the employer's work force and range from $50,000 for employers having 15 to 100 employees to $300,000 for employers having 500 or more employees.

Adverse Impact. In an adverse impact case, the plaintiff must identify a specific employment practice as the cause of discrimination. If the employee is successful in this effort, the burden of proof then shifts to the employer who must "demonstrate that the challenged practice is job related for the position in question and consistent with business necessity."

Protection in Foreign Countries. The Act amends Title VII and the Age Discrimination in Employment Act by extending protection from employment discrimination to U.S. citizens working in a foreign facility owned or controlled by a U.S. company. The employer is not required to comply with U.S. discrimination laws, however, if to do so would violate the law of the host country.

Racial Harassment or Other Post-hiring Conduct. The Civil Rights Act of 1866 was amended to broaden the term "make and enforce contracts" to encompass not only the making, performance, modification, and termination of contracts, but also the enjoyment of all benefits, privileges, terms, and conditions of the contractual relationship.

Challenges to Consent Decrees. Challenges to consent decrees or other orders by individuals who had notice of the proposed judgment, a reasonable opportunity to present objections, and whose interests were adequately represented and protected by another party who challenged the decree on the same grounds are barred. In other words, nonparties to the original suit cannot mount a legal challenge to previously decided enforcement actions.

Mixed Motive Cases. Under the Civil Rights Act of 1991, a finding of discrimination is not negated even though the employer demonstrates that the same decision would have been reached without the influence of the discriminatory factor. On the other hand, if the employer can show that the same decision would have been reached without using the discriminatory factor, the court may not assess damages or require rehiring, reinstatement, or promotion of the plaintiff.

Seniority Systems. Seniority systems that intentionally discriminate can, under the Act, be challenged within 180 days at any of three points: (1) when the system is adopted, (2) when a protected class member becomes subject to the system, or (3) when a person is actually injured by the system.

Race Norming. The Act makes it unlawful "to adjust the scores of, use different cutoff scores for, or otherwise alter the results of employment-related tests on the basis of race, color, religion, sex, or national origin."

Expert Witness Fees. Expert witness fees are recoverable, along with attorneys' fees, under Title VII and are not considered separate elements of litigation expenses.

Protection of U.S. Senate Employees and Appointed Officials. The Act extends employment discrimination protection to protected class employees of the U.S. Senate, political appointees of the president, and staff members employed by elected officials at the state level.

Glass Ceiling Commission. The Civil Rights Act of 1991 established the Glass Ceiling Commission and charged it with the responsibility of investigating the barriers to advancement of women and minorities in the workplace and making recommendations for the purpose of eliminating those barriers.

The Family and Medical Leave Act of 1993

The Family and Medical Leave Act of 1993 (FMLA) was the first piece of legislation signed by former President Bill Clinton when he took office in January 1993. Congress had twice passed similar legislation that the President George H. W. Bush had on each occasion vetoed.

The Act guarantees up to 12 weeks of unpaid leave per year for birth or adoption of a child; caring for an ill child, spouse, or parents; or the employee's own serious health condition. Where practical, employees must give the employer a 30-day notice of intent to take leave. Employers must maintain health insurance benefits during the leave period. Additionally, employees are guaranteed the right to return to their same or comparable jobs when their leaves are over. Employers can require workers to provide medical certification of serious injuries as well as a second medical opinion. A company may exempt from FMLA coverage the top 10 percent of its highest paid employees.

To be eligible for leave under FMLA, an employee must have been on the job for at least one year and have worked a minimum of 1,250 hours during the preceding 12-month period.

Employers may require that covered employees use vacation and sick leave first before the period of unpaid leave begins, provided that vacation and sick leave are compensated at the rates normally used by the company.

There are four methods of determining the 12-month period constituting the period in which FMLA leave may be taken: any calendar year; any fixed-month leave year, such as a fiscal year; the 12-month period as measured by the employee's first FMLA leave; or a rolling 12-month period measured backward from the date an employee uses any FMLA leave. The calculation method selected must be applied consistently and uniformly to all covered employees.

FMLA applies to private sector firms that employ 50 workers, including part-time workers, within a 75-mile radius; i.e., not all 50 employees are required to work at any one job site for an employer to be covered. Public sector employers that are subject to the provisions of the Fair Labor Standards Act of 1938 are also covered as well as the federal government.

It is estimated that only 5 percent of U.S. employers are affected by FMLA. Approximately 40 percent of all employees are covered.[27]

Uniformed Services Employment and Reemployment Rights Act of 1994, as Amended

The Uniformed Services Employment and Reemployment Act (USERRA) was signed into law in October 1994. It was subsequently amended in 1996, 1998, and 2000. The expressed purposes of the Act are the following:

(1) to encourage noncareer service in the uniformed services by eliminating or minimizing the disadvantages to civilian careers and employment which can result from such service, (2) to minimize the disruption to the lives of persons performing service in the uniformed services as well as to their employers, their fellow employees, and their communities, by providing for the prompt reemployment of such persons upon their completion of such service, and (3) to prohibit discrimination against persons because of their service in the uniformed services.

As specified in the Act, uniformed services include the Army, Navy, Marine Corps, Air Force, Public Health Service Commission Corps, reserve components of the aforementioned services, as well as the National Guard and Air National Guard.

Under USERRA employers must hold open jobs of employees away on military service and not discriminate against such employees in any way because of their military service. Upon return from a period of military service lasting up to five years, the employee is entitled to whatever position he or she would have attained with reasonable certainty had the employee's military service not interfered with the person's tenure in the employing organization. In other words, promotions the employee would have earned or pay increases the employee would have received must be considered in ascertaining where the employee is to be placed in the company upon return from military service. An employee returning from military service may not be terminated or subjected to adverse employment action, except for cause (e.g., a bona fide reduction in force), for 12 months after the date of his or her reinstatement. USERRA provides that employers must offer up to 18 months of health coverage to employees who are away on military duty. Upon return from military service, the employee must immediately be covered under the employer's health insurance plan if the employee was covered prior to military service. Seniority under an employer's pension or retirement plan must continue to accrue while the employee is on military duty and to the extent the employer funds the retirement plan, the employer must continue to fund the employee's participation in the plan. Generally speaking, if a benefit has to do with length of service that would have accrued had the employee not been away on military service, the employer must award the benefit to the returning employee as if he or she had not been away. USERRA protection is extended to all types and varieties of employees. For Family and Medical Leave Act purposes, all of an employee's months of military service must be credited toward FMLA eligibility.[28]

In the event a returning employee is disabled, the employer must make reasonable accommodation to reinstate, retrain, and retain the employee. Whereas the Americans with Disabilities Act requires only that employers make reasonable accommodations for individuals who can perform the essential functions of a job, USERRA requires employers to make reasonable accommodations in the form of training and retraining returning employees so that they may become qualified to perform essential functions of jobs to which they may be entitled.

USERRA prohibits employers from requiring that employees leaving for military service use accrued vacation, sick, or other types of leave time for military service.

USERRA covers almost all private and government employers. It is administered by the Department of Labor through its Veterans' Employment and Training Service (VETS).

As the foregoing review of federal employment statutes has indicated, the field of human resource management has become quite legalistic in nature. Consequently, a general awareness of the legal framework surrounding the management of people is imperative for staffing specialists in order to avoid employment practices that are proscribed by law.

EXECUTIVE ORDERS

An Executive Order is a directive issued by the president of the United States, without legislative authority, stipulating the terms and conditions under which the federal government will do business with private sector employers or regulating the employment practices of the government itself. Executive Orders cover only those private employers who do business with the government and have thus entered into a contract whereby they agree, as a condition of the contract, to abide by the terms and conditions set forth by the government.

The Executive Order that has had the most impact on employment practices of firms doing business with the federal government is Executive Order 11246 as amended by Executive Order 11375.

Executive Order 11246, as Amended by Executive Order 11375

Executive Order 11246 was signed by President Lyndon Johnson on September 24, 1965.[29] This Executive Order makes it the policy of the government to provide equal opportunity in federal employment for all qualified persons. Discrimination in employment because of race, creed, color, or national origin is prohibited. The Order also requires promoting the full realization of equal employment opportunity in the federal sector through a positive, continuing program of affirmative action in each executive department and governmental agency. The policy of equal opportunity applies to every aspect of federal employment policy, procedure, and practice.

A major provision of Executive Order 11246 requires that all executive departments or agencies that issue contracts to employers or that administer programs involving federal financial assistance to employers must make certain those employers adhere to a policy of nondiscrimination in employment as a condition for the approval of a contract, grant, loan, insurance, or guarantee. The "equal opportunity clause" in the contract or grant stipulates that the employer, as follows: (1) will not discriminate against any applicant or employee because of race, creed, color, or national origin; (2) will take affirmative action to increase the number of minorities or protected classes in the employer's work force; (3) agrees to follow the rules, regulations, and requirements set forth by Executive Order 11246; (4) will furnish all information that may be required by federal agencies; (5) state its policy of nondiscrimination in employment advertisements; (6) notify any union with which it has a labor agreement of its policy of nondiscrimination and its intention to follow the requirements of the Executive Order; and (7) include an equal opportunity clause in each subcontract it issues.

Employment practices covered by this regulation include recruiting, employment advertising, selecting, promoting, demoting, transferring, layoffs, terminations, rates of pay and other compensation, and selection for training, including apprenticeship programs. Employers are also required to post notices, in conspicuous places in their facilities such as employee bulletin boards, concerning their nondiscriminatory policies.

In the event of noncompliance, contracts can be canceled, terminated, or suspended in whole or part, and the contractor may be declared ineligible for further government contracts.

In 1968, Executive Order 11246 was amended by Executive Order 11375. The word "creed" was changed to "religion" and sex discrimination was added to the other prohibited forms of discrimination.

All first- or second-tier government contractors with contracts in excess of $10,000 are covered under this regulation. Contractors with contracts of $50,000 or more must also file EEO-1 reports (to be discussed in Chapter 4) and develop a written affirmative action plan. It is interesting to note that these affirmative action requirements are not established by the Executive Order itself, but by OFCCP regulations. Contractors having contracts of $1 million or more must meet all of the previous stipulations and must undergo an on-site pre-award compliance review.

The secretary of labor established the Office of Federal Contract Compliance Programs and gave it the power and responsibility for administering and enforcing Executive Order 11246.[30] The OFCCP has set forth regulations that apply to both federal contractors and subcontractors. Under Executive Order 12086 issued by President Jimmy Carter in 1978, OFCCP has the responsibility for conducting equal employment opportunity compliance reviews for contracts issued by the Department of Defense and other federal departments and agencies. When there is reason to believe that a contractor has violated the equal opportunity clause in a contract, the director is empowered to institute proceedings to correct the violation. The contractor in question must be given a full hearing in front of an administrative law judge before OFCCP can impose any sanctions against the contractor. As previously stated, OFCCP can cancel or suspend contracts for failure to comply with equal opportunity requirements. OFCCP also has the power to prohibit federal agencies from entering into new contracts with contractors who have been declared ineligible.

COMMON LAW TORTS

Today's aggrieved employees are increasingly turning to use of common law torts as vehicles for redress of their employment complaints against employers. When the first edition of this text was published, tort causes of action in employment disputes were atypical because most lawsuits were filed under federal or state statutes. Currently common law employment tort cases are commonplace. Consequently, human resource professionals must become familiar with yet another facet of the complex, rapidly changing environment of employment law.

Common law originated in England and was later applied in the United States. It is based on judicial precedents rather than legislative statutes. Common law is derived from "comprehensive principles based on justice, reason, and common sense" rather than "absolute, fixed, and inflexible rules." [31] The principles of common law "have been determined by the social needs of the community and have changed" as "conditions, interests, relations, and usages" have occurred in society.[32] Common law is dynamic and subject to modification as the expectations of society expand. Thus, it is an area of employment law that can be expected to be used more widely in the future.

A tort is defined as a noncontractual

private or civil wrong or injury resulting from a breach of a legal duty that exists by virtue of society's expectations regarding interpersonal conduct . . . The essential elements of a tort are . . . a legal duty owed by a defendant to a plaintiff, breach of that duty, and a causal relation between defendant's conduct and the resulting damage to plaintiff.[33]

As applied in the employment arena, a tort is a private or civil wrong inflicted by an employer on an employee as a result of a breach of society-imposed obligations owed by the employer to the employee.

Employment torts are of particular concern to human resource managers and staffing specialists because not only the organization but also individual managers may be held liable for compensatory, consequential, and punitive damages.

Types of Employment Torts

There are a number of employment torts frequently used as causes of action by aggrieved employees. Some of the more commonplace are assault, battery, false imprisonment, invasion of privacy, defamation, negligence, and intentional infliction of emotional distress.

Assault. Assault is defined as "an attempt or threat, with unlawful force, to inflict bodily injury upon another accompanied by the apparent present ability to give effect to the attempt if not prevented." [34] Even a threat intended as a "joke" may be considered an assault if the victim is placed in reasonable fear. For example, if a supervisor pulls back a fist and says to an employee, "I'm going to knock some sense into you," the supervisor has committed an assault if the employee perceives the gesture as a threat accompanied by an ability to carry it out and experiences reasonable fear of harm. In instances of sexual harassment, gestures and statements may be construed as assault.

No actual touching or physical injury is needed to establish an assault. Legally, an assault may be both a tort and a criminal offense.

Battery. This tortious act is defined as the touching of another person, willfully or in anger, against his or her wishes. Battery also extends to "anything so closely attached that it is customarily regarded as part" [35] of the person, e.g., the person's clothing, the person's automobile, or the person's desk. Offensive, but harmless, touching may entitle the person touched to nominal damages. A manager who slams an item down on an employee's desk or who purposely knocks an item off that desk may be committing battery. As in assault, battery has both criminal and tort aspects.

False Imprisonment. False imprisonment occurs when a person is intentionally and unjustifiably detained. Mere obstruction, stopping a person, or locking a person out of his or her office is not sufficient to constitute false imprisonment. The restraint must be so total that it amounts to an imprisonment; however, the duration of such restraint may be of any appreciable period of time. The use of physical force is not required to establish a cause of action. If the victim reasonably believes that he or she has been restrained against his or her will, a cause of action has occurred. No actual damages have to be proved in a false imprisonment case.

Invasion of Privacy. Although the U.S. Constitution does not specifically guarantee the right to privacy,[36] tort law protects an individual's private concerns against wrongful intrusion by other individuals or the government. Unwarranted exploitation of personal information or publicity that causes mental suffering or humiliation is actionable under tort law. In general, employers are entitled to intrude on an applicant's or employee's "personal life no more than is necessary for legitimate business interests." [37] Areas in which employers may find themselves violating an employee's privacy include credit reports, drug tests, medical records, off-the-job behavior, and unreasonable searches of lockers.

Defamation. The publication of anything injurious to a person's reputation or good name or anything that tends to bring a person into disrepute constitutes defamation. A defamation in writing is libel; a defamation delivered orally is slander. While technically "there is no legal cause of action called defamation," [38] libel and slander as actual causes of action are based on defamation. Although establishing "a prima facie case of defamation requires a false statement, even a vague statement that casts doubt on the reputation of an individual by inference can cause difficulties for an employer if the statement cannot be substantiated." [39] Furnishing references is the primary area where employers are at risk for violations of this type. Self-compelled disclosure is another form of defamation that has been more frequently used over the past few years. When an employee is given a false or defamatory reason for his or her termination and is subsequently required to reveal this reason to prospective employers, defamation is deemed to have occurred.

Negligence. Negligence is the "failure to exercise that degree of care which a person of ordinary prudence would exercise under the same circumstances." [40] In other words, negligence is conduct that does not provide for the proper protection of others against reasonable risk of harm.

Of particular importance to human resource professionals are the five forms of negligence that have been used as causes of action in cases involving staffing activities: negligent hiring, negligent retention, negligent training, negligent supervision, and negligent referencing.

An employer has a continuous and nondelegatable duty to furnish an adequate force of competent workers for performing the duties of the workplace with relative safety. If an employer hires an individual who is incompetent or unfit for the position for which he or she was hired and thereby poses a potential risk of injury to other workers, the employer runs the risk of a negligent hiring claim. Or if an employer knowingly hires an individual who poses a danger to other employees, customers, vendors, etc., the employer is open to charges of negligent hiring. It is imperative that staffing specialists exercise due diligence in checking references and backgrounds of all prospective employees. In the absence of due diligence or reasonable care in the hiring of employees, an employer may be open to claims of negligence in the hiring process.

Another possible negligence claim is negligent retention: the failure to terminate an employee once it has come to light that the person in question poses a risk to others. For example, a taxicab company that knowingly retains a cab driver previously convicted of sexual assault may be liable for negligent retention because the company failed to assume its obligation to transfer, retrain, reassign, reschedule, or discharge an employee who in his present position posed a potential danger to others.

Negligent training may arise in situations where an employer has provided insufficient training to enable an employee to safely perform job duties without posing a risk to others. Assume that a recently hired worker is given 2 hours training in how to operate a forklift and the normally prescribed training period is 20 hours. Further assume that in using the forklift the employee injures a fellow employee. The employer may be held liable for negligent training because the employer had reason to believe that the shortened training period was insufficient and that injuries could occur if an operator was improperly trained.

Negligent supervision may occur in situations where supervisors fail to provide reasonable care and protection for employees. In one particular case, a supervisor failed to take steps to prevent "a vicious case of racial harassment" by coworkers of a minority employee. The supervisor was held liable because he knew or should have known about the harassment and did not take steps to end it.

Negligent referencing involves the giving of false or misleading information about a former employee by a former employer when the former employer knew that the information was incorrect and that, if hired, the former employee would pose a danger to others in the new workplace. For example, if the referencing company fails to reveal that the previous employee has a history of violence, including violence on the premises of the past employer, the company providing the information may be held liable for negligent referencing inasmuch as it knew that it was withholding important information and thereby putting others at risk.

Intentional Infliction of Emotional Distress. This common law tort involves intentional conduct on the part of an employer that is so "extreme and outrageous" as to cause emotional distress on the part of the employee. In one case, an employer and an individual supervisor were held liable for intentional infliction of emotional distress after describing an employee's sales meetings as "cult-like" and "satanic." An employer exercising its legal right to take action against an employee, such as in a discipline or termination situation, does not intentionally inflict emotional distress even though the employer knows that its actions will cause emotional harm. In other words, an employer's conduct must be patently egregious for its actions to constitute an intentional infliction of emotional distress.

STATE AND LOCAL LAWS

In addition to federal legislation, administrative regulations, and common law torts governing staffing practices, there are numerous state and local laws that affect human resource management.[41] Some states, such as Michigan, Wisconsin, Illinois, New York, and California, frequently serve as trendsetters, passing state statutes on employment rights well before Congress enacts similar federal legislation. At times, state legislation is even more stringent than federal legislation. For example, in New York the protected age group is 18 years of age and older and an employer cannot discriminate against anyone in that group on the basis of age. Age-based retirement is illegal except in a few occupations. However, in the majority of instances, federal legislation sets the pattern for subsequent state statutes.

A number of states and even some municipalities have passed fair employment practice laws that prohibit discrimination on the basis of race, color, religion, sex, or national origin. Some cities such as San Francisco have ordinances that protect individuals from sexual orientation discrimination. Several states also have antidiscrimination laws protecting the disabled. When federal legislation conflicts with state or local employment practices regulations, the law that most favors the employee or the protected class of employees is the one that will be followed. This means that federal statutes are the ones adhered to in the majority of cases.

One area in which variances between federal legislation and state legislation is being seen with greater frequency is required hourly minimum wages. Table 2.1 shows a list of those states that have higher mandated minimum wages than set by the federal government.

Because state and local laws vary greatly, it is outside the scope of this book to attempt to examine or compare them. It is important, though, that human resource personnel (and staffing specialists in particular) familiarize themselves with the

Table 2.1
States with Minimum Wages in Excess of Federal Minimum Wage as of 2008

Washington	8.07
Massachusetts	8.00
California	8.00
Oregon	7.95
Arizona	7.90
Illinois	7.75
Vermont	7.68
Connecticut	7.65
Michigan	7.40
Rhode Island	7.40
Hawaii	7.25
Iowa	7.25
New Hampshire	7.25
West Virginia	7.25
Alaska	7.15
Delaware	7.15
New Jersey	7.15
New York	7.15
Pennsylvania	7.15
Colorado	7.12
Maine	7.00
Ohio	7.00
Florida	6.79
Missouri	6.15
Federal Minimum Wage (2008)	6.55
Federal Minimum Wage (2009)	7.25

Source: U.S. Department of Labor.

numerous state and local regulations relative to employment practices in the locales where their companies conduct business. Failure to do so may make an already complicated legal environment even more difficult to contend with.

NOTES

1. Howard C. Lockwood, "Equal Employment Opportunities," in *Staffing Policies and Strategies,* ed. Dale Yoder and Herbert G. Heneman (Washington, DC: Bureau of National Affairs, 1974), 4–252.

2. Barbara Lindermann Schlei and Paul Grossman, *Employment Discrimination Law,* 2nd ed. (Washington, DC: Bureau of National Affairs, 1983), 692.

3. R. Wayne Mondy and Robert M. Noe, *Personnel: Human Resource Management,* 6th ed. (Upper Saddle River, NJ: Prentice-Hall, Inc., 1996), 467.

4. Donld L. Caruth, *Compensation Management for Banks* (Boston: Bankers Publishing Company, 1986), 252–253.

5. "The Federal Hourly Minimum Wage Since Its Inception," *HR-News,* December 1999, 34.

6. George T. Milkovich and Jerry M. Newman, *Compensation,* 6th ed. (Boston: Irwin-McGraw-Hill, 1999), 542–548.

7. "Job Out of Bounds," *HR Magazine,* October 1999, 59.

8. Mondy and Noe, *Human Resource Management,* 468.

9. Kenneth J. McCulloch, *Selecting Employees Safely under the Law* (Englewood Cliffs, NJ: Prentice-Hall, 1981), 182–183.

10. Mondy and Noe, *Human Resource Management,* 61.

11. Ibid., 61.

12. Schlei and Grossman, *Employment Discrimination Law,* 507–517.

13. Mondy and Noe, *Human Resource Management,* 62.

14. Schlei and Grossman, *Employment Discrimination Law,* 276.

15. Mondy and Noe, *Human Resource Management,* 62.

16. Wayne F. Cascio, *Managing Human Resources,* 4th ed. (New York: McGraw-Hill, Inc., 1995), 97.

17. *Employment Coordinator* (Deerfield, IL: Clark Boardman Callaghan, 1996), 124, 311.

18. Steven Mitchell Sack, *From Hiring to Firing* (Merrick, NY: Legal Strategiers, Inc., 1995), 286.

19. Ibid., 287.

20. Dawn D. Bennett-Alexander and Laura B. Pincus, *Employment Law for Business* (Chicago: Richard D. Irwin, Inc., 1995), 401.

21. Ibid.

22. Ibid.

23. Ibid., 401–404.

24. Mack A. Player, *Federal Law of Employment Discrimination,* 3rd ed. (St. Paul, MN: West Publishing Company), 45.

25. The six cases are Wards Cove v. Antonio (490 U.S. 642 [1989]); Price Waterprice v. Hopkins (409 U.S. 22 [1989]); Patterson v. McClean Credit Union (491 U.S. 164 [1889]); Martin v. Wilks (490 U.S. 755 [1989]); West Virginia Hospitals v. Casey (55 F.E.P. Case 353 [1989]); and Lorance v. AT&T Technologies (490 U.S. 900 [1989]).

26. Bennett-Alexander and Pincus, *Employment Law for Business,* 574.

27. Ibid., 251.

28. *Especially for Texas Employers* (Austin, TX: Texas Workforce Commission, 2008), 95.

29. Mondy and Noe, *Human Resource Management,* 71.

30. Ibid., 71–72.

31. Steven H. Gifis, *Law Dictionary,* 3rd ed. (Hauppauge, NY: Barron's Educational Services, Inc., 1991), 82.

32. Ibid.

33. Ibid., 492.

34. Ibid., 30.

35. Ibid., 44.

36. Ibid., 372.

37. Barbara Kate Repa, *Your Rights in the Workplace* (Berkeley, CA: Nolo Press, 1994), 6/2.

38. Gifis, *Law Dictionary,* 35.

39. Bennett-Alexander and Pincus, *Employment Law for Business,* 315.

40. Gifis, *Law Dictionary,* 315.

41. Mondy and Noe, *Human Resource Management,* 69–70.

3

Significant Federal Court Decisions

Because law is a dynamic thing that changes as the courts interpret, reinterpret, and apply it in various cases, human resource practitioners must know much more than just the letter of the law as expressed in employment statutes. They must also understand the spirit of the law as defined by the courts. Interpretation of the law is revised from time to time as new court decisions are rendered, even though the statutes in question may not have been altered by further legislative action. Consequently, it is imperative for human resource professionals to understand how the courts have applied and interpreted the law in previous situations. Thus, it is appropriate to review some of the more significant federal court decisions and indicate the requirements imposed by these decisions. We will first examine decisions handed down by the Supreme Court and then consider those rendered by the various federal Circuit Courts of Appeal.

SUPREME COURT DECISIONS

As the final interpreter of the law, the Supreme Court actually decides how federal statutes or Constitutional provisions will be applied. Decisions rendered by the Court become, in effect, the "law of the land" and are binding on all entities in the country. It is vitally important, therefore, to understand how the Court has ruled on the application of federal statutes relative to staffing. A review of several major cases will illustrate the Court's interpretation of what it sees as the spirit of the law in employment situations.

Griggs v. Duke Power Company

Decided by the Supreme Court in March 1971, *Griggs* is the landmark case in human resource management and has had the most far-reaching impact on employment practices of any case decided by the Court. At issue was the question of whether the company could use a high school diploma and a passing score on a standardized intelligence test as bona fide requirements for employment or promotion. The petitioner was able to demonstrate that in the relevant labor market for the company 34 percent of white males had a high school diploma as opposed to only 12 percent of black males. The petitioner was also able to establish that there were people who were successfully performing the job in question who did not have a high school diploma. Additionally, *Griggs* was able to prove that there was no demonstrable relationship between test scores and job performance.

As it often does, the Court used *Griggs* to interpret existing laws broadly and specify legal principles.[1] The decision affirmed the following points:

- It is not necessary to prove that an employer intended to discriminate in order to substantiate the existence of discrimination. The result of an employment practice and not the employer's intention is sufficient to establish the existence of discrimination.
- Employment practices that appear neutral on the surface or that appear neutral in intent are illegal if their effect on protected classes is unequal.
- Tests or other employment practices must be removed if they discriminate on the basis of race or any other protected Title VII classification.
- Tests or other measuring devices can be used only when they can be shown to have a demonstrable relationship to actual job performance.
- It is the responsibility of the employer to show that tests are job related.

The immediate impact of the *Griggs* decision was felt in the area of pre-employment testing. Many employers abandoned the use of tests altogether; others retained industrial psychologists or psychometricians to establish a statistical relationship between employment tests and actual job performance. Concomitantly, employers began to examine other pre-employment practices that had a tendency to eliminate higher percentages of minorities and women than of white males from hiring consideration.

Overlooked to a great extent in the immediate concern with pre-employment practices was the fact that the Court had laid down requirements for *all* employment practices. Any employment practice, as clarified in later Court decisions, must meet job relatedness and nondiscriminatory standards.

Phillips v. Martin Marietta Corporation

In another 1971 decision, the Court ruled that the company had discriminated against a female because she had young children. This was the first decision involving the issue of "sex-plus" discrimination, i.e., discrimination on the basis of sex due to a subset of gender.

The company had a rule of not hiring women with school-age children; no such rule was imposed on males. The company argued that it did not preclude all women from job consideration; in fact, the company's work force was 75 percent female. Martin Marietta contended that the rule was a business necessity because women with school-age children were likely to be absent more frequently than those without children.

The Court rejected the company's argument and ruled that an employer cannot have one hiring policy for women and another hiring policy for men. The major implication of this decision is that hiring standards must be uniform for both sexes and that the employer cannot use a subset of sex (such as having children) unless it is applied equally to both men and women.

Espinoza v. Farah Manufacturing Company

In 1973 the Court ruled that Title VII does not prohibit discrimination on the basis of lack of citizenship. The Equal Employment Opportunity Commission had previously said that it was discriminatory to refuse to hire anyone who was a noncitizen since this selection standard was likely to have an adverse impact on individuals of foreign national origin. Inasmuch as 92 percent of the employees at the Farah facility in question were Mexican-Americans or native Mexicans who had become American citizens, the Court held that the company had not discriminated on the basis of national origin when it refused to hire a Hispanic who was not a U.S. citizen.

Albermarle Paper Company v. Moody

In this 1975 case, the Court reaffirmed its position on the use of employment tests by ruling as follows:

- Any test used in selection or promotion must be validated if its use has been shown to discriminate against a protected class.
- The burden of proof for demonstrating that a test is valid rests entirely upon the employer.
- Any selection device used by an employer must be shown to measure what it actually purports to measure.
- Performance appraisals that do not have a job-related content base have a built-in bias.
- A job analysis conducted by an employer is admissible as evidence that the employer has made a good faith attempt to validate selection and promotion tests.
- Performance appraisals by supervisors that are based on vague and inadequate standards of job relatedness are open to subjective interpretations and do not meet the guidelines for test validity.

The decision in this case makes clear the following: (1) tests must be job related, (2) performance appraisal is an employment test and the system of appraisal used must be validated in terms of actual job content, (3) it is the employer that must substantiate the job relatedness of any test, and (4) job analysis can be used as evidence to show that performance appraisal or any other test measures what it actually purports to measure.[2]

Washington v. Davis

In 1970 two black police officers in the District of Columbia filed suit alleging that the promotion policies of the District's police department were racially discriminatory. To be accepted by the department and to enter an intensive 17-week training program, a police recruit was required to satisfy certain physical and character standards, to be a high school graduate or the equivalent, and to receive a grade of at least 40 on "Test 21," an examination developed by the Civil Service Commission and widely used throughout the federal service.[3]

The validity of Test 21, designed to measure verbal ability, vocabulary, reading, and comprehension, was the issue in question. However, the District Court in trying the case noted that, since August 1969, 44 percent of the new police force recruits had been black. This percentage represented the proportion of blacks on the police force and was roughly equivalent to the percentage of 20- to 29-year-old blacks residing in the department's 50-mile recruiting radius. The District Court rejected the contention that Test 21 was culturally biased to favor whites over blacks. It found the test to be reasonable and directly related to the requirements of the police-recruit training program and that it was neither designed nor operated so as to discriminate against blacks. The test sampled material that recruits would be exposed to in the training program. Moreover, a positive relationship was found to exist between success in the training program and success on the job. However, it was also found that blacks and women failed the test at a much higher rate than did white males.

The Court of Appeals overturned the District Court ruling and held that lack of discriminatory intent was irrelevant since four times as many blacks as whites failed the test—a disproportionate impact that evidenced the existence of discrimination.

In 1976 the Supreme Court reversed the decision of the Court of Appeals and upheld the decision of the District Court. It ruled that there was no indication that the test was racially biased or that it had been used for the purpose of excluding blacks from the police force. A major conclusion in this case is that if a test is specifically job related and racially neutral, it may be used as a selection device even though it has a disproportionate impact on protected classes.

Weber v. Kaiser Aluminum Corporation

In 1974 the United Steelworkers of America and Kaiser Aluminum and Chemical Corporation entered into a master collective bargaining agreement covering the terms and conditions of employment at 15 Kaiser plants. The agreement contained an affirmative action plan designed to eliminate racial imbalances in Kaiser's almost exclusively white craft work force. Hiring goals for black craft workers were set at each Kaiser plant. The hiring goals were equal to the percentages of blacks in each of the respective labor markets for the 15 plants. To enable the plants to meet these goals, on-the-job training programs were initiated to train unskilled production workers, both black and white, in the skills needed to become craft workers. The plan agreed to reserve 50 percent of the openings in these newly created in-plant training programs for blacks.

In 1974 only 1.83 percent of the skilled craft workers at the Gramercy, Louisiana, plant were black, although the work force in the local labor market was approximately 39 percent black. Thirteen craft trainees were selected from the Gramercy plant's production work force for the new training program—seven blacks and six whites. The most junior black employee selected for the program had less seniority than several of the white workers whose bids for admission were rejected. Brian Weber, one of the rejected white workers, subsequently filed a class action suit alleging that Kaiser and the United Steelworkers had discriminated against him and other white workers.

Although the lower courts agreed with Weber's allegation of discrimination, the Supreme Court did not and reversed the rulings of the lower courts. In reaching its decision, the Court relied heavily upon what it considered to be the underlying intent or spirit of Title VII—the opening of job opportunities for blacks. The Court recognized that while there was no history of discrimination against blacks at the company, there was a serious underutilization of blacks in the craft work force. Also, the plan had been voluntarily entered into by Kaiser and the United Steelworkers and did not, per se, create a bar to employment or advancement of white workers. Moreover, the plan was temporary in nature and would terminate when the percentage of black workers in the crafts was equal to the percentage of blacks in the labor market. Under these conditions, the Court felt that there was no violation of Title VII.[4]

Dothard v. Rawlinson

In this 1977 case the Court addressed minimum height and weight requirements. Rawlinson, a 22-year-old female college graduate whose major course of study had been correctional psychology, was denied employment as a correctional counselor trainee because she failed to meet the state of Alabama's minimum weight requirement of 120 pounds for the position of correctional counselor. The Court held that minimum height and weight requirements have a discriminatory impact on females where there is no evidence to attest to the necessity of these requirements for satisfactory job performance.

Regents of the University of California v. Bakke

This highly publicized 1978 case was the first Supreme Court case to address the issue of reverse discrimination.[5]

The medical school of the University of California at Davis had an admissions program wherein a minimum number of places (16 out of 100) in the first year medical class were reserved for racial minorities. Allen Bakke, a while male, was denied admission twice to the medical school even though he scored higher on the admission criteria than some minority group members who were admitted. Bakke filed suit in state court charging that he had been discriminated against because of his race. In 1976, ruling in Bakke's favor and issuing a decree requiring his admission to the medical school, the California Supreme Court held that a preferential selection program was unconstitutional. The U.S. Supreme Court, acting on a request from the regents of the University of California, agreed to review the state court's decision.

The Court reached its decision on June 28, 1978. In a five-to-four decision, the University was ordered to admit Bakke to medical school. He subsequently received his degree in 1982 and later became an anesthesiologist.

Even though deciding in Bakke's favor, the Court failed to clarify or settle the issue of reverse discrimination. On the question of whether or not the racial quota system at the university was acceptable in deciding who should be admitted, four of the Justices said yes. On the question of whether or not an applicant's race can ever be considered in admission decisions, five of the Justices said yes. Apparently, affirmative action programs that require government contractors covered by Executive Order 11246 to utilize racial hiring goals and timetables to correct the past effects of discriminatory practices are acceptable, but individual decisions to discriminate against specific white applicants in order to remedy past effects of employment practices are not. Rather than saying that no consideration of race is acceptable in hiring or admission programs, the Court seemed to suggest that race may be taken into consideration as a factor as long as it is not the *sole* factor in making a selection decision.

American Tobacco Company v. Patterson

This 1982 decision allows seniority and promotion systems established after Title VII to stand although they unintentionally affect minority workers adversely. Under *Griggs* a *prima facie* violation of Title VII may be established by policies or practices that are facially neutral and neutral in intent but that nevertheless discriminate against a particular protected class. A seniority system would fall under the *Griggs* rationale were it not for Section 703(h) of the Civil Rights Act of 1964. That section provides the following:

Notwithstanding any other provision of this subchapter, it shall not be an unlawful employment practice for an employer to apply different standards of compensation, or different terms, conditions, or privileges of employment pursuant to a bona fide seniority or merit system ... provided that such differences are not the result of an intention to discriminate because of race, color, religion, sex, or national origin, nor shall it be an unlawful employment practice for an employer to give and to act upon the results of any professionally developed ability test provided that such test, its administration or action upon the results is not designed, intended, or used to discriminate because of race, color, religion, sex, or national origin.

Thus, the Court ruled that a bona fide seniority system adopted after Title VII may stand even though it has a discriminatory impact. It should be noted that the Supreme Court has generally taken a "hands off" position where bona fide labor agreements between company and union are involved as long as the agreement does not intend to discriminate.

County of Washington v. Gunther

At issue in this case was the question of whether or not employees who fail to satisfy "the equal pay for equal work" standard of the Equal Pay Act are precluded from pursuing action under Title VII on a claim of sex-based pay discrimination.

A group of women who were employed as guards in the female section of the jail of the County of Washington, Oregon, filed suit for back pay and other relief claiming, among other things, that they had been paid lower wages than male guards in the male section of the jail and that part of this differential was attributable to intentional sex discrimination. Based on the County's own wage and salary survey, male guards were compensated at a rate of 100 percent of the evaluated worth of their jobs. Female guards were compensated at a rate of 70 percent of the evaluated worth of their jobs even though the County had previously determined that their jobs should be compensated at a rate of 95 percent of their evaluated worth. The District Court rejected the female guards' claim, ruling that a sex-based wage discrimination charge cannot be brought under Title VII unless it satisfies the equal pay for equal work standard of the Equal Pay Act. "[T]he District Court found that male guards supervised more than ten times as many prisoners per guard as did the female guards, and that females devoted much of their time to less valuable clerical duties." Since equal pay for equal work was not in question because the jobs were unequal, the female guards' claims were rejected.

The Ninth Circuit Court of Appeals reversed the decision of the lower court, holding that persons alleging sex discrimination "are not precluded from suing under Title VII to protest . . . discriminatory compensation practices" simply because their jobs were not equal to higher paying jobs held by members of the opposite sex.

The Supreme Court ruled on June 8, 1981, in a five-four decision that "claims of discriminatory undercompensation are not barred by . . . Title VII merely because respondents do not perform work equal to that of male jail guards." In essence, the Court's decision clearly indicates that gender motivated pay differences are a violation of Title VII even if the work of males and females is not "equal" within the meaning of the Equal Pay Act.

Connecticut v. Teal

In a 1982 decision in which the Court split five to four, the majority opinion stated "that Connecticut's non-discriminatory 'bottom line' was no answer, under the terms of Title VII, to respondents' *prima facie* claim of employment discrimination." In this case, four black employees of the Department of Income Maintenance of the State of Connecticut had been promoted provisionally to positions as Welfare Eligibility Supervisors and had served in that capacity for almost two years. To attain permanent status as supervisors, however, these individuals had to participate in a selection process that required, as the first step, a passing score on a written examination. On the examination, 54.17 percent of the black candidates passed while 79.54 percent of the white candidates passed. The four blacks who had been promoted provisionally failed. In April 1979, the four individuals filed suit alleging that Title VII had been violated by the state's imposing, as an absolute condition for consideration for promotion, that applicants pass a written test that excluded blacks in a disproportionate number. They further alleged that the test was not job related.

More than a year after the suit was filed, and approximately one month before the case went to trial, promotions were made from the eligibility list generated by the written examination. In choosing persons for that list, past work performance, recommendations from the candidates' supervisors, and seniority were considered. After the selection process was completed this time, 22.9 percent of the identified black candidates were promoted and 13.5 percent of the identified white candidates were promoted. Connecticut argued that it is this "bottom line" result, more favorable to blacks than to whites, that should be considered.

The Court ruled against Connecticut and stated that each step of the hiring process is open to scrutiny and that the final result of the selection process—the bottom line—is not sufficient evidence to prove nondiscrimination. In short, the Court ruled that each step in the selection process could be examined to show adverse impact on protected classes.[6]

Newport News Shipbuilding & Dry Dock Co. v. EEOC

In September 1979, one of the company's male employees filed a discrimination charge with EEOC alleging that the company had unlawfully refused to provide full insurance coverage for his wife's hospitalization necessitated by pregnancy. A month later the United Steelworkers of America filed a similar charge on behalf of other employees. The company then filed suit against EEOC, the male employee, and the United Steelworkers challenging EEOC's guidelines relative to health care coverage, which state that

Where an employer provides no coverage for dependents, the employer is not required to institute such coverage. However, if an employer's insurance program covers the medical expenses of spouses of female employees, then it must equally cover the medical expenses of spouses of male employees, including those arising from pregnancy-related conditions.

EEOC in turn filed an action against Newport News Shipbuilding alleging discrimination on the basis of sex against male employees in the provision of hospitalization benefits.

After passage of the Pregnancy Discrimination Act of 1978, the company had revised its health insurance plan to provide its female employees with hospitalization coverage for pregnancy-related conditions to the same extent as hospitalization benefits for all other medical conditions. It differentiated, however, between female employees and spouses of male employees in its provision of pregnancy-related benefits. In effect, female employees were completely covered while spouses of male employees were only covered to the extent of $500 for hospitalization expenses and were fully covered for all reasonable and customary delivery and anesthesiologist's charges.

The company contended that Title VII did not extend to pregnant spouses because that statute applies only to discrimination in employment and the spouses affected were not employees of the company. The District Court upheld the lawfulness of the company's benefit plan and dismissed EEOC's complaint. On appeal, the Fourth Circuit Court overturned the lower court's decision and ruled that, "The pregnancy limitation in petitioner's amended health plan discriminates against male employees."

On further appeal, the question facing the Supreme Court was whether or not the company discriminated against its male employees relative to their compensation, terms, conditions, or privileges of employment because of their sex. The Court ruled that the company's benefit plan did, in fact, discriminate against male employees on the basis of their sex. According to the Court,

There is no merit to petitioner's argument that the prohibitions of Title VII do not extend to discrimination against pregnant spouses because the statute applies only to discrimination in employment . . . The Pregnancy Discrimination Act has now made clear that . . . discrimination based on a woman's pregnancy is . . . discrimination because of her sex. And since the sex of the spouse is always the opposite of the sex of the employee, it follows inexorably that discrimination against female spouses in the provision of fringe benefits is also discrimination against male employees.

Arizona Governing Committee for Tax Deferred Annuity and Deferred Compensation Plans v. Norris

A female employee of an Arizona state agency filed a class action suit alleging that the state's deferred compensation plan for its employees discriminated on the basis of sex. Under the plan, employees were given the opportunity to postpone a portion of their wages until retirement. By doing so, participating employees could delay paying federal income tax on the amounts deferred until after retirement. The state selected several insurance companies to participate in this plan. Employees had to select one of the approved insurance companies. Many of the companies offered three payout options at retirement: (1) a single lump-sum payment, (2) periodic payments of a fixed sum for a fixed period of time, and

(3) monthly annuity payments for the remainder of the employee's life. All of the companies selected to participate used sex-based mortality tables that paid larger monthly amounts to males than to females, even when the amount of deferred compensation and retirement age were the same for either sex.

The Court held that this practice constitutes discrimination on the basis of sex and is a violation of Title VII. Several statements from the Court's majority opinion may help clarify its reasoning: (1) "We have no hesitation in holding . . . that the classification of employees on the basis of sex is no more permissible at the pay-out stage of a retirement plan than at the pay-in stage." (2) "An employer that offers one fringe benefit on a discriminatory basis cannot escape liability because he also offers other benefits on a nondiscriminatory basis." (3) "Title VII requires employers to treat their employees as individuals, not as simply components of a racial, religious, sexual, or national class." (4) "[I]f it would be unlawful to use race-based actuarial tables, it must also be unlawful to use sex-based tables." (5) "[A] scheme that uses sex to predict longevity is based on sex; it is not based on any other factor than sex." (6) "Congress has decided that classifications based on sex, like those based on national origin or race, are unlawful." (7) "An individual woman may not be paid lower monthly benefits simply because women as a class live longer than men."

It is abundantly clear from *Arizona v. Norris* that employers cannot offer any benefit to one protected class that is not offered on an equal basis to all other protected classes. Furthermore, broadly interpreting the Court's logic in this case, it would appear that any preferential treatment accorded to one protected group cannot be provided at the expense of other protected groups.

Firefighters Local Union No. 1784 v. Stotts et al.

In this 1984 decision the Supreme Court reaffirmed its position that bona fide seniority plans entered into by an employer and a union, in the absence of intent to discriminate, are solid and binding.

In 1977 a black fire-fighting captain in the Fire Department of the City of Memphis, Tennessee, filed a class action suit charging that the department and certain city officials "were engaged in a pattern or practice of making hiring and promotion decisions on the basis of race in violation of . . . Title VII." The District Court combined this suit with that of another black firefighter who claimed he had been denied a promotion because of his race. A consent decree was approved and entered by the Court in April 1980.

The stated purpose of the decree was to remedy hiring and promotion practices of the Fire Department with regard to the employment of blacks. The city agreed to promote 13 individuals as well as provide back pay to 81 employees of the department. While not admitting to any past violations of applicable laws, regulations, or rules, the city agreed to adopt a long-term goal of increasing the proportion of minority representation in each job category in the Fire Department. An interim departmental hiring goal was established wherein 50 percent of all new employees hired would be black. Moreover, it was agreed that the department would attempt to promote blacks at a rate of 20 percent in each job category. Unfortunately, the decree did not contain any provisions for layoffs or reductions in force.

When, subsequently, the city announced that budget deficits necessitated a reduction in the number of employees, the District Court issued an order enjoining the city from following the seniority system outlined in its labor agreement with the Firefighters Union. The Court stated that adhering to that system would have a racially discriminatory impact (more blacks that whites would be laid off) and declared that the seniority system was not a bona fide one. A modified layoff plan was approved whereby white employees with more seniority would be laid off rather than black employees with less seniority. The Sixth Circuit Court of Appeals, despite holding that the District Court had erred in declaring the seniority system in the labor agreement not bona fide, affirmed the lower court's decision.

The Supreme Court, in a six-to-three ruling, reversed the decision of the Circuit Court. Justice White, delivering the majority opinion, stated that "Title VII protects seniority systems . . . [and] since neither the union nor the white employees [affected] were parties to the suit when the consent decree was entered, the entry of such decree cannot be said to indicate any agreement by them to any of its terms."

In effect, the Court held that a bona fide seniority system cannot be overturned arbitrarily by a consent decree. All affected parties—employer, union, and employees—must agree to the terms of the decree whenever changes are made in a bona fide seniority plan. Again, the Court clearly stated that labor-management agreements, in the absence of intent to discrimination, must be given great deference by the courts.

Meritor Savings Bank, FSB v. Vinson

Mechelle Vinson was hired in 1974 by what later became Meritor Savings Bank as a teller trainee. The vice president who hired her, Sidney Taylor, was also branch manager for the office where Vinson was hired to work.

Vinson later testified that during her probationary period Taylor "treated her in a fatherly way and made no sexual advances. Shortly thereafter, however, he invited her out to dinner and, during the course of the meal, suggested that they go to a motel to have sexual relations. At first she refused, but out of what she described as fear of losing her job she eventually agreed." Vinson "estimated that over the next several years she had intercourse with Taylor some 40 or 50 times." Additionally, she claimed that Taylor "fondled her in front of other employees, followed her into the women's restroom . . . exposed himself to her . . . forcibly raped her on several occasions" as well as "touched and fondled other women employees of the bank." Taylor's actions toward her ceased in 1977 when Vinson began dating "a steady boyfriend."

In District Court, where subsequently it was ruled that the plaintiff "was not the victim of sexual harassment . . . and was not the victim of sexual discrimination" because the "relationship was a voluntary one having nothing to do with her continued employment . . . or her advancement or promotions," Taylor denied all allegations and maintained that he had never had sexual relations with Vinson.

The District Court also held that the bank was not liable for the conduct of its supervisor since it had no knowledge of the alleged behavior. The Circuit Court of Appeals for the District of Columbia reversed the decision of the lower court on grounds that a violation of hostile environment sexual harassment had not been considered. The lower court had considered only *quid pro quo* sexual harassment. The Circuit Court also maintained that if the evidence otherwise showed that [the supervisor] made Vinson's toleration of sexual harassment a condition of her employment, her alleged voluntary behavior had no materiality whatsoever.

The Supreme Court, in a June 1986 unanimous decision, upheld the concept of hostile environment sexual harassment regardless of whether or not such harassment is connected to possible economic gain or loss. Under Title VII, according to the Court, employees are entitled to a work environment "free from discrimination, intimidation, ridicule, or insult." However, for hostile environment harassment to occur, such harassment must be sufficiently "severe or pervasive" enough to alter the victim's conditions of employment. The Court further stated that "mere utterance of an . . . epithet which engenders offensive feelings in an employee" is not sufficient in itself to alter an employee's terms or conditions of employment.

Once the victim of harassment has indicated that sexual advances are inappropriate, voluntary participation by the victim is no longer an issue. Vinson's notice to Taylor that his advances were unwelcome also constituted notice to the bank inasmuch as Taylor was an agent for the bank. According to the Supreme Court, "the fact that sex-related conduct was voluntary in the sense that the complainant was not forced to participate against her will, is not a defense to a sexual harassment suit brought under Title VII." In determining whether or not sexual harassment has occurred, courts must examine "the record as a whole" and consider "the totality of circumstances." The Court also held that a charge of hostile environment sexual harassment was actionable under Title VII, thus establishing the validity of hostile environment claims in addition to *quid pro quo* causes of action.

In *Meritor* the Supreme Court applied concepts of common law agency principles to determine the culpability of an employer. If an employer has specific policies against sexual harassment and definitive procedures to address any complaints in this area—provided they do not include an initial step of reporting the harassing behavior to the harasser—the company is absolved from liability. Vinson had not followed the bank's grievance procedure (which was also not specific relative to sexual harassment) because the first step involved reporting any complaints to her supervisor, who, in this instance, was also the cause of the problem.

UAW v. Johnson Controls, Inc.

The Supreme Court, in this 1991 decision, reaffirmed its previous position that BFOQs must be narrowly rather than broadly interpreted. At issue was a fetal protection policy Johnson Controls implemented in its battery manufacturing process after eight of its employees became pregnant while maintaining blood lead levels exceeding the standards of the Occupational Safety and Health Administration.

The Court held that "Title VII, as amended by the Pregnancy Discrimination Act (PDA), forbids sex-specific fetal protection policies." It went on to state that, "By excluding women with childbearing capacity from lead-exposed jobs, the respondent's policy creates a facial classification based on gender and explicitly discriminates against women on the basis of their sex." Johnson Control's policy, according to the Court, was not neutral because it did not apply to males in the same way despite evidence about the debilitating effect of lead on the male reproductive system.

The company's fetal protection policy was not based on the ability or inability of women to perform the job in question: it was based on pregnancy or the ability to become pregnant—a violation of the Pregnancy Discrimination Act. Moreover, the Court dismissed any safety issues by asserting that concern for the unborn fetus was not relevant because the question of safety did not involve third parties or customers. Reiterating its earlier opinion in *Dothard v. Rawlinson,* the Court stated that "danger to a woman herself does not justify discrimination." Citing other previous cases, it also maintained that fetal safety is best left to the mother, not the employer.

Harris v. Forklift Systems, Inc.

Teresa Harris was an equipment rental manager for Forklift Systems, Inc. from April 1985 until October 1987. During her tenure with the company, as established by the District Court, the company's president, Charles Hardy, often insulted her because of her gender and made her the target of sexual innuendoes. On several occasion in front of other employees, Hardy stated, "You're a woman, what do you know?" and "We need a man as the rental manager." He once told her she was "a dumb ass woman." In front of others he also suggested that the two of them "go to the Holiday Inn to negotiate [Harris's] raise." Furthermore, it was established that Hardy occasionally asked Harris and other female employees to retrieve coins from his front pants pockets, threw objects on the ground in front of Harris and other female workers and asked them to pick the objects up, and made sexual innuendoes about Harris's and other women's clothing.

In August 1987, Harris complained to Hardy about his behavior. He was surprised that she was offended, claimed that he had only been joking, apologized for his conduct, and promised it would stop. In September, Hardy's previous behavior surfaced again. In front of other employees, as well as one of Forklift's customers with whom Harris was arranging a deal, he asked her, "What did you do, promise the guy some [sex] Saturday night?" On October 1, Harris collected her paycheck and quit.

Harris filed suit in Federal District Court claiming that the Hardy's treatment of her constituted an "abusive work environment in violation of Title VII." The District Court, however, concluded that the comments in question did not create an abusive environment because they were not "so severe as to . . . seriously affect [Harris's] psychological well being" or lead her to "suffer injury." The Sixth Circuit Court of Appeals affirmed the decision of the lower court.

On November 9, 1993, in a unanimous decision, the Supreme Court held that "to be accountable as abusive work environment harassment, conduct need not seriously affect . . . psychological well-being or lead the plaintiff to suffer injury." The Court further stated that "Title VII is violated when the workplace is permeated with discriminatory behavior that is sufficiently severe or pervasive enough to create a . . . hostile or abusive working environment . . . This standard requires an objectively hostile or abusive environment—one that a reasonable person would find hostile or abusive—as well as the victim's subjective perception that the environment is abusive . . . whether or not" such an environment exists "can be determined only by looking at all the circumstances," which include "frequency of the . . . conduct; its severity; whether it is physically threatening or humiliating, or a mere offensive utterance; and whether it unreasonably interferes with an employee's work performance . . . But while psychological harm, like any relevant factor, may be taken into account, no single factor is required."

The Court's decision was intended to offer a middle ground between conduct that is merely offensive and conduct requiring proof of psychological injury. A mere offensive remark is not enough to constitute a cause of action under Title VII nor must a person wait until psychological damage has been done before filing a complaint or suit. According to the Court, for conduct or behavior to create a hostile or abusive working environment it must be "severe or pervasive." Moreover, the decision established a standard of conduct that a "reasonable person would find hostile or abusive."

In his concurring opinion, however, Justice Scalia expressed concern that what a reasonable person would find hostile or abusive was not a very clear standard and would open "more expansive vistas of litigation."

Oncale v. Sundowner Offshore Services, Inc.

For many years a nagging question in sexual harassment cases had been whether or not a member of one sex could harass a member of the same sex. Different courts had viewed this issue in varying ways without arriving at a uniform, consistent answer. The Supreme Court finally resolved this issue in 1998.

In October 1991 Joseph Oncale worked as a roustabout for Sundowner Offshore Services, Inc. on an oil platform in the Gulf of Mexico. He was a member of an eight-man crew supervised by the crew's driller, Danny Pippen, and the crew's crane operator, John Lyons. On several occasions Oncale "was forcibly subjected to sex-related, humiliating actions by" Lyons and Pippen along with Brandon Johnson, another crew member, in the presence of the other crew members. On another occasion Oncale was "physically assaulted in a sexual manner . . . and threatened with rape" by Lyons. When Oncale reported these incidents to the company's Safety Compliance Clerk, Valent Hohen, Hohen informed Oncale that he, too, had also received sexual harassment and abuse from Pippen and Lyons. Oncale turned in his resignation and asked "that his pink slip reflect that he 'voluntarily left due to sexual harassment and verbal abuse.' " Later when asked why he left the company, he stated "I felt that if I didn't leave my job, that I would be raped or forced to have sex."

Oncale's suit in District Court was dismissed on summary judgment. His appeal to the Fifth Circuit Court of Appeals was denied because, as stated by the Court, "Mr. Oncale, a male, has no cause of action under Title VII for harassment by male co-workers." The case was then appealed to the Supreme Court.

In March 1998 the Supreme Court ruled that "same-sex sexual harassment is actionable under Title VII" and that the occurrence of sexual harassment is not dependent upon the harasser and the target of harassment being of different sexes. The Court's ruling in Oncale ended years of discussion and disagreement concerning same-sex sexual harassment. In effect, the Court concluded that sexual harassment, as long as it meets the statutory requirements, is sexual discrimination, regardless of whether both or only one sex is involved in the harassing action.[7]

Faragher v. City of Boca Raton

Between 1985 and 1990 Beth Ann Faragher, while attending college, worked part time as well as in summers as an ocean lifeguard for the City of Boca Raton, Florida. During her service with the Marine Safety Section of the Parks and Recreation Department, Faragher had three immediate supervisors. She resigned her job in June 1990.[8]

In February 1986 the city formally adopted a sexual harassment policy and distributed this policy to all employees via a memorandum from the city manager. The city revised its sexual harassment policy in May 1990 and issued a statement to that effect. However, as indicated in the records of the District Court, the city "completely failed to disseminate its policy among employees of the Marine Safety Section." As a result, supervisors and lifeguards were unaware of the policy statement.

Faragher filed suit against two of her former supervisors, Bill Terry and David Silverman, and the City of Boca Raton in 1992. Faragher alleged that the two supervisors, acting as agents for the city, had created a hostile work environment by making lewd remarks to her and other women, speaking of women in offensive terms, sexually propositioning her as well as other women, and repeatedly subjecting her and other female employees to "uninvited and offensive touching." As reported in the District Court proceedings, one supervisor, Bill Terry, told Faragher, "Date me or clean the toilets for a year." During the trial numerous other instances of alleged sexual harassment were presented. The city's main line of defense was that the supervisors were acting outside the scope of their job duties when the alleged harassment occurred and therefore the city had no responsibility for the behavior of Terry and Silverman.

The District Court found for Faragher and ruled that the alleged sexual harassment was severe and pervasive. The Court also held that the city was vicariously liable for the conduct of its supervisors under traditional agency law principles since the city had "constructive knowledge" of the supervisors' behavior.

On appeal, the Eleventh Circuit Court of Appeals overturned the ruling of the District Court that the city was liable. The Circuit Court found the following: (1) the city had no constructive knowledge of the supervisors' behavior, (2) the supervisors were acting outside of an agency relationship and engaged in a "frolic" unrelated to their authorized tasks, and (3) the severe and pervasive nature of the harassment was not established in fact.

In a rather lengthy opinion written by Justice David Souter, the Supreme Court reversed the judgment of the Circuit Court and reinstated the judgment of the District Court. The Supreme Court held that an employer is vicariously liable for the actions of its supervisors even though the employer may not have known of such actions. The Court, however, indicated that employers may use an affirmative defense against vicarious liability where the employer can show that it developed and disseminated to all employees a sexual harassment policy that includes a reasonable compliant procedure and that the employer tracks the behavior of its supervisors working in remote areas. Interpreting the Court's findings broadly, it is readily apparent that large employers must exercise due diligence in developing and disseminating to all employees and supervisors a comprehensive sexual harassment policy. Care must also be taken to ensure that the behavior of supervisors or managers in remote locations is adequately monitored.

Burlington Industries, Inc. v. Ellerth

Kimberly Ellerth worked for Burlington Industries from March 1993 until May 1994 in a two-person office in Chicago. Administratively she reported to her office colleague who in turn reported to a Burlington vice president, Ted Slowik, in New York.[9]

"Against a background of repeated boorish and offensive remarks and gestures," Ellerth alleged three specific incidents by Slowik that she construed as threats to deny her tangible job benefits. First, in the summer of 1993 Slowik invited Ellerth to meet him at a hotel lounge. As she later admitted, she felt compelled to accept this invitation because Slowik was her boss. When, during the meeting, remarks were made about her breasts and Ellerth offered no encouragement, she was informed by Slowik "Kim, I could make your life very hard or very easy at Burlington."

The second incident reported by Ellerth occurred in a March 1994 interview when she was being considered for a promotion. Slowik expressed concerns about her promotion because she was not "loose enough." Slowik's reaching out and rubbing Ellerth's knee followed this comment. She did receive the promotion but was informed by Slowik when he called her to announce it to her, "you're gonna [*sic*] be out there with men who work in factories, and they certainly like women with pretty butts/legs [*sic*]."

The third incident occurred in May 1994 when Ellerth called Slowik to ask for permission to insert a customer's logo in a fabric sample. He informed her that he did not have time to talk to her "unless you want to tell me what you're wearing." As Ellerth later reported, she quickly terminated the call. She called Slowik back a few days later to ask again for permission to include the logo in a sample. Permission was denied this time but during the conversation Slowik asked if Ellerth was "wearing shorter skirts, yet, Kim, because it would make your job a whole lot easier."

Shortly after this last exchange Ellerth resigned from Burlington, citing reasons unrelated to any sexual harassment allegations. About three weeks later Ellerth sent Burlington a letter stating that she had terminated her employment because of Slowik's sexually harassing behavior.

During her 15 months of employment at Burlington, Ellerth did not inform anyone in the company about Slowik's behavior despite her knowing that Burlington had a policy against sexual harassment.

After receiving a right to sue letter from EEOC, Ellerth filed suit in October 1994 alleging that sexual harassment at Burlington had led to her constructive discharge. While finding that Slowik's behavior was severe and pervasive enough to create a hostile environment, the District Court held that Burlington neither knew about nor should have known about Slowik's behavior. The Court also dismissed Ellerth's claim of constructive discharge. The Court of Appeals in a decision producing "eight separate opinions and no consensus for a controlling rationale" reversed, *en banc,* the decision of the District Court.

Citing the need to create uniform standards for employers to follow in sexual harassment cases, the Supreme Court accepted the case for review. It handed down its decision in June 1998. In its decision the Court established the following guidelines: (1) *quid pro quo* sexual harassment encompasses only cases where an employee suffers tangible job action as a result of threats by a supervisor— all other forms of sexual harassment fall under the category of hostile environment; (2) hostile environment cases are actionable only if the practices are sufficiently severe and pervasive; (3) employers are strictly liable for the acts of supervisors that result in adverse employment actions against an employee; and (4) employers may offer an affirmative defense against hostile environment sexual harassment by supervisors where the employer can show the exercise of reasonable care to prevent and correct such conditions and can demonstrate the development and promulgation of an antiharassment policy and complaint resolution procedures.

Grutter v. Bollinger

In two cases decided on the same day, June 23, 2003, the Supreme Court arrived at different opinions concerning affirmative action admission programs at the University of Michigan.

Barbara Grutter, a Caucasian resident of Michigan, was denied admission to the University of Michigan Law School. Initially Grutter, who possessed an undergraduate GPA of 3.8 and a LSAT score of 161, had been placed on the Law School's admissions waiting list, but her application was later rejected. In December 1996 Grutter filed suit against the University, alleging that she had been discriminated against on the basis of race in violation of the Equal Protection Clause of the Fourteenth Amendment and Title VI of the Civil Rights Act of 1964, as amended. According to Grutter, the Law School used race as a predominant factor in admission decisions wherein applicants of certain racial and ethnic groups (African Americans, Hispanics, and Native Americans) were afforded "a significantly greater chance of admission than students with similar credentials from disfavored racial groups." [10]

In its efforts to create "a critical mass" of student diversity that would enrich the educational experience of students, the Law School did, in fact, consider race as a factor in admissions decisions, but race was not the sole factor considered nor was it the deciding factor in admissions. The Law School admitted that race was a "plus factor" in admissions but emphasized that race was only one of several factors considered in an individualized scrutiny of each applicant's file. The Law School did not use quotas or percentages in its admission decisions and the term "critical mass," as applied to diversity, was not defined in quantifiable terms, but rather was based on a nebulous concept of the proper amount of student diversity that would enrich the overall educational experience of all students.

In its first educational affirmative action admission case since *Bakke,* decided over 25 years earlier, the Court was faced with answering two fundamental questions: (1) was achieving a critical mass of student body diversity a "compelling state interest" that required the Law School to take steps to ensure that the student population reflected a sufficient amount of diversity required to enhance the overall educational experience? and (2) was the Law School's use of race in admissions decisions narrowly tailored enough so as not to unnecessarily interfere with students who were not members of racially advantaged classes?

As to the first question, a finding of no compelling state interest in achieving diversity would have invalidated the Law School's admissions program; however, the Court found "that student body diversity is a compelling state interest that can justify the use of race in university admissions." The Court went on to say "When race-based action is necessary to further a compelling government interest, such action does not violate the constitutional guarantee of equal protection so long as the narrow-tailoring requirement [of the use of race] is also satisfied."

In reference to the second question facing the Court—the use of race in admission decisions—the Court held that universities could not use racial quota systems or similar approaches that put racial minorities on a separate admissions track. Where race is used it must be used flexibly "in consideration of each and every applicant." The Law School's use of a critical mass approach to achieving diversity allowed it to be flexible in admissions decisions, thereby assuring that each applicant was considered in some individualized fashion. In fact, the number as well as the percentage of minority students admitted under the critical mass approach varied considerably from year to year. The Court ruled that the Law School's use of affirmative action in admissions was of such a nature to ensure adequate consideration of all applicants.

Gratz v. Bollinger

Jennifer Gratz and Patrick Hamacher, both Caucasian residents of the state of Michigan, were denied admission to the University of Michigan's undergraduate College of Literature, Science, and the Arts (LSA) Gratz applied for admission to the University in 1995 and was considered by LSA to be a well-qualified candidate for admission. Hamacher, who was considered by LSA to be within the range of qualified applicants, applied for admission in 1997. The University's Office of Undergraduate Admissions (OUA) used written guidelines that considered such factors as "high school grades, standardized test scores, high school quality, curriculum strength, geography, alumni relationships, leadership, and race." African Americans, Hispanics, and Native Americans were deemed by the University to be underrepresented minority groups and each qualified individual from these groups was "automatically awarded 20 points of the 100 needed to guarantee admission." During the time period in question virtually every qualified applicant from these minority groups was admitted to the University.[11]

Gratz and Hamacher filed a class action suit against the University "alleging that the University's use of racial preferences in undergraduate admission violated the Equal Protection Clause of the Fourteenth Amendment [and] Title VI of the Civil Rights Act of 1964." Title VI is that section of the Civil Rights Act of 1964 pertaining to educational institutions receiving any form of funding from the federal government.

The Court announced its decision the same day it announced its Grutter decision, June 23, 2003, ruling that the University's broadly applied use of race in undergraduate admissions violated the Equal Protection Clause of the Fourteenth Amendment as well as Title VI of the Civil Rights Act of 1964. The Court found that awarding 20 points for admission status made race the decisive factor for every minimally qualified applicant. As in its earlier *Bakke* decision, the Court seemed to suggest that race could be used as a factor in admission decisions as long as it was not the sole or decisive factor in making decisions. In the present instance, the awarding of 20 points out of 100 to minority applicants made race the dominating factor in admissions.

Equal Employment Opportunity Commission v. Waffle House, Inc.

In this 2002 decision the Court addressed the issue of whether or not an arbitration agreement between employee and employer to submit all employment-related disputes to binding arbitration precludes or limits EEOC's ability to pursue, through legal action, discrimination charges arising under Title VII or ADA.

Eric Baker began work at one of the company's restaurants on August 10, 1994. In his employment application Baker agreed that any dispute or claim arising from his employment with Waffle House would be settled through mandatory binding arbitration rather than through the court system. All prospective company employees signed similar agreements. Sixteen days after beginning work Baker suffered a seizure on the job and was subsequently terminated. Baker did not initiate arbitration proceedings either at the time of his termination or in the years that followed. He did, however, file a timely discrimination charge with EEOC, alleging that his discharge by Waffle House violated provisions of the Americans with Disabilities Act of 1990. After investigation and an unsuccessful conciliation attempt, EEOC filed suit against Waffle House seeking injunctive relief to eradicate the effects of past and present discriminatory practices of the company. EEOC also sought back pay, reinstatement, and damages, both compensatory and punitive, for Baker.[12]

The Court of Appeals held that where a valid and enforceable arbitration agreement between employee and employer existed EEOC was limited to injunctive relief only and was not entitled to pursue victim-specific relief for individual employees; i.e., EEOC could require an employer to correct past discriminatory practices and require actions to prevent future discrimination, but EEOC could not seek reinstatement, back pay, or damages for individual employees. The Supreme Court overturned the Circuit Court's decision on victim-specific damages and ruled that EEOC could seek victim-specific damages as well as injunctive relief in discrimination cases involving Title VII and ADA. The Court reasoned that victim-specific damages in the form of compensatory and punitive damages "also serve an obvious public function in deterring future violations" by the company itself as well as other companies. While upholding the right of companies and employees to enter into binding arbitration agreements relative to employment disputes, the Court stated that EEOC was not bound by such agreements because it was not a party to them. Therefore, EEOC may take action against a company despite the fact that the company and its employees have agreed to settle employment disputes through arbitration.

Ledbetter v. Goodyear Tire & Rubber Company, Inc.

In 2003 the Court was asked to deviate from its previously established precedent concerning the time period for filing a discrimination charge with EEOC under Title VII. The Court had previously held that, under terms of Title VII, a discrimination charge must be filed within 180 or 300 days, depending on the particular state in which the charge was filed, of the alleged discriminatory act.[13]

Lilly Ledbetter worked for the Goodyear Tire & Rubber Company at its Gadsden, Alabama, plant from 1979 until her early retirement in 1998. Salaried plant employees were typically given or denied pay increases based on performance evaluations conducted by their supervisors. In July 1998 Ledbetter filed a formal discrimination charge with EEOC alleging sex discrimination in pay under Title VII and the Equal Pay Act. According to Ledbetter, by the end of her employment with Goodyear she was being paid significantly less than any of her male coworkers.

The District Court dismissed her claim under the Equal Pay Act but allowed Ledbetter to pursue other charges under Title VII. On appeal the Eleventh Circuit Court ruled in favor of Goodyear and held that Ledbetter's allegations had not been filed in a timely fashion.

The crux of Ledbetter's argument in this case was that pay discrimination is an ongoing form of discrimination that is not bound by the specific date at which pay decisions were made initially. It was Ledbetter's contention that every time she received a paycheck she was, in fact, being discriminated against; hence each paycheck she received was a discriminatory act in itself.

The Supreme Court disagreed with Ledbetter and held "that any unlawful employment practice, including those involving compensation, must be presented to the EEOC within the period prescribed by law." In other words, all alleged Title VII discriminatory employment violations must be filed with EEOC within 180 or 300 days of their occurrence or they are time-barred from being filed. (The 180-day period applies to states without a state antidiscrimination deferral agency and the 300-day period applies to states with such a deferral agency.) Because Ledbetter had not met the statutory filing requirements, her discrimination charge was denied.

SIGNIFICANT FEDERAL CIRCUIT COURTS OF APPEALS DECISIONS

After a case is tried in federal district court, if a party to the case is dissatisfied with the decision, normally the next step is to appeal the decision to a federal circuit court of appeals. There are 12 such courts in this country and each state and the District of Columbia is assigned to one of the circuits. Rulings at this level have a significant effect on employment practices since the Supreme Court hears only the cases it elects to hear. Thus, a circuit court ruling may or may not be open to further appeal. While circuit court decisions are binding only in that particular circuit, they are often used as precedents. Some of the more interesting decisions to come from these courts are discussed below. The presentation of circuit court decisions is intended to be illustrative rather than exhaustive. Decisions from several circuits have been included for the purpose of providing a sampling of opinions from the various courts.

Diaz v. Pan American World Airways

This 1971 decision of the Fifth Circuit Court ruled that being a female is not a bona fide occupational qualification for the position of flight attendant. The *Diaz* ruling established the concept of business necessity as the basis for a BFOQ as opposed to business convenience or customer preference. Discrimination based on sex is valid only when the essence of the business operation would be undermined by not hiring members of one sex exclusively.

According to the Court:

The primary function of an airline is to transport passengers safely from one point to another. While a pleasant environment, enhanced by the obvious cosmetic effect that female stewardesses provide as well as, according to the finding of the court trial, their apparent ability to perform the non-mechanical functions of the job in a more effective manner than most men, may all be important, they are tangential to the essence of the business involved. We do not mean to imply, of course, that Pan Am cannot take into consideration the ability of individuals to perform the non-mechanical functions of the job. What we hold is that . . . Pan Am cannot exclude all males simply because most males may not perform adequately.

In general, the Court stressed the importance of making judgments about the qualifications of people as individuals, not as members of a group.

Spurlock v. United Airlines, Inc.

In this case the Tenth Circuit Court held that United Airlines could use as selection criteria a college degree and a minimum of 500 hours flying experience even though these requirements eliminated a greater percentage of black applicants than white applicants. United's contention, supported by statistics, was that applicants who have a greater number of flight hours are more likely to succeed in its rigorous training program. The Court agreed. The Court also accepted United's argument that the high cost of the training program rendered it necessary to have as many individuals as possible who enter the program complete it. The Court also agreed with this line of reasoning as an example of business necessity. Moreover, United was able to show a direct correlation between having a college degree and successfully completing the training program. The Court ruled that the airline "met the burden of showing that its requirement of a college degree was sufficiently job related to make it a lawful pre-employment standard."

Spurlock illustrates that the courts will accept rigorous pre-employment requirements if those requirements are logical and are supported by factual evidence; they will not, however, accept requirements based on subjectivity, intuition, and generalizations.

Richardson v. Hotel Corporation of America (5 FEP 323)

This case, decided by the Fifth Circuit Court, addressed the matter of considering conviction records for specific crimes as a selection criterion. The Court found that the hotel did not discriminate on the basis of race when it discharged Richardson, a newly hired black bellhop, after learning that he had previously been convicted of theft and receiving stolen property. The hotel had a policy of rejecting applicants for employment in "security sensitive" positions if they had been convicted of a serious crime. As a bellhop the complainant would have had keys to the rooms in the hotel. The Court ruled for the hotel on grounds of business necessity, in spite of the contention that more blacks than whites are convicted of serious crimes and that discharge based upon criminal record is therefore inherently racially discriminatory.

According to the Court: (1) people who have been convicted of serious crimes are more likely to engage in future criminal conduct than those who have never been convicted, (2) it is reasonable for the company to require persons having access to valuable property of others to be relatively free from convictions related to theft of property, (3) the hotel applied its policy to both blacks and whites, (4) similar requirements are not imposed on employees who do not have access to property, and (5) the hotel has had an excellent record of providing equal opportunity in jobs at all levels to minority group members.

In short, conviction records can be used as selection criteria or grounds for dismissal if they are job related.

Rowe v. General Motors Corporation

This case decided by the Fifth Circuit Court involved performance appraisal. The company's evaluation system was used as the basis for determining promotions, with the immediate supervisor's recommendation on promotability the key factor in deciding whether the employee would be promoted or not. The appraisal standards used by General Motors were vague and supervisors were given no written instructions for conducting the appraisals. The decision reached in this case emphasized the following points:

- Subjective, unstructured evaluation systems that result in a disparate adverse effect on minorities have been unanimously condemned by the courts and found discriminatory.
- Objective measures of performance accomplish the goals of performance appraisal better than subjective means such as interviews or vague evaluations by supervisors.
- Written instructions on the use of appraisal criteria and the qualifications for promotion should be furnished to the evaluators.
- Where all of the appraisers are white and all of those being appraised are minority group members, the appraisers cannot be expected to evaluate fairly the performance of those being evaluated. As the Court stated, "We and others have expressed a skepticism that

black persons dependent on decisive recommendations from whites can expect non-discriminatory action."

- A review process, wherein performance evaluations given by supervisors are examined by the next level of management, provides a safeguard in performance appraisal systems that may avert discriminatory practices.

Interpreting *Rowe* broadly, it would appear that a firm's performance appraisal system, if it is to avoid potential discrimination, must be objective, provide written instructions to appraisers, establish a review procedure by another level of management, and exercise care to see that evaluators are not all from one class while those being evaluated are all from another, protected class.

Brito v. Zia Company

In this Tenth Circuit case performance appraisals were used as the basis for an employee layout. Fifteen employees were terminated in a reduction in force at the company on the basis of unsatisfactory performance. Twelve of those discharged were Hispanics and three were white.

The decision by the Court indicated the following:

- The company's performance appraisals were based on the best judgments and opinions of the evaluators and not on any identifiable quality or quantity of work criteria.
- The subjective appraisal system adversely affected a protected class in determining who would be laid off.
- No performance records were maintained by the company, nor was there any documentation to substantiate the ratings given to employees.
- Performance of the employees was not observed on a daily basis by the evaluators.
- Evaluations were neither administered nor scored in a controlled and standardized fashion; thus, they were susceptible to subjective interpretation.
- The company failed to validate its performance appraisal system under EEOC guidelines for employment test validation.

It is apparent from *Brito* that face or even content validity is not sufficient evidence to demonstrate the validity of a performance appraisal system; the system must be validated in terms of job requirements and content inasmuch as performance appraisal is in actuality an employment test.

Hodgson v. Greyhound Lines, Inc.

In 1974 the Seventh Circuit Court ruled that Greyhound did not violate the Age Discrimination in Employment Act when it refused to hire persons 35 years of age or older as intercity bus drivers. The Court found that Greyhound had a rational basis in fact to believe that the elimination of its hiring age policy would increase the likelihood of risk or harm to its passengers. The company provided statistical evidence showing that the company's safest driver is one who has between 16 and 20 years of driving experience with the company and is between 50 and 55 years of age—a blend of experience with the company and age that could never be attained in hiring applicants 40 or older. Greyhound also presented evidence concerning degenerative physical and sensory changes that humans undergo at about age 35 that have a detrimental effect upon driving skills and that are not detectable by physical tests. Thus, age can be a bona fide occupational qualification where it is reasonably necessary to the essence of the business and the employer has a rational or factual basis for believing that all or substantially all people within the age class would not be able to perform satisfactorily.

Wade v. Mississippi Cooperative Extension Service

Unlike most discrimination cases, *Wade* was not filed under contemporary employment statutes; it was filed under the equal protection clause of the Fourteenth Amendment. At issue in this Fifth Circuit case was the Extension Service's performance appraisal system. In its decision the Court ruled as follows:

- In a performance appraisal system, general characteristics such as "leadership, public acceptance, attitude toward people, appearance and grooming, personal conduct, outlook on life, ethical habits, resourcefulness, capacity for growth, mental alertness, loyalty to organization" are "susceptible to partiality and to the personal taste, whim, or fancy of the evaluator" as well as "patently subjective in form and obviously susceptible to completely subjective treatment" by those conducting the appraisals.

- The Extension Service had not used performance evaluation ratings consistently as a basis for promoting employees or adjusting their salaries.

- Trait-rating performance appraisal systems are subjective and biased because they are not usually based on a study of job content.

- Where a trait is used in an appraisal system, there must be a clear relationship between that trait and the work performed in the job.

- When subjected to legal challenge, the employer must be able to demonstrate the relationship between the performance appraisal instrument used and job content.

Wade emphasizes the requirement for specifically relating performance appraisal factors to actual job content. Broadly speaking, this case also stresses the importance of job analysis, since it is through job analysis that job content is determined.

Hillebrand v. M-Tron Industries, Inc.

Ernest Hillebrand, a 60-year-old vice president of operations for M-Tron Industries, was terminated by the company as part of an alleged reduction in force. Prior to his termination, Hillebrand had no knowledge of any plans to reduce the size of the work force. No other top-level manager was discharged in

1984, the year of Hillebrand's termination. His responsibilities were assumed by the company's comptroller, a 40-year-old male who was not, by his own admission, experienced in manufacturing or plant operations—the areas of Hillebrand's expertise.

Hillebrand filed suit under the Age Discrimination in Employment Act of 1967, maintaining that the company's reason for terminating him was "pretextual" inasmuch as no other high level manager was so affected. He also cited instances in which he had been referred to as "a gray-haired old man," a person of "questionable usefulness" to the company, and an individual who had "outlived his usefulness" to the organization.

The District Court granted summary judgment in favor of the defendant M-Tron, stating that the plaintiff had not established a case of age discrimination.

The Eighth Circuit Court overturned the lower court's decision and remanded the case back to the District Court for trial. According to the Circuit Court, "Knowing that discrimination is difficult to prove by direct evidence, the Supreme Court has interpreted employment discrimination cases as requiring simplified proof from a claimant in order to create an inference of discrimination and thereby establish a prima facie case." The Court went on to state that, "Once the inference is created, the law is clear that the burden of proof is placed on an employer to show a non-discriminatory reason" and "In proving a prima facie case, the plaintiff is not required to adopt as part of his case the reason given by the employer as to the discharge."

The Circuit Court also ruled that, in an age discrimination case, "A plaintiff need not be replaced by a person outside the protected age group to make out a prima facie case under ADEA; the plaintiff need only be replaced by a younger person."

This case clearly illustrates two points: (1) Neither a preponderance of evidence nor definitive evidence of discriminatory intent is requisite for a person to establish a cause of action in an age discrimination case. All the plaintiff need do is establish "an inference" of possible discrimination. Once this inference is created, the burden of proof then shifts to the employer to show that there was no discriminatory intent or impact. (2) In an age discrimination case, the fact that a terminated individual was replaced by another person in the same protected class is insufficient proof for refuting an age-related discrimination charge.

NOTES

1. Donald L. Caruth, *Compensation Management for Banks* (Boston: Bankers Publishing Company, 1986), 222–223.

2. Ibid., 225–226.

3. Richard D. Arvey, *Fairness in Selecting Employees* (Reading, MA: Addison-Wesley, 1979), 74–76.

4. R. Wayne Mondy and Robert M. Noe, *Human Resource Management,* 6th ed. (Upper Saddle River, NJ: Prentice-Hall, Inc., 1996), 68.

5. Barbara Lindemann Schlei and Paul Grossman, *Employment Discrimination Law,* 2nd ed. (Washington, DC: Bureau of National Affairs, 1983), 786–802.

6. R. Wayne Mondy and Robert M. Noe, *Personnel: The Management of Human Resources,* 3rd ed. (Boston: Allyn and Bacon, 1987), 80.

7. Dawn D. Bennett-Alexander and Laura P. Hartman, *Employment Law for Business,* 5th ed. (Boston: McGraw-Hill/Irwin, 2007), 386–389.

8. Ibid., 347–357.

9. Ibid., 346–349.

10. Ibid., 205–207.

11. Ibid., 206.

12. Ibid., 57–58.

13. Kristine E. Kwone, "Supreme Court Holds that Later Effects of Past Discrimination Don't Restart EEOC Charge-Filing Clock," *HR Watch* (May/June 2007): 1.

4

EEOC Compliance and Affirmative Action Programs

While an understanding of employment legislation, Executive Orders, and federal court decisions is imperative for staffing specialists, additional knowledge is required to ensure that employment practices, policies, and procedures are implemented and followed in a manner that reflects not only the letter but also the spirit of the law. The additional knowledge that staffing specialists must have is a thorough understanding of the Equal Employment Opportunity Commission's guidelines and compliance requirements for lawful employment practices. This includes an understanding of what constitutes an employment test, the definitions and interpretations of disparate treatment and adverse impact, and the meaning and application of guidelines relative to sexual harassment, national origin discrimination, and religious discrimination. Additionally, staffing specialists whose organizations are federal contractors or receive federal monies must have knowledge of the requirements of affirmative action programs as specified by the Office of Federal Contract Compliance Programs (OFCCP). These broad areas are the subjects of this chapter.

UNIFORM GUIDELINES ON EMPLOYEE SELECTION PROCEDURES

Prior to the development and publication of the *Uniform Guidelines on Employee Selection Procedures,* employers had to comply with several different sets of employment and selection guidelines promulgated by different federal agencies. To eliminate this confusing situation and provide employers with a single set of standards, the Equal Employment Opportunity Commission, the Office of Personnel Management (formerly the Civil Service Commission), the

Department of Justice, and the Department of Labor adopted and issued the *Uniform Guidelines on Employee Selection Procedures*. The *Guidelines* cover the major federal equal opportunity statutes and Executive Orders. While the courts are not bound by the *Guidelines,* they do tend to afford these interpretive rules "great deference" in the decisions the courts make.[1]

The *Guidelines* set forth a single set of principles designed to assist employers, labor organizations, employment agencies, and licensing and certification boards in complying with requirements of federal law prohibiting employment practices that discriminate on the basis of race, color, religion, sex, and national origin. Age and disability discrimination have since been added to the EEOC's enforcement responsibilities. The *Guidelines* are designed to provide a framework for determining the proper use of tests and other selection devices and procedures. The *Guidelines* provide a basis for making lawful employment decisions relative to hiring, promotion, demotion, referral, retention, licensing, and certification. Recruiting procedures, under the *Guidelines,* are not considered selection procedures and are therefore not covered;[2] however, inferences can be made from the *Guidelines* that suggest what is proper or improper practice in recruiting.

One of the most important clarifications contained in the *Guidelines* is the definition of an employment test:

Any measure, combination of measures, or procedures used as a basis for any employment decision. Selection procedures include the full range of assessment techniques from traditional paper and pencil tests, performance tests, training programs, or probationary periods and physical, educational, and work experience requirements through informal or casual interviews and unscored application forms.[3]

Under this broad, comprehensive definition, virtually *any* factor used in making *any* employment decision is a test. From the time a person's resume or application crosses the organization's threshold to the time that person leaves the institution, any evaluation for any purpose—hiring, promoting, appraising, rewarding, training, terminating—is, in fact, an employment test under the *Guidelines.* Unfortunately, many organizations apparently have not fully grasped EEOC's all-inclusive definition of employment test.

Prior to the issuance of the *Guidelines,* the only means for establishing the job relatedness of a test was through validation of each test used. The *Guidelines* do not require validation in all cases. The fundamental principle underlying the *Guidelines* is that employer policies or practices that have an adverse impact on employment opportunities for classes of individuals protected under Title VII or Executive Orders are illegal unless justified by business necessity. Adverse impact occurs when members of a protected class receive unequal consideration for employment. As specifically defined by the *Guidelines,* adverse impact occurs if protected groups are not hired at a rate of at least 80 percent of the rate for the best achieving group. This 80 percent selection factor is also known as the four-fifths rule.

Assuming that adverse impact has been shown, employers have two avenues available to them if they still desire to use a particular selection device, procedure, or standard. First, employers may validate the selection device used to show that it is indeed a predictor of success on the job. When the device has been proven to be a valid, reliable indicator of on-the-job performance, an employer has established business necessity as the basis for its use. In the event that the firm's selection tool has not been validated, business necessity may be demonstrated in another manner. The employer can show that there is a strong relationship between the selection device and job performance and that, without using this specific selection procedure, the firm's training costs would be prohibitive.

The second avenue available should adverse impact be shown is the *bona fide occupational qualification* defense. The BFOQ defense means that certain qualifications are needed for job performance and that the majority of the members of one or more protected classes cannot reasonably be expected to possess the necessary qualifications. Because it has often been based on stereotyping and vague generalizations, the courts have narrowly interpreted the BFOQ defense. For example, the courts have rejected the contention that since most women cannot lift 150 pounds all women can be excluded from consideration for a job involving such lifting requirements. Employers electing to use the BFOQ defense for their selection procedures must have significant evidence to substantiate their position.

Creators of the *Guidelines* adopted, in essence, a "bottom line" approach in assessing whether a firm's employment practices are discriminatory. If a number of selection procedures are used in making a selection decision, for example, the enforcement agencies are likely to focus (*Connecticut v. Teal* notwithstanding) on the result of the combined practices to determine the existence of adverse impact. Essentially, EEOC is more concerned with what is occurring—the bottom line—as opposed to how it occurred. Admitting that discriminatory practices may exist that cannot be validated by an employer, EEOC's focus tends to be on the net effect produced by the procedures that are used.

ADVERSE IMPACT

Unlawful employment discrimination, as established through various Supreme Court decisions, can be divided into two broad categories: disparate treatment and adverse impact. Adverse impact is in reality discrimination that results from a facially neutral employment practice that affects protected classes differently than it affects the white majority class. It is a form of discrimination that can be detected statistically. Three approaches that have been developed to determine the existence of adverse impact: the four-fifths rule, the standard deviation method, and the Chi-Square Test.

The four-fifths or eighty-twenty rule is outlined in the *Guidelines* and should generally be used first since it is accepted in most instances by both EEOC and OFCCP. If adverse impact is shown under the four-fifths rule, other statistical methods may then be used. It should be remembered that the eighty-twenty rule is itself a rule of thumb; it is not a hard-and-fast criterion. Some courts have adopted it as an appropriate standard, while "others have criticized the rule as an arbitrary standard that fails to take into account deficiencies in sample sizes and test results in the applicant population." [4] The Supreme Court clearly stated in *Watson v. Fort Worth Bank and Trust* that it has never relied on mathematical precision to determine adverse impact but that it does rely on significant statistical evidence in determining adverse impact.

A second method for assessing adverse impact is the standard deviation approach. This method was tested in the Supreme Court decision in *Hazlewood School District v. United States*. The Chi-Square Test, the third possible method of measuring adverse impact, has not yet received widespread judicial acceptance but it is a test of statistical significance that may be used by employers.

Establishing Job Pools

The first step in conducting an adverse impact analysis is to establish job pools. A job pool is a group of jobs having essentially the same minimum level of qualifications. An organization may decide to create separate pools for accountants, systems analysts, machine operators, or salespeople. The key to establishing a reliable job pool is the similarity of minimum qualifications for each job in the pool. Computer technician and computer programmer jobs, for example, would not be placed in the same pool because qualifications required for these two types of jobs are dissimilar.

Once job pools have been identified, the second step is to collect the following data: (1) the total number of qualified applicants in the pool, (2) the number of applicants selected, (3) the number of applicants classified as to protected class status and majority status (usually Caucasians), and (4) the number of applicants selected by protected class status and majority status (usually Caucasians). These data are then analyzed to determine the existence or nonexistence of adverse impact.

Four-Fifths Rule

The general formula for computing adverse impact using the four-fifths or eighty-twenty rule is the following:

$$\frac{\text{Protected Group Selection Rate}}{\text{Best Achieving Group Selection Rate}} = \text{Protected Group Selection Ratio}$$

The selection rate for protected class applicants is determined by dividing the number of protected class members hired by the total number of qualified protected class applicants within a given period of time. Selection rates should be calculated for all protected classes for the same periods of time.

To illustrate how the four-fifths formula for calculating adverse impact works, assume that during a 12-month period 400 individuals were hired for the job of machine operator. Of the total number hired, 300 were white males and 100 were African American males. There were a total of 1,500 applicants: 1,000 white males and 500 African American males. The selection rate for white males is 30 percent (300 ÷ 1000 = .30), and the selection rate for African Americans is 20 percent (100 ÷ 500 = .20). Applying these numbers to the formula for calculating adverse impact, we arrive at a selection ration of 66.67 percent for the protected class involved.

$$\frac{\text{Protected Group Selection Rate}}{\text{Best Achieving Group Selection Rate}} = \text{Protected Group Selection Ratio} = \frac{20\%}{30\%} = 66.67\%$$

Inasmuch as the selection ratio for African American males is 66.67 percent of the selection ratio for white male machine operators, adverse impact exists under the four-fifths rule that requires a selection ratio for protected classes of 80 percent of the selection ratio for the best achieving group.

Evidence of adverse impact is, obviously, more that the total number of protected class workers hired. The total number of applicants is also important. Assume, for instance, as a second example of the four-fifths rule, that 300 African American applicants were hired and 300 white applicants were hired, but that 1,500 African Americans and 1,000 whites applied for job openings. Using these numbers, we see that adverse impact still exists:

$$\frac{300}{1,500} = 20\% \text{ African American Selection Rate}$$

$$\frac{300}{1,000} = 30\% \text{ White Selection Rate}$$

$$\frac{20\%}{30\%} = 66.67\% \text{ Protected Group Selection Ratio}$$

Even though 200 more African Americans were hired in the second example as compared to the first example, there were 1,000 more African American applicants. Thus, the selection ratio indicates that African American applicants still are not hired at a rate that approaches 80 percent of the selection rate for white males. The total number of protected class members hired is insufficient evidence to refute a claim of adverse impact. EEOC is concerned with the comparative rate, not the sheer numbers, at which protected class members are hired.

It must be emphasized again that the four-fifths rule is intended to be a guideline, not a hard-and-fast indicator of adverse impact. Protected class selection ratios well below 80 percent may be acceptable in some cases, while selection ratios considerable above 80 percent may not be acceptable in other cases. According to the *Guidelines:*

Smaller differences in selection rate may nevertheless constitute adverse impact, where they are significant in both statistical and practical terms or where a user's actions have discouraged applicants disproportionately on grounds of race, sex or ethnic group. Greater differences in selection rates may not constitute adverse impact where the differences are based on small numbers and are not statistically significant, or where special recruiting or other programs cause the pool of minority or female candidates to be atypical of the normal pool of applicants from the group.[5]

For all practical purposes, EEOC reserves the "right to excuse an employer that fails the four-fifths rule or hold in violation an employer that satisfies the four-fifths rule."[6]

What determines how the rule will be applied? In essence, it is the number of applicants involved. When the numbers are small, statistical chance alone may produce a violation of the four-fifths rule. But, when large numbers of applicants are involved, adverse impact may exist even if the selection ratio for protected classes is considerably above 80 percent.[7] In the latter instance, EEOC may conclude that systemic discrimination is present in the organization and adversely affects a significant number of protected classes. An employer must, consequently, pay attention not only to the rate at which protected class members are selected but also to the overall numbers hired, using the four-fifths rule as a baseline for the likely acceptance of selection practices by EEOC.

Standard Deviation Formula

As previously indicated, the standard deviation formula has been court tested as a method for determining adverse impact. The standard deviation approach uses the following formula:

$$\text{Standard Deviation} = \sqrt{\frac{\text{Total Black Applicants}}{\text{Total Applicants}} \times \frac{\text{Total White Applicants}}{\text{Total Applicants}} \times \frac{\text{Total Number of Workers Selected}}{}}$$

This formula is known as a two-tailed standard deviation formula in that it indicates whether there has been discrimination against either the protected group or the group used as the basis for comparison.[8] The expected number, plus or minus two standard deviations, constitutes the acceptable hiring range for employers. Two standard deviations are used because, statistically speaking, the possibility of error due to chance is reduced to 4.6 times out of 100 occurrences. The *Guidelines* suggest that at least a .05 error rate be used; consequently, two standard deviations are within the suggested range of error.

An example will illustrate how this formula is applied in actual practice. Assume that there were 300 applicants for a particular job. Of the total number of applicants, 100 were African American and 200 were white. Assume also that 90 individuals were hired: 25 African Americans and 65 whites. Inserting these numbers into the formula, we would arrive at the following:

$$\text{Standard Deviation} = \sqrt{\frac{100}{300} \times \frac{200}{300} \times 90}$$

$$= \sqrt{20}$$

$$= 4.47$$

The number of African Americans we would expect this employer to hire, on the basis of the indicated selection ratio, is 30 ($100 \div 300 \times 90 = 30$). Therefore, the acceptable hiring range would be $30 \pm (2 \times 4.47)$, or 21.06 to 38.94. Since the actual number of African Americans hired was 30, a number that falls within the acceptable range, no adverse impact exists. If the number hired was less that 21, the conclusion would be that adverse impact exists. Because two standard deviations are used, if the number of African Americans hired was outside the range of 21.06 to 38.94, there would be less than a 5 percent probability that it was due to chance.

Chi-Square Test

When the Chi-Square Test of adverse impact is used, the selection rates of various subgroups are compared. This test assists in determining if differences exist between the selection rates for subgroups. An advantage of the Chi-Square approach is that it is sensitive to differences in sample size. Unfortunately, the four-fifths rule does not distinguish between a selection rate of 10 out of 20 or 1,000 out of 2,000.[9]

In using Chi-Square, a contingency table is prepared that shows the number of individuals in the various subgroups. Such a table might look like the following:

	Selected	Not Selected
Men	A	B
Women	C	D

The formula for calculating Chi-Square would be as follows:

$$\text{Chi-Square} = \frac{N(AD - BC)^2}{(A + B)(C + D)(A + C)(B + D)}$$

Assume that for the position of machine operator 50 men and 50 women apply. Of this total number of applicants, nine men and six women are hired. Using these figures in the Chi-Square Test would result in the following:

	Selected	Not Selected	Total
Men	9	41	50
Women	9	44	50
Totals	15	85	100

$$\text{Chi-Square} = \frac{100(396 - 246)^2}{(50)(50)(15)(85)} = 0.71$$

This value calculated must be interpreted based upon the degrees of freedom that may be found in most textbooks on statistics. For one degree of freedom, Chi-Square values less than 3.84 are not considered to be statistically significant at the .05 level inasmuch as 5 times out of 100 the difference may be due solely to chance. Because the *Guidelines* advocate a .05 significance level and the Chi-Square value in this example is less than 3.84, it is apparent that the selection rates for men and women are not significantly different. Therefore, there is no indication of adverse impact.

DISPARATE TREATMENT

Disparate treatment is the most easily understood form of discrimination: an employer simply treats a person or a group of people less favorably than others because of race, religion, sex, national origin, age, etc. Disparate treatment is direct, intentional discrimination. For example, an employer may favor males over females or an employer may prefer whites rather than African Americans. The crux of disparate treatment is different treatment of different groups of people on the basis of some nonallowable criterion. Common forms of disparate treatment include selection rules with a racial, sexual, or other premise; prejudicial actions by managers or supervisors; unequal treatment on an individual basis; and different hiring standards for different groups.

McDonald v. Santa Fe Trail Transportation Company offers an excellent example of disparate treatment. Three of the company's employees, two whites and one African American, had allegedly misappropriated 60 gallons of antifreeze. Santa Fe took disciplinary action against the workers by terminating the two whites, but not the African American employee. The discharged white workers filed suit against the company, charging that their termination violated both Title VII and the Civil Rights Act of 1866. The Supreme Court agreed with the plaintiffs and ruled that they had been the recipients of unequal treatment on the basis of their race. In other words, the two white males were the victims of disparate treatment.

Central to disparate treatment is the matter of proof. The plaintiff alleging illegal treatment must first be able to establish a *prima facie* case, and, second, he or she must be able to establish that the employer was acting on the basis of a discriminatory motive. Once a *prima facie* case is established, the burden of proof shifts to the employer.

Adverse impact, as previously discussed in this chapter, occurs when facially neutral or neutrally applied employment procedures affect different groups differently. Unlike disparate treatment, adverse impact does not require proof of a discriminatory motive or intent on the part of the employer. It is only necessary, in adverse impact cases, to show that employment practices in question affect different groups differently.

ADDITIONAL GUIDELINES

After the publication of the *Uniform Guidelines* in 1978, a number of modifications were made to the stipulated regulations. Some of these changes resulted from Supreme Court decisions; others were made in an attempt to clarify further or add to the interpretation of the *Guidelines*. Topics covered in these modifications include sexual harassment, discrimination based on national origin, and religious discrimination. Each of these three subjects is addressed in a separate set of *Guidelines*.

Guidelines on Sexual Harassment

The Equal Employment Opportunity Commission published its first guidelines on sexual harassment in 1980. The Office of Federal Contract Compliance Programs issued similar guidelines in 1981. The EEOC developed these sex discrimination guidelines because of the belief that sexual harassment is a widespread problem in the workplace.[10] Attesting to this problem is one study that reported that 59 percent of the female employees interviewed in the study indicated experiencing one or more incidents of sexual harassment in the workplace.[11] This particular issue is one of continued concern today and is likely to remain an area of major importance in the years to come because of the increasing numbers of women in the workplace.

Sexual harassment is defined by EEOC as follows:

Unwelcome sexual advances, requests for sexual favors, and other verbal or physical conduct of a sexual nature . . . when (1) submission to such conduct is made either explicitly or implicitly a term or condition of an individual's employment, (2) submission to or rejection of such conduct by an individual is used as the basis for employment decisions affecting such individual, or (3) such conduct has the purpose or effect of unreasonably interfering with an individual's work performance or creating an intimidating, hostile, or offensive working environment.[12]

As further clarified by the courts and the EEOC, sexual harassment may take one of two forms: *quid pro quo* or hostile environment. In *quid pro quo* (a Latin term meaning essentially "something for something"), the employee is requested to engage in some form of sexual activity in exchange for some job benefit such as promotion, pay increase, training, or continued employment. This is a direct form of harassment that is not difficult to recognize. Hostile environment sexual harassment is an indirect form of harassment that produces a work climate that is offensive or abusive. Obscene jokes, loud and vulgar remarks, sexual references to anatomy, and displays of pinup calendars are some of the elements that may create a hostile environment. For the courts to uphold a finding of hostile environment, several conditions must be met: (1) the harassment must be unwelcome, (2) it must be based on gender, (3) it must be severe or pervasive enough to create an abusive work environment, (4) it must affect a term or condition of employment, and (5) the employer knew of or should have known of the hostile environment and took no action.

According to EEOC, employers are totally responsible for the acts of their supervisors and managers with respect to sexual harassment regardless of whether they were aware of such acts. Where coworkers are concerned, the employer is responsible for acts of sexual harassment if it knew or should have known of the harassing conduct, unless the employer can show that it took immediate and appropriate corrective action to deal with the problem once it was made known.

Another interesting aspect of the EEOC's interpretation of sexual harassment is that employers may also be responsible for acts of sexual harassment committed in the workplace by nonemployees—vendors, consultants, delivery personnel, etc. To be held responsible for the acts of nonemployees, however, the employer or its supervisors must have knowledge of the conduct or should have known that such conduct was occurring and failed to take immediate corrective action. In determining the liability of the employer for the acts of nonemployees, EEOC will take into consideration "the extent of the employer's control and any other legal responsibility which the employer may have with respect to the conduct of such non-employees." [13]

There have been a number of court cases involving sexual harassment in the workplace. In *Miller v. Bank of America,* the U.S. Court of Appeals for the Ninth Circuit held the employer to be liable for a supervisor's sexually harassing behavior even though the employer had a policy prohibiting such conduct and had no knowledge of the harassment. The Court "reasoned that, just as an employer is liable for the negligence of its employees in operating motor vehicles, an employer should be held liable for adverse action taken by its supervisors because of sexual harassment." [14] In *Barnes v. Costle,* the Circuit Court for the District of Columbia ruled that the employer was not entitled to exoneration because the supervisor's behavior was, in the eyes of the employer, a "personal escapade." The importance of immediate and appropriate action in dealing with sexual harassment once the employer has knowledge of it was underscored in *Tomkins v. Public Service Electric & Gas Co.* The Third Circuit Court held that the employer's failure to take action was a sufficient basis to establish a claim against the company. In *Meritor Savings Bank, FSB v. Vinson,* the first sexual harassment case to reach the Supreme Court, the court affirmed the use of hostile environment as the basis for sexual harassment claims. Hostile environment was also more recently addressed in *Harris v. Forklift Systems, Inc.* wherein the Supreme Court ruled that the standard for determining hostile environment was what a "reasonable person" would find offensive; however, the Court did not articulate a definition of reasonable person.

In general, the courts have held that sexual harassment in and of itself is a violation of Title VII. The victim, moreover, is not required to prove that she resisted sexual harassment or that she was penalized if she did offer resistance. [15]

The need for company policy statements and training programs dealing with sexual harassment is essential. According to the EEOC:

Prevention is the best tool for the elimination of sexual harassment. An employer should take all steps necessary to prevent sexual harassment from occurring, such as affirmatively raising the subject, expressing strong disapproval, developing appropriate sanctions, informing employees of their right to raise and how to raise the issue of harassment under Title VII, and developing methods to sensitize all concerned.[16]

Firms must investigate all complaints, either formal or informal, alleging sexual harassment and, after investigation, take prompt and appropriate action to correct the situation.[17]

For many years an interesting question was whether or not a member of one sex could harass a member of the same sex. The Supreme Court finally resolved this issue in 1998 in its *Oncale v. Sundowner Offshore Services, Inc.* decision in which the Court ruled affirmatively that same sex sexual harassment could occur and was actionable under Title VII.

National Origin Discrimination

Title VII, while establishing national origin as a protected class, does not define what is meant by the term; thus, for many years there was confusion as to discrimination on the basis of national origin. It was this confusion the EEOC sought to eliminate with its guidance on discrimination because of national origin. National origin discrimination is defined "broadly as including, but not limited to, the denial of equal employment opportunity because of an individual's, or his or her ancestor's, place of origin; or because an individual has the physical, cultural, or linguistic characteristics of a national origin group." [18]

Both EEOC and the courts have interpreted national origin protection under Title VII as extending far beyond discrimination against individuals who came from or whose forebears came from a particular country. National origin protection also includes: (1) marriage or association with a person of a specific national origin; (2) membership in, or association with, an organization identified with or seeking to promote the interests of national groups; (3) attendance at, or participation in, schools, churches, temples, or mosques generally used by persons of a national origin group; (4) use of an individual's or spouse's name that is associated with a national origin group.[19]

Because height and weight requirements used as selection criteria tend to exclude some applicants on the basis of national origin, employers must evaluate these items for adverse impact. In effect, height and weight requirements are exceptions to the bottom-line concept normally adhered to by EEOC.

Two other selection procedures that may be discriminatory on the basis of national origin are fluency in English and training or education requirements.

Certainly, a questionable practice is denying employment opportunities to individuals because of their accent or inability to communicate fluently in English. In instances where this practice is continually followed by employers, EEOC's position is that the practice is a presumed violation of Title VII warranting further investigation. An employer may require, however, that employees speak only in English at certain times if it is necessary to the performance of the employee's duties and thereby constitutes a business necessity.

Denying employment opportunities to individuals because of their foreign training or education or requiring individuals to be foreign trained or educated may also be the basis for discrimination on grounds of national origin if adverse impact on a particular national origin group can be shown and if the requirements are not job related.

Harassment on the basis of national origin such as ethnic slurs or derogatory remarks is also interpreted as a violation of Title VII if such conduct has the purpose or effect of creating an intimidating, hostile, or offensive working environment, interferes with an individual's performance of his or her job, or adversely affects an individual's employment opportunities with an organization.[20] Generally speaking, the same standards are applied to national origin harassment as are used in sexual harassment.

Guidelines on Religious Discrimination

Under the 1972 amendments to Title VII, "The term 'religion' includes all aspects of religious observance and practice, as well as belief." EEOC's position is that it will define religious practices as including moral or ethical beliefs that are held with the strength of traditional religious views.[21]

The 1972 amendments to Title VII also require that employers make reasonable accommodations for employees' religious practices and observances unless the employer can demonstrate that such accommodation would place undue hardship on conducting the employer's business.

In determining whether an accommodation would constitute undue hardship, EEOC will give consideration to the size and operating costs of the employer as well as the number of individual employees who actually need the accommodation. EEOC recognizes that regular payment of premium wages in the form of overtime compensation would probably constitute undue hardship, whereas such payments on an infrequent or temporary basis would not. Undue hardship would likewise exist if the accommodations required the employer to deviate from its seniority system under the terms and conditions of a bona fide union contract.

EEOC has identified several methods for accommodating religious practices. Some of the methods suggested are the following: (1) voluntary substitutes (one employee electing to work in the place of another employee who needs time off for religious purposes); (2) flexible scheduling that allows an employee to take a particular day off and work another day in its place; (3) lateral transfers to units where work schedules do not interfere with religious observances; and (4) changes in job assignments.

Some collective bargaining agreements include a provision that each employee must join the bargaining unit or pay the union a fee equivalent to the amount of dues for the bargaining services the union renders. Where an employee's religious practices or beliefs do not permit compliance with this provision, the labor union should make an attempt to accommodate the employee by allowing him or her to donate an equivalent amount, in lieu of union dues, to a charitable organization of the individual's choosing.

RECORD-KEEPING AND REPORTING REQUIREMENTS

Title VII, referring to record-keeping requirements on the part of covered organizations states:

Every employer, employment agency, and labor organization subject to this title shall (1) make and keep such records relevant to the determinations of whether unlawful employment practices have been or are being committed, (2) preserve such records for such periods, and (3) make such reports therefrom as the Commission shall prescribe by regulation or law.

For purposes of Title VII and the Americans with Disabilities Act, EEOC has not promulgated any specific requirements that particular records be made or be kept. Under the Age Discrimination in Employment Act EEOC requires that covered employers make and retain for three years certain payroll-type records that contain the employee's name, address, date of birth, occupation, pay rate, and amount of compensation earned each week. For Equal Pay Act purposes employers are required to make and keep such records as required of employers under the Fair Labor Standards Act.

Where records are made under Title VII or the ADA, EEOC requires that these records be kept for a minimum period of one year from the time the record was made or from the time of the personnel action involved. If a record becomes involved in an EEOC charge, it must be maintained until final disposition of the charge has been reached.

Simply because certain records must be maintained for a stipulated period of time does not mean that the employer has to keep these records under active consideration or in an active file. For example, employment applications must be retained, but the employer has no obligation to continue active review of these beyond its customary period of 30 to 60 days.

Moreover, because records must be maintained does not mean that all of the documents "should be made available to any investigator from any agency." [22] An EEOC investigator who is examining a claim of sex discrimination is not automatically entitled to see company records pertaining to racial composition of the work force, promotion rates by race, and so forth. Employers with 100 or more employees are required to file an employer information report, commonly referred to as an EEO-1 by September 30 of each year. This report indicates the relationship of female and minority employees to the employer's total work force by specified job categories. Knowingly submitting false information on EEO reports is punishable by fine or imprisonment.

AFFIRMATIVE ACTION

The term "affirmative action" was first used informally during President Dwight Eisenhower's administration. The first official use of the term occurred in March 1961, when President John Kennedy signed Executive Order 10925 directing all federal contractors to "take affirmative action to ensure that all applicants are employed, and that employees are treated, during employment, without regard to their race, creed, color, or national origin." [23]

The Office of Federal Contract Compliance Programs defines affirmative action as "a set of specific and result-oriented policies and procedures to which a contractor commits itself to apply every good faith effort. The objective of those procedures plus such efforts is equal employment opportunity." In other words, affirmative action is "a program undertaken by an organization to improve job opportunities for and increase the utilization of protected classes in its work force." It is important to note that affirmative action is understood to refer to qualified individuals within protected classes. Consequently, affirmative action should not be viewed as either a mandate to employ unqualified applicants or to afford preferential treatment for one protected class at the expense of another protected class. An affirmative action plan, therefore, is any program undertaken by an organization to improve job opportunities for and increase utilization of protected classes in its work force. Such a program may be originated voluntarily by a company (or a company and its union) or it may be imposed by federal regulations, court order, or EEOC action.

An organization may elect, on its own, to initiate an affirmative action plan to correct imbalances in its work force such as underutilization of minorities in certain jobs or occupations. By doing so, the organization is not admitting to discriminatory practices; rather, it is attempting to correct deficiencies in the hiring and promotion of women and minorities that have resulted from legitimate selection procedures. A voluntary program is likely to be based on an employer's recognition of its social responsibility to the community in which it operates.

There is, however, a risk attached to a voluntary affirmative action plan—the possibility of reverse discrimination. While the Supreme Court has, as discussed in Chapter 3, addressed this issue several times (*Regents of the University of California v. Bakke, Weber v. Kaiser Aluminum Corporation, Gratz v. Bollinger,* and *Grutter v. Bollinger*), it has yet to give a clear-cut answer on reverse discrimination. Nevertheless, interpretation of the Court's decisions in these and other rulings would seem to suggest certain principles to which voluntary affirmative action plans must conform:

- The plan must be remedial in nature and designed to open job opportunities in occupations that have traditionally been closed to women and minorities.
- The plan must not trammel the interests of Caucasian or male employees.
- The plan must not create a bar to the advancement of Caucasian or male employees.
- The plan must not require the discharge of Caucasians or males to create job openings for minorities.
- The plan must be temporary in nature.

Inasmuch as *Weber* addressed the issue of reverse racial discrimination, the terminology used by the Court in specifying plan requirements reflects racial consideration. It seems clear, however, that the guidelines promulgated in the majority opinion apply equally as well to other protected classes.

While the potential for charges of reverse discrimination exist in any voluntary affirmative action plan, the charges are almost certain to come from majority employees since "employers can be sure the federal government is not going to prosecute them for reverse discrimination because it has never done so." [24]

The vast majority of affirmative action plans are originated under mandatory requirements. There are three situations that require employers to develop such plans: (1) the employer is a government contractor with a contract of $50,000 or more, in which case the need for such a plan is mandated by EO 11246, as amended by EO 11375; (2) the employer has been found guilty of discrimination and ordered by a federal court to develop and implement a plan; or (3) a discrimination suit brought against the employer by EEOC shows the existence of discrimination, and the employer has entered into a consent decree with EEOC whereby the employer will establish an affirmative action plan.

CONTENTS OF AN AFFIRMATIVE ACTION PLAN

The procedures established by the Office of Federal Contract Compliance Programs for developing and implementing affirmative action programs were originally published in the *Federal Register* on December 4, 1974. Today the requirements and regulations are published in the *Federal Contract Compliance Manual (FCCM)* issued by the Department of Labor, Employment Standards Administration, Office of Federal Contract Compliance Programs in November 1998. Although the following discussion is based on the requirements for affirmative action outlined by OFCCP, the same requirements would generally apply to plans mandated under different regulations or by other agencies. [25]

Development or Reaffirmation of Equal Opportunity Policy

The organization's policy statement should reflect the employer's attitude regarding equal employment opportunity, assign overall responsibility for EEO within the company, and provide for monitoring and reporting procedures. The policy should state the firm's intentions to recruit, hire, train, and promote persons in all job titles without regard to race, color, religion, sex, age, disability, veteran status, or national origin, except where sex is a bona fide occupational qualification. It should also state that all employment decisions will be made in consistency with equal employment opportunity principles. Moreover, the policy should ensure that promotion decisions impose only valid requirements. The policy, finally, should guarantee that all human resource actions involving such areas as compensation, benefits, transfers, layoffs, return from layoff, company-sponsored training, education, tuition assistance, and social and recreational programs will be administered without regard to protected class status.

Dissemination of Policy

An organization's equal employment opportunity policy must be widely disseminated throughout the enterprise. The organization should

- Include it in the company's policy manual.
- Include it in the company's human resource manual.
- Conduct special meetings with executive, management, and supervisory personnel to explain the intent of the policy and individual responsibility for effective implementation, making clear the chief executive officer's attitude on equal opportunity.
- Schedule special meetings with all other employees to discuss the policy and explain individual employee responsibilities.
- Discuss the policy thoroughly in both employee orientation and management training programs.
- Meet with union officials (if the company has a union) to inform them of the policy and request their cooperation.
- Include nondiscrimination clauses in all union agreements and review all contractual provisions to ensure that they are nondiscriminatory.
- Publish articles covering EEO programs, progress reports, promotions, and so forth of protected classes in company publications.
- Post the policy on company bulletin boards.
- Feature both minority and nonminority men and women in product or consumer advertising, employee handbooks, or similar publications.
- Communicate to employees the existence of the organization's affirmative action program and make available such elements of the program as will enable employees to know of and avail themselves of its benefits.

There are also additional requirements for disseminating the policy externally. These are as follows:

- Inform all outside recruiting sources, verbally as well as in writing, of the organization's policy, stipulating that they will actively recruit and refer all protected classes for all positions listed.

- Incorporate the equal opportunity clause in all purchase orders, leases, contracts, etc., covered by Executive Order 11246, as amended, and its implementing regulations.
- Notify minority and women's organizations, community agencies, community leaders, secondary schools, and colleges of company policy, preferably in writing.
- Communicate to prospective employees the existence of the organization's affirmative action program and make available such elements of the program as will enable prospective employees to know of and avail themselves of its benefits.
- Picture both minority and nonminority men and women in consumer or help wanted advertising.

Responsibility for Implementation

An individual should be appointed as director or manager of the organization's equal employment opportunity program. This person should be accorded the necessary top management support to accomplish this assignment effectively. Among the minimum level of responsibilities associated with the task of EEO manager are the following:

- Developing policy statements, affirmative action programs, and internal and external communication techniques.
- Assisting in the identification of problem areas.
- Assisting line managers in arriving at solutions to problems.
- Designing and implementing audit and reporting systems.
- Serving as liaison between the organization and outside enforcement agencies.
- Serving as liaison between the company and minority organizations, women's organizations, and other community action groups concerned with employment opportunities for protected classes.
- Keeping management informed of the latest developments in the area of equal employment opportunity.

OFCCP also imposes some requirements on an organization's line management in regard to affirmative action programs. These include:

- Assistance in the identification of problem areas and establishment of local and unit goals and objectives relative to equal employment.
- Active involvement with local minority organizations, women's organizations, community action groups, and community service programs.
- Periodic audit of training programs, hiring, and promotion patterns to remove impediments to the attainment of goals and objectives.
- Regular discussions with local managers, supervisors, and employees to ensure that the company's equal opportunity policies are being followed.
- Review of the qualifications of employees to ensure that protected classes are given full opportunities for transfers and promotions.

- Career counseling for all employees.
- Periodic audits to ensure that each location or company facility is in compliance with the affirmative action plan.
- Ensuring that supervisors understand that their work performance is being evaluated on the basis of their equal employment opportunity efforts and results as well as other criteria.
- Ensuring that supervisors understand that it is their responsibility to take actions to prevent harassment of employees assigned to their units through affirmative action efforts.

Utilization Analysis

An acceptable affirmative action program must include an analysis of areas where the organization is deficient in its utilization of protected classes. The first step in conducting a utilization analysis is to complete a work force analysis. To do this, each job title is listed as it appears in applicable collective bargaining agreements or payroll records and ranked from the lowest paid job to the highest paid job within each department or other similar organizational unit. For each job title, the total number of incumbents for each of the following groups must be given: total African American male and female, Hispanic Americans male and female, American Indians male and female, and Asian Americans male and female. The wage rate or salary range for each job title must also be given.

The second step involves an analysis of all major job groups at each facility or location where the company operates, with an explanation if minorities or women are currently being underutilized. A job group, for this purpose, is defined as one or more jobs or groups of jobs having similar content, wage rates, and opportunities. Underutilization is defined as having fewer minorities or women in a particular job group than would reasonably be expected by their availability in the labor market. Utilization analysis is important to the affirmative action concept because the percentage figure calculated will determine whether underutilization exists. For example, if the utilization analysis determines the availability of African Americans for a certain job group to be 30 percent, then the organization must have 30 percent African Americans in that job group. If 30 percent of the job group is not African American, underutilization exists and the company must set a goal of reaching the level of 30 percent African Americans in that job group within a reasonable period of time.

In determining whether there is underutilization of minorities, the Office of Federal Contract Compliance Programs states that the organization should consider the following factors:

- The minority population of the labor market surrounding the facility.
- The amount of minority unemployment in the surrounding labor market.
- The percentage of the minority work force, as compared to the total work force, in the immediate labor market area.

- The general availability in the immediate area of minorities having requisite skills.
- The availability of minorities having requisite skills in an area from which the company can be reasonably expected to recruit.
- The availability of promotable and transferable minorities within the organization.
- The existence of training institutions capable of training people in the requisite skills.
- The degree of training the company is reasonably able to undertake as a means of making all job classes available to minorities.

In determining whether there is underutilization of women, OFCCP takes a slightly different approach and considers the following factors:

- The size of the female unemployed work force in the labor area surrounding the facility.
- The percentage of the female work force as compared to the total work force in the immediate area.
- The general availability in the immediate area of women having requisite skills.
- The availability of women having requisite skills in an area from which the company can reasonably be expected to recruit.
- The availability of women seeking employment in the labor market or recruiting area of the organization.
- The availability of promotable and transferable female employees within the organization.
- The existence of training institutions capable of training people in the requisite skills.
- The degree of training the company is reasonably able to undertake as a means of making all job classes available to women.

If underutilization of minorities or women is occurring, a further study should be made to identify the cause of the problem. OFFCP identifies the following possible causes of underutilization:

- Underutilization of minorities or women in specific job groups.
- Lateral and/or vertical movement of minority or female employees occurring at a rate lower than that of nonminority or male employees.
- A selection process that eliminates a significantly higher percentage of minorities or women than nonminorities or males.
- Application forms or other preemployment forms not in compliance with federal legislation.
- Job descriptions that are inaccurate in relation to actual job duties and functions.
- Formal or scored selection procedures that are not validated as required by the *Uniform Guidelines*.
- Test forms that are not validated by location, work performance, and failure to include minorities and women in the sample.

- Referral ratio of minorities or women to the hiring supervisor or manager indicating that a significantly higher percentage are being rejected as compared to nonminority or male applicants.
- Minorities or women are excluded from or are not participating in company-sponsored activities or programs.
- *De facto* segregation that is still in existence in some facilities.
- Seniority provisions that contribute to overt or inadvertent discrimination; that is, a disparity by minority group status or sex exists between length of service and types of jobs held.
- Nonsupport of company policy by managers, supervisors, or employees.
- Minorities or women underutilized or significantly underrepresented in training or career improvement programs.
- No formal techniques established for evaluating the effectiveness of EEO programs.
- Lack of access to suitable housing that inhibits recruiting efforts or employment of qualified minorities.
- Lack of suitable transportation, either public or private, to the workplace.
- Labor unions and subcontractors not notified of their responsibilities in affirmative action efforts.
- Purchase orders not containing an EEO clause.
- Equal employment opportunity posters not prominently displayed.

Establishment of Goals and Timetables

Central to any affirmative action program is the concept of goals and timetables. These goals and timetables represent minority and female hiring or promotion levels that are realistic and attainable in terms of the organization's utilization deficiencies and its affirmative action program. In establishing goals and setting timetables, the organization should consider the results that it can reasonably expect to achieve by putting forth good faith, positive efforts to increase the size and utilization of its minority and female work force.

Both human resource managers and line managers should be involved in the process of developing goals and timetables. There are two goals that must be established regarding underutilization: an annual goal and an ultimate goal. The annual goal is one that moves toward elimination of underutilization, whereas the ultimate goal is, of course, the abolishment of any underutilization. Both of these goals should be specific in terms of planned results and related to realistic timetables for their accomplishment. However, goals should not be rigid or inflexible. Nor should they be quotas. Rather, they should be reasonably attainable targets that can be met through positive action by the employer.

Development and Execution of Programs

Employers should conduct detailed analyses of job descriptions to ensure that these documents accurately reflect job requirements and content. In other words, an effective affirmative action program requires that a comprehensive job analysis program be in place and operating. Additionally, all job specifications should be validated in terms of the job itself. Special attention should be given to academic, experience, skills, and physical requirements. If a job specification screens out a disproportionate number of protected class members, the requirements need to be validated in accordance with the procedures specified in the *Uniform Guidelines.*

When a job opening occurs, all members of management who are involved in the recruiting, screening, selecting, and promotion processes should be notified. Also, any individual involved in recruiting, screening, selecting, promotion, disciplinary, and related processes should be carefully trained so as to eliminate potential bias in any human resource action.

The organization's entire selection and employment process should be carefully evaluated to ensure freedom from discrimination or bias. Any procedures that adversely affect the hiring of protected classes must be scrutinized carefully and revised or eliminated if there is a possibility that such procedures result in discrimination or exclusion of these classes from employment opportunities.

Particularly important in an effective affirmative action program are efforts to increase the number of protected class members who apply for job openings. OFCCP suggests some techniques that are designed to improve recruitment efforts and increase the flow of minority and female applicants. These actions include:

- Identifying referral organizations for minorities and women.
- Holding formal briefing sessions with representatives of referral organizations.
- Encouraging minority and female employees to refer applicants to the company.
- Including minorities and women on the human resource staff.
- Permitting minorities and women to participate in career days, youth motivation programs, and related activities in their communities.
- Actively participating in job fairs and giving company representatives the authority to make on-the-spot commitments to qualified minorities and women.
- Actively recruiting at schools having predominantly minority or female enrollments.
- Recruiting efforts at other schools that utilize special approaches to reach minorities and women.
- Using special employment activities such as co-op programs, after school jobs, work-study jobs, summer employment, and so forth that increase employment opportunities for protected classes.
- Pictorially presenting minorities and women in recruiting brochures.
- Placing help wanted ads in minority news media and women's interest media.

To ensure that minorities and women are given equal opportunity for promotion within the organization, OFCCP suggests that companies do the following:

- Post or otherwise announce internally promotional opportunities.
- Inventory current minority and female employees to determine academic, skills, and experience levels of individual employees.
- Initiate necessary remedial, job training, and work-study programs.
- Develop and implement formal employee evaluation programs.
- Validate all job specifications in terms of job-related performance criteria.
- Require supervisory personnel to submit written explanations when apparently qualified minorities or females are rejected for promotion.
- Establish formal career counseling programs.
- Review seniority practices and seniority clauses in union agreements to ensure that such practices or clauses are nondiscriminatory and do not have a discriminatory effect.
- Ensure that facilities and company-sponsored social and recreational activities are integrated and actively encourage all employees to participate in all company-sponsored events and activities.
- Encourage child care, housing, and transportation programs appropriately designed to improve employment opportunities for minorities and women.

Internal Audit and Reporting Systems

Organizations should monitor records of referrals, placements, transfers, promotions, and terminations at all levels to ensure that a nondiscriminatory policy is carried out effectively. Additionally, the company should require formal reports from unit managers on a regularly scheduled basis specifying the degree to which corporate or unit goals and timetables relative to affirmative action are met. Report results should be reviewed with all levels of management.

DEVELOPMENTS IN AFFIRMATIVE ACTION

In 1996 voters in California, by a wide margin, approved Proposition 209, an initiative to end state-sponsored race and sex preferences in public hiring, contracting, and education. The state of Washington approved a similar plan in 1998, as did Michigan in 2006. In 1999 the state of Florida, through executive order and pressure on the governing boards of the state's universities, curtailed affirmative action preferences in state government as well as university admissions. Five other states—Arizona, Colorado, Missouri, Nebraska, and Oklahoma—are set to vote in November 2008 on initiatives to restrict state-sponsored affirmative action efforts. There is some speculation that these anti-affirmative action activities may be the result of a backlash against illegal immigration. Regardless of its specific cause, this trend toward the restriction of affirmative action within the states bears careful watching.

The Supreme Court has also taken actions that portend a rethinking of affirmative actions programs may be in order. The Court held in *Adarand Constructors, Inc. v. Pena* that in federal government affirmative action programs race preferences created by the government will be subjected to "the strictest judicial standard" and programs that do not meet the standard of "compelling governmental interest" violate the Constitution. In effect, *Adarand* ended minority "set aside" programs in federal contracting. While *Adarand* does not apply to private organizations and thus has limited practical significance for the private sector, it suggests that the courts may in the future be more willing to apply strict standards to other affirmative action efforts.

In 1996 the Supreme Court refused to hear an appeal of the Fifth Circuit Court's decision in *Hopwood v. State of Texas* and let stand a decision that prohibits consideration of race in higher education admissions, scholarships, and loans. Cheryl Hopwood, a Caucasian female, and three other Caucasian males had sued the University of Texas claiming that the Law School's admission process violated the Fourteenth Amendment by giving raced-based preferences exclusively to African Americans and Hispanic Americans. The Circuit Court agreed. Although the decision applies only to states in the Fifth District—Texas, Louisiana, and Mississippi—it may have broader implications eventually.

In another development with potentially far-reaching implications, the Department of Defense announced in 2007 that it was considering changes in regulations that would end the ability of the nation's military service academies to favor female and minority applicants by offering them an additional year of academic preparation if they are deemed unprepared to enter the service academies directly. This change could have a significant impact on the academies. The Air Force Academy, for example, estimates that about 40 percent of its minority students are admitted only after they have completed a ten-month regimen at a preparatory school that operates on its campus in Colorado Springs.

While no definitive conclusions can be drawn from the examples cited above, it seems safe to suggest that affirmative action programs will continue to be the topic of debate in the coming years.

NOTES

1. *Employment Discrimination Coordinator* (Deerfield, IL: Clark, Boardman Callaghan, 1995), 25,102.

2. Ibid.

3. *Uniform Guidelines on Employee Selection Procedures,* Section 1607.16Q.

4. Gary Dessler, *A Framework for Human Resources Management,* 4th ed. (Upper Saddle River, NJ: Pearson Prentice Hall, 2006), 40.

5. *Uniform Guidelines,* Section 1607.4D.

6. James Ledvinka and Vida G. Scarpello, *Federal Regulation of Personnel and Human Resource Management,* 2nd ed. (Boston: PWS-KENT Publishing Company, 1991), 144.

7. Ibid.

8. Kenneth J. McCulloch, *Selecting Employees Safely Under the Law* (Englewood Cliffs, NJ: Prentice-Hall, 1981), 68.

9. Robert J. Haertel, "The Statistical Procedures for Calculating Adverse Impact," *Personnel Administrator* (January 1984): 56–58.

10. Michelle Hoyman and Ronda Robinson, "Interpreting the New Sexual Harassment Guidelines," *Personnel Journal* (December 1980): 996.

11. Barbara Hagler, Testimony before House Judiciary II Committee, State of Illinois, March 4, 1980, 5.

12. *Guidelines on Discrimination Because of Sex,* Section 1604.11.

13. Ibid.

14. Barbara Lindemann Schlei and Paul Grossman, *Employment Discrimination Law,* 2nd ed. (Washington, DC: Bureau of National Affairs, 1983), 423.

15. Ledvinka dn Scarpello, *Federal Regulation,* 74.

16. *Discrimination Because of Sex,* Section 1606.1.

17. R. Wayne Mondy and Robert M. Noe III, *Personnel: The Management of Human Resources,* 3rd ed. (Boston: Allyn and Bacon, 1987), 83.

18. *Guidelines on Discrimination Because of National Origin,* Section 1606.1.

19. Schlei and Grossman, *Employment Discrimination Law,* 306.

20. Mondy and Noe, *Personnel,* 84.

21. Schlei and Grossman, *Employment Discrimination Law,* 207.

22. McCulloch, *Selecting Employees Safely,* 300.

23. Nancy Kruh, "Insight Politics," *The Dallas Morning News,* July 11, 1996, 4.

24. Ibid., 72.

25. Discussion on affirmative action programs is based on material taken from U.S. Department of Labor, Employment Standards Administration Office of *Federal Contract Compliance Manual,* Vols. 1–4, Washington, DC, May 2002.

5

Job Analysis

Broadly defined, job analysis is the process of collecting, interpreting, and reporting pertinent facts about the nature of a specific job. This process encompasses determining the duties and responsibilities that comprise the job; identifying the skills, abilities, knowledge, experience, and other factors required of a worker to be able to perform the job; and preparing job descriptions and job specifications.[1]

Job analysis is the most fundamental of all human resource management activities because all other human resource functions, especially staffing, depend to a large extent on the successful execution of this one activity. Human resource planning requires job analysis data to determine the types of jobs and skills that will be needed by the organization in the future. Recruiting needs job analysis information to be able to attract people with the proper experience and skill mix. Since selection of employees, for logical as well as legal reasons, must be based on job-related criteria, job analysis is essential to effective selection. Career planning and development, performance appraisal, and staffing administration also require information provided by job analysis. The information gathered, synthesized, and reported through this process will form the basis upon which significant staffing decisions will be made. Consequently, it is of vital importance that job analysis be performed carefully and accurately.

OVERVIEW OF THE JOB ANALYSIS PROCESS

Before considering the job analysis process in detail, an explanation of some of the terminology used in this activity is necessary. Three terms that warrant definition are task, position, and job.

A *task* is a duty; it exists whenever effort must be expended for a specific purpose such as typing a letter. A *position* is a group of tasks assigned to one employee. In any organization, there are as many positions as there are workers. A *job,* on the other hand, is a group of positions that are identical as far as their major or significant tasks are concerned. In a small organization, where every position differs from every other position, a position is also a job.[2]

Job analysis, in essence, consists of five major components: (1) identification of each job in the organization; (2) collection of information about duties, responsibilities, and working conditions of each job; (3) delineation of essential job functions and marginal or nonessential job functions; (4) determination of the human qualifications needed to perform the job; and (5) preparation of job descriptions and job specifications.

Job Identification

Before any job can be analyzed, it is necessary to determine what and how many jobs exist in the organization. To do this, a list of all positions is usually compiled. In a large organization the list would be assembled department by department; in a small organization, the list would be compiled for the total company. There are several ways this list can be constructed: by studying the organizational chart, by reviewing payroll records, by examining personnel directories, by talking to supervisors and managers, or by observing the actual work performed in each organizational unit. The final list of positions should equal the total number of employees in each department, if it has been compiled department by department; or it should equal the total number of employees in the organization if it has been compiled in aggregate fashion.

Once the list of positions has been completed, the next step is to develop a list of jobs. If, for example, an organization has six employees who function as information technology analysts and they all perform the same duties, it is clear that "information technology analyst" constitutes one job. But, if an organization has three individuals designated as "engineer" and one performs electrical and electronic engineering duties, one carries out mechanical engineering duties, and the other performs chemical engineering duties, it is clear that there are three separate jobs, not one. Should any doubt exist as to whether two or more positions are actually similar in nature, they should be listed as separate jobs until further analysis can clarify the situation.

After the tentative list of jobs has been completed, it is good practice to standardize job titles so that they conform to universally accepted and recognized titles. Frequently, organizations create job titles that are unique to the organization and have little or no meaning outside the institution. The *Dictionary of Occupational Titles,* originally a publication of the U.S. Department of Labor but now privately maintained, contains a list of standardized, commonly used, and widely accepted job titles. The *Dictionary of Occupational Titles* is available online as well as in printed form from a number of nongovernment sources. The Department of Labor has replaced *DOT* with *o*net,* which can also be used as a source of standardized job titles. Wherever possible, standardized job titles should be used in the interest of uniformity and consistency.

Collection of Data on Job Duties and Responsibilities

After determining which jobs exist in an organization, the major task of analysis begins: ascertaining the specific duties, responsibilities, essential functions, and nonessential functions of each job. Techniques for accomplishing this vital task are examined in subsequent sections of this chapter.

Delineation of Essential Job Functions

An essential job function is a task, duty, or responsibility that must be performed by the job incumbent with or without reasonable accommodation. Essential job functions are activities that are intrinsic to the job; they are the reasons the job exists. Employers are typically allowed fairly wide latitude in determining what is an essential job function. Specific job duties not identified as essential become, by definition, nonessential or marginal job functions.

Determination of Needed Human Qualifications

One of the most difficult parts of job analysis is determining the skills, abilities, experience, and other qualifications needed to perform a job successfully. A great deal of judgment, discretion, and expertise is required on the part of the individual performing the job analysis. While input from supervisors and managers is helpful, there is a tendency for these individuals to describe the qualifications that an *ideal* job incumbent should possess rather than a person who can perform job duties successfully. Employees, especially those who have been performing a job for a while, also tend to overstate the qualifications needed. The task of the job analyst is to sort through preferred qualifications and determine the minimally appropriate level of skills needed for successful job performance.

Preparation of Job Descriptions and Job Specifications

The final phase of job analysis is the preparation of written documents that enumerate the duties, responsibilities, and functions of the job (job descriptions) and specify the skills, abilities, and other qualifications required to perform the job (job specifications.)

The following sections cover the purposes and uses of job analysis information. Later sections examine in greater detail how the information is gathered and reported.

PURPOSES AND USES OF JOB ANALYSIS

As a basic tool of human resource management, job analysis provides information that can be used in a number of ways to satisfy organizational purposes. The information provided through this activity can be used as follows:

- To assist in human resource planning. Through job analysis, data relative to future skills and needs are determined. The organization knows not only what jobs will be needed in the future but also the qualifications individuals will need to fill these jobs successfully.
- To establish definitive criteria for making staffing decisions. Under the provisions of Title VII and the *Uniform Guidelines,* all selection standards and procedures used must be job related. Job analysis is the vehicle through which this is accomplished.
- To indicate the need for training of present as well as future job incumbents in the performance of job duties and responsibilities.
- To establish a basis for appraising the performance of employees in terms of actual job duties.
- To assist in the career planning and development process by identifying the qualifications employees must have to progress to positions of greater responsibility.
- To reallocate work from one job to another if the workload is too heavy in one job or if it could be performed better in another job.
- To correct unsafe or undesirable working conditions in a job before such conditions cause injury or illness to workers.
- To determine which jobs are exempt from the payment of overtime compensation and which jobs are not.
- To evaluate jobs relative to each other, thereby establishing a system of internal equity that can be used for compensation purposes.
- To establish groups or classes of similar jobs for compensation or performance appraisal purposes.
- To create a factual basis for determining promotions, transfers, terminations, or demotions.
- To establish a basis that assists in research efforts attempting to distinguish successful from less successful employees.
- To protect the organization in the event of legal challenge. The courts have typically held that a job analysis made in good faith is admissible as evidence that the organization has attempted to validate certain of its human resource procedures and practices.[3]

The preceding list is intended to be illustrative rather than exhaustive. However, it demonstrates that there are a number of reasons why all organizations should perform job analysis. Not the least of these reasons is the creation of a foundation, through development of job descriptions and job specifications, for effective staffing.

IMPACT OF ADA ON JOB ANALYSIS

The Americans with Disabilities Act of 1992 (ADA) has had a significant impact on the preparation of job descriptions. This Act requires that *essential functions* of a job be differentiated from *marginal* or nonessential job functions. Essential job functions are those job duties that are intrinsic to the position. They are, in essence, the reasons a position exists. Evidence of an essential function in a particular job includes the following: (1) the employer's judgment of its essentiality, (2) written job descriptions that suggest the essential nature of a job function, (3) the amount of time a job incumbent spends performing the specified function, (4) the consequences of not requiring the employee to perform the function, (5) the work experience of previous employees in the job, and (6) the current work experience of employees in similar jobs.[4] Marginal or nonessential functions are job functions that may be performed in a job, but are not key reasons for the performance of a job.

Since the enactment of ADA, it has become incumbent upon employers to separate essential job functions from marginal or nonessential job functions inasmuch as the Act precludes employers from discriminating against qualified individuals with disabilities who can, with or without reasonable accommodation, perform the essential functions of the job. As stated in Section 101(8) of the ADA: "consideration shall be given to the employer's judgment as to what functions of a job are essential, and if an employer has prepared a written job description before advertising or interviewing applicants for the job, this description shall be considered evidence of the essential functions of the job."

Well-written, comprehensive job descriptions that separate essential job functions from nonessential functions help protect an organization from charges of disability discrimination in hiring, promotion, transfer, or other employment decisions.

TYPES OF JOB ANALYSIS INFORMATION

A thorough, effectively performed job analysis can collect a wealth of information. The specific information generated depends largely upon its potential uses as well as the methods used to collect the data. As a general rule, it is preferable to collect as many job facts as possible so as not to overlook any important items. Table 5.1 presents examples of the types of data by category that can be gathered through job analysis.[5]

Certainly, job duties, responsibilities, essential functions, nonessential functions, and human qualifications are crucial items that must be identified for staffing purposes. But it is also important to identify organizational relationships and contexts in which the job is performed.

Table 5.1
Types of Information Collected by Job Analysis

1. **Job Duties**
- General purpose of the job.
- Duties performed daily and the approximate time spent on each.
- Duties performed only at stated periods such as once a week or once a month and the approximate time spent on each.
- Duties performed infrequently or irregularly, such as fill-in for another worker, and the approximate time involved.
- Most difficult or complex parts of the job, and why they are difficult or complex.
- Essential functions of the job: those duties that are the basic purpose of the job.
- Marginal functions, or peripheral duties, that are not the primary reason for the job's existence.

2. **Job Responsibilities**
- Nature and extent of responsibility for money, property, equipment, or other types of assets.
- Nature and extent of responsibility for materials or supplies.
- Nature and extent of responsibility for people.
- Number of workers supervised, directly or indirectly.
- Job title of workers supervised, directly or indirectly.
- Nature and extent of access to or usage of classified, confidential, or proprietary information.
- Nature and extent of decision-making authority.

3. **Machines, Equipment, Tools, and Materials Used**
- Machines and equipment operated and degree of proficiency required.
- Tools used and degree of proficiency required.
- Types of materials used, how they are used, and what is done to them.

4. **Controls over Work**
- Type of instructions received on how work is to be performed, and from whom they are received.
- Tasks that must be checked by others, and by whom and how they are checked.
- Decisions that must be referred to supervisor.
- Policies or procedures used.

5. **Performance Standards or Output Expectations**
- Output requirements.
- Quality requirements.
- Time schedules, deadlines, or other time requirements that must be met.

6. **Interactions with Others**
- Nature and frequency of contacts with coworkers or other organizational personnel.
- Nature and frequency of contacts with people outside the organization.
- Types of circumstances under which contacts within or outside the organization are normally made.
- Number of people contacted in a typical workday.

7. **Organizational Relationship**
• Job title of immediate supervisor.
• Department and unit to which job is assigned.
• Type of supervision received.
• Type of supervision given.
• Job from which individual is typically promoted to present job.
• Job to which individual is typically promoted from present job.

8. **Physical Factors and Job Environment**
• Percentage of time spent sitting, standing, and walking.
• Amount and type of physical exertion required.
• Environmental conditions in which work is performed.
• Typical work schedule, including overtime requirements.
• Job factors that produce fatigue.

9. **Education, Training, Experience, and Personal Requirements**
• Minimum level of education needed.
• Specialized courses required.
• Licenses or certifications required.
• Minimum level of experience required.
• Types of jobs in which required experience is usually gained.
• Personal requirements needed, such as oral or written communication skills, and mathematical or mechanical aptitude.
• Other qualifications, skills, or characteristics.

TRADITIONAL JOB ANALYSIS METHODS

Over the years, four traditional methods of job analysis have evolved: (1) questionnaires, (2) interviews, (3) observations, and (4) some combination of the preceding three methods. These approaches, despite their deficiencies, are still the ones most commonly used by most organizations.

Questionnaires

One of the simplest and quickest ways to collect a substantial amount of data on many jobs simultaneously is to administer a structured questionnaire to employees. Questionnaires are also the most economical data collection method. With this approach each employee in a job—or if there are many employees performing the same job, a representative sample of employees—is given a questionnaire and instructed to provide certain kinds of information about his or her job. While the specific types of data requested depend largely upon how the organization plans to use the job analysis information, the worker is typically asked to elaborate on the kinds of things shown in Table 5.1.

Administering a job analysis questionnaire to employees is customarily done in one of three ways: (1) the job analyst meets with all employees of a work unit and explains how to complete the questionnaire; (2) the job analyst meets with work unit supervisors to explain how to complete the instrument and the supervisors, in turn, explain it to their employees; or (3) the questionnaire is distributed with an accompanying memorandum that contains instructions needed for completing it. From an effectiveness standpoint, the first approach would seem to be the best since it offers the greatest opportunity to answer questions, provide clarification, and eliminate problems that may affect the quality or quantity of the information produced by questionnaires.

Once the employee completes the questionnaire, it is usually reviewed by his or her supervisor for completeness and accuracy, and then returned to the job analyst.

Designing a questionnaire that will produce the data needed for a thorough analysis of jobs is not an easy matter. The types of information needed, how the information will be used, and other factors must be considered before a sound instrument can be constructed. In many instances, one questionnaire cannot be used for all the jobs in an organization; several may be required. It may be necessary, for example, to design one questionnaire for manufacturing personnel, another for administrative employees, and another for technical personnel.

Obviously, the questionnaire approach to job analysis has some disadvantages: (1) it may interfere with normal work routine since employees will typically complete it during working hours; (2) it may produce inaccurate information due to the tendency of employees to overstate the importance of their jobs; (3) it may generate insufficient data if employees completing the instrument are not verbally facile; (4) it may be viewed by some employees as an imposition or interference with their normal work duties; and (5) it may, if used on a large number of jobs simultaneously, produce a mass of data for a job analyst to examine, interpret, synthesize, and report in a meaningful fashion.[6] Nevertheless, the questionnaire remains the most widely used job analysis method.

Interviews

The second traditional method of conducting job analysis is to interview employees performing the work. When this method is used, a structured interview guide is utilized so that the same questions are asked of each job incumbent and the same areas are covered in every interview conducted. Such a guide is especially critical when several individuals will be doing the interviewing. In effect, the interview method is much like the questionnaire approach except that the information is given to the analyst orally instead of in writing.

Job analysis interviews may be conducted in several different ways. They may be held with an individual employee, a group of employees performing the same job, the supervisor of a section or department, the individual employee and then the supervisor, or a group of employees and then the supervisor.[7] The most common procedure is to interview the job incumbent individually and then verify the information received by interviewing the employee's supervisor.

Interviews can be a very effective means of collecting job analysis information because most workers enjoy talking about their jobs. A skillful interviewer can often probe a job in much greater depth than could ever be achieved through a questionnaire.

Interviews have certain limitations: (1) they are time-consuming and therefore more expensive than questionnaires; (2) the quality of the information gathered is highly dependent upon the interviewer's skill; (3) they are often disruptive to the work routine because they take employees away from their assigned tasks; (4) they may be viewed as threatening by employees; and (5) even though the interviewer may be highly skilled, the quality and quantity of information obtained may suffer if the employee is not orally expressive.[8] Yet in most instances, the information provided by interviews may be far superior to what can be collected by questionnaires.

Observations

Job analysis can also be conducted by observing employees as they perform their jobs. The analyst watches the worker and records information about the various tasks being performed and the kinds of skills used to perform them. In order not to miss infrequent or irregular tasks, it may be necessary to observe a number of work cycles over an extended period of time.

The biggest advantages of observations are that the analyst can see firsthand the conditions under which the work is performed, note the level of complexity or difficulty involved, and gain greater insight into the job than might be possible through other methods.

However, relying solely upon observations as a job analysis method has serious drawbacks: (1) observations require a highly trained individual who can recognize task difficulties and variations of skill requirements; (2) many jobs are largely mental rather than physical and there is not actually much to observe; (3) it is easy to overlook infrequently performed job duties that require greater skill and effort than those performed on a daily basis; (4) observations can be very time-consuming and thus expensive; (5) observations can be threatening to employees; and (6) observations may disrupt normal work routine, not only for the worker being observed but also for others in the work unit who are uncomfortable with an outside observer in their midst.

Certainly, there is a place for observation in the collecting of job analysis information, but its place is secondary rather than primary.

Combination

Of all the traditional approaches to job analysis, a combination method is probably the best because it minimizes the disadvantages and maximizes the advantages of any one approach used by itself. Of the possible combination approaches, the two used most often are the following: (1) questionnaires and interviews, and (2) questionnaires, interviews, and limited observations used to determine the conditions under which work is performed.

As indicated earlier, one of the advantages of the questionnaire is that it produces a great deal of data rather quickly. But the job analyst often encounters difficulty in analyzing or interpreting questionnaire data accurately. Employees may use jargon, shoptalk, or technical terms that mean little to the analyst. In addition, employees may provide very sketchy information that has little or no value to an outsider. Interviews, conducted with the employee's completed questionnaire in hand, give the job analyst an opportunity to seek clarification or obtain additional clarifying job information.

The job analysis interview itself can be conducted more expeditiously when workers have already supplied written material because the analyst does not have to cover every aspect of each job, but only those parts where additional explanation is needed. Interview time is likely to be considerably less when the discussion with the worker is conducted from a completed job analysis questionnaire.[9]

A job analysis that combines questionnaires, interviews, and observation of the job and physical environment collects the most complete information. Observation often reveals factors about a job that are not uncovered through questionnaires or interviews, for example, poor lighting, an inefficiently designed workstation, excessive or irritating noise, or unusual physical motions required for task performance—items that may affect the subsequent selection of workers for the job.

Utilizing questionnaires, interviews, and observations provides the advantage of seeing a job from different perspectives; consequently, the information obtained in this fashion not only tends to be more complete, but also more valid.

THE PRODUCTS OF JOB ANALYSIS

Two major written products result from job analysis: a job description and a job specification. The job description delineates duties, responsibilities, essential functions, and nonessential functions; the job specification sets forth the human skills and qualifications needed to be able to perform a specific job. In practice, job specifications are commonly included as a section in the description itself. However, from a conceptual standpoint it is beneficial to envision these two end products as separate items that serve different purposes. By doing so, greater emphasis is placed on accurately describing the job and correctly specifying the skills required for effective job performance.

Job descriptions and job specifications are crucial to effective staffing; they serve as guidelines for hiring that ensure an organization is selecting the right kinds of individuals to perform the work of the institution, Additionally, job descriptions establish a factual basis for determining rates of pay, establishing performance standards, and delineating career paths or progression ladders.

Job Descriptions

Writing a good job description is not a simple matter. An effective job description must be specific, concise, complete, accurate, meaningful, and readable.[10] Whoever writes the description—job analyst, manager, or supervisor—must have an understanding of the content needed, the manner in which the information is to be presented, and effective writing techniques.

Content. The specific content of a job description varies from one organization to another, depending upon the uses to be made of the description, the format selected, and the nature of the job being described. Despite content differences, three requisites must be satisfied: job identification, job definition, and job delineation.

Job identification consists of information that differentiates one job from another job. Commonly used identifiers include job title, departmental location of the job, specific unit to which the job is assigned, exempt or nonexempt status, and title of the position to which the job reports. In large organizations additional identifiers may also be used, for example, job number, labor grade or job class, and number of job incumbents.

Careful thought should go into selecting a job title since it is the primary job identifier. The title chosen should reflect as clearly as possible the nature of the work performed, be distinct enough to differentiate the job from other similar jobs, and be consistent with other titles used in the organization. Job titles, unfortunately, are often misleading. An *executive secretary* in one organization may be little more than a highly paid clerk while a job with the same title in another organization may identify an incumbent who is an *administrative assistant* to a chief executive officer and does little or no clerical work as such. As mentioned earlier, the *Dictionary of Occupational Titles* or *o*net* can be of invaluable assistance in standardizing job titles. *DOT,* although now maintained by nongovernment sources but still widely used, contains thousands of standardized job titles as well as job descriptions. Each job title includes a numeric code that categorizes a job by different dimensions such as major job category, subsection of the major category, the job's relationship to data, people, and things, and an alphabetical listing within the job category.

Job definition is usually accomplished by means of a summary of the job that sets forth the purpose or nature of the job, why it exists, and how it relates to other organizational jobs. A good job summary usually provides, in two to four sentences, a succinct statement of the job's function and assists in differentiating it from other jobs in the organization.

Job delineation is the actual heart of the job description; it is the section of the job description in which duties, responsibilities, essential functions, nonessential or marginal functions, reporting relationships, and other tasks or activities are enumerated. It is, obviously, the longest part of the job description. Sufficiently detailed information must be provided about actual job duties, but the temptation to be verbose or pompous must be vigorously resisted. The job should be described so that duties, responsibilities, essential functions, etc., can be clearly understood by users of the job description.

Format. There is no universal job description format; nevertheless, the three requisites for job content—job identification, job definition, and job delineation —provide a reasonable indication of the basic format that should be followed.

Variations in job description format are most frequently found in the job delineation portion. Often, duties, responsibilities, and functions are subdivided into several sections to provide clarity and call attention to important job factors—financial responsibility, decision-making authority, controls over work, and interactions with others, for example. This is a sound practice because it not only clarifies duties, responsibilities, and functions, but also improves the readability of the job description.

Whatever format is used should be consistent from job to job for each particular group of jobs; for instance, all manufacturing jobs should be described according to the same format, and all managerial jobs should be described according to the same format. Additionally, the format used should parallel the use for which the description is intended. Where the job description is to be used as the basis for job evaluation, each compensable factor in the job evaluation plan must be clearly addressed in the job description. Where the job description is to be used as a basis for performance evaluation, each performance factor must be indicated.

Writing Techniques. Many job descriptions used in today's organizations are often poorly written; they can be excessively wordy, imprecise, or difficult to read. A job description should be an action-oriented document that states precisely, concisely, and clearly the duties performed and responsibilities carried out in a particular job. Careful attention to clarity of expression is essential. The following guidelines should be observed when writing a job description:

- Start each duty or responsibility statement with an action verb such as *analyze, calculate, compute, file, issue, prepare, reconcile, sort, tabulate,* or *transmit.* Words of this kind identify what is actually done in a job. (See Figure 5.1 for a list of suggested action words to use in job descriptions.)
- Avoid imprecise terminology. Words such as *handles, coordinates,* or *utilizes* are vague and open to different interpretations by different readers.
- Avoid shoptalk, jargon, or acronyms wherever possible because they are confusing to people who are not intimately familiar with the job.
- Use short, easy-to-read sentences.
- Use a style that specifies *who* does *what, when* it is done, *why* it is done, *where* it is done, and *how* it is done.
- Be detailed, but not wordy. Excess verbiage not only tends to confuse, but may also imply a degree of complexity that does not exist in a job.
- Use an outline form. With the exception of the job summary, which is normally in paragraph form, a job description is not a narrative. Each job duty, responsibility, or function identification statement should make a specific point.

Figure 5.1
Selected Action Words for Job Descriptions

Accomplish	Contact	Help	Prescribe
Accumulate	Contribute	Identify	Prevent
Acknowledge	Control	Implement	Process
Acquire	Convert	Import	Procure
Adjust	Convert	Improve	Promote
Advise	Correct	Inform	Provide
Affix	Correlate	Initiate	Purchase
Allot	Correspond	Innovate	Quantify
Alter	Create	Insert	Question
Amend	Decide	Inspect	Rate
Analyze	Delegate	Integrate	Read
Answer	Delete	Interpolate	Receive
Answer	Deliver	Interpret	Recommend
Apply	Describe	Interview	Reconcile
Appraise	Design	Investigate	Record
Approve	Determine	Issue	Refer
Approve	Develop	Itemize	Register
Approve	Devise	Join	Regulate
Arrange	Dictate	Justify	Reject
Assemble	Dispatch	Lead	Relate
Assist	Display	List	Release
Assure	Disseminate	List	Remit
Attach	Distribute	Locate	Remove
Attend	Divide	Maintain	Report
Authorize	Edit	Make	Request
Balance	Elaborate	Manage	Require
Batch	Eliminate	Match	Rescind
Budget	Employ	Measure	Research
Build	Encourage	Merge	Revise
Calculate	Endorse	Modify	Route
Cancel	Enforce	Monitor	Scan
Check	Engage	Move	Schedule
Clarify	Establish	Negotiate	Search
Classify	Estimate	Notify	Secure
Close	Examine	Nullify	Select
Collate	Exchange	Observe	Sell
Collect	Exclude	Obtain	Show
Communicate	Execute	Occupy	Solve
Compare	Expedite	Operate	Sort
Compile	Extend	Organize	Specify
Comply	Extract	Originate	Standardize
Compose	Extract	Outline	Summarize
Compute	Facilitate	Participate	Tabulate
Concentrate	File	Perform	Terminate
Condense	Formulate	Permit	Transcribe
Conduct	Furnish	Persuade	Transmit
Confirm	Gather	Place	Update
Consolidate	Generate	Post	Verify
Construct	Give	Predict	Weigh
Consult	Guide	Prepare	Write

- Enumerate each duty and responsibility in the general order of its overall importance to the job.

- Differentiate accurately essential functions from nonessential functions.

- Keep the user in mind. In the staffing process one of the key users of the job description is likely to be the screening interviewer, who must make a quick decision as to whether or not an applicant is sufficiently qualified for further consideration. If the job description is not clear, qualified candidates may be eliminated, and unqualified candidates may be recommended for further employment consideration. Select words and make statements that the user will understand.

Figure 5.2 presents a job description that follows the preceding guidelines. While the job described is one that is not specific to any organization, the same style and format can be used for almost any job.

Job Specifications

Job specifications outline the minimum qualifications, such as education, experience, or skills, a person should possess to perform a job satisfactorily. Job specifications should always reflect the minimum rather than the ideal qualifications for a particular job. In many instances there is probably a tendency for organizations to overstate qualifications. Because the information on job qualifications is usually gathered from supervisors or employees, organizations often overstate qualifications. Supervisors may describe the ideal candidate while employees may describe their own skills. Several problems can result if specifications are inflated. First, if specifications are set so high that they systematically eliminate minorities, women, individuals with disabilities, or other protected class members from consideration for jobs, an organization runs the risk of discrimination charges. Second, compensation costs will increase because ideal candidates expect to be compensated more than candidates with minimum skills. Third, job vacancies will be harder to fill because ideal candidates are more difficult to find than minimally qualified candidates.

Ascertaining the appropriate qualifications for a job is undoubtedly the most difficult part of job analysis. It requires a great deal of probing on the part of the job analyst as well as a broad understanding of the skills needed to perform varieties of work. Because of the problems associated with job specifications, it is preferable for an organization to underspecify rather than to overspecify qualifications.

Figure 5.3 shows the specifications for the position of Administrator, Human Resources that was described in Figure 5.2.

OTHER JOB ANALYSIS METHODS

Although the majority of organizations in this country probably use one of the traditional approaches to job analysis described previously in this chapter, there

Figure 5.2
Job Description

Human Resource Management Systems
Job Description

Position Title: Administrator		**Reports To:**	Director
Department: Human Resources		**Date Prepared:**	January 7, 2008
FLSA Status: Exempt		**Job Code:**	HRMS-HR001

Purpose of Position: Responsible for assisting with a comprehensive human resource function including employment, employee benefits, compensation, training and development, employee relations, and records management. Encourages understanding, cooperation, and support; recognizes employees as individuals with emotional and practical needs and seeks opportunities to build alignment among the people resources and the company's mission. Brings focus to the countless personal and compelling issues that each individual employee encounters and assures that the Firm expresses itself as a caring employer through equal employment opportunities, compensation and benefits programs, employee training and professional development objectives, proactive employee relations practices, health and safety programs, and records management.

Essential Functions:
1) Handles daily activity regarding insurance questions and insurance paper flow between employees and carriers to insure efficient use of employee benefits.
2) Assists with the preparation of human resource forecasts to project future employment needs.
3) Handles recruitment, screening, interviewing, applicant referrals, and placement in compliance with current litigation in order to effectively staff with the most qualified employee.
4) Maintains records of applicant flow to determine results of recruitment and selection programs in accordance with Firm's EEO objectives and applicable employment regulations.
5) Plans and conducts new employee orientation programs.
6) Assists with the development and implementation of the compensation program. Maintains salary administration program and pay policies, performance appraisal program, and communication of the employee benefit program in order to retain a highly qualified staff in compliance with Department of Labor and ERISA regulations. Coordinates the Firm's professional development and employee training programs to maintain optimal performance and motivation.
7) Maintains personnel records related to promotions, transfers, disciplinary action, and terminations.
8) Maintains a proactive approach to employee relations by (1) conducting exit interviews to determine reasons for separations, (2) maintaining two-way communication with departments, (3) acting as liaison between top management and employees with regard to employment issues, and (4) promoting continual communication efforts at all levels. Provides assistance in identifying, evaluating, and resolving work related problems within the Company to facilitate communication, improve employee relations, and achieve optimum employee performance.
9) Develops and maintains a human resource information system to meet the needs of key managers and supervisors for reports and reporting purposes.
10) Maintains and communicates human resource policies and procedures to promote equal employment opportunities and to ensure company-wide compliance.
11) Oversees the analysis, maintenance, and communication of records required by law or by local governing bodies to ensure compliance.
12) This job description includes, but is not limited to, the above functions. May temporarily perform other assigned duties to maintain operations and services.

Marginal Functions:
Marginal Functions will vary with the specific assignment and depend on the particular unit or function for which the person is responsible. Consideration will be given on a case by case basis and reassignment of marginal duties will be made when appropriate.

Supervision of Personnel:
None.

---

have been ongoing attempts to develop more systematic, standardized approaches to improve the quality and consistency of job analysis information. Three of these approaches—the Position Analysis Questionnaire (PAQ), the Job Analysis Schedule (JAS), and Functional Job Analysis (FJA)—are described briefly in this section. While other new approaches continue to be developed,

Figure 5.3
Job Specification

Human Resource Management Systems
Job Specification

Knowledge, Skills, Abilities, and Other Requirements:

A bachelor's degree in human resource management or related field required. Must have a minimum of two (2) to three (3) years working experience in human resources as a generalist or one (1) to two (2) years working experience as a specialist in benefits. Certification as a Professional in Human Resources (PHR) preferred. Individual with strong computer skills helpful. Good communication skills, both written and oral, essential.

- **Normal Ambulatory Requirements:** Ability to move in and around personal work space and to and from other areas of the office or building using wheelchair or other aid to attend meetings, deliver or retrieve materials, conduct interviews, or other activities outside of personal work space.
- **Normal Cognitive Requirements:** Ability to learn, remember, and integrate rules, policies, or practices guiding the performance of an activity.
- **Normal Speech/Communication Requirements:** Ability to communicate verbally with supervisors, co-workers, and clients to gather information and/or explain procedures.
- **Normal Written Communications Requirements:** Ability to continually record information such as draft correspondence/reports/documents/policies/procedures, conduct interviews recording information, prepare case narratives, or prepare other lengthy documents using handwritten or mechanical means.
- **Normal or Corrected Reading Vision Required:** Ability to read with attention to details.
- **Normal or Corrected Hearing Required:** Ability to hear and understand speech to interact with co-workers/clients/customers on a routine or frequent basis with the use of amplifying equipment/hearing aids.

Physical/Mental/Environment:

- **Physical Demands:** Normal office activity of sitting, standing, walking, and carrying small items.
- **Environment/Hazard Demands:** Pleasant working conditions.
- **Travel Demands:** Moderate travel requirements, ability to travel for activities such as out-of-town meetings or training sessions.
- **Lifting Demands:** May lift office equipment and supplies on occasion.

PAQ, JAS, and FJA are the most widely recognized and frequently used nontraditional job analysis methods.

Position Analysis Questionnaire

The PAQ was developed at Purdue University and resulted from more than ten years of research by psychologists who studied thousands of jobs.[11] The PAQ is a structured job analysis questionnaire that uses a checklist approach to identify job elements. There are 194 job descriptors that relate to job-oriented or worker-oriented elements. Proponents of PAQ believe that the ability of the checklist to identify job elements, behaviors required of job incumbents, and other job characteristics makes it possible to use this procedure for virtually any type of job.[12]

The 194 job elements used in PAQ are grouped into 27 division job dimensions and 5 overall job dimensions. These 32 dimensions are further divided into 6 major job activities: information input, mental process, work output, relationships with other persons, job context, and other job characteristics. Each job descriptor is evaluated on a specified scale such as *extent of use, importance of job, possibility of occurrence,* and applicability.

Computer scoring allows each job studied to be analyzed very quickly relative to the 32 different job dimensions. The score derived represents a profile of the job that can be compared with standard profiles to group the job into known job families, that is, jobs of a similar nature. In essence, PAQ identifies significant job behaviors and classifies jobs. Using PAQ, job descriptions can be prepared based on the relative importance and emphasis given to various job elements.

The PAQ is completed by an employee or employees familiar with the job being studied—typically an experienced job incumbent or the immediate supervisor. Job analysts then prepare the profiles and job descriptions. As can be deduced from this brief description, PAQ is a comprehensive, complex form of job analysis that requires an individual trained in its use if it is to produce the desired results.

Job Analysis Schedule

For many years, the U.S. Department of Labor worked on the development and refinement of a systematic means of analyzing and classifying job content: the Job Analysis Schedule (JAS).[13] Many federal, state, and local governmental agencies as well as private enterprises use this approach or some variation of it.

The JAS is an instrument for gathering data on five categories that can be used to define satisfactory job performance: worker functions; work fields; machines, tools, equipment, and work aids; materials, products, subject matter, and services; and worker traits.

Worker functions describe what workers do in the performance of a job with data, people, and things. The JAS includes a scale of values that ranks the complexity of worker functions. The 24 identifying activities for the three worker function areas are shown in Figure 5.4. The highest combination of the three areas establishes the relative importance of the job. Normally, reading down a column, each successive function includes each lower function. For example, in the column *Data,* if the highest activity identified is compiling, it is assumed that the job also requires computing, copying, and comparing. Note that the numerical values assigned the functions are the reverse of what might be expected in a typical value scale. With JAS, the lower the numerical value, the higher the level of activity.

The work fields, which are classified into 99 different categories, describe the mechanical, technological, or socioeconomic requirements of the job. The category of machines, tools, equipment, and work aids identifies the instruments and devices of a mechanical nature that are used to carry out the job. The category of materials, products, subject matter, and services describe the type or kind of materials worked on, the end products, the knowledge required to perform the job, and the nature of the services rendered. Worker traits are primarily concerned with job specifications. They are divided into five components: training time, aptitude, temperament, interests, and physical demands. Obviously, effective use of the JAS requires a highly trained and skilled job analyst.

Figure 5.4
Job Analysis Schedule Worker Functions

Data		People		Things	
0	Synthesizing	0	Mentoring	0	Setting-up
1	Coordinating	1	Negotiating	1	Precision Working
2	Analyzing	2	Instructing	2	Operating-Controlling
3	Compiling	3	Supervising	3	Driving-Operating
4	Computing	4	Diverting	4	Manipulating
5	Copying	5	Persuading	5	Tending
6	Comparing	6	Speaking-Signaling	6	Feeding-Offbearing
		7	Serving	7	Handling
		8	Taking Instruction and Helping		

Functional Job Analysis

This approach to job analysis, a modification of the JAS, is a comprehensive approach that concentrates on the interactions among the work, the worker, and the work organization.[14] Functional Job Analysis (FJA) is a worker-oriented approach to job analysis that identifies what a worker actually does rather than what the worker is responsible for.

FJA utilizes a modified version of the worker functions scales contained in the job analysis schedule. In fact, the two scales are almost identical except that FJA adds a *no significant relationship* to the data, people, and things categories of worker functions and reverses the numerical coding.

The basic premises and fundamental elements of FJA are the following:

1. A distinction is made between what gets done and what a worker must do to get it done. As far as job analysis is concerned, it is probably more important to know the latter. For example, an airline pilot does not fly passengers; he or she performs a multitude of tasks to take an airplane from one location to another.

2. What a worker does in a job is related to only three basic elements: data, people, and things. These are, in fact, the materials as well as the results of all work that is performed in any organization.

3. In relation to data, people, and things, workers function in unique ways. In essence, *data* draw on mental resources; *people* draw on interpersonal resources; and *things* draw on physical resources.

4. Every job requires that a worker relate to data, people, and things.

5. Although worker behavior or task performance can be described in an almost infinite number of ways, there are only a few definite and identifiable functions connected with data, people, and things. These basics are those shown in Figure 5.4.

6. The functions performed by workers proceed from the simplest to the most complex. For instance, the least complex form of *people* would be *serving* while the most complex would be *monitoring*. Consequently, if an upper level function is required, all of the lower-level functions are also required.

7. The three hierarchies for data, people, and things provide two measures for a job: level and orientation. Level is a measure of complexity in relation to data, people, and things. Orientation is a measure of involvement with data, people, and things.[15]

Proponents of FJA claim that, in addition to being a useful means of analyzing jobs, it also establishes criteria that can be used to evaluate the worth of a job (set compensation rates) and appraise the performance of workers in each job.

As with the other newer approaches to job analysis, FJA is more complex than the traditional methods and requires a well-trained job analyst.

CONCLUDING OBSERVATIONS ABOUT JOB ANALYSIS

Job analysis, despite efforts to increase the levels of sophistication with which it is performed, will probably always remain somewhat subjective because it is a process that requires human judgment. Consequently, it seems important to offer a few concluding caveats about this basic human resource management activity.

- Not all job analysis methods will yield the same results. Some methods yield sophisticated, detailed data, while others yield more general and less defined results.

- Complex methods of job analysis do not necessarily produce more accurate results. The complexity of a method is not automatically a guarantee of the usability of its results.

- Job analysis tends to produce static rather than dynamic results. Job analysis describes a job as it is done, not how it might be done more effectively. Thus, the results tend to preserve the ways things have always been done, not how they might be done best.

- Different job analysts tend to produce different results. Judgment and subjectivity on the part of different analysts often lead to different conclusions.

- No one method of job analysis is clearly superior to all other methods. Different methods can produce equally usable results.

- Information gathered by job analysis may be influenced by input from job incumbents. More experienced incumbents may tend to make a job appear more complex or demanding than it really is. Less experienced incumbents may lead an analyst to describe a job in more simplistic terms than it actually deserves.

Care must always be taken to ensure that the results of job analysis produce the results an organization desires and can use.

NOTES

1. Donald L. Caruth and Gail D. Handlogten, *Staffing the Contemporary Organization,* 2nd ed. (Westport, CT: Quorum Books, 1997), 102.

2. Donald L. Caruth, *Compensation Management for Banks* (Boston: Bankers Publishing Company, 1986), 37.

3. Sidney A. Fine, Robert J. Harvey, and Steven F. Cronshaw, "FJA Strategies for Addressing O *Net Limitation in a Post-DOT Environment," Symposium presented at the Annual Conference of the Society for Industrial and Organizational Psychology, Chicago, 2007.

4. Joan Ackerstein, *The Americans with Disabilities Act: What Supervisors Need to Know* (Burr Ridge, IL: Business One Irwin/Mirror Press, 1994), 22.

5. Caruth, *Compensation Management,* 256–262.

6. Ibid., 40.

7. Ibid.

8. Ibid., 41.

9. Ibid., 43.

10. Donald L. Caruth and Gail D. Handlogten, *Managing Compensation (and Understanding It Too)* (Westport CT: Quorum Books, 2001), 64–66.

11. Ernest J. McCormick, Paul R. Jeanneret, and Robert Mecham, "A Study of Job Characteristics and Job Dimensions as Based on the Position Analysis Questionnaire (PAQ)," *Journal of Applied Psychology* (August 1972): 347–368.

12. Joseph Tiffin and Ernest J. McCormick, *Industrial Psychology,* 6th ed. (Englewood Cliffs, NJ: Prentice-Hall, 1974), 53.

13. U.S. Department of Labor, Manpower Administration, *Handbook for Analyzing Jobs* (Washington, DC: U.S. Government Printing Office, 1972).

14. Caruth and Handlogten, *Managing Compensation,* 71.

15. Ibid., 71.

6

Human Resource Planning

In far too many instances, human resources do not receive the same meticulous attention that management devotes to other organizational resources. Nowhere is this more evident than in planning for future personnel needs. Physical and financial resources are usually planned for well in advance. The need for new facilities, equipment, or capital may be anticipated years ahead of the time they will actually be required. Costs will be calculated, sources will be determined, rates of return will be computed, and other analyses will be performed. Yet when it comes to people resources, it is common to find many organizations relying on the "faith principle"—the assumption that sufficient quantities and qualities of human resources will be available as needed to staff the new facilities and operate the new equipment. In most cases, people planning occurs after the fact. The new plant is opened, the new machinery is installed, and the scramble to find employees to staff the facility and operate the equipment just begins. To neglect planning for human resources, however, is to invite disruptions and delays if sufficient numbers of properly trained people do not materialize when they are needed.

Fortunately, a number of organizations have recognized, and others are beginning to recognize, the essentiality of planning for personnel needs. The reason, according to one author, is that "strategic planning for human resources makes good business sense [because many institutions] have at least half of their financial resources continuously committed to the acquisition, development, maintenance, and use of human resources." [1] In sum, effective human resource planning is an important factor in the formulation and implementation of an organization's overall strategy and success. [2]

DEFINITION OF HUMAN RESOURCE PLANNING

Human resource planning may be defined in several ways. It may be thought of as (1) "a process and set of activities undertaken to forecast an organization's labor demands (requirements) and internal labor supply (availabilities), to compare these projections to determine employment gaps, and to develop action plans for addressing these gaps";[3] (2) "a systematic process for setting policies governing the acquisition, use, and disposition of personnel in order to achieve organizational objectives";[4] or (3) the "process of determining the human resource needs of an organization and ensuring that the organization has the right number of qualified people in the right jobs at the right time."[5] Some common threads are apparent in these definitions. First, human resource planning is a process, an ongoing activity. Second, the purpose of human resource planning is to aid the organization in reaching its goals and objectives. Third, human resource planning is not haphazard; it is a systematic, analytical activity. And fourth, the goal of human resource planning is to have the right people in the right jobs at the right time.

By combining these definitions and their common elements, human resource planning can now be more specifically defined as a systematic, ongoing activity that ensures that an organization has the right number and kind of people in the right jobs at the right time so that the institution can achieve its stated objectives.

STRATEGIC BUSINESS PLANNING AND HUMAN RESOURCE PLANNING

The determination of future human resource requirements logically stems from the organization's strategic business plan. This is the document that identifies the direction in which the firm intends to move, in the long run as well as the short run.

Through strategic business planning, an institution clarifies its mission and purpose, sets its goals and objectives, and develops courses of action that it hopes will lead to goal accomplishment and mission fulfillment. In the past, it was not unusual for the human resource manager to be left out of the strategic planning process or for human resource planners to forecast personnel requirements without referring to the business plan. Nor was it unusual for management to formulate goals and strategies without explicit information on the potential availability of human resources to carry out the firm's plans. Today, this situation is changing. More organizations are recognizing that well-formulated business plans cannot be developed without input from human resource professionals. Strategic planning and human resource planning are being increasingly viewed as interactive processes that rely heavily upon each other.[6] To construct viable plans, strategists need information on the availability of personnel; to forecast requirements and availability of personnel, human resource planners need information on anticipated expansions or contractions of the organization. Only through an interactive linkage can both strategic planning and human resource planning become truly effective.

In recent years, many organizations have wrestled with the issue of determining the appropriate size for the institution. *Downsizing, restructuring, reengineering,* and, most recently, *rightsizing* have become commonplace terms in the lexicon of management. By whatever term it may be called, changes in size are a result of organizational efforts to create effective, efficient, streamlined organizations that employ the right number of people—no more and no less—needed to achieve its goals. As a result, human resource planning has increased in importance as a vehicle for ascertaining appropriate institutional size.

THE HUMAN RESOURCE PLANNING PROCESS

Figure 6.1 shows a generalized model of the human resource planning process. After the organization's strategic plan has been developed—with the full participation of the human resource department—the determination of specific future personnel needs can begin.

As the model indicates, there are three basic phases involved in human resource planning. The first phase is concerned with identifying the number and kinds of employees the firm will need in the future. This is the requirements forecasting stage. The strategic business plan may necessitate the creation of new jobs, the elimination of existing jobs, no changes in jobs, or increases or decreases in organizational positions (that is, number of employees). Additionally, the requirements forecast must consider the number of employees who will be lost through normal attrition, such as terminations and retirements. After all of the factors that influence requirements have been considered and the human resource planners have ascertained the personnel necessary to fulfill the business plan, the anticipated organizational structure of the future is created.

The second phase of human resource planning entails the determination of the availability of qualified people to staff the organization of the future. At this time, planners must look inside the enterprise to identify individuals who could be promoted or transferred to new jobs or positions. They must also look outside the firm, through the examination of demographic data and other factors, to forecast the number of qualified individuals who will be available to meet the future staffing needs. Personnel requirements are then matched with personnel availability. Although all steps in the human resource planning process are crucial, comparing needs and availability is especially important because it identifies the staffing situation that will confront the organization in the future and suggests actions that will have to be taken to equate the demand for and supply of human resources.

The final phase of human resource planning is the development of specific courses of action to assure the institution that it will have the appropriate number and kind of people in the right places at the right times to carry out the strategic business plan.

Figure 6.1
The Human Resource Planning Process

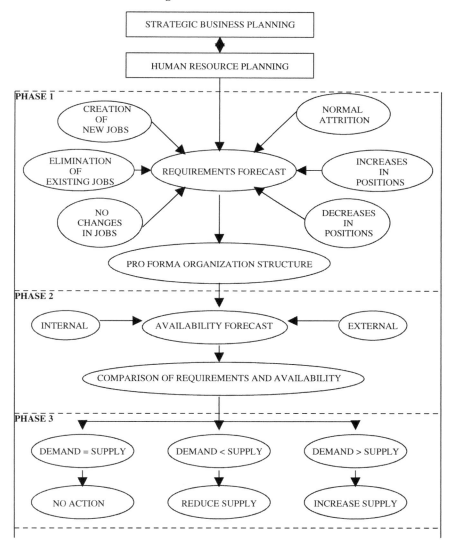

Each phase in the human resource planning process requires careful thought and analysis. Some steps are very complex and require the use of statistical methods. Other steps are highly subjective and depend upon the exercise of creativity. Different approaches to planning may be used at different times or by different organizations. In some instances, planning may be carried out entirely by specialists. In other cases, operating management may bear the bulk of the responsibility. The following sections examine the human resource planning process in greater detail.

REQUIREMENTS FORECASTING

A requirements forecast is an estimation of the number and kind of employees the organization will need at future dates to meet its objectives. It is important to remember two points about forecasting personnel requirements. One, while estimating the total number of employees that will be needed is necessary, a forecast that provides only a total number and does not furnish a breakdown of that number, job by job, is incomplete. Identifying the mix of jobs is critical; the combination of needed skills lays a foundation upon which effective staffing activities can be built. Although the discussion of forecasting presented in this chapter tends, for the sake of clarity and simplicity of presentation, to center on obtaining a single number, forecasting actually results in a series of job-by-job numbers that reflect the diversity of future personnel requirements. Two, even with the most sophisticated computerized statistical techniques, forecasting is an imprecise endeavor at best. There is no generalized procedure or set of techniques that automatically produces usable results. Judgment plays a sizable role in forecasting and influences the usefulness of the results.

Human resource forecasting techniques may be divided into two broad categories: (1) subjective and (2) quantitative. Subjective techniques rely heavily on qualitative information supplied by managers, supervisors, human resource planners, and others to develop an estimation of personnel needs. Quantitative approaches utilize mathematical procedures to predict requirements.

Subjective Techniques

Managerial estimates, the Delphi technique, and zero base forecasting are three subjective approaches used by organizations to forecast human resource requirements. The most widely used is managerial estimates. While these techniques depend on informed judgment, they may also employ quantitative data to substantiate or support subjective findings.

Managerial Estimates. This is essentially a *bottom up* approach to determining personnel requirements. It is based on the premise that each individual manager in an organization is the person most knowledgeable about the number and kind of people needed to run his or her unit effectively at various levels of activity. Beginning with the lowest level work units in the organization, each unit manager makes an estimate of human resource needs for the time period encompassed by the planning cycle. As the process moves upward in the company, each successively higher level of management in turn makes its own estimates of needs, incorporating the input from each of the immediately preceding levels. The result, ultimately, is an aggregate forecast of needs for the entire organization.

This process is often highly interactive since estimated requirements from the previous level are discussed, negotiated, and reestimated with the next level of management as the forecast moves upward through the institution. The interactive aspect of managerial estimating is one of the advantages of this procedure because it requires managers to justify their anticipated staffing needs.

Figure 6.2 shows an illustration of a typical form used at the work unit level to estimate personnel needs. This example deals only with total requirements. In actual practice, estimates would be made for each job in the unit and then combined into one document that enumerates requirements job by job, as well as by total work unit. The supervisor or manager, in order to make realistic estimates, will have to have information about such factors as future production levels, changes in products or functions, and turnover rates. The needed information normally comes from the strategic business plan and from human resource specialists.

In Figure 6.2, the supervisor of the unit in question anticipates losing seven employees over the course of the planning period—six employees through normal attrition and one through a reduction in the number of positions in the unit. At the same time, however, changes in products or services will result in the creation of two new jobs, necessitating a staffing level of 37 employees. If the supervisor anticipates that one employee will be transferred into the unit and another one will be promoted into the unit, a total of seven employees will have to be hired to achieve the projected staffing level of 37 employees.

Admittedly, this example is simplistic, but it does indicate the basic thrust of managerial estimating. If supervisors and managers have sufficient information on which to base their anticipated requirements, and the process is interactive and adequately justifies projected staffing levels, this approach can provide an organization with reasonably accurate forecasts of human resource requirements.

The Delphi Technique. This technique consists of using a panel of experts to independently offer their estimates of the future human resource demands of the organization. Once each expert gives his or her forecast, an intermediary presents each expert's forecast to the entire panel and each expert is then allowed to revise his or her forecast, if desired. The goal is to reach some sort of consensus among the experts, providing the organization with a single forecast upon which to base human resource planning efforts.[7]

Zero Base Forecasting. This technique uses the organization's current staffing level as the starting point for estimating future requirements.[8] The key to zero base forecasting is the necessity of justifying, quantitatively or otherwise, the filling of any vacant position or the creation of any new positions or jobs. If any employee leaves the organization for any reason, the vacant position is not automatically filled. The supervisor or manager must conduct an analysis and offer substantive justification for filling the position. Likewise, when a new position is created, justification for its existence must be provided or the position will not be approved. The primary advantage to this approach is the thorough analysis of human resource needs required for additions to staff or replacements to current

Figure 6.2
Human Resource Forecasting Form

I.   CURRENT STAFFING   35

II.   ANTICIPATED LOSSES

     A.   Normal Attrition

        1.   Termination   -1
        2.   Retirements   -3
        3.   Deaths   -0
        4.   Lateral Transfers out of Unit   -0
        5.   Promotions out of Unit   -2
        6.   Demotions out of Unit   -0

        Total Attrition Losses   **-6**

     B.   Changes in Staffing

        1.   Reductions in Positions   -1
        2.   Job Eliminations   -0

        Total Staffing Losses   **-1**

     C.   Total Losses   **-7 (35 – 7 = 28)**

III.   ANTICIPATED GAINS

     A.   Attrition Replacements: Internal

        1.   Lateral Transfers into Unit   +1
        2.   Promotions into Unit   +1
        3.   Demotions into Unit   +0

     B.   Total Internal Gains   **+2 (28 + 2 = 30)**

IV.   NET HIRING NEEDS   **+5 (30 + 5 = 35)**

V.   POSITION AND JOB INCREASES

     A.   Increases in Positions   **+0**
     B.   Anticipated New Jobs   **+2 (35 + 2 = 37)**

VI.   TOTAL HIRING NEEDS   **+7 (30 + 7 = 37)**

VII.   PROJECTED STAFFING LEVEL   37 staffing. As yet, this technique has not become a major procedure for forecasting human resource requirements. It is more commonly used in combination with other approaches.

Quantitative Techniques

Although the use of judgment in forecasting human resources requirements has been addressed in this chapter, quantitative approaches can provide a more solid basis for making good judgments. The primary quantitative technique used in organizations involves correlation and regression analysis. Some large institutions, because of the number of jobs and the complexity of forecasting requirements, use computer simulation models to predict personnel needs.

Correlation and Regression Analysis. Correlation measures the relationship between two or more variables. Regression analysis measures the value of one variable in terms of the value of another variable. For example, since there is often a direct relationship between employment levels and a firm's sales, output, or assets, correlation and regression analysis can be used to determine the degree of relationship and forecast the number of employees that will be required at different levels of sales, output, or assets.

A detailed example will show how these statistical procedures work. Assume that a firm believes its staffing requirements are dependent upon total sales. The first step is to test that assumption to determine whether there is a direct relationship between the dependent variable (number of employees) and the independent variable (sales). This is done through correlation. The degree of relationship is expressed as a coefficient of correlation (r), ranging from −1.0 to +1.0 in value. The closer the correlation value is to plus or minus 1.0, the stronger the relationship between the two variables. A coefficient of exactly +1.0 or −1.0 would indicate a perfect relationship—the first completely positive and the second completely negative. A coefficient of zero would indicate no relationship exists between the two variables.

Table 6.1 contains all of the data that will be used in this correlation and regression analysis example. The first two columns contain data on the number of employees and sales volumes for ten periods. The other columns contain calculations that will be used in the correlation and regression formulas.

The statistical formula for calculating the correlation coefficient is

$$r = \frac{n(\Sigma XY) - (\Sigma X)(\Sigma Y)}{\sqrt{\left[n\left(\Sigma X^2\right) - (\Sigma X)^2\right]\left[n\left(\Sigma Y^2\right) - (\Sigma Y)^2\right]}}$$

Inserting the values from Table 6.1 into this equation would result in r = +0.91488. Inasmuch as a perfect positive correlation has a value of +1.0, we now know that there is an extremely strong positive relationship between sales and the number of employees; that is, the number of employees the firm needs

Table 6.1
Correlation and Regression Analysis Data

Period	Number of Employees Y	Sales in (00,000) X	XY	X_2	Y_2
1	10	15	150	225	100
2	16	19	304	361	256
3	20	30	600	900	400
4	28	22	616	484	784
5	32	41	1,312	1,681	1,024
6	42	40	1,680	1,600	1,764
7	42	50	2,100	2,500	1,764
8	47	53	2,491	2,809	2,209
9	49	45	2,205	2,025	2,401
10	61	53	3,233	2,809	3,721
x	347	368	14,691	15,394	14,423

is linked very closely to variations in sales volume. Thus, sales dollars are likely to be a good predictor of total human resource requirements for this organization.

Having established the usefulness of sales as an indicator of personnel needs, the next step is to calculate a regression line that establishes the linear relationship between changes in sales and employee requirements. To do this, a scatter diagram such as the one shown in Figure 6.3 is constructed. Then a line of *best*

Figure 6.3
Scatter Diagram

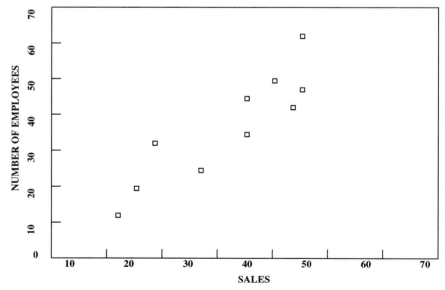

fit is computed to graphically show the relationship of employees to sales. The most frequently used method for determining this line is the *least squares* method, which minimizes the sum of the squares of the distance between each unit of data and its corresponding point on the assumed line. The basic formula for a straight line is

$$Y = a + bX$$

where

$$Y = \text{number of employees}$$

$$a = \text{the point of origin of the line}$$

$$b = \text{the rate of change}$$

$$X = \text{sales}$$

To solve for *a* and *b* the following formulas are used:

$$a = \frac{\Sigma Y - b\Sigma X}{n}$$

$$b = -\frac{n(\Sigma XY) - (\Sigma X)(\Sigma Y)}{n(\Sigma X^2) - (\Sigma X)^2}$$

Using the data in Table 6.1 to solve these equations, we find that

$$a = -3.58725$$

$$b = 1.037697$$

A line can now be drawn through the data as shown in Figure 6.4.

Once the line has been statistically fitted to historical data, it can then be extrapolated into the future to show potential staffing needs at different sales levels. Figure 6.5 shows that when sales reach $6 million, 60 employees will probably be needed.

Although the calculations for correlation and regression analysis seem laborious (in fact, they are if done manually), statistical software packages put this approach to forecasting human resource requirements within the reach of practically every manager. All of the calculations used in the preceding example, including the scatter diagram and the regression line, were generated on a personal computer and printed in hard copy within a matter of minutes.

The principal disadvantage of correlation and regression analysis as a forecasting technique is that staffing projections are based on the assumption that the future will resemble the past. In many cases, because of technological changes, economic conditions, strategic maneuvers, or a host of other factors, this may not be a valid assumption. Yet statistical forecasting does establish a sound point of departure upon which anticipated staffing changes can be based.

Figure 6.4
Scatter Diagram with Regression Line

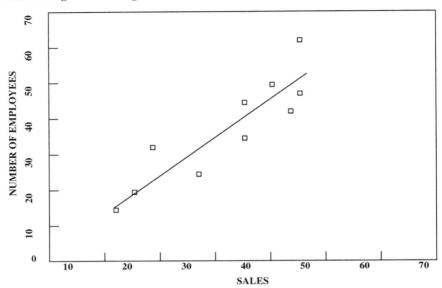

Simulation

Simulation relies on the use of models to forecast human resources requirements. A model, simply defined, is a representation of reality that includes key
features or variables relative to what it purports to represent. In simulation, a
computer is used to assist in duplicating a real-world situation through mathematical logic and manipulating important variables so that an approximation
of reality under varying conditions can be predicted and analyzed. Simulation
assists human resource planners in answering "what if" questions. Typical questions of this nature that impact the number of people employed are the following:
"What if sales increase by 15 percent?" "What if 20 percent of the work force is
put on overtime?" "What if a policy of no new hiring is implemented?" By developing a model that shows the many complex interrelations between several different variables, human resource planners can obtain insights into many staffing
situations and possibilities before they actually occur. However, the quality of
these insights depends on the sophistication of the model and the identification
and quantification of the variables that influence staffing levels.

Simulation is not an approach that can be used by all organizations. It requires
a powerful computer and software to manipulate a number of variables under different conditions. Furthermore, the process of building an accurate model is time-
consuming and expensive, and it depends on the expertise of individuals skilled
in both human resources and computer programming. More widespread use of

Figure 6.5
Extrapolated Regression Line

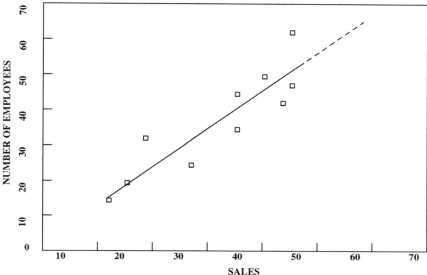

this approach is expected in the future, but at the present it remains a forecasting option for primarily large institutions.

The *Pro Forma* Organization Structure

After human resource requirements have been determined, the next logical step in the forecasting process is to develop an organization structure or series of structures that reflect the form the enterprise will assume in the future. The strategic business plan may necessitate creation of new departments or geographical units, elimination of existing offices, or a variety of other changes. The purpose of the *pro forma* structure is to show not only these changes but also the human resource needs required to accommodate them. While the organization structure of the future may resemble the traditional organization chart, effective human resource planning carries the chart one step further: it identifies, function by function, department by department, and unit by unit, the number and kind of jobs made necessary by the future structure. To accomplish this task, staffing tables, such as the one presented in Figure 6.6, are often created for each existing or anticipated organizational unit.

Even though the staffing table shown here is simplistic, close examination reveals its usefulness in identifying the points at which jobs will be created or additional employees will be needed for existing jobs. This knowledge permits an organization to begin its requisite staffing activities well in advance of actual

Figure 6.6
Staffing Table

WORK CENTER: Final Assembly	PRODUCTION VOLUME									
DEPARTMENT: Production	NUMBER OF UNITS ASSEMBLED (In Thousands)									
STAFFING REQUIREMENTS	2.0	2.1	2.2	2.3	2.4	2.5	2.6	2.7	2.8	2.9
Supervisor	1	1	1	1	1	1	1	1	1	1
Assistant Supervisor	-	-	-	-	-	-	-	1	1	1
Leadperson	-	-	-	-	1	1	1	1	1	1
Clerical Assistant	-	-	-	-	1	1	1	1	1	1
Expeditor	-	-	-	-	-	1	1	2	2	2
Inventory Control Clerk	1	1	1	1	1	1	1	1	1	1
Assembler "A"	9	9	9	10	10	11	11	12	12	13
Assembler "B"	4	4	4	4	4	4	4	4	5	5
Assembler Trainee	-	1	2	2	2	3	3	3	4	4
Total Staff	15	16	17	18	20	23	23	26	28	29

need, thereby ensuring that sufficient qualified people will be available when needed.

AVAILABILITY FORECASTING

The requirements phase of the human resource planning process provides the organization with knowledge of how many and what kinds of employees will be needed and when they will be needed. However, the organization must also determine if it will be able to obtain employees with the necessary skills and from what sources these individuals may be secured. This is the task of availability forecasting. The demand for employees may be met by either obtaining people from within the company or resorting to external sources of supply, or both.

Internal Sources

Many of the employees who will be needed to fill future positions are already employed by the institution. Through transfer and promotion, these individuals can be shifted laterally to other jobs or elevated to positions of greater responsibility. The major problem for large firms is being able to identify available internal talent so that this talent can be matched with the company's needs. Two approaches that are valuable in the identification and matching process are skills inventories and management inventories.

Skills Inventories. Information maintained on nonmanagerial employees concerning their availability and preparedness to move into higher-level or lateral positions is referred to as a skills inventory. The purpose of the inventory is to enable the organization to readily determine which employees may be shifted from one job to another in order to meet the changing employment needs of the firm. Essential data maintained in such a record would include, but not be limited to, the following:

- Educational background.
- Work experience in the organization or elsewhere.
- Specific work skills, such as the ability to operate particular pieces of equipment.
- Licenses or certifications held.
- Biographical data, including protected class status.
- Previous performance appraisal evaluations.
- Internal or external training programs completed.
- Career goals and aspirations.

The popularity of skills inventories has increased thanks to computerization.[9] Essential information on employee skills can easily be maintained and updated on electronic human resource information systems. In the smallest of organizations, inventories can be maintained manually. With this information, the organization is less likely to overlook the best source of employees for future positions —those already employed by the enterprise.

Management Inventories. Managerial talent is a critical resource for every organization. Thus, it is more common for firms to maintain data on managers than it is for them to keep the same detailed records on lower-level employees. A management inventory, very simply defined, is a collection of information about managerial employees and typically includes brief assessments of past performance, strengths, weaknesses, and the potential for advancement to higher-level positions.[10] Essentially, this type of inventory provides information for replacement and promotion decisions. It differs from a skills inventory primarily in terms of the amount of information maintained and the detailed nature of that information. Typically included in a management inventory would be data pertaining to the following:

- Work history and experience.
- Educational background.
- Assessment of strengths and weaknesses.
- Developmental needs.
- Promotional potential at present or with further development.
- Current job performance.
- Field of specialization.
- Job preferences.
- Geographical preferences.

- Career goals and aspirations.
- Anticipated retirement date.
- Personal history, including any psychological assessments.

As with the employee skills inventory, this kind of information can be maintained either electronically or manually.

Both skills and management inventories are valuable tools that assist a company in making the best possible use of its present human resources. Effectively utilized, inventories can also have a positive effect on morale because they signify an organization's interest in, and commitment to, a promotion-from-within policy. Inventories help ensure that talented employees will not be overlooked when promotional opportunities become available. For these tools to function properly, however, the informational databases must be kept current through frequent updating.

Ongoing Training and Development Programs. Where organizations have various training programs in operation, program graduates can fill new job openings. While these programs are frequently technical in nature and designed for operative-level employees, on occasion in-house programs are used to develop new supervisors or lower-level managers.

External Sources

Because not all demands for human resources can be met internally, an organization will, from time to time, have to resort to external sources for skilled workers. Anticipating the number and kind of skilled people who will be available is no easy task for human resource planners. Many environmental factors influence the potential availability of employees. Planners must carefully analyze each factor and assess its likely impact on the supply of workers the firm may need. Among the items that must be considered are the following:

- Demographic changes.
- Population shifts from one part of the country to another.
- Changes in the total work force.
- Composition of the work force.
- Increasing educational levels.
- Societal attitudes toward particular careers, industries, and institutions.
- Economic conditions.
- Technological changes.
- Political conditions.
- Governmental regulations.[11]

Much of the needed information is available from federal agencies such as the U.S. Bureau of Labor Statistics, which publishes monthly, quarterly, and annual reports on current and expected conditions in various labor markets. The U.S. Census Bureau is another good source, issuing periodic reports and projections on population changes and many other items of interest to human resource planners. Many trade associations also publish data on trends in specific industries. The task of the human resource planner is to sift through the tremendous amount of information to determine how the future availability of personnel for a particular organization is likely to be affected by changes in the overall environment. Of necessity, forecasting availability of employees is a continuous function of human resource planning. Rapid employment of new employees is difficult. Consequently, a firm must be capable of determining not only the number of employees required but also where and when they can be obtained. Specific external sources of supply are discussed in detail in the following chapter.

Requirements and Availability Comparison

Although a rather simple step in the planning process, the requirements-availability comparison is nevertheless quite important because it reveals the staffing situation that will confront the enterprise in the future. Knowledge of the impending situation then sets the stage for taking appropriate action to ensure that the organization will have the right number and kind of individuals in the right jobs and at the right time.

The comparison may reveal that: (1) the demand for employees will be equal to the supply, (2) the demand for personnel will be less than the supply, or (3) the demand for human resources will be greater than the anticipated supply. Since the basic purpose of human resource planning is to equate labor demand to labor supply, each of these three situations calls for developing different courses of action. Specific actions that may be taken are described in the following section.

EQUATING HUMAN RESOURCE DEMAND TO SUPPLY

The first two phases of human resource planning are analytical and conceptual in nature. The third phase is action-oriented; it is during this phase that steps are formulated and implemented to obtain a balance between the number and kind of employees needed and the number and kind available.

Demand Equals Supply

Should labor demand equal labor supply—a situation that could occur in very small firms operating in a stable environment, but is not likely to happen in large organizations facing dynamic conditions—no action needs to be taken. The company can simply continue doing what it is doing; nothing else is required, at least in the short run. No intensification of recruiting is needed; no layoffs are necessary; no additional training programs have to be implemented; no early retirements have to be encouraged. Maintenance of the status quo is sufficient.

Demand Is Less than Supply

As an increasing number of large organizations downsize, rightsize, restructure, reengineer, and outsource to cut costs, increase efficiency, improve productivity, and remain competitive,[12] the potential demand for employees to be less than the available supply is a distinct possibility. In such a situation, a firm must focus on maintaining sufficient people in the organization to produce its goods or services, while simultaneously reducing the total number of employees. Several methods are available for equating demand and supply when faced with this condition.

Restricted Hiring. A simple way of reducing the number of employees, provided the surplus is not too great, is to let normal attrition take its course and not replace employees who leave the company. Knowledge of the attrition rate would indicate how long it should take to achieve the desired reduction in the work force by this method. Exceptions will, of course, have to be made to a no-hiring policy. The criticality of the position is the deciding factor in determining which departing employees will be replaced. For example, the loss of one general production worker would likely pose no problem because the overall decrease will more than likely be picked up by other workers. However, the departure of a tool and die maker might cause disruptions in the production process since the position is very specialized, requires greater skill, and is vital to the production flow. Workers essential to maintaining company operations would be replaced under a hiring freeze, others would not. Where the surplus of personnel is large, other measures will have to be taken in addition to restricted hiring to reduce the firm's employment level.

Reduced Hours. By reducing the number of hours worked, reductions in hourly workers can be effectively accomplished without permanently cutting the work force. Instead of continuing a standard workweek of 40 hours, a workweek of 35 hours may be instituted. A cut in working hours of this magnitude is equivalent to a 12.5 percent decrease in the total number of salaried employees.

Job Sharing. A more contemporary approach to achieving work force reductions is job sharing, wherein two employees work half-time to staff a single position. An obvious drawback to this approach is the drastic reduction in income each worker experiences. Consequently, this approach is best used only in short-term situations.

Early Retirement. Reductions in the number of employees can also be accomplished through the use of incentives that encourage employees to retire at an earlier than normal age. An additional advantage to this approach is that employees who are eligible to retire early are generally higher-paid employees. Consequently, the organization not only reduces the number of workers, but also reduces its higher-level personnel expenses.

Layoffs. When faced with an acute surplus of personnel, an organization may have no choice other than a layoff. Layoffs may be used in an across-the-board fashion, commonly referred to as a reduction in force, in which case a stipulated percentage of employees in each department is laid off. Layoffs may also be used to reduce only the number of workers in specific departments where excess personnel can be readily identified. In nonunionized firms, layoffs can be used at the discretion of the employer; in unionized companies, strict procedures, as spelled out in the labor agreement, must be followed.

Personnel reductions are extremely sensitive matters that may affect an organization's future staffing efforts. They should always be approached carefully and deliberately so as to minimize the potential impact of unsought consequences.

Demand Is Greater than Supply

Faced with a shortage of personnel, an organization must intensify its efforts to obtain the necessary supply of people to meet the needs of the firm. Several actions may be implemented.

Creative Recruiting. A shortage of personnel may mean that new approaches to recruiting will have to be tried. The organization may have to recruit in different geographical areas than in the past, explore new methods, and seek different kinds of candidates. Creative recruiting may take many forms. For example, a large builder of single-family homes in the Southwest, faced with a serious shortage of construction workers, experimented with several approaches. This company broadened its recruiting area for skilled workers from its normal local area to locales across the country where there were surpluses of workers. The company advertised its hiring needs on radio stations and billboards. These efforts, unusual for a local construction company, secured employees who otherwise might not have applied for jobs with the organization.[13]

Compensation Incentives. With other firms competing for skilled workers in a short-supply, high-demand situation, a company may have to rely on compensation incentives. Premium pay is one obvious method, but this approach may trigger a bidding war that the organization cannot sustain for an extended period. More subtle forms of compensatory rewards may be required to attract employees to a firm, such as four-day workweeks, flexible working hours, telecommuting, part-time employment, and child care centers. The number of incentives that could be offered is limited only by the imagination of human resource specialists.

Training Programs. Acute shortages of personnel may necessitate the implementation of special training programs to prepare previously unemployable individuals for positions with a firm. Remedial education and skills training are two types of programs that may help attract individuals to a particular company. The construction company mentioned above, in addition to its creative recruiting efforts, also implemented its own in-house ten-week training program to satisfy the need for bricklayers to build its tract homes. This unique effort, reported in the media and spread by word of mouth, resulted in additional applicants seeking employment with the company in order to take advantage of its skills-training program.[14]

Different Selection Standards. Another approach to dealing with shortages of required human resources is lowering of employment standards. Selection criteria that screen out certain workers may have to be altered to ensure that enough people are available to fill jobs. This means of coping with a personnel shortage may be coupled with training programs to ensure that employees are qualified to perform the jobs for which they are hired.

SUMMARY

Human resource planning is a complex endeavor, but an essential one for organizations in today's uncertain environment. Admittedly, this chapter has only scratched the surface of what is involved with anticipating personnel requirements and ensuring that those requirements are met. The pivotal point is that requirements must be anticipated and actions taken to ensure that an organization will have the requisite human resources on hand when they are needed. All other staffing activities depend upon the accuracy of the information concerning personnel requirements.

NOTES

1. Donald W. Jarrell, *Human Resource Planning* (Englewood Cliffs, NJ: Prentice-Hall, 1993), 109.

2. Charles R. Greer, *Strategic Human Resource Management: A General Managerial Approach,* 2nd ed. (Upper Saddle River, NJ: Prentice-Hall, 2001), 121–123.

3. Herbert G. Heneman III and Timothy A. Judge, *Staffing Organizations,* 5th ed. (Middleton, WI: Mendota House, 2006), 93.

4. Guvenc G. Alpander, *Human Resources Management Planning* (New York: AMACOM, 1982), 2.

5. Lloyd L. Byars and Leslie W. Rue, *Human Resource Management,* 9th ed. (New York: McGraw-Hill Irwin, 2008), 87.

6. Greer, *Strategic Human Resource Management,* 121–123.

7. Byars and Rue, *Human Resource Management,* 92.

8. R. Wayne Mondy and Robert M. Noe III, *Human Resource Management,* 5th ed. (Boston: Allyn and Bacon, 1993), 150.

9. Byars and Rue, *Human Resource Management,* 94.

10. Ibid.

11. James W. Walker, *Human Resource Planning* (New York: McGraw-Hill Book Company, 1980), 5.

12. Raymond A. Noe, John R. Hollenbeck, Barry Gerhart, and Patrick M. Wright, *Human Resource Management: Gaining a Competitive Advantage,* 6th ed. (New York: McGraw-Hill Irwin, 2008), 87–90, 706–710.

13. Based on one of the author's experiences as a manager with this organization.

14. Ibid.

7

The Recruiting Process

Recruiting involves locating individuals, with appropriate qualifications and in sufficient numbers, and encouraging them to apply for jobs with a particular organization. The basic purpose of recruiting is to ensure a sufficient pool of applicants from which the most qualified individuals may be selected. Recruiting is an essential activity for any firm regardless of its size. In most medium and large organizations, the human resource department is responsible for all recruiting activities. In small companies, individual managers often conduct their own recruiting efforts. Whether conducted by operating managers or staffing specialists, effective recruiting is crucial because sufficient qualified applicants are needed to ensure that selection can be accomplished successfully.

A GENERALIZED RECRUITING MODEL

Figure 7.1 depicts a basic model of the recruiting process. The need to recruit is triggered by either the human resource planning function or the human resource administration function. The former provides information on the number and kinds of new positions to be filled, while the latter identifies existing positions that must be filled due to terminations, promotions, retirements, and the like. New or open positions may be filled from within the organization, from outside the firm, or by using alternative methods such as overtime, contracting, or temporary employees secured from external agencies. If positions cannot be filled from within or if the use of alternative methods is not feasible, the organization must look to the labor market for the people it needs. Sources of employees must be identified, methods to reach these sources must be selected, and qualified

Figure 7.1
A Model of the Recruiting Process

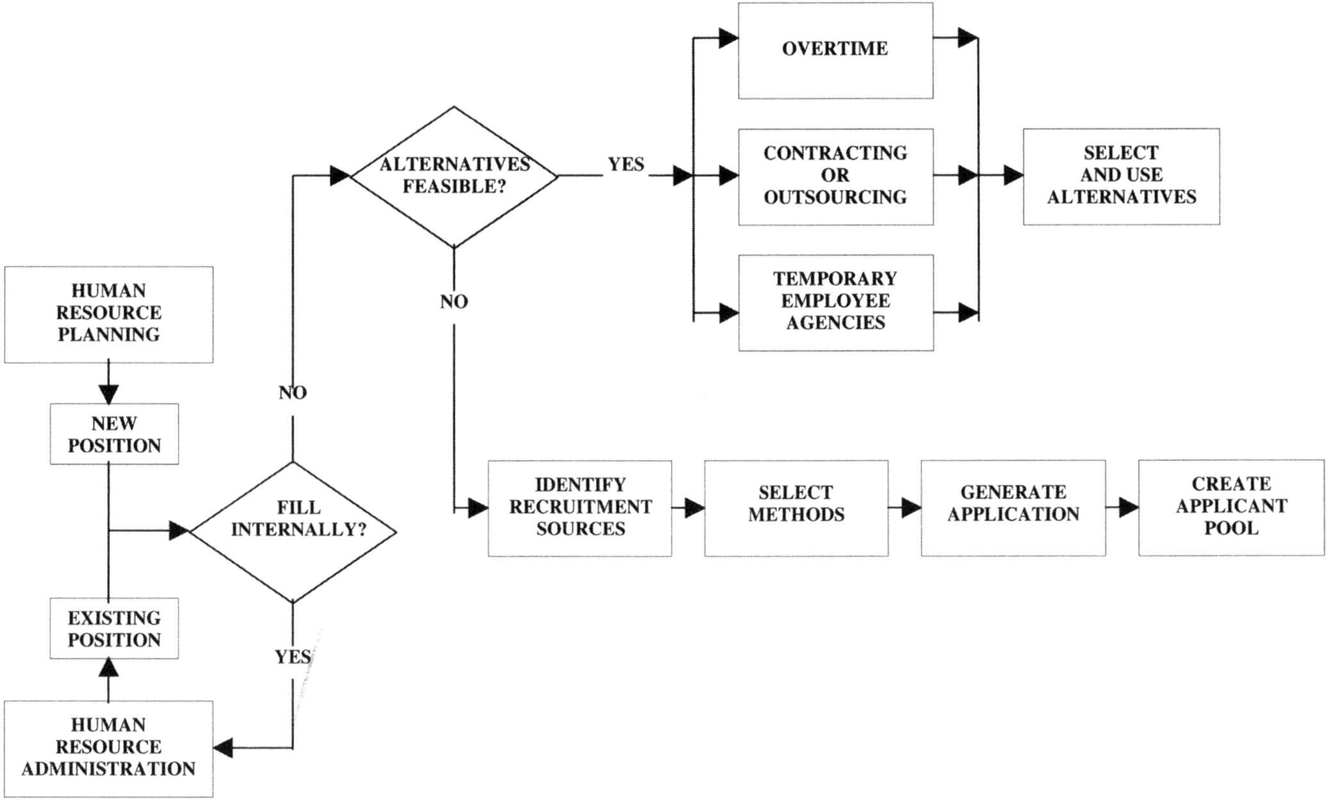

individuals must be encouraged to apply for job openings in order to create a sufficient pool of applicants.

Typically, the first step in filling a position is for a department manager to initiate an employee requisition. This document specifies various details such as job title, department, date employee is needed, and justification for filling the position. A copy of the job description and job specifications is often attached to the requisition, particularly if the position is a new one. This information then sets in motion the series of actions leading to filling the job.

ALTERNATIVES TO RECRUITING

When there is a need for additional or replacement employees, a firm may choose to explore alternatives to recruiting. Recruitment costs can be high. Moreover, once employees are placed on the payroll, they may be difficult to remove even if their performance is marginal. Consequently, an organization is well advised to consider alternatives to adding full-time staff members. Three viable options are increasing the use of overtime, contracting work to other organizations (frequently today, the use of outside contractors, subcontractors, and consultants is referred to as outsourcing), and utilizing temporary employees provided by firms specializing in this service.

Overtime

The most common approach to meeting requirements for additional personnel, especially when the need is generated by short-term increases in work volume, is overtime. Both employer and employee may benefit from overtime: the employer avoids the cost of recruiting, selecting, and training while the employee gains an increase in compensation.

Overtime, however, is not without its disadvantages. Many managers feel, and justifiably so, that when employees are required to work extra hours over an extended length of time, the organization pays more and receives less production per hour in return. This situation may become worse if excessive overtime is required; employees may become fatigued and lack the energy to perform at normal levels.

Two other potential problems are related to prolonged overtime. First, employees may, consciously or unconsciously, pace themselves during normal hours so that overtime is ensured. Second, employees tend to become accustomed to the added income resulting from overtime pay and may even elevate their standard of living to the level permitted by this additional income. When overtime is no longer required and the paycheck shrinks to its normal level, employees may become disgruntled at what they perceive as a cut in pay.

An interesting problem with overtime in contemporary organizations is that many employees, particularly younger ones, do not want to work more than the required 40 hours a week. Because of changes in values, leisure time is more important to a growing number of workers than is the prospect of earning additional income by working longer hours.

Despite its potential drawbacks and problems, the use of overtime does offer an alternative to increasing an organization's full-time staff and should be evaluated carefully when the need for additional employees arises.

Contracting

When faced with an increased demand for its goods and services, an organization may decide against expanding its work force and opt to contract work to another company. This alternative becomes particularly attractive when the increased demand is expected to be short run in nature. Even in the long run, though, contracting can be beneficial as a means of avoiding increases in a company's employment level.

Two essential considerations in the use of contracting are the costs involved and the maintenance of quality standards in the firm's goods or services. To be a feasible alternative, contracting should be cost effective; that is, the contractor should be able to perform the necessary work at a lower cost than if the employing organization increased the size of its work force to handle increased production demands. The contractor must also be capable of maintaining quality levels specified by the using organization. It would be self-defeating to attempt to save staffing costs if the result was a product or service of an inferior nature.

Increasingly today, American companies are contracting out all or most of their manufacturing operations because they can be performed at lower costs in other countries. Nike, Inc., one of the most widely recognized athletic apparel and footwear companies in the United States, does not manufacture a single item of apparel or a single pair of shoes—all manufacturing for Nike is done by other companies!

Several American companies are also outsourcing the services that they provide. As with manufacturing, lower costs is the reason for contracting out service jobs to other countries. The majority of the customer service call centers for Dell Computers, a Texas-based company, are located in India.

Many organizations use contracting not only for major products or services (including the entire human resource management function) but also for ancillary activities such as in-house cafeteria operations, security work, and custodial services—functions that are frequently performed more efficiently and inexpensively by outside firms. Increasingly, too, professional services such as the human resource management function are being contracted out or "outsourced."

The use of consultants on a project basis is another form of contracting that enables a firm to keep from expanding its core work force. Consultants can be retained to provide a specialized service such as development of a salary administration plan or installation of a computer system. They bring needed expertise to an organization, focus on a specific assignment, and leave when the assignment is completed.

Temporary Employees

Another alternative to work force expansion, especially in the short run, is the use of temporary help. It is estimated that as many as nine out of ten companies in this country have used temporary help firms as sources of employees.[1] Temporary help companies usually assist their client organizations by assigning their own employees (technically, the employee works for the temporary help firm but does not get paid unless he or she is given an assignment with a client) to handle excess or special workloads of the client. The temporary help firm fulfills all obligations associated with being an employer. The user organization avoids the expense of recruitment and the cost of employee benefits as well as absenteeism and turnover.

Not all aspects of using temporary help are positive. Oftentimes, the permanent and temporary employees do not get along well. Permanent workers may feel as if the temporary staff does not possess the knowledge and experience required to perform the job effectively, are assigned easier tasks because of their lack of knowledge and experience, and lack the commitment that a permanent employee exhibits.[2] It is possible that temporary employees may lack required specialized training. Providing this training may take more time than can be justified and also cause feelings of resentment among regular employees who have to conduct the training. There may also be feelings of resentment among all of the permanent staff if they perceive that their jobs could be threatened by temporary workers. Moreover, since temporaries are not on the client's payroll, their loyalty or commitment to the organization may not be as strong as that of regular employees.[3]

One very positive benefit, however, of using temporaries is that it gives the company an opportunity to preview and evaluate the performance of individuals. In a study exploring the reasons why employers utilize flexible staffing arrangements, 21 percent of the organizations reported that they use temporary agencies as a way to screen potential employees for permanent positions.[4] Many companies end up hiring temporaries as regular employees. Temporary employees also see the benefits of this type of staffing arrangement. According to the 2008 statistics provided by the American Staffing Association, 88 percent of staffing employees reported that temporary assignments made them more employable and 77 percent reported that such assignments were a good way to eventually obtain a permanent position.[5]

A variation of the temporary help firm is the "job shopper"—an independent worker who takes assignments with organizations on a contractual basis. The job shopper is usually a skilled professional such as an engineer, draftsperson, systems analyst, or computer specialist who is willing to work on a nonpermanent basis because of the high rate of pay involved. Job shoppers are very prevalent in aerospace, defense, and high technology industries, where companies often face the need for additional highly skilled employees on a short-run basis to meet project deadlines or demands.

Professionals in the field estimate that contingent workers represent approximately 20 percent of the average organization's total work force.[6] These percentages are expected to grow in the years to come, indicating that the use of contingent workers is an increasingly popular alternative for satisfying staffing needs.

SELECTING AND USING ALTERNATIVES

Overtime, contracting or outsourcing, and using temporary employees are all viable options for satisfying increased work needs. Each organization must fully analyze its particular situation to determine which of these alternatives is the most appropriate and cost effective to implement. It is possible that none of these alternatives will be feasible to use. If an organization is unable to utilize any of these alternatives, it will have to fill the work need in a more permanent way. When an organization needs to fill a position permanently, it can search for potential candidates either internally or externally.

INTERNAL ENVIRONMENTAL RECRUITMENT FACTORS

An organization's own internal practices and policies affect the recruiting process. A major factor that can influence the success of a recruiting program is whether the firm engages in human resource planning. In most instances, an organization cannot attract prospective employees with the required skills in sufficient numbers overnight. It takes time to examine the options concerning the appropriate sources of applicants and the most productive methods for encouraging individuals to apply for open positions. Once the best alternatives have been identified, recruiting plans may be made. Thus, effective human resource planning that indicates in advance when employees will be needed and what kinds of skills they must possess greatly facilitates recruiting efforts.

An organization's promotion policy can also have a significant impact on its recruiting program. Basically, there are two approaches an organization may follow. It can stress a policy of promotion from within or it can adhere to a policy of filling the majority of positions with individuals from outside the company. There is a logical rationale for each approach.

When an organization emphasizes promotion from within, its employees have increased incentive to strive for advancement. As they witness promotions occurring within the company, employees become increasingly aware of their own opportunities. Consequently, a promotion from within policy enhances motivation and leads to a relatively high level of morale. However, a strictly applied promotion from within policy is not always possible or practicable because a firm may need fresh ideas or new skills that can only be obtained from outsiders. In any event, a promotion policy that first considers insiders before looking at outsiders boosts morale and motivation and should be standard practice for all organizations.

A distinct advantage of filling positions internally is that the institution is already aware of its employees' capabilities. While a person's past performance in a given job may not, by itself, be a reliable criterion for promotion, nevertheless, many personal and job-related qualities are known since the person has established a track record with the company. An outsider is always an "unknown quantity" to some extent.

Yet it is unlikely that any firm can or would desire to adhere rigidly to a practice of promotion from within because such a practice eventually leads to inbreeding, a lack of new ideas, and a lack of creativity. Management may believe that new blood is badly needed to provide new ideas and innovation. In such cases, even organizations that emphasize internal promotion periodically have to look outside for new talent.

Another problem of promotion from within is that it may trigger a series of promotions, thus necessitating additional efforts to fill other positions vacated by promoted individuals. If so, the organization is faced with the need of identifying not just one, but two or more candidates for vacant positions. There is also the matter of training. Every time a person is promoted, he or she has to be trained in the new job. Promotion from within may create the need for training several individuals in their new job duties.

METHODS USED IN INTERNAL RECRUITING

Management must be able to identify current employees who are capable of filling higher-level positions as these positions become available. Helpful tools used for internal recruitment include management and skills inventories and job posting and bidding procedures. As mentioned in Chapter 6, management and skills inventories permit organizations to determine whether needed qualifications are possessed by current employees. As an internal recruitment device, these inventories have proven to be extremely valuable to organizations in locating talent, provided, of course, that inventories are maintained on an up-to-date basis. Also, their use strongly supports the concept of promotion from within.

Dependent upon the upkeep of management and skills inventories is the method of forecasting. Organizations should be continuously collecting data regarding the current supply of labor that they have within the organization. They should also be analyzing labor and market trends, economic conditions, and other variables in order to more accurately forecast the future supply and demand of labor within the organization. A succession plan is a basic internal supply forecast that helps organizations be prepared to readily fill job openings with the most qualified internal candidate.[7] Trying to anticipate and prepare for future labor demands is vital to the effective and efficient recruitment and placement of quality candidates in new job positions.

Another excellent internal recruiting approach is a job posting and bidding system. The purpose of job posting is to communicate to employees the fact that job openings exist. Job bidding permits individuals in the organization to apply for any job for which they believe they have the qualifications. Some firms provide their employees with a weekly list of jobs available within the organization. Typically today, this is done through computers or automated telephone "job lines." All open positions should also appear on an organization's company Web site, providing they have one. Other firms post lists of job openings on bulletin boards. Job posting and bidding minimizes the complaint commonly heard in many companies that insiders never hear of an opening until it has been filled with an outsider. Numerous organizations have a policy that requires a job to be posted for a specified length of time, usually two weeks, before any effort is made to fill the vacancy from outside.

When properly administered, a job posting and bidding system reflects a management philosophy of openness and genuine interest in advancement of its employees. Additionally, this system can often assist in outside recruitment efforts because it demonstrates a firm's interest in career advancement and individual growth of its employees. Job posting and bidding also increases upward mobility opportunities for an institution's protected classes.

EXTERNAL SOURCES OF JOB APPLICANTS

Inevitably, an organization must look to outside sources for additional employees. This is especially true when a company is expanding its work force on a permanent basis. The following circumstances generally necessitate external recruiting: (1) creation of new entry level jobs, (2) vacancies in entry level jobs created by internal promotions, (3) need to acquire skills not possessed by current employees, (4) desire for new ideas, (5) opening of additional facilities, (6) expansion into new product or service lines, and (7) expansion into new geographic areas.

Some of the most common sources of new employees are high schools, community colleges and vocational schools, colleges and universities, competitors and other organizations, and unsolicited applicants.

High Schools

High schools are one of the major sources of applicants for entry level or unskilled positions. Many schools sponsor career days where local area employers visit the school and explain career opportunities in their organizations. Cooperative education programs, where a student goes to school part of the day and works the remainder of the day, also afford employers the opportunity to tap this source of employees. Some companies find it advantageous to familiarize high school counselors with job opportunities so that counselors can refer students to the prospective employer.

Community Colleges and Vocational Schools

Typically, community colleges serve two functions: preparing students for completion of a four-year degree program, or preparing students for a specific occupation such as auto mechanic, draftsperson, secretary, or computer programmer. A number of these colleges have done an outstanding job of defining the employment needs in their areas and have designed programs that produce students to fill these needs. Often, these colleges work in conjunction with local employers so that the courses students take fit the needs of specific occupations. Employers frequently offer internship programs to enable students to gain practical work experience. For many entry level jobs, community colleges are an excellent source of potential employees.

Vocational schools train individuals for specific occupations. Because they normally offer placement assistance to their students, vocational schools maintain working relationships with employers in their local areas, thus functioning as a good source of trained applicants for entry level positions—especially technical ones.

Colleges and Universities

Colleges and universities represent a major source of recruitment for many organizations. A substantial number of entry level professional, technical, and managerial employees are found in these institutions. College recruiters who visit campuses on an annual or semiannual basis are commonly used as the vehicle for reaching this source of potential employees. Because schools differ widely in terms of their curricula and specifications, the key to using this recruiting source effectively is to determine which colleges or universities provide the proper training or educational experiences to fulfill the organization's employment needs.

Placement directors, faculty, and administrators are potentially helpful to organizations attempting to take advantage of this source of applicants. For instance, the large retailer, Bloomingdale's, has improved its credibility on college campuses by making personal contacts with business professors, providing grants for studies, and offering internships. The company has also used alumni to establish relationships with college placement offices and to recruit students.[8]

Since college recruitment is mutually beneficial, both employers and universities should take steps to develop and maintain close working relationships. Once a company has established a college recruiting program, it is important that contacts and visits be continued year after year to ensure an effective relationship.

Competitors and Other Organizations

Competitors and other organizations in the industry or in the area are the most important sources of applicants for positions requiring experience. It is estimated that at any given time about 5 percent of the working population is actively seeking or is receptive to a change in employment. Furthermore, one out of every three people—especially managers and professionals—change jobs every five years.[9] These facts underscore the importance of other employers as a potential source of applicants.

Even where promotion from within is the rule, organizations are sometimes forced to "raid" other organizations to fill important positions or acquire expertise that is not available internally. This practice is not a rare occurrence nor is it an unethical one, per se. Small firms in particular look for employees who have been trained by larger organizations that have the resources needed to support extensive training and development programs.[10]

It is common for organizations to recruit professionals and managers from the public accounting and management consulting firms that provide services to these organizations. As one executive with an international accounting firm once confided to one of the authors, "We run the world's largest employment agency. We didn't plan it that way. It just happened." Accountants or consultants familiar with an organization are, potentially, a good source of employees.

Unsolicited Applicants

If an organization is well known, has high visibility, or has a reputation as a good place to work, it will usually be able to attract prospective employees without engaging in extensive recruiting efforts. High quality individuals may seek out a specific company on their own initiative to apply for a job. Unsolicited applicants often prove to be a valuable source of potential employees for positions ranging from entry level to top level managers. However, it is not advisable for an organization to rely on this source exclusively. Unsolicited applicants are likely to be an intermittent source—they may not appear when employees are needed or they may appear in great numbers when an organization has no job openings.

The Working Retired

Another way in which some organizations are filling vacant positions is by recruiting retired employees. Individuals who have retired from an organization are an excellent source of labor because they are already familiar with the organization and already know how to do the job. This saves the company time and money that would be associated with training somebody completely new. Several organizations hire these former employees in a part-time or consultant capacity, in which case they can avoid paying the high cost of benefits. Organizations may also hire retired individuals who have not worked in these particular organizations in the past. Retired individuals, regardless of where they were previously employed, still bring a wealth of experience and a proven work ethic to the table.

RECRUITING METHODS

An analysis of recruitment sources enables organizations to determine where potential job applicants are likely to be found. Recruiting methods are then used to encourage potential candidates to seek employment with the company.

Recruiting methods such as advertising, employment agencies, and employee referrals may be effective in attracting virtually any type of candidate. College recruiters, job fairs, and internships are designed basically to attract entry level professionals, although job fairs may be used for high level technicians and professionals, too. Executive search firms and professional associations are helpful in the recruiting of managerial and professional employees.

Advertising

One of the most widely used recruiting methods is advertising, primarily in newspapers and on the Internet. The answers to several questions provide the basis for successful employment advertising planning. These questions include:

- Who does the organization want to hire?
- How many applicants must be attracted to ensure a sufficient applicant pool?
- When will the new employee(s) be needed?
- What message should the advertising convey?
- What specific journals or publications should be used?
- What has been the organization's previous experience with advertising?
- What is the anticipated cost effectiveness of advertising?

Job descriptions and specifications answer the first question. The organization's past experience, based on the typical ratio of hires to qualified applicants generated, assists in determining the number of responses needed to achieve an adequate applicant pool. While advertising produces a number of applicants, not all of them will be qualified; thus, previous experience relative to the number of qualified applicants is more important than simply the total number of responses produced.

When employees will be needed is contingent upon human resource planning or the existence of vacancies within the organization. Recruitment through advertising should be planned well in advance of anticipated openings, where possible, to avoid the crisis situation of needing employees "yesterday." Selections made under the pressure of time often result in poor employment decisions.

In determining the content of the advertising message, an organization has to decide upon the image it wants to project. Obviously, prospective applicants should be given a clear and honest picture of the job and the organization—something that may be difficult to achieve in a short piece of advertising copy. At the same time, an attempt should be made to determine what advertising appeals to the self-interest of potential applicants. The advertisement must communicate to the prospect why he or she should be interested in the job and the organization. The message should also clearly indicate how the applicant is to respond; that is, in person, by submitting a resume, by telephone, by letter, by fax, or by online methods.

The advertising medium to be used is purely an organizational decision. The firm's previous experience with various media suggests what publications or approaches should be taken for specific kinds of jobs.

As far as cost effectiveness is concerned, the most inexpensive form of advertising that typically generates the greatest number of responses is newspaper advertising. The biggest problem with this approach, however, is the number of responses from individuals who are not qualified for the position—although each response will have to be evaluated, an organization will not have to respond to each individual if it uses a blind box number in its advertisement. But if a blind box number is used, the organization does not have the advantage that accrues from using its name in the advertisement.

An effective employment advertisement should avoid generalities and provide concise information about the job, the organization, and possibilities for career mobility. It is not enough to simply say that the company has a particular position open; thus, advertisements must be written with considerable thought if they are to be effective in producing sufficient responses from qualified applicants.

Advertisements placed in publications such as *The Wall Street Journal* are reserved for managerial, professional, and high-level technical positions. The reading audience of this periodical is largely composed of individuals who are likely to be qualified for these kinds of positions. Consequently, there is less likelihood of receiving responses from marginally or even totally unqualified applicants when this publication is used for the aforementioned types of job openings.

Virtually every professional group publishes a journal or newsletter that is widely read by its members. When advertising for human resource executives, for example, *HR Magazine* or *Resource,* both publications of the Society for Human Resource Management, are excellent media for reaching the desired target audience.

Trade journals are widely used for employment advertising, but this medium is not without problems. For example, since regional editions usually are not available, these journals may not be very useful to employers desiring to avoid relocation expenses. Also, journals lack scheduling flexibility: deadlines for black and white copy are usually 30 days prior to the issue date and may be even further in advance for four-color copy. Since staffing needs cannot always be anticipated far in advance nor can long delays be tolerated in filling positions, the use of trade journals for recruiting may be inappropriate at times.

Recruiting advertisers assume that qualified employment prospects read newspapers and trade journals and that they are dissatisfied to the extent that they peruse employment ads. This is not always the case, particularly for those individuals who are not currently considering a job change. Therefore, in high demand situations, a firm should consider all available media, not just newspapers and journals.

Other advertising media that can be used for recruiting purposes include radio, billboards, handbills, television, and increasingly, the Internet. While some of these approaches may be more expensive than newspapers or journals, they have been used quite successfully in specific situations.[11] A regional medical center, for instance, was able to attract registered nurses by using billboards. A large manufacturing firm was successful in attracting production trainees with radio spot advertisements. An electronics firm used television advertising to attract experienced engineers when the company opened a new facility and needed a number of engineers immediately. In situations where hiring needs are urgent, radio and television can provide much faster results than print media. However, radio broadcasting used alone may not be sufficient. It can alert people to the fact that an organization is seeking recruits, but it is limited in its ability to provide data such as company address, telephone number, and contact person inasmuch as many people are not prepared to write down these items when they are listening to the radio. For this reason, broadcasting and print are often used in conjunction with each other.

The fastest growing advertising medium for recruitment purposes is the Internet. Several organizations are using the Internet as part of their strategic recruitment process.[12] As reported in 2001, 90 percent of major U.S. companies were using the Internet as a recruitment tool.[13] It is likely that the percentage has risen even higher since then. These companies maintain Web sites that contain detailed information regarding the company itself, the positions that are open, and the recruitment process. The amount of information that can be conveyed via this medium far exceeds the amount that can be communicated with the more traditional recruitment advertising. Both the company and the potential applicant can benefit from this high level of information sharing. Another advantage for job seekers is the fact that several thousand job search sites exist today, some of the most popular being Monster.com and CareerBuilder.com. Web-based methods also reduce recruitment costs for the employer[14] and application costs for the prospective employee.[15] The Internet has definitely expanded and improved recruitment options for both the recruiter and the job seeker.

While most organizations use advertising in their recruiting efforts, evidence suggests that it may be somewhat ineffective. Sources indicate that regional newspapers continue to be one of the most effective recruiting methods, but word-of-mouth and internal recruitment methods are just as, if not more, successful.[16] While newspaper ads continue to be popular and are considered effective, research indicates that applicants recruited via job ads have higher turnover rates than applicants recruited via referrals.[17] The research concerning the effectiveness of some of the other types of advertising media is minimal or nonexistent. It is important that organizations conduct their own research to determine which advertising methods work best for them.

Private Employment Agencies

A private employment agency is a company that assists firms in recruiting employees and, at the same time, aids individuals in their attempts to locate jobs.

Agencies perform many recruiting and selecting activities for employers such as advertising job openings, reviewing resumes, obtaining application blank data, conducting screening interviews, and testing.

Private agencies are used by companies for filling virtually every type of job opening, although they are best known for their role in recruiting white collar personnel. Although the private employment agency industry has an unfavorable reputation in some respects, there are a number of highly reputable agencies that have been in operation for decades. One difficulty that poses problems for agencies is that there are few industry standards. The quality of a particular agency is dependent upon the professionalism of its management and employment counselors.

Regardless of problems, private agencies are a method for bringing qualified applicants and job openings together. Because of the recruiting and selecting functions it performs, an agency can save an employer a great deal of time in finding potential employees.

Agencies work on a fee basis, charging either the company or the individual a certain percentage of annual gross salary of the position being filled. In the past, this fee was normally paid by the employee, but increasingly today employers pay the fee.

In using private agencies, organizations may list job openings with several agencies or use one agency exclusively. Using several agencies tends to broaden the scope of recruiting efforts. Working with a single agency allows a company the opportunity to develop a relationship that may lead to better referrals from the agency since the agency comes to know more about the company and the kinds of employees it needs.

Public Employment Agencies

While public employment agencies are operated by each state under guidelines set by that state, they receive overall policy direction from the U.S. Employment Service. Historically, public employment agencies have been best known for their efforts in recruiting and placing individuals in blue collar jobs. Recently they have become increasingly involved with filling technical, professional, and managerial positions. Thus, public agencies now represent a good source of applicants for all types of positions—a source that should not be overlooked by employers in their recruiting efforts.

Public agencies perform many of the same recruiting and selecting activities for employers as are performed by private agencies. In some instances computerized job matching systems are used to facilitate the recruiting process. The services provided by public agencies are supported by payroll taxes levied on employers. The employer pays no additional charge for listing job openings and securing employees through this source. The services are provided free of charge to job seekers.

Company Recruiters

The most common use of company recruiters is with vocational schools, community colleges, and colleges and universities. The key contact for the recruiter is usually the director of student placement at the school. The placement director assists the recruiter by identifying qualified candidates, scheduling interviews, providing interviewing facilities, and, in some cases, maintaining student files that include resumes, references, and other types of information.

The company recruiter obviously plays a vital role in attracting applicants for an organization. The recruiter's actions may be viewed by students as reflecting the attitudes, philosophy, and character of the company the recruiter represents. If the recruiter is dull, the company represented may be considered dull; if he or she is apathetic, discourteous, or vulgar, all of these negative characteristics may well be attributed to the firm doing the recruiting. It is imperative that both company and recruiter be cognizant of the potential impact that may be made when recruiting on school campuses.

Recruiters determine which individuals possess the required qualifications and encourage them to continue exploring job opportunities with the organization. In achieving this purpose, the recruiter becomes involved in a two-way communication process by providing information about the company, its products or services, its general organizational structure, its policies, the duties and responsibilities of the job to be filled, compensation and benefits, and so forth.

Considering the importance of the occasion, the campus interview is often extremely short, averaging about 30 minutes. Thus, it is important that:

- The interview begin on time.
- The recruiter be well prepared.
- The interview take place in an area free from distractions.

It is important that recruiters be thoroughly trained to seek useful information from applicants and keep the interview focused on obtaining this information. Aptitude, motivation, judgment, analytical ability, and interpersonal skills are the kinds of information the recruiter should gather.[18]

Special Events

The two most commonly used special events in recruiting are job fairs and open houses. Job fairs are normally sponsored by a group of organizations that pool their efforts to bring together a large number of applicants at the same time and place in a convention-like atmosphere. The advantage to the job seeker is obvious: he or she can visit with a variety of institutions in a limited amount of time. The advantage to employers is that a greater number of applicants are generated than could be generated by any one employer alone. Newspaper ads, radio spots, and billboards are the normal vehicles for announcing a job fair. While traditional job fairs take place in some type of convention center or exhibition hall, advancements in technology have made virtual job fairs a reality. Job seekers are able to participate in job fairs from remote locations via the Internet.[19] However, the effectiveness of this virtual method has yet to be evaluated against the effectiveness of the old-fashioned job fair.

An open house is a special event conducted by a single company. Typically, an open house is held on a Saturday to ensure maximum turnout of applicants. Company representatives from different departments are available to explain various job opportunities. Newspaper ads and radio spots are also used to alert applicants to an open house.

Special events are best suited for use as recruiting methods when a company needs to employ substantial numbers of people in relatively short periods of time.

Internships

Internships are recruiting methods that have value not only to the firm involved, but also to students and schools. Internships may involve temporary jobs during the summer, part-time jobs during the school year, or alternating periods of employment and school attendance, in which case the internship is called a co-op arrangement. Often, interns are paid for the time they work; in some instances, they are not. During the period of working with a company, students are given the opportunity to learn something about a particular business as well as make a contribution to the company by performing needed tasks. Through this relationship, the student can determine whether the organization would likely be a suitable employer after graduation. Likewise, the organization can make a better judgment about the qualifications of the individual because it has the opportunity to evaluate the person in the work situation.[20] This method of recruiting is limited in scope since any one organization can utilize only a limited number of interns at one time. Moreover, it is not feasible for many types of jobs. It can, though, be highly effective where it is practicable.

Executive Search Firms

Executive search firms are used by organizations to locate experienced professionals and top level executives. These firms "are retained to search for the most qualified executive available for specific positions, only on assignment from the company seeking a specific type of individual."[21]

While executive search firms appear to function like employment agencies, there are differences other than the fact that they recruit exclusively for high-level and high-paying positions. A main difference between the two is that executive search firms do not work for individuals; they are retained and compensated by the client organizations they serve. Executive search firms also provide a higher level of confidentiality for hiring companies and job seekers. The quality of an executive search firm is partially judged on how ethically they handle the sensitive information they have gathered via their close working relationships with their clients.[22]

Over the past quarter of a century, the executive search industry has evolved from a basic recruitment service to a highly sophisticated profession filling a greatly expanded role. Search firms are now serving as sounding boards to assist organizations in determining their human resource needs, establish compensation ranges, and provide advice concerning organizational structures.[23]

Firms in this business often visit their clients' offices to interview company management. This enables them to gain a clear understanding of company goals, requirements of the position, and qualifications needed by a candidate. After this information is obtained, the search firm seeks out potential candidates, reviews their resumes, conducts interviews, and performs background checks. As a general rule, the best three or four candidates will be referred to the client organization for the actual selection decision.

The search firm's fee is usually a stipulated percentage of the individual's annual income. However, the manner in which the fee is earned may differ from firm to firm. Some firms operate on a contingency basis, receiving their fee only if the organization hires one of the referred candidates. Other firms agree to furnish three or four well-qualified candidates and the organization agrees to pay the search fee regardless of whether or not it actually hires one of the candidates. Some firms charge an hourly rate for the actual hours expended on the search. Expenses incurred in the search are customarily added to any agreed upon fees.

Perhaps the key problem in executive searches is poor communication between the client and the search firm. Reaching agreement on job specifications and qualifications is absolutely essential if the search firm is to do its job effectively.

Professional Associations

Associations in business professions such as finance, marketing, computer systems, and human resources frequently provide placement services on a national, regional, or local basis for their members. (For example, the Dallas Human Resource Management Association provides a "Resume Book Service" for its members wherein members seeking employment send copies of their resumes to a central source for consideration by member companies seeking human resource professionals.) Associations act as clearinghouses and maintain lists of positions that member companies are attempting to fill and lists of individual members seeking new jobs. The association's role is limited to one of simply providing information. Where an opening needs to be filled in a specific profession, companies may want to consider this low-cost method of recruiting.

Religious and Other Special Interest Groups

Another method for recruiting employees is to contact religious or other special interest groups. Job opportunities are sometimes advertised in the religious organization's bulletins, posted in areas where members gather, or announced during weekly services. Members may also pass along information about job openings to other members. The same is true of other special interest groups. Job openings may be advertised in printed materials distributed by the group, posted in meeting areas, announced at meetings, or passed along by word of mouth. As with professional associations, the opportunities for networking among group members help recruiters fill vacant positions and help individual group members find jobs.

Networking

Discussing job opportunities in professional, religious, and other special interest groups helps employers find employees and vice versa. This type of networking can also take place over the Internet. Job information can be shared in chat rooms, and Web sites such as LinkedIn provide a platform upon which professionals can share and learn about employment opportunities.

Employee Referrals

Many organizations have found that their employees can assist in the recruitment process by actively soliciting applications from their friends and associates. This recruitment method has been proven to be very effective. In fact, employee referrals have emerged as one of the best sources of long-tenure employees.[24] Some organizations reward referrals by paying the referring employee a bonus if the applicant is hired and stays on the job for a stipulated length of time.

One potential problem with referrals that an organization should be aware of is that referrals tend to perpetuate the current composition of the work force; that is, if the present work force is largely composed of white males, the majority of referred applicants will be white males because people tend to refer others who are similar to themselves.[25] As one company discovered to its dismay in a groundbreaking case, relying solely on referrals can result in a situation that has discriminatory impact even though there is no intent to discriminate.[26]

Rehires

Yet another option for dealing with the need to fill open positions is to rehire former employees. If an employee left on good terms and his or her skills and abilities can be utilized, the organization can try to get that employee back. As soon as business starts to increase again, organizations often attempt to rehire employees that they were forced to lay off due to an economic downturn. Organizations need to be cautious when rehiring former employees, especially those who were laid off, because these employees could be harboring some feelings of resentment.

MATCHING METHODS TO SOURCES

Organizations differ widely and, because they do, the types and qualifications of workers needed to fill various positions also differ. Recruitment efforts, if they are to be successful, must be tailored to meet the specific needs of an organization. Realistically, each job opening may require identifying different sources of potential employees and using different methods of recruiting to secure personnel from these sources.

A staffing specialist must first identify the source—where people are likely to be found—before the methods—how to attract people to the organization—can be chosen. Suppose, for example, that a large firm has an immediate need for a computer systems manager with a minimum of five years experience managing a substantial computer operation. Studying the sources, it is clear that this individual must come from competitors or other companies. Once the source of recruiting has been identified, the staffing specialist must next choose the method or methods of recruiting that will have the best chance of encouraging qualified candidates to apply for the job. Several choices are available in this example: (1) an advertisement in the employment section of *The Wall Street Journal,* (2) an ad in *Computerworld,* (3) attendance at meetings of professional associations, (4) an executive search firm, (5) employment agencies that specialize in computer systems management personnel, or (6) the Internet. Some methods would not be appropriate at all for trying to fill this position—public employment agencies, college recruiters, special events, internships, and employee referrals.

On the other hand, suppose that a firm has a need for an entry level machine operator and the firm is willing to train the person to operate the equipment. High schools, vocational schools, and unsolicited applicants are likely recruiting sources. Effective recruiting methods might include newspaper advertisements, public employment agencies, employee referrals, and recruiter contact with schools.

The specific methods used in recruiting also depend upon external environmental factors, such as labor supply and demand. Because of the differences in companies, some methods may prove satisfactory for one organization but be virtually useless for another. To match methods to sources effectively, each organization should maintain records on recruiting efforts and conduct research to determine the best methods to use for specific job categories.

RECRUITMENT RESEARCH

If a company has information revealing where its employees were recruited, statistics on present and past employees may be used to indicate the best sources of recruiting. For instance, a firm may discover that graduates from a particular college or university adapt well to the firm's environment. One large farming equipment manufacturer has achieved excellent success in recruiting from schools located in rural areas. Managers in this firm believe that since many of the students in these schools come from a farming environment, they can adapt more quickly to the firm's type of operations.

Other organizations have identified sources of employees by determining where their current employees live. This type of research, however, is likely to be more revealing where entry level production or clerical workers are concerned. If a firm discovers that the majority of its lower level employees reside within 20 miles of the workplace, recruiting efforts for these kinds of employees should be concentrated within that geographical area.

Recruiting research can assist not only in identifying sources of employees but also in predicting what types of individuals are more apt to succeed in the organization. When a regional medical center, located a fairly good distance from a large metropolitan area, reviewed its personnel records, it discovered that registered nurses who were born and raised in smaller towns adapted better to the small town environment in which the center was located than did those who grew up in large metropolitan areas. Based on this study, the hospital modified its recruiting efforts.[27]

Examples of improper recruiting are numerous. Managers of a large convenience store, for example, were disturbed that their employee turnover was high. Upon analyzing their recruiting efforts, they learned that the majority of short-term employees had merely seen a sign in the store window advertising a job opening. The individuals hired in this manner were often unemployed and highly transient. The source of supply and the recruiting method used practically ensured a high turnover rate. Once these facts were discovered, new sources of supply and new methods were used and employee turnover decreased significantly.

Because recruiting is expensive—in terms of both direct and indirect costs—it is essential that organizations conduct research in this area to ensure that recruiting efforts are as effective as possible.

EQUAL EMPLOYMENT OPPORTUNITY AND RECRUITING

Although recruiting is not expressly mentioned in Title VII of the Civil Rights Act of 1964, as amended, the manner in which recruiting is carried out can potentially lead to discrimination or to the perpetuation of historical patterns of discrimination. When an organization operates under an affirmative action plan, the recruiting effort must not only be free from discrimination, but also take actions above those normally employed to ensure that sufficient utilization of protected classes in the work force is attained.

Analysis of Recruiting Procedures

To ensure that its recruiting program is nondiscriminatory, a firm must thoroughly analyze its recruiting procedures and practices. It might, for example, be unwise to use employee referrals as a primary method and unsolicited applicants as a main recruitment source. These actions tend to perpetuate the traditional composition of an organization's work force. Particularly where protected classes are not well represented at all organizational levels, the courts have ruled that reliance on these practices is discriminatory.

In identifying sources of continuing discrimination, it is helpful to develop a record of applicant flow. (Such a record, of course, may be a requirement if an organization has to file an EEO-1 report, has been found guilty of discrimination, or operates under an affirmative action plan.) This record should include minority status and job-related data concerning each applicant; it should indicate whether a job offer was extended. If no job offer was made, a written explanation must be provided. Records including this kind of information facilitate the analysis of recruiting practices relative to protected classes and enable an organization to modify the ways it recruits.

Utilization of Protected Classes

Each individual who engages in recruiting must be trained to use objective, job-related standards. Two objective measures pertaining to job relatedness are specific skills and work experience. Recruiting based on these kinds of standards goes a long way toward eliminating discrimination.

Recruiters themselves play a critical role in either encouraging or discouraging protected class members to apply for employment with an organization. In this regard, qualified minorities and women should be utilized as much as possible in key recruiting activities. Using minorities as college recruiters or in job fairs and open houses is a way of suggesting to other minority group members that they, too, are potential candidates for employment with the organization.

Pictures of protected class employees in employment advertisements and recruiting brochures also help an organization establish credibility as an equal employment opportunity employer.

All of these things must, however, be underscored by a genuine commitment on the part of management to increase protected class participation.

Advertising

With few exceptions, jobs must be open to all individuals. Consequently, all advertisements must be free from discriminatory preferences unless the reason for preferring a particular type of individual over another has been firmly established as a bona fide occupational qualification. Some of the terms that must be avoided in employment advertising are the following:

- Young
- Boy
- Girl
- Age 25 to 35
- Age over 50

- Attractive lady
- Real sharp girl
- Career minded men
- College student
- Recent college graduate
- Retired person

The courts have ruled that each of the preceding terms is discriminatory on the basis of either sex or age.[28] The Equal Employment Opportunity Commission has issued policy statements concerning age and sex referent language in employment advertising. The use of both blatant and subtle trigger words in advertising is banned. "Junior executive," "energetic," "meter-maid," and "patrolman" are examples of words and phrases that would discourage potential applicants from applying because of their age or sex.[29]

To ensure that advertisements reach an adequate number of minorities, organizations must do more than place a help wanted ad in the major local newspaper; they must advertise in places and through media that will reach the target group. Potentially effective media include ethnic newspapers, urban contemporary radio stations, and Hispanic radio stations.

All advertising copy used in print media should also contain the phrase "Equal Opportunity Employer, M/F" to convey the idea that job opportunities are available not only to traditional minorities but also to women. Many people have the mistaken impression that "EEO Employer" suggests only racial nondiscrimination.

Employment Agencies

An organization should emphasize its nondiscriminatory recruitment practices when placing job orders with employment agencies. Inasmuch as employment agencies are covered under Title VII, the potential employer cannot go so far as to say, "We want a black ... an Hispanic ... a woman ... someone over 50 ... for this position." By specifying protected class status desired for a job opening, the organization is open to discrimination charges. Likewise, the agency that screens individuals on this basis is engaging in discriminatory practices. Complete nondiscrimination must be the rule in recruiting.

Jobs at all levels should also be listed with the local state employment agency. Often, these agencies can provide valuable assistance to organizations seeking to fulfill affirmative action goals.

Other Affirmative Action Recruiting Approaches

Personal contacts should be made with counselors and administrators at high schools, vocational schools, and colleges with large minority or female enrollments to indicate that an organization is actively seeking minorities and females for job openings. The possibilities of internships and summer employment for students of these schools should be carefully explored and provided wherever possible.

Organizations engaged in affirmative recruitment should develop positive working relationships with minority, women's, ethnic, and other community organizations. While the most productive sources may vary in each locality, some helpful organizations to contact include: National Association for the Advancement of Colored People, National Urban League, League of United Latin American Citizens, American Business Women's Association, American Association of University Women, Federation of Professional Women's Talent Bank, National Council of Negro Women, and the local Veterans Administration. Regional offices of the Equal Employment Opportunity Commission will assist employers in locating appropriate agencies.

NOTES

1. R. Wayne Mondy and Robert M. Noe III, *Human Resource Management,* 5th ed. (Boston: Allyn and Bacon, 1993), 76.

2. Herbert G. Heneman III and Timothy A. Judge, *Staffing Organizations,* 5th ed. (Middleton, WI: Mendota House, 2006), 119.

3. David Biggs and Stephen Swailes, "Relations, Commitment and Satisfaction in Agency Workers and Permanent Workers," *Employee Relations* 28, no. 2 (2006): 130–143.

4. Susan N. Houseman, "Why Employers Use Flexible Staffing Arrangements: Evidence from an Establishment Survey," *Industrial and Labor Relations Review* 55 (2001): 149–170.

5. http://www.americanstaffing.net/statistics/facts.cfm

6. Jeffrey A. Joerres, "Engaging the Total Workforce," *Human Resources Magazine* 11, no. 2 (2006): 2–7.

7. Wayne F. Cascio, *Managing Human Resources: Productivity, Quality of Work Life, Profits,* 7th ed. (New York: McGraw-Hill Irwin, 2006), 181.

8. Mondy and Noe, *Human Resource Management,* 185.

9. Dan Lionel, "Dow Jones Tests Recruitment Weekly," *Editor and Publisher* (May 24, 1980): 29.

10. Mondy and Noe, *Human Resource Management,* 185.

11. Jo Bredwell, "The Use of Broadcast Advertising for Recruitment," *Personnel Administrator* (February 1981): 45–49.

12. Richard T. Cober, Douglas J. Brown, Alana J. Blumental, Dennis Doverspike, and Paul Levy, "The Quest for the Qualified Job Surfer: It's Time the Public Sector Catches the Wave," *Public Personnel Management* 29, no. 4 (2000): 479–494.

13. Peter Cappelli, "Making the Most of On-line Recruiting," *Harvard Business Review* 79 (2001): 139–146.

14. In Lee, "E-Recruiting: Opportunities and Challenges," *Information Management* 19, no. 3/4 (2006): 24–25.

15. Cappelli, *Harvard Business Review,* 139–146.

16. Nick Martindale, "First Steps," *Personnel Today* (Spring 2007): 5–7.

17. Sara L. Rynes, Amy E. Colbert, and Kenneth G. Brown, "HR Professionals' Beliefs about Effective Human Resource Practices: Correspondence between Research and Practice," *Human Resource Management* 41 (2002): 149–174.

18. Richard A. Fear, *The Evaluation Interview,* 3rd ed. (New York: McGraw-Hill Book Company), 74–75.

19. "The Virtual Job Fair," *HR Professional* 25, no. 1 (December/January 2008): 15.

20. Herbert G. Heneman III and Robert L. Heneman, *Staffing Organizations* (Middleton, WI: Mendota House, 1994), 254.

21. Richard J. Cronin, " Executive Recruiters: Are They Necessary?" *Personnel Administrator* (February 1981): 32.

22. "Recruiters on Recruiting," *HR Magazine* 53, no. 1 (January 2008): 48–49.

23. Thomas C. Amory, "Searching for a Search Firm," *Personnel Journal* (February 1983): 114–116.

24. Michael A. Zottoli and John P. Wanous, "Recruitment Source Research: Current Status and Future Directions," *Human Resource Management Review* 10, no. 4 (2000): 353–382.

25. *Employment Coordinator,* vol. 14 (Deerfield, IL: Clark Boardman Callaghan, 1996), PM-10,408.

26. A. Prakash Sethi, *Up Against the Corporate Wall* (Englewood Cliffs, NJ: Prentice-Hall, 1971), 84–106.

27. Van M. Evans, "Recruitment Advertising in the '80's," *The Personnel Administrator* (December 1978): 23.

28. Barbara Lindemann Schlei and Paul Grossman, *Employment Discrimination Law* (Washington, DC: Bureau of National Affairs, 1983), 486.

29. Heneman and Heneman, *Staffing Organizations,* 279.

8

The Selecting Process

Selecting is the process of choosing from a group of applicants the individual deemed to be best qualified for a particular job opening. An organization's success in its recruiting activities significantly affects the efficiency and effectiveness of selection. An adequate pool of applicants provides an organization with greater latitude in choosing employees; an inadequate pool reduces the amount of latitude and may result in the employment of marginally qualified candidates.

Selecting is, at best, a difficult process because it involves making judgments about people. Three essential questions must be answered if the most qualified person is to be selected: "What is the applicant's *can do* ability?" "What is the applicant's *will do* ability?" "How well will the applicant *fit* into the organization?" *Can do* ability refers to experience and education required to perform a specific job; *will do* ability refers to the level of motivation the person will actually exert in performing the job; *fit* refers to how well the individual will conform to the sociopsychological environment or culture of the organization. Making these determinations requires skill, effort, and time. Moreover, in an effective selection process, such decisions must be carefully made.

Mistakes made during the selection process can be costly. Hiring individuals who cannot or will not do their jobs leads to output and quality problems, and ultimately to employee turnover. Hiring individuals who do not fit into the organization well leads to the same problems and may also adversely affect the morale of other employees. Consequently, selecting must be done carefully in order to minimize potential negative impacts, financial and otherwise, on the organization.

As emphasized throughout this book, the entire human resource management function operates in an increasingly legalistic environment. Nowhere is it more open to potential discrimination charges and lawsuits than in selection. The challenge to an organization in selecting employees thus is twofold: (1) to select the best qualified individual and (2) to make the selection decision in accordance with the letter and spirit of the law.

Selecting is such an important activity that three chapters of this book are devoted to it. This chapter presents an overview of the entire selection process. The following two chapters examine crucial elements of the process: testing and interviewing, respectively.

A GENERALIZED SELECTING MODEL

A generalized model of the selecting process is depicted in Figure 8.1. Selection begins where recruiting ends—with the applicant pool—and proceeds through five stages: (I) initial screening, (II) secondary screening, (III) candidacy, (IV) verification, and (V) final decision. Selection procedures vary from organization to organization; consequently, the steps outlined may not be followed in the described sequence by every firm. Moreover, an applicant may be rejected at any point during the first four stages. The purpose of the model is to illustrate, in a logical sequence, the basic steps that are typically followed in evaluating and ultimately hiring a job applicant.

Once individuals are interested in applying for employment, they may do so by submitting a resumé (a common procedure for technical, professional, or managerial positions), by completing an employment application (standard procedure for entry level, operative, clerical, or other nonexempt positions), or by doing both. During Stage I, the majority of applicants will be screened out based on an individual evaluation of the resumé or the employment application. Applicants who submitted a resumé may be asked to complete an employment application if their credentials survive the initial review.

The two components of Stage II are the screening interview and testing. The purpose of the screening interview is to eliminate from further consideration those individuals whose qualifications, although passing preliminary inspection, do not measure up to the standards of the position. Based on the screening interview, applicants for certain types of positions may be asked to take employment tests. Applicants passing the screening interview who have not yet completed an employment application will be asked to do so at this stage. On occasion, applicants may move from the completion of the employment application in Stage I directly into employment testing before the screening interview takes place—a common procedure for keyboardists or machine operators. If the test results are favorable, the screening interview then takes place.

Since the vast majority of applicants are eliminated in Stages I and II, only genuinely qualified candidates, assuming that the previous selection procedures are working effectively, enter Stage III. The basic component of this stage is the employment interview or series of employment interviews, which focus on an in-depth evaluation of the applicant's qualifications. In some organizations, individuals successfully completing their employment interviews are sent to an

Figure 8.1
A Model of the Selecting Process

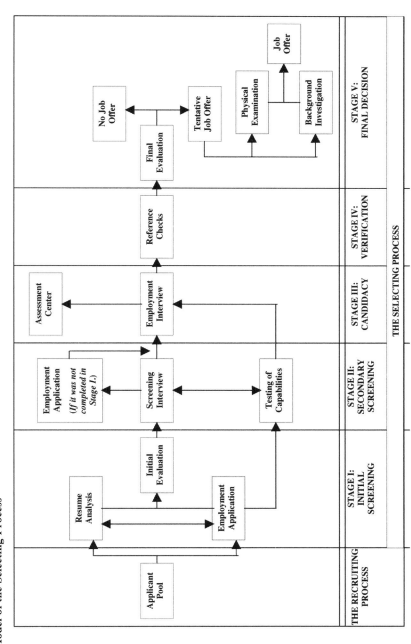

assessment center where they may complete batteries of tests and engage in various simulations to further assess their capabilities. Applicants completing Stage III are potential employees.

Stage IV is concerned with verifying information furnished by applicants. Because of the increasing number of negligent hiring cases, organizations must be careful to exercise due diligence in verifying and documenting references.

State V is the decision-making stage. The information furnished by the applicant and gathered by the organization is evaluated. If the information is favorable, a job offer is made; if the information is unfavorable, no job offer is extended. The tentative job offer is subject to physical examination (typically including a drug screen) and a background investigation. If the candidate successfully completes these two final hurdles, a final job offer is made. The physical examination is delayed until this stage so as to avoid any possible discrimination based on disability. The background investigation is delayed for similar reasons—to avoid any potential charge of discrimination based on non-job-related factors.

In reviewing the generalized selecting model, note that the least time-consuming and least expensive selection activities are performed first. The most time-consuming, most expensive activities are performed later in the process. This sequencing helps ensure the cost effectiveness of selection.

FACTORS AFFECTING THE SELECTING PROCESS

While a generalized selection model is helpful in showing the series of logical steps that are usually taken in choosing employees, specific procedures do vary from firm to firm. Additionally, there are other organizational variables and influences, as discussed below, that may affect the process.

Organizational Hierarchy

The selection process would be greatly simplified if a single standardized procedure could be developed—and followed—for all applicants. Deviations from predetermined steps, however, are often necessary to accommodate the needs of specific situations. In particular, variations are appropriate, even required, when filling positions at different levels in the organizational hierarchy. For instance, consider the differences that exist in hiring a top-level executive as opposed to a secretary. Exhaustive interviewing of the potential executive, followed by extensive background checks to verify experience, education, and personal implacability are essential for a senior-level position. On the other hand, an applicant for a secretarial position may only take a keyboarding test and be subjected to a short employment interview.

As a general rule, the higher or more sensitive the position, the more involved and complicated the selection process. The lower the position, the less likely the full series of steps specified by the model will be followed. The findings of a recent study support this rule, indicating that when the skill requirements for a job are greater (as would generally be for a higher-level position) the selection methods used by the organization tend to be more extensive.[1]

Speed of Decision Making

The time available for making a selection decision can also exert a major influence on the selecting process. Suppose, for instance, that a firm's only two quality assurance technicians terminate without advance notice. Filling these positions immediately is a matter of critical importance. Consequently, the algorithmic steps in the selection process are likely to be truncated. Since speed is of the essence, a few telephone calls and two short interviews may comprise the entire selection process. Conversely, when the need for filling a position is known well in advance, more time can be spent rigidly following the normal selection procedure steps.

Applicant Pool

The number of applicants for a particular job also affects the selecting process. An organization can be highly selective if there are many applicants for a specific position. It cannot be as selective or uncompromising in its requirements if few applicants are available. In the latter case, selection becomes largely a matter of choosing whoever is available.

The number of persons hired for a particular job compared to the number of qualified individuals in the applicant pool is known as the selection ratio. This ratio is determined as follows:

$$\frac{\text{Number of Individuals Hired for a Particular Job}}{\text{Number of Qualified Applicants Available}} = \text{Selection Ratio}$$

A selection ratio below 1.0 indicates that there are more qualified applicants than there are jobs; a selection ratio above 1.0 indicates that there are more jobs than there are applicants. Obviously, the lower the ratio, the more choice an organization has; the higher the ratio, the less choice it has. Thus, the applicant pool generated by recruiting has a significant impact on selection.

Type of Organization

The specific kind of enterprise where individuals are to be employed—private, not-for-profit, or governmental—can also affect the selection process. A business in the private sector is profit-oriented, and prospective employees—especially professionals and managers—are likely to be screened with regard to potential contributions they can make toward helping the organization achieve its profit objectives. Profit-making enterprises, consequently, are apt to be more stringent in their selection criteria.

Governments—federal, state, and local, but especially federal—typically identify qualified applicants through competitive examinations. Often, the hiring manager is permitted to select only from the three top qualifying applicants for a given position. A manager in the governmental sector may not have the prerogative to interview candidates other than the top scorers on the competitive examination.

In not-for-profit organizations such as the American Heart Association, the Boy Scouts of America, or the YWCA, the situation is different. Because salary levels in these types of organizations are not normally competitive with those in industry or government, selection must focus on not only the applicant's qualifications for job performance but also on an assessment of the applicant's dedication to the kind of work the institution does.

Clearly, the type of organization involved affects both the sorts of individuals who will be attracted as well as the selection criteria that will be used in making a hiring decision. A firm that has a good reputation typically attracts a greater number of applicants who possess desirable characteristics, creating a larger, more talented applicant pool.[2]

Probationary Period

Many organizations use a probationary period that provides for evaluation of an employee's ability to perform, before longer-term employment is offered. The probationary period may be a substitute for, or supplement to, the use of other selection procedures. The rationale for using a probationary period in lieu of other selection measures is that if a person can successfully perform the job during the trial period, tests or other predictors of success are not needed. However, accurate measures of performance are essential to the use of a probationary period.

Even though a firm may be unionized, a new employee typically is not protected by the labor-management agreement until after completing a probationary period—usually 30 days. During this time, the employee may be terminated with minimum justification. However, once the probationary period is over, it may prove to be quite difficult to terminate even a marginal employee who belongs to a union. Selection under these conditions requires careful identification of qualified workers and realistic evaluation of their performance during the probationary period.

STAGE I: INITIAL SCREENING

Employment Applications

For the majority of positions, the selecting process begins with the prospective employee completing an application form. The application is then reviewed (either by someone in the human resource department or by the hiring manager, depending upon how selection is carried out in a particular organization) to determine if there appears to be a possible match between the applicant and the open position. Traditionally, individuals completed hard copy applications at the organization's physical site. Nowadays, more and more people complete their applications online. While applying for a job via the Internet is convenient for applicants, privacy concerns over supplying sensitive information is an issue.[3]

The specific types of information requested on employment applications vary from company to company, and even by job groupings within an organization. Sections of an application typically include personal data such as name, address, and telephone number; educational background; work experience; specific job qualifications; and possibly military service. It is becoming increasingly important, because of possible legal ramifications, to include several consent or acknowledgment statements on the application just above the applicant's signature. These items include: (1) an acknowledgment of job status as employment-at-will (i.e., the organization has the right to terminate employees at any time); (2) consent to drug and alcohol testing prior to employment or during employment; (3) consent to undergo physical testing where the job has physical requirements that are essential to effective performance; (4) permission for the organization to conduct a background investigation; (5) permission to conduct a credit investigation (provided that an applicant's credit record is directly related to the job); and (6) an acknowledgment that any false, inaccurate, omitted, or misleading statements or information are grounds for rejection of an application or termination of employment.[4]

The employment application must reflect the firm's informational needs and also adhere to federal legislation and Equal Employment Opportunity Commission's (EEOC) *Guidelines*. A sample of a properly designed application is provided in Figure 8.2.[5] Note that many traditional informational requests that are potentially discriminatory have been eliminated. Among the missing items are such things as sex, race, age, number of children living at home, and credit references. An organization can inquire about convictions, but questions relating to a person's arrest record are illegal, and if they appear on an application they may be regarded as a prima facie violation by EEOC. While there are no other questions that are illegal per se, there are numerous informational requests and questions that may expose an organization to discrimination charges. Some of the items and questions that should be considered as inappropriate for an employment application are the following:

• Race	• Spouse's Place of Employment
• Sex or Gender	• Dependents Other than Children
• National Origin	• Length of Time on Job for Spouse
• Native Language	• Nature of Military Discharge
• Religion	• Date Graduated from High School
• Disability Status	• Date Graduated from College

Figure 8.2
Sample Employment Application

Employment Application

PLEASE PRINT ALL INFORMATION REQUESTED EXCEPT SIGNATURE

APPLICATION FOR EMPLOYMENT

PLEASE COMPLETE PAGES 1-5.   Date _____

Name _____

      Last   First   Middle   Maiden

Present Address _____

      Number   Street   City   State   Zip

How long have you lived at your present address? _____ Social Security No. _____ – _____ – _____

Telephone: (   )

If under 18, please list age: _____

                                                   Days/hours available to work:
Position applied for (1): _____   Monday _____ Friday _____
and salary desired (2): _____   Tuesday _____ Saturday _____
(Be Specific)   Wednesday_____ Sunday _____
                                                   Thursday _____ No Preference _____

How many hours can you work weekly? _____ Can you work nights? _____

Employment desired: ❑FULL-TIME ONLY   ❑PART-TIME ONLY   ❑FULL- OR PART-TIME
When are you available for work? _____

TYPE OF SCHOOL	NAME OF SCHOOL	LOCATION (Complete mailing address)	NUMBER OF YEARS COMPLETED	MAJOR & DEGREE
High School				
College				
Bus. or Trade School				
Professional School				

HAVE YOU EVER BEEN CONVICTED OF A FELONY?   ❑ No   ❑ Yes

If yes, please explain. _____

_____

- Date of Birth
- Height
- Weight
- Marital Status
- Number of Children
- Spouse's Name
- Spouse's Position

- Have you ever been injured?
- Do you have any defects in hearing?
- Do you have any defects in vision?
- Do you have any defects in speech?
- List any physical defects.
- What is your general physical condition?
- Credit References

The information in a completed employment application should be compared with the job description and job specifications to determine the degree of match

Figure 8.2 (continued)
Sample Employment Application

PLEASE PRINT ALL INFORMATION REQUESTED EXCEPT SIGNATURE	

APPLICATION FOR EMPLOYMENT

DO YOU HAVE A DRIVER'S LICENSE?   ❑ Yes   ❑ No

What is your means of transportation to work? _____

Driver's License
Number _____ State of Issue _____   ❑ Operator   ❑ Commercial (CDL)
❑Chauffeur

Expiration Date _____

Have you had any accidents during the past three years?   How many?
_____

Have you had any moving violations during the past three years?   How Many?
_____

OFFICE ONLY

	❑ Yes				❑ Yes	Word	❑ Yes		
Typing	❑ No	_____ WPM		10-key	❑ No	Processing	❑ No	_____ WPM	
Personal	❑ Yes	PC ❑		Other					
Computer	❑ No	Mac ❑		Skills					

Please list two references other than relatives or previous employers.

Name _____	Name _____
Position _____	Position _____
Company _____	Company _____
Address _____	Address _____
_____	
Telephone ( )	Telephone ( )

Use the space below to summarize any additional information necessary to describe your full qualifications for the specific position for which you are applying.

Figure 8.2 (continued)
Sample Employment Application

PLEASE PRINT ALL INFORMATION REQUESTED EXCEPT SIGNATURE	

APPLICATION FOR EMPLOYMENT

MILITARY

HAVE YOU EVER BEEN IN THE ARMED FORCES?   ❑ Yes ❑ No

ARE YOU NOW A MEMBER OF THE NATIONAL GUARD?   ❑ Yes ❑ No

Specialty _____ Date Entered _____ Discharge Date

Work Experience	Please list your work experience for the past five years beginning with your most recent job held. If you were self-employed, give firm name. Attach additional sheets if necessary.

Name of Employer	Name of Last Supervisor	Employment Dates	Pay or Salary
Address			
City, State, Zip Code		From	Start
Phone Number		To	Final
	Your Last Job Title		

Reason for Leaving (Be Specific)

List the jobs you held, duties performed, skills used or learned, advancements or promotions while you worked at this company.

Name of Employer	Name of Last Supervisor	Employment Dates	Pay or Salary
Address			
City, State, Zip Code		From	Start
Phone Number		To	Final
	Your Last Job Title		

Reason for Leaving (Be Specific)

List the jobs you held, duties performed, skills used or learned, advancements or promotions while you worked at this company.

between an applicant and the job. This is often a difficult task. Applicants may exaggerate their qualifications in order to present themselves in a more favorable light. Estimates concerning the number of job seekers who enhance their previous work experiences range from 40 to 70 percent.[6] Also, it is hard to compare duties and responsibilities of previously held positions with those of the position the applicant is seeking. Job titles can also be misleading. A person who has the title of vice president in one organization, for example, may actually perform few managerial tasks while a person with the same title in another organization may have extensive managerial responsibility.

Figure 8.2 (continued)
Sample Employment Application

PLEASE PRINT ALL INFORMATION REQUESTED EXCEPT SIGNATURE	

APPLICATION FOR EMPLOYMENT

Work Experience	Please list your work experience for the past five years beginning with your most recent job held. If you were self-employed, give firm name. Attach additional sheets if necessary.

Name of Employer	Name of Last Supervisor	Employment Dates	Pay or Salary
Address			
City, State, Zip Code		From	Start
Phone Number		To	Final
	Your Last Job Title		

Reason for Leaving (Be Specific)

List the jobs you held, duties performed, skills used or learned, advancements or promotions while you worked at this company.

Name of Employer	Name of Last Supervisor	Employment Dates	Pay or Salary
Address			
City, State, Zip Code		From	Start
Phone Number		To	Final
	Your Last Job Title		

Reason for Leaving (Be Specific)

List the jobs you held, duties performed, skills used or learned, advancements or promotions while you worked at this company.

May we contact your present employer? ❏ Yes ❏ No

Did you complete this application yourself?   ❏ Yes ❏ No

If not, who did? _____

The purpose of reviewing the application is not, however, to make a selection decision. It is to eliminate from further consideration those applicants who do not possess the minimum qualifications.

Resumé Analysis

Resumés often play a significant role in the selection process. For managerial, professional, and technical positions, they are commonly the first information received from job applicants. A resumé is a relatively short, detailed account of the candidate's work history, educational background, and other qualifications.

Figure 8.2 (continued)
Sample Employment Application

AGREEMENT (PLEASE READ CAREFULLY BEFORE SIGNING)

I certify that all the information on this application is accurate and complete to the best of my knowledge and understand that misleading or false statements will constitute sufficient cause for refusal of hire or termination of my employment.

I understand that neither the acceptance of this application nor the subsequent entry into any type of employment relationship with [the Company] creates an actual or implied contract of employment. I understand that, if I accept employment with [Company Name], it will be on an at-will basis. This means that either [Company Name] or I have the right to terminate the employment relationship at any time, for any reason, with or without cause.

I agree to submit to drug and alcohol testing, if requested by [Company Name]. I release [Company Name], and its employees, plus other persons or companies, from any and all liability arising out of or related in any way to such testing.

I authorize [Company Name] to investigate information concerning my education, employment experiences and all other aspects of my background relevant to my proposed employment. I release [Company Name] and its employees from all liability arising from such investigation.

Signature of Applicant_____ Date: _____

[Company Name] is an equal employment opportunity employer. We adhere to a policy of making employment decisions without regard to race, color, religion, sex, sexual orientation, national origin, citizenship, age or disability. We assure you that your opportunity for employment with [Company Name] depends solely on your qualifications.

A common mistake in reviewing a resumé is to assume that all of the data shown are accurate and true. In fact, a survey conducted through Career-Builder.com in June 2006 estimates that 57 percent of hiring managers found lies in submitted job applications. The managers indicated that applicants lied about the actual dates of their past employment, their past employers, academic degrees and institutions, technical skills and certifications, and accomplishments.[7] For example, a seminar attended may show up on a resumé as a certification when in reality, no legitimate certification was ever granted. Consequently, resumé reviewers should not accept a resumé at face value. Rather, they should examine it carefully, note any inconsistencies or questionable data, and identify other items that warrant later verification. Conducting a background check can help identify any misinformation.

There are several things that should be viewed as *red flags* in a resumé, signaling the need for a closer inspection of the information (or lack thereof) presented. Among the most prominent of these red flags are the following:

• Incomplete Information
• Gaps in Employment History
• Frequent Job Moves
• Several Job Moves for Lesser Pay
• Short Periods of Employment
• Regression in Job Titles or Job Duties

• Obscure Colleges or Universities Attended
• Questionable Certifications
• Nonpertinent Certifications or Degrees
• Poor Presentation: Appearance, Paper Quality, Grammar, Nonreverse Chronology, Misspellings, etc.

Each of these items is an indication that the resumé should be examined very closely. Their existence is not, however, a sign that the applicant should not be considered for employment. The applicant may have a good reason for such red flags. For example, gaps in employment history could be explained by an illness, family obligations, or a return to school.

The major thrust in reviewing a resumé is the same as for an employment application: Does the applicant seemingly possess the necessary qualifications for the job? Job descriptions and job specifications are used to compare the person's reported experience and background with the requirements of the position for which he or she is applying.

A resumé also should be viewed as an advertising brochure. The reviewer should evaluate how well the applicant presents himself or herself in print. Thus, there are some other considerations the reviewer should note in order to determine if the resumé is worthy of in-depth review.[8] These are as follows:

- *Positive image conveyed.* Does the applicant present positive factors first? Is the overall tone positive or is it negative? What is the general appearance of the resumé?
- *Evidence of contributions.* Does the applicant emphasize the contributions he or she has made to previous organizations or does the applicant simply list job duties?
- *Logical presentation.* Are the data presented in a logical, easy to follow manner? Is work history listed in reverse chronological order so that most recent experience is shown first?
- *Carefully written.* Is the resumé carefully written and free of grammatical mistakes and typographical errors or does it appear to be hastily compiled with little thought given to writing style?
- *Specifics rather than generalities.* Does the resumé deal with previous experience in terms of specifics or does it deal with experience in vague generalities that could be interpreted several ways?

Many individuals also post their resumés on the Internet. When utilizing this method, it is beneficial to use many details, avoid touchy subjects (i.e., political or religious affiliations), use key words that make it "search friendly," use abbreviations, and always proofread prior to posting.[9] Also, it is important to remember that the resumé file you upload from your computer may not display as intended on the Internet. The formatting may be distorted, so it is important to view the way in which your resumé is actually displayed online to make sure it looks as it should, nicely formatted with the right information in the right places.

STAGE II: SECONDARY SCREENING

The Screening Interview

The purpose of the screening interview is to identify tentatively viable employment candidates. The initial screening of the employment application or the resumé eliminates many applicants; those not eliminated by this review process are then screened to see if they do, in fact, possess the necessary qualifications. The screening interview reduces the number of applicants to a more manageable number.

The typical screening interview is relatively short. In fact, one of the authors once witnessed a screening interview that could not have lasted over 15 seconds. At the end of the interview, the applicant was referred to the hiring supervisor for a final interview and employment decision. A few straightforward questions are asked during the screening interview: "Do you know how to—? Have you ever operated a—? What is your experience with—? Do you have a—?" If the applicant does not have the required experience, know-how, or background, any further consideration in the employment process would benefit neither the individual nor the organization.

In addition to quickly eliminating obviously unqualified job applicants for specific positions, screening interviews may produce other positive benefits. It is likely that the position for which the individual is applying is not the only one available. In the process of screening for one position, a skilled interviewer may be able to identify prospective employees for other open positions in the firm. The fact that the applicant does not qualify for one job does not mean that he or she is not qualified for other jobs. For example, an applicant may be obviously unqualified to fill the position of senior programming analyst, but may very well possess the necessary skills to work as a computer operator. The person doing the screening must remember that his or her responsibility is not only to eliminate candidates for one position but also to identify candidates for other positions. Recognizing this dual responsibility, the interviewer can build goodwill for the employer as well as maximize recruiting and selecting efforts.

While screening interviews lead to several positive outcomes, there are some drawbacks. As with every step in the hiring process, interviewers must be careful not to make judgments based on characteristics such as race and gender. They must focus only on questions concerning characteristics related to the job (i.e., knowledge, skills, and abilities). It is common to use perceptual shortcuts such as biases and stereotypes when decisions must be made in a short amount of time,[10] as is the case with screening interviews. Another drawback is that interviewing is a costly screening procedure, even when the interview lasts only a few minutes. Conducting interviews over the phone saves organizations some time and money.[11] Some organizations are even starting to use computerized screening to make the initial screening process more efficient and to reduce costs. Such automated hiring technologies are expected to greatly reduce the hiring cycle time.[12]

Evaluating Background and Biographical Information

Over the years, there have been many studies examining the relationship between application form data and success or failure in particular jobs. One study found that the biodata included on a typical application (i.e., basic demographic and personal information, a list of social activities, a record of employment, and a record of academic qualification) was a predictor of future performance in entry-level professional positions.[13] With respect to an applicant's academic record, one large firm discovered that the single most reliable indicator of a college graduate's success in the organization was the person's rank in his or her graduating class. Additionally, this firm found that class ranking was even more important as a predictor than the actual college attended.[14] These studies suggest that the employment application can be a valuable predictive device for certain types of positions. The weighted application blank and regression analysis, two specific approaches to evaluating background and biographical data, are discussed below.

Weighted Application Blank

The oldest and perhaps best known technique for identifying factors that differentiate between successful and less successful employees is the weighted application blank (WAB). When the WAB is used, an attempt is made to identify factors on the application that differentiate between long- and short-term employees, productive and less productive employees, or satisfied and less satisfied employees. One such variable, "years on last job," is shown in Figure 8.3.

Previews

Although there are several techniques that can be applied to calculate the weights to be used, the simplest approach is the horizontal percent method.[15] In using this method, a large sample of current employees is used to construct

Figure 8.3
Example of a Weighted Application

Item: Years on Last Job	Number of Responses:			%	
	Short-Term Employees	Long-Term Employees	Total Employees	Long-Term Employees	Weight
Less than 1	18	3	21	14%	1
1 to 1 1/2	42	12	54	22%	2
1 1/2 to 2 1/2	46	23	69	33%	3
2 1/2 to 3	17	13	30	43%	4
More than 3	10	11	21	52%	5
Total	133	62	195		

weights that are then used as a means of assessing later applicants for employment. Examining Figure 8.3, we can see how the calculations are made. The two groups of employees are classified as to the length of time spent with their previous employer. Short-term employees are those who left previous organizations after a limited tenure, usually within the first year or two of employment. Long-term employees are those who stayed on the job longer than one or two years. The percentage of long-term employees is then determined by the years spent on the last job. In this example, we see that only 14 percent of the long-term employees were with their last employer less than one year, whereas 52 percent had three or more years of job service with their last employer. The weight for each category of years on last job is determined by moving the decimal point one place to the right; thus, less than one year on the previous job has an actual weight of 1.4 and more than three years on the last job has an actual weight of 5.2. To simplify weighting, the number is customarily rounded off to the nearest whole number, so the weight for less than one year on the last job is 1 and the weight for more than three years on the last job is 5.

Once weights for all variables on the application blank have been computed, applicants can be screened based on the point total they receive on the WAB. Applicants with the highest point totals are considered to have the highest potential for success on a particular job or with the organization. With respect to Figure 8.3 for example, an individual who worked at his or her previous job for two years would earn 3 points for this item on the WAB.

In specific instances, the WAB has been proven to be very accurate. One study recently found that the WAB method was able to predict performance, distinguishing successful from unsuccessful police academy applicants.[16] At most other times, however, it has been only marginally useful. Consequently, the vast majority of companies continue to use the traditional application form rather than the WAB.

Regression Analysis

Regression analysis, mentioned in Chapter 4 as a human resource planning technique, has also been used successfully for evaluating employment application data. Regression analysis establishes the relationship between two or more variables so that one variable can be predicted from the other variables.[17]

In some instances, organizations may desire to determine whether employee productivity can be estimated from information available on the employment application. In regression analysis terminology, the productivity level, in this example, is referred to as the dependent variable. Any item or items on the application used to predict or estimate the productivity level are called independent variables. Commonly used independent variables that may be predictive of productivity are work experience and education.

Although the potential for successful use of regression analysis in the selection process appears to be significant, it is used by few organizations. First of all, in order to use regression analysis to help with selection decisions, the organization must have somebody that is capable of performing the advanced statistical technique and interpreting the results of the analysis. Another limitation of its use is that a significant database is required for any degree of statistical significance to be established. Moreover, since regression analysis should be conducted on specific jobs or job categories, only very large companies are able to accumulate sufficient data.

An additional drawback of regression analysis is that a model developed for one company cannot be used by another company; the model must be tailored to fit each organization. When utilized in different geographical areas, a regression model becomes less accurate because of cultural or labor market factors. The model must also be continually updated with current employment applications data or its accuracy is likely to diminish. Despite the problems associated with this analytical tool, it can be of assistance in making selection decisions.

Employment Testing

Testing is frequently used early in the selecting process to determine if an applicant is qualified for a particular job. Keyboarding or other work sample tests are commonly used for lower-level positions. Because of the complex issues involved in employment testing, the following chapter is devoted to an examination of this area. As a step in the selection process, testing may be advantageous as a means of verifying specific skills.

STAGE III: CANDIDACY

The Employment Interview

One of the most critical steps in the selection process is the employment interview. Applicants reaching this step are considered to be qualified for a position; unqualified or marginally qualified applicants have already been eliminated from serious consideration. The employment interview is essentially an in-depth probing of the candidate's background that provides substantial evidence upon which to base the hiring decision. Employment interviewing is thoroughly examined in Chapter 10.

Assessment Centers

An assessment center is a selection technique for identifying management potential. Because of its expense, this technique is primarily utilized as an internal selection and development device for managerial positions. However, it is sometimes employed in the selection of external candidates.

In assessment centers, candidates are subjected to a variety of exercises constructed to simulate the job for which they are applying. These exercises, or test batteries on occasion, are developed through thorough job analyses of positions.

Candidates participate in a series of activities similar to those they may be expected to encounter in the actual job. Commonly used activities include in-basket exercises, management games, case analyses, leaderless discussion groups, mock interviews, and other simulations. A team of assessors observe and evaluate the participants.

The time and costs involved severely limit assessment centers as a means for selecting new employees. It has been estimated that the cost of an assessment center is between $750 and $1,000 per hire.[18] Other sources suggest that the cost can rise above $2,000, but that the quality of the person hired through this method more than compensates for the hiring cost.[19]

STAGE IV: VERIFICATION

Reference Checks

As indicated earlier, job applicants sometimes record inaccurate information on employment applications and resumés in order to present a more positive image. The purpose of reference checks is to verify the accuracy of the data furnished. Typically, applicants are required to provide names of previous supervisors or names of several business references. Checks on these references are then made by letter or telephone. Because of possible legal ramifications, reference information provided by one organization to another organization is usually limited to neutral information such as job title, dates of employment, and possibly wage or salary. When conducted by telephone, other information may be gathered: for example, absentee record, promotions and demotions, compensation, and stated reasons for termination. Even though limited information may be obtained through reference checking, it is essential that an organization demonstrate a good faith effort and exercise due diligence in checking all employee references in order to protect itself against possible lawsuits from employees alleging negligent hiring and negligent referencing.

Employers are very concerned about the legal ramifications of providing information regarding the performance of former employees, fearing that release of sensitive information could lead (as it often has) to charges of defamation or self-compelled defamation by previous employees who receive a less than satisfactory recommendation. Several states have recognized this employer dilemma and have passed legislation to exempt employers from liability in providing information as long as they are acting in good faith. Currently, 32 states provide this legal protection to organizations.[20]

Since the passage of the Federal Privacy Act of 1974, a person who has been employed by the federal government has the legal right to review reference checks that have been made concerning his or her employment unless the person has waived this right. There have been instances where applicants have sued and won court cases when it was proven that the reference information given out was biased or incorrect. Because of the possible extension of the Privacy Act to the private sector, many firms and individuals are now reluctant to provide any kind of negative reference information on former employees or business associates. However, providing only positive reference information for a former employee who had posed a potential safety risk led the California Supreme Court to impose damages on that former employer after the employee molested a student at his new place of employment.[21] Reference checking has proven to be a very complicated task because of all of the legal and moral issues accompanying it.

Another problem with references is that the applicant normally provides them. Applicants may selectively choose their references to ensure that only positive information is furnished. It is unlikely, except where the names of previous supervisors are requested, that an applicant would list anyone who might give an unfavorable report. Thus, references tend to be biased in a positive manner.

Since some individuals are reluctant to state their opinions about former employees or colleagues in writing, many organizations prefer to use the telephone when checking references. Since there is no written record of the conversation, more information may be collected. However, there is still a potential problem with bias—the individual providing the reference is just as likely to offer a negatively biased as a positively biased opinion. One way to improve the validity of telephone reference checks is to structure the reference-checking procedure.[22] This structured format should help individuals focus on gathering information that is solely related to qualifications for the job in question, reduce bias, and avoid legal repercussions.

Some suggestions for improving the reference checking process are as follows:

- *Train employment specialists.* Telephone interviewing techniques, how to ask questions, and how to probe for information are some of the topics that should be covered.
- *Communicate preferences to applicants.* Indicate the kinds of references preferred (i.e., former supervisors or business colleagues). Tell the applicant how references will be contacted.
- *Communicate preferences to recruiting sources.* Outside parties such as employment agencies can often obtain additional reference information on applicants if they know the kinds of information the organization is seeking.
- *Provide feedback to references.* Thank-you letters build goodwill for the company and help ensure cooperation from those who may be regular suppliers of reference information.[23]

STAGE V: FINAL DECISION

After all information has been obtained from appropriate selection devices, the most critical step in the entire process—the decision to hire or not to hire—takes place. The other stages in the selecting process have been used to narrow the number of candidates. The final decision is made from among those individuals who are still being considered after reference checks, background investigations, physical examinations, and drug and alcohol screening have been completed.

The human resource department is normally involved in all phases leading up to the final employment decision. The selection decision is usually the prerogative of the operating manager, who may or may not seek the advice of staffing specialists. The rationale for permitting the manager or supervisor to make the final selection decision is obvious: this is the individual who will be responsible for the new employee. Yet there are times when it is a collective decision, most notably when an employee will have to interface with others across organizational lines.

In some cases, the human resource manager may have strong influence on the decision. If the organization is attempting to meet minority hiring goals under an affirmative action plan, a recommendation from the personnel manager may have considerable bearing on the candidate hired. It is important that the human resource manager refrain from exerting too much pressure on the decision because this may undermine the operating manager's authority.

No Job Offer: Rejecting Candidates

Applicants may, of course, be rejected at any stage of the selection process. If the process is functioning properly, only a few candidates—ideally three to six—will reach the selection decision stage.

When an individual makes an application for employment, he or she is essentially saying, "I think I am qualified for this job. Will you hire me?" Tension increases as the applicant progresses through the selection process. If the person is eliminated early in the process, there is likely to be only a minimum amount of ego damage to the individual. The company, in fact, may even be able to inform the individual of other jobs in the organization that better match his or her qualifications.

For many people, the employment interview is not a pleasant experience. Taking tests that affect a person's career can also cause high anxiety. Suffering through all of these experiences only to be told at the end, "There does not appear to be a proper match between your qualifications and our needs," may be extremely painful. Many firms recognize these facts and take deliberate actions to protect the applicant's self-esteem. Still, it is quite difficult to tell people that they are not going to be hired.

All organizations should recognize that both firm and candidate have invested considerable time in the selection process. Rejected candidates are entitled to some explanation as to why they were rejected. Form letters or callous expressions that imply "don't call us, we will call you" must be avoided. The treatment afforded a rejected applicant can have an impact on company goodwill as well as future recruiting efforts. Organizations should remember that today's rejected candidate may be tomorrow's stellar employee.

Rejections can be handled effectively in one of three ways: (1) a personal conference with the applicant, (2) a telephone conversation, or (3) a personalized letter. The most effective practice is the personal conference. It is also the most time-consuming and expensive. At times, it may not even be practicable because of the geographical separation between applicant and company. When it can be used, it offers the opportunity to carefully explain why the applicant was not hired. It provides information to the applicant that may be useful in further job searches, and it suggests the organization's genuine interest in people. Unfortunately, this approach is the very rare exception rather than the rule in American industry.

Personal telephone calls serve essentially the same purposes as the conference approach, offering an opportunity for explanation and building goodwill for the company. Individuals receive more extensive information and have the chance to ask clarifying questions about the information they receive, as they do with the face-to-face, personal conference.

If for some reason applicants must be rejected by letter, the letter should be personalized; it should be written so as to reduce the stigma of rejection and lessen the chance that the applicant will resent the firm's actions. Postcard notices of rejection, which have become very common, should be avoided at all costs because they make rejection a matter of public knowledge, especially in smaller communities where postal employees may read them.

No matter which rejection method is used, rejected candidates should be notified as quickly as possible so that they may pursue other employment opportunities. All too often, organizations keep candidates in a state of suspense for an undue amount of time before informing them they will not be hired.

Making a Tentative Job Offer

Once the decision to hire has been made, the candidate is customarily notified by telephone and then sent a letter confirming in writing all of the aspects of the job offer, such as starting date and rate of pay. If the individual is currently employed by another firm, the reporting date must be set far enough in advance so that the person can give his or her current employer sufficient notice of termination—two weeks in most cases, but possibly much longer for high-level professional or managerial positions. Even after this notice, the individual may need some personal time to prepare for the new job, especially if the job requires moving to another city.

The firm itself may also want to delay the date of employment. If the new employee's first assignment upon joining the firm is to attend a particular training school, the organization may request that the person delay joining the firm until perhaps a week before the school begins. This prevents having idle, nonproductive, and possibly bored employees on the payroll.

Because there is no guarantee that the person offered the job will accept, the organization should make sure that it has placed candidates in rank order. If the first candidate declines the offer, the offer can then be extended to the applicant ranked second on the list.

Physical Examinations

One of the final steps in the selecting process is the physical examination. In fact, under current legislation it is advisable to use physical examinations only after a tentative job offer has been made. This examination serves three purposes. First, it screens out individuals who have contagious or communicable diseases that make them unfit for the work to be performed—an applicant for the position of salad chef who has hepatitis or tuberculosis, for example. Second, the examination assists in determining if an applicant is physically capable of performing the work. In the construction industry, where some jobs involve considerable bending, stooping, lifting, and carrying, spinal x-rays are customarily taken to see if the applicant's back is free of defects that might preclude them from performing the job. Third, physical examination information can be used to determine if there are certain physical capabilities that differentiate between successful and less successful performers. Because of the requirements of Title VII and the Americans with Disabilities Act, if a physical quality is specified in the job description, it must be shown to be job-related. The examination is a means of collecting data to make this sort of determination.

Physical examinations are increasingly being used for purposes of drug and alcohol screening, particularly in the federal government and the defense industry. Applicants for positions that require the operation of public vehicles—taxis, buses, trains, trucks, ships, and airplanes—are also required to be screened for drug usage at the time of employment and on a random basis thereafter.[24] The intent of such testing is to eliminate applicants who potentially pose a risk to themselves or to others or who pose a risk to security. Both employers and employees can benefit from drug and alcohol tests because screening for substance abuse generally leads to a safer working environment and higher performance among employees.[25] Drug and alcohol screening has become an issue of major national importance. It is likely that in the near future the majority of private sector organizations in this country will require such testing for all applicants, either as a pre-employment requirement or as a condition of continued employment.

Background Investigations

Although a reference check often provides information to verify certain statements on an employment application or resumé, there are times when it does not. Often, it is necessary to perform a background investigation of the applicant's past employment history. Two key reasons for conducting background investigations are the following: (1) to verify the accuracy of all information provided by the applicant and (2) to uncover derogatory information such as criminal record, bankruptcy, or a suspended driver's license.[26] This investigation may be helpful in determining if past work experience is related to the qualifications needed for the new job. As noted previously, job titles are quite deceptive when attempting to evaluate past work experience.

In the defense industry, background investigations are required if the individual must have a security clearance to perform job duties. This type of investigation is quite thorough and includes checking into the personal life and habits of the person. The federal government also conducts extensive background checks for many of its positions. In addition to defense and government jobs, background testing is also performed for occupations in law enforcement, private security, and nuclear power.[27]

Background investigations have become more important and prevalent because of the increasing number of applicants who misrepresent themselves on their applications and resumés, lying about items such as their criminal history and credentials.[28] One management firm, specializing in background investigation services, estimated that between 7 and 10 percent of job applicants were not what they presented themselves to be, claiming degrees, certifications, and other credentials that they did not possess.[29] Many employers, unfortunately, still accept such misrepresentations even when simple logic might suggest otherwise. For example, in a particular governmental agency, a person reporting directly to the president of that institution claimed to have a certification in employment law even though the person was not an attorney and had, in fact, only attended a five-day seminar open to the general public and received a certificate of completion. The facts, in this instance, should have spoken for themselves inasmuch as one cannot have a legal certification of any kind without first having a law degree and passing a state bar exam. Background investigations are useful in combating this kind of misrepresentation.

Job Offer

After the applicant successfully completes the physical examination and background investigation, the organization finalizes its job offer to the candidate. If the applicant does not pass both of the examinations, the tentative job offer is rescinded and the candidate is not offered employment. Placing the physical examination and background investigation at the end of the selection process protects the organization from charges of discrimination that might arise if physical limitations or other non-job-related items were taken into consideration before the extension of a tentative job offer. In effect, the organization first makes a hiring decision based on the applicant's qualifications and then extends a final job offer after physical limitations or other background factors have been eliminated.

Realistic Job Interviews

Many candidates have unrealistic expectations about a prospective job or employer.[30] These inaccurate perceptions can have negative consequences for an organization if such candidates are hired, such as job dissatisfaction, absenteeism, and turnover. Unrealistic expectations are often created by hiring organizations as they attempt to portray the company and the job in the most favorable light possible. To correct this situation, it is suggested that at some point in the selection process applicants be afforded a realistic preview of both the job and the company. This preview may take place either before or during the employment interview. It is crucial, however, that it occurs before a job offer is made. That way, the applicant has all of the information about the job and the organization that he or she needs to make a quality decision about whether to accept the offer.

A realistic job preview conveys important job and organizational information to an applicant in an unbiased, objective manner. Such a preview requires that an individual is told about the nice things a job has to offer, as well as the unpleasant aspects of that job.[31] Describing negative and positive features allows applicants to develop a more accurate perception of the job and the firm. Research studies indicate that newly hired employees who receive realistic job previews have greater job survival and higher job satisfaction rates.[32] At the same time, this approach does not reduce the flow of qualified applicants. A comparison of the results of traditional job preview procedures with those of realistic job preview procedures is shown in Figure 8.4. Certainly, every organization

Figure 8.4
Comparison of Results: Traditional versus Realistic Job Previews

TRADITIONAL JOB PREVIEW	REALISTIC JOB PREVIEW
1. Job is generally viewed as highly attractive (because only positive information is shared). ↓	1. Job may be viewed as attractive or unattractive (because both positive and negative information is shared). ↓
2. Job expectations are set too high. ↓	2. Job expectations are set more realistically. ↓
3. Rate of job offer acceptance is high. ↓	3. Rate of job offer acceptance is more moderate. ↓
4. Experience on job may not accord with employee's expectations. ↓	4. Experience on job tends to accord with employee's expectations. ↓
5. Employee realizes job is NOT matched to his or her needs. ↓	5. Employee realizes job is matched to his or her needs. ↓
6. Dissatisfaction with job. ↓	6. Satisfaction with job. ↓
7. Low rate of job survival.	7. High rate of job survival.

Source: Adapted from John P. Wanous, "Tell It Like It Is at Realistic Job Previews," *Personnel,* vol. 52(4), July-August, 1975, p. 54.

desires to present itself in a positive manner. However, it should not overemphasize positive aspects nor should it downplay negative features. Realism in describing the employment situation must always be the objective.

NOTES

1. Steffanie L. Wilk and Peter Cappelli, "Understanding the Determinants of Employer Use of Selection Methods," *Personnel Psychology* 56 (2003), 103–124.

2. Daniel B. Turban and Daniel M. Cable, "Firm Reputation and Applicant Pool Characteristics," *Journal of Organizational Behavior* 24 (2003): 733–751.

3. Talya N. Bauer, Donald M. Truxillo, Jennifer S. Tucker, Vaunne Weathers, Marilena Bertolino, Berrin Erdogan, and Michael A. Campion, "Selection in the Information Age: The Impact of Privacy Concerns and Computer Experience on Applicant Reactions," *Journal of Management* 32, no. 5 (2006): 601–621.

4. James Walsh, *Rightful Termination* (Santa Monica, CA: Merritt Publishing, 1994), 311–312.

5. Adapted from http://www.cose.org/PDF/usefulForms/Sample_Employment%20 Application.rtf

6. Joey George and Kent Marett, "The Truth about Lies," *HR Magazine* 49, no. 5 (May 2004), 87–91.

7. Jacqueline Durett, "Redoing Your Resumé? Leave Off the Lies," *Training* 43, no. 12 (December 2006): 9.

8. Adapted from Robert Half, "How to Write (or Read) a Resumé," *Practical Accountant* (May 1981): 63–64.

9. Sarah E. Needleman, "Posting a Job Profile Online? Keep It Polished; Presentation Can Be Critical in Getting Sought Out by Managers and Recruiters," *Wall Street Journal* (Eastern Edition), August 29, 2006, B.7.

10. Stephen P. Robbins and Timothy A. Judge, *Organizational Behavior,* 12th ed. (Upper Saddle River, NJ: Pearson Education, Inc., 2007), 152–153.

11. Herbert G. Heneman III and Timothy A. Judge, *Staffing Organizations,* 5th ed. (Middleton, WI: Mendota House, 2006), 384.

12. Linda Thornburg, "Computer-Assisted Interviewing Shortens Hiring Cycle," *HR Magazine* 43, no. 2 (February 1998): 73–79.

13. J. E. Harvey-Cook and R. J. Taffler, "Biodata in Professional Entry-Level Selection: Statistical Scoring of Common Format Applications," *Journal of Occupational and Organizational Psychology* 73 (2000): 103–118.

14. Wayne F. Cascio, *Applied Psychology in Personnel Management,* 2nd ed. (Reston, VA: Reston Publishing Company, 1982), 192–193.

15. David G. Lawrence, Barbara L. Salsburg, John Dawson, and Zachary D. Fashman, "Design and Use of Weighted Application Blanks," *Personnel Administrator* (March 1982): 47.

16. James H. Browne, Stuart H. Warnock, and Nancy J. Boykin, "Predicting Success of Police Officer Applicants Using Weighted Application Blanks," *Journal of American Academy of Business, Cambridge* 6, no. 1 (March 2005): 26–31.

17. John Neter, Michael H. Kutner, Christopher J. Nachtscheim, and William Wasserman, *Applied Linear Regression Models,* 3rd ed. (Chicago, IL: Irwin, 1996), 3.

18. Lisa McDaniel, "Group Assessments Produce Better Hires," *HR Magazine* 40, no. 5 (May 1995): 73.

19. Wayne F. Cascio and Val Silbey, "Utility of the Assessment Center as a Selection Device," *Journal of Applied Psychology* 64, no. 2 (1979): 107–118.

20. Jane Easter Bahls, "Available upon Request," *HR Magazine* 44, no. 1 (January 1999): 206.

21. Rex M. Edwards and Brian H. Kleiner, "Conducting Effective and Legally Safe Background and Reference Checks," *Managerial Law* 44, no. 1/2 (2002): 136–150.

22. Paul J. Taylor, Karl Pajo, Gordon W. Cheung, and Paul Stringfield, "Dimensionality and Validity of a Structured Telephone Reference Check Procedure," *Personnel Psychology* 57 (2004): 745–772.

23. Adapted from Bruce D. Wonder and Kenneth S. Deleman, "Increasing the Value of Reference Information," *Personnel Administrator* 29, no. 3 (March 1984): 102–103.

24. Mark A. de Bernardo, "Random Alcohol Testing of 7.4 Million Workers Required by 'Final' Transportation Rule," *Legal Report,* Society for Human Resource Management (Fall 1994): 1–6.

25. William F. Current, "Drug Testing: How Both Employers and Employees Benefit," *Occupational Hazards* 64, no. 12 (December 2002): 76–78.

26. Seymour Adler, "Verifying a Job Candidate's Background: The State of Practice in a Vital Human Resources Activity," *Review of Business* (Winter 1993): 3.

27. Herbert G. Heneman III and Timothy A. Judge, *Staffing Organizations,* 5th ed. (Middleton, WI: Mendota House, 2006), 380.

28. Louis Barani, "Background Investigations: How HR Stays on the Cutting Edge," *HR Focus* 70, no. 6 (June 1993): 12.

29. Scott T. Rickard, "Effective Staff Selection," *Personnel Journal* 60, no. 6 (June 1981): 477.

30. John P. Wanous, "Organizational Entry: From Naïve Expectations to Realistic Beliefs," *Journal of Applied Psychology* 61 (1976): 22–29.

31. Wayne F. Cascio, *Managing Human Resources: Productivity, Quality of Work Life, Profits,* 7th ed. (New York: McGraw-Hill Irwin, 2006), 220.

32. Jean M. Phillips, "Effects of Realistic Job Previews on Multiple Organizational Outcomes: A Meta-Analysis," *Academy of Management Journal* 41, no. 6 (1998): 673–690.

9

Selection Tests

Psychological tests are objective, standardized measures of behavior samples. The types of behavior measured may range from general intelligence to interests, from aptitudes to levels of achievement, from personality to eye-hand co-ordination. When used in the selection process, tests measure behavior that indicates which individuals possess the needed skills or qualifications for specific jobs. The extent to which psychological tests are used in the private sector as selection aids is not known; however, it is known that the use of such devices had been declining until the mid-1990s because rigid government standards concerning tests created a situation in which potentially useful instruments had been discarded along with the poor ones. Because of the more recent concern with workplace violence, there is some reason to believe that tests have reemerged as potentially useful selection devices.

Passage of the Civil Rights Act of 1964 and subsequent court interpretations of its provisions initially produced a sharp decline in the use of employment tests. In the landmark *Griggs v. Duke Power Company* decision, as discussed earlier, the Supreme Court ruled that selection tests must show a relationship to job performance. In *Albermarle v. Moody,* the Court again ruled that any test used in selection or promotion decisions must be validated if its use has had an adverse impact on protected classes. Additionally, the *Uniform Guidelines* promulgated standards to which tests must adhere if they are to be considered nondiscriminatory. In the wake of these decisions, many employers, rather than conduct validation studies, dropped selection testing altogether, while others cut back on test usage.

By curtailing use of what are commonly considered tests, some employers apparently felt that their selection procedures would be immune from validation studies or legal challenge. However, as the *Uniform Guidelines* make abundantly clear, *any* selection device, method, or procedure, and not just psychological assessment instruments, is considered a test subject to the same validation requirements as paper-and-pencil tests. While many staffing specialists distrust tests and many organizations are fearful of potential legal implications in the use of employment tests, tests may well be one of the most valid predictors of job success available to managers. Recognition of this fact, coupled with increased awareness of the interview's fallibility and heightened concern with the legal ramifications of hiring individuals with a propensity for violence, has recently produced a resurgence of test usage in the selection process.

Research suggests several things about test usage in the employment arena: (1) tests are more widely used in the public sector than they are in the private sector, (2) large to medium size companies are more likely to use tests than small companies, (3) larger enterprises are more likely to have trained specialists running their testing programs than are other companies, and (4) tests are more apt to be used to fill office and administrative positions than other types of jobs—more than 80 percent of the companies in one survey use them for office and administrative jobs, 20 percent for manufacturing jobs, and only 10 percent for sales and service jobs.[1]

ADVANTAGES OF SELECTION TESTS

Selection tests, used as one of several and not the sole criterion for hiring individuals, are valuable in the overall selection process because their judicious use can assist an employer in making better hiring and placement decisions. Among the advantages claimed for tests are the following:

- *Objectivity*. Test results are not influenced by the test evaluator. Thus, they are not prone to subjective interpretation as are other parts of the selection process such as the interview. The test scores speak for themselves.

- *Cost-effectiveness*. Tests can be an inexpensive way to choose workers and improve organizational productivity. Studies tend to suggest that significant cost savings can result from effective employment testing.

- *Quality of information*. Tests can provide information about individuals that cannot be acquired adequately through other selection devices. Aptitudes, abilities, and skills are not always uncovered by resumes, application blanks, or interviews. On the contrary, they can be misrepresented, faked, or even omitted. Tests offer a method of determining what an individual can really do and whether the person has the necessary qualifications to perform the job successfully.

- *Validity*. Because tests provide quantitative data, they lend themselves more readily to objective statistical validation in terms of job performance than do other selection approaches.

- *Legally defensible*. Where validation studies that establish a demonstrable relationship between test scores and job performance are conducted, the organization has a solid basis for defending any legal challenges to its use of tests. The same cannot be said as easily for other selection methods.

It is important to remember that tests can serve a useful purpose in selection decisions. Their use should not be avoided simply because of certain limitations placed on their role in selection by the courts or federal agencies.

DISADVANTAGES OF SELECTION TESTS

If selection tests were perfect predictors of future job performance, there would be little or no need for interviews, reference checks, and the like. There are, however, definite disadvantages to using selection tests.

- Tests do not measure motivational levels. Successful performance on any job is essentially dependent on two variables: "can do" ability and "will do" ability. The first ability refers to the skills necessary to perform the job, while the second ability refers to the person's willingness to exert the motivation required to get the job done. Tests are more accurate at measuring "can do" than they are at ascertaining "will do." There are numerous examples in almost every organization of individuals who have the ability and potential to succeed in a job, but for some reason never do. Lack of motivation, poor relationships on the job, personal problems, and other factors that are not readily measurable through testing, not lack of ability, account for unwillingness to perform the job at the expected level.

- Tests are more accurate at predicating failures than successes. Studies can establish the minimum level of ability needed to perform a job and indicate that people with less than this level of ability are apt to fail in the job. But, as mentioned above, tests may be totally inadequate measures of who, on an individual basis, will actually succeed in a job.

- Tests are more predictive for groups than they are for specific individuals. Again, this is primarily related to the motivational level of individuals. Of a total group of people taking a test, the test can reveal with some certainty which subgroup is likely to perform well, but it cannot identify which individuals are most likely to perform well.

- Some tests are susceptible to dishonesty. Personality tests, interest inventories, or honesty tests, for example, may not be responded to truthfully. The test taker may answer the questions in such a manner as to convey the impression he or she wants to create or respond in accordance with the answers he or she believes the organization desires. Although some tests have built-in lie detection scales, the problem of faking answers still exists.

- Tests often create anxiety on the part of the test taker. Individuals seeking employment may become more nervous or tense when confronting another hurdle that could eliminate them from further employment consideration. Consequently, test results may not accurately reflect the actual abilities of certain individuals.

- Tests are subject to legal challenge. Perhaps because they are highly visible or because many applicants are suspicious of them, tests are often open to charges of discrimination.

In deciding whether to use selection tests as part of the overall selection process, organizations should carefully weigh the advantages of tests against the disadvantages. Even with the best tests available, errors in predicating job success will be made. Nevertheless, tests may provide additional information that can be used effectively in conjunction with other selection criteria.

CHARACTERISTICS OF PROPERLY DESIGNED TESTS

A well-designed selection test is one that is standardized, objective, based on sufficient normative data, and valid. Tests that do not possess these five characteristics should never be used in the selection process.

Standardization

Standardization refers to the uniformity of the procedures and conditions involved in administering and scoring tests. For the results to be useful, the test should be given to all individuals under conditions that are as similar as possible. Even the physical environment of the testing room should be the same for all test takers. If some individuals take the test in a noisy, drafty, or poorly lit room, while others take it in a quiet, pleasant atmosphere, test results may be distorted. Standardization also means that the same materials must be used each time, the same time limits employed, identical instructions given to the individuals, and so forth. Even the way oral instructions are given and preliminary questions are answered should be identical.[2] Ensuring standardized conditions is the responsibility of the test administrator—a responsibility that requires detailed advance preparation.[3]

Objectivity

Objectivity refers to the scoring of test results. If all persons scoring a given test obtain the same results, the test is said to be objective. The most objective of all employment tests are those that use multiple-choice or true-false answers since the test taker either chooses the correct answer or does not. Scoring, in this instance, is then largely a clerical process that can be performed by individuals with little training. Often, tests of this nature are machine scored or computer scored.

There are some tests—not widely used in the selection process—that are highly subjective as far as their scoring is concerned. The Rorschach "inkblot" test and the Thematic Apperception Test (TAT) are two such subjective instruments open to different interpretations by different scorers. With the Rorschach, the applicant is shown a series of cards containing inkblots of varying sizes, shapes, and colors and asked to offer an explanation of what he or she perceives in the inkblot. Obviously, there can be no uniform scoring here because there are no uniform answers. The scorer has to interpret the applicant's answers. In the TAT, applicants are shown pictures of real-life situations and asked to provide their interpretations of each picture. Again, there are no standardized answers. The scorer utilizes a great deal of judgment in deciphering the responses. The highly subjective nature of these two tests requires trained psychologists as scorers or interpreters, and even so, the psychologists often differ from each other in interpreting the results. Such tests are not looked upon with great favor by EEOC as selection devices and should be avoided in the selection process.

Normative Data

Normative data provide a frame of reference for comparing an applicant's performance on a test with that of a representative group of similar individuals who have previously taken the test. The test performance of the representative or sample group thus becomes the standard or norm by which the scores of future test takers will be evaluated or interpreted. Norms, more specifically, reflect the distribution of many scores obtained from a large sample group.

Typically, the scores from the sample group will be distributed according to a normal probability (bell-shaped) curve with approximately 68.3 percent of the scores falling within one standard deviation of the mean (arithmetic average). Applicants scoring within one standard deviation—a measurement of the dispersion of the data from the sample group—would be considered average relative to the sample population. Applicants scoring outside the range of two standard deviations would be considered to be unlikely performers if the two standard deviations were less than the mean or to be likely high performers if the standard deviations were more than the mean.

Normative data may also be developed by using percentile scores. Percentile scores are expressed in terms of the percentage of the sample group who fall below a specified raw score on the test. A percentile ranking thus indicates the test taker's relative position in terms of the sample group taking the test. Percentile standings are calculated from the bottom up so that the lower the individual's percentile, the lower the person's standing as compared to the sample population; the higher the individual's percentile, the higher the person's standing relative to the group.

Developers of commercially distributed employment tests usually provide employers with detailed normative data since this adds to the usefulness of the instrument as a selection device. Organizations that have sufficient numbers of employees performing similar work may elect to develop their own norms, although this is not usually the case. Where the developers of the test have computed statistically sound norms, these are generally used. In any event, a test must have sufficient normative data for it to be considered a usable selection tool.

Reliability

The reliability of a selection test is the extent to which it provides consistent results.[4] If a person takes the same test several times, his or her actual scores will, of course, vary; this variance is referred to as the standard error, and is a measurement of the extent to which differences in scores are due to chance error. The closer the scores are to each other in repeated takings of the test, the more reliability the test has; the farther apart the scores are, the less reliability the instrument has. If a test has low reliability, its usefulness as a predictor of job success will be questionable inasmuch as the applicant takes the test only once and his or her actual score may not be reflective of actual ability—it may be due entirely to chance error. Reliability of a test is expressed as a coefficient of correlation. Ideally, this coefficient should exceed +0.801 for a test to be considered reliable enough to be used as a selection instrument.

The actual reliability of a particular instrument can be determined in one of three ways: test-retest, equivalent forms, or split-halves.

Test-retest. This method of reliability determination requires giving the test twice to the same group of people and correlating the scores from the two testing instances. A perfect positive correlation would be +1.0, indicating that the instrument is as reliable as possible, statistically speaking. The closer the reliability coefficient is to +1.0, the more consistent the test results are and, therefore, the more useful the test is as a selection method.

There are several problems associated with the test-retest approach: the costs of administering the test twice, the necessity of ensuring that group composition is identical on both occasions, the possibility that test takers may recall test questions if the retest is given too soon after the original test, and the learning that may have taken place between test administrations that could affect the results. Despite these problems, this approach is a sound one for ascertaining reliability.

Equivalent Forms. A second method of determining reliability involves using two tests that are similar but not identical. The scores on each test are then correlated to establish the reliability of the first instrument. While this approach overcomes some of the difficulties associated with test-retest, there is a definite problem of finding or developing two tests that are essentially the same, yet not the same.

Split-Halves. This method examines the reliability of a test by dividing it into two parts and then correlating the results from each half. In its simplest form, odd-numbered items from the test constitute the first half and even-numbered items constitute the second half. The two scores for each person taking the test are then correlated to arrive at a reliability coefficient.

Unmistakably, such an approach can eliminate the problems involved with either test-retest or equivalent forms. The biggest difficulty in split-halves is ensuring that the two halves are equal in content, difficulty, and nature.

Validity

The *sine qua non* of any test, psychological or otherwise, is that it actually measures what it purports to measure. This is referred to as validity. If a selection test does not actually measure ability to perform a job, it is useless as a selection tool and, as stated previously, is vulnerable to successful legal challenge in the courts under existing federal statutes and the *Uniform Guidelines*. Test validity is, has been, and probably always will be, a proper concern of organizations using selection tests. In recent years, because of the emphasis given to employment of women and minorities, greater emphasis has been placed on establishing test validity.

Validity is usually expressed as a correlation coefficient that indicates the relationship between two variables: test scores and actual job performance. A coefficient of 0 would indicate no relationship between the variables, while a coefficient of +1.0 or −1.0 would indicate a perfect relationship—the former a completely positive one and the latter a completely negative one. Certainly, no selection test will ever be 100 percent valid, but organizations using tests should strive for the highest possible coefficient of validity. If a test is designed to be a predictor of job success and validity studies show a high correlation coefficient, an organization can be reasonably assured that applicants who score high on the test are apt to be successful on the job. Valid tests enable an employer to select better qualified, potentially more productive workers.[5]

Employers are not automatically required to validate the selection tests they use. Generally, validation is required only when the instrument used or the selection process as a whole results in adverse impact on a protected class. While validation of selection tests is expensive, it is something that must be done. Otherwise, an organization cannot know whether a test is actually measuring the qualities and abilities that it is supposed to measure.

VALIDATION STUDIES

The *Uniform Guidelines* identifies three methods that may be used to validate selection tests: criterion-related validity studies, content validity studies, or construct validity studies.

Criterion-related Validity

Criterion-related validity indicates the efficacy of a test in predicting an individual's performance in specified situations. Performance on the test is compared with a criterion—an independent measure of what the test is designed to predict. If, for example, a keyboarding test is used, the criterion might be subsequent job performance as a keyboardist in producing quantity or quality of work. A high correlation between the test score and both work volume and work quantity would suggest that the test is valid.

The two basic forms of criterion-related validity are concurrent validity and predictive validity. With concurrent validity, the test scores and the criterion information are collected at basically the same time. Assume, for the sake of illustration, that a company wants to validate a mechanical aptitude test for use in selecting machine operators. The concurrent methodology would entail giving the test to all currently employed machine operators while at the same time collecting information about each operator's job performance. The test scores and job performance criterion would then be correlated to determine the relationship between the two items. If the correlation coefficient is high (that is, workers who score high on the test are the most productive and workers who score low on the test are the least productive), the test would be a valid predictor of job success or performance. If there was little or no relationship between test scores and job performance, the test would not be valid.

A potential problem that could affect the results obtained from this validation procedure comes from changes that may have occurred within the work group before the study was conducted. The less productive employees may already have been terminated because of poor performance while the most productive workers may have been promoted out of the group.

The major difference between concurrent and predictive validity studies is the time interval between administering the test and collecting the criterion data. For example, a particular test might be given to all computer programmers hired, but the test results would not be used in making selection decisions. At a later time, performance data would be collected and correlated with test scores to ascertain whether the employer could predict success on the job from the test scores.

Predictive validity is considered by some to be the soundest method for assessing the validity of a test,[6] but there are problems associated with this approach. First, many organizations do not have the time or the resources to conduct a study that extends over a long period. Second, if legally challenged on the use of a test, a company may have to establish the test's validity very quickly. The longitudinal nature of the predictive validity method precludes obtaining results in a short time span.

Content Validity

Content validation involves the systematic examination and analysis of test content to determine whether the test contains a representative sample of the behaviors, skills, and knowledge required for job performance. The classic example of content validity is a typing test in which an applicant would be required to type samples of the same kinds of items that would be typed on the job.

A content validity study normally involves three steps.[7] First, a thorough job analysis is conducted to identify basic tasks, responsibilities, and skills involved in the job. The relevancy, importance, and frequency of task performance and skill usage are also determined. Second, test items are written or representative "work samples" of the job are developed. Third, test items or work samples are reviewed by individuals familiar with the job to determine if the test items are accurate reflections of job content.

Although content validity is far less statistically oriented than the other two approaches to validity, many human resource practitioners believe it to be a more sensible approach to validation.[8]

Construct Validity

Construct validity is a method used to determine the extent to which a test measures some theoretical construct or trait such as intelligence, mechanical comprehension, or verbal ability. Because it deals with fairly abstract behaviors, "construct validity requires the gradual accumulation of information from a variety of sources." While several different techniques may be used to validate a construct, the complexity of this approach, its time-consuming nature, and the degree of psychometric expertise required make it an infrequently used procedure in the validation of employment tests.

ESTABLISHING CUTOFF SCORES

Once a test has been validated, it is necessary to set an appropriate cutoff score. The cutoff score is that test score below which an applicant will not be accepted. The actual cutoff score used on a particular test may be altered from time to time, depending upon the organization's selection ratio. During periods when there are a great number of applicants applying for jobs, higher cutoff scores will be used because the firm can afford to be more selective in the employees it hires. When there are fewer applicants, the cutoff score may be lowered so that job vacancies can be filled. Regardless of where they are set, cutoff scores should always reflect a reasonable expectation of success on the job.

Establishing cutoff scores is not as easy as it may seem. Validation studies will typically show that some employees who scored low on a test are actually successful on the job while some employees who scored high were unsuccessful in job performance. Figure 9.1 illustrates the nature of the problem. In examining the data presented, it can be seen that successful employees scored between 40 and 60 on the test and unsuccessful employees scored between 25 and 50. It is the area of overlapping scores that produces the difficulty in setting a cutoff score. In this example, several possibilities exist. One, the organization could set the cutoff score at 50, thereby assuring itself that it would be hiring only employees who would be good performers. But, setting the score at this point would also eliminate a sizable percentage of other applicants who are likely to be successful. Two, the organization could set the cutoff at 40—the lower limit for successful employees—but if it did so it would hire many applicants who would be poor performers. Third, the organization could compromise and set the score somewhere between 40 and 50, recognizing that some successful performers will be eliminated by the test and some unsuccessful performers will not. In the illustration it is this third option that has been exercised. With a cutoff score of 45 the majority of unsuccessful employees will be eliminated by the test along with a few successful ones.[9]

Obviously, since no test is a perfect predicator, establishing a cutoff score is a gray area. When tests are used, therefore, they should be used as only one of several selection criteria and not as a sole basis for the selection decision.

Figure 9.1
Cutoff Score for a Validated Test

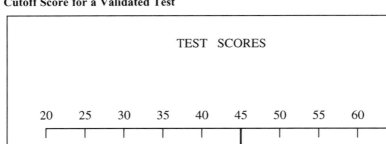

Prior to 1991 it was not unusual to find organizations using different cutoff scores for different protected class groups—a practice referred to as "race norming." The Equal Employment Opportunity Commission, in fact, was supportive of differential test validation (validation for the overall testing population as well as minority subgroups) and the use of adjusted cutoff scores.[10] The Civil Rights Act of 1991 prohibits this practice. It is no longer legal to use cutoff scores based on race, gender, religion, or national origin. In the event that adverse impact occurs, however, "employers of 100 or more employees are required to maintain records to ascertain the validity of tests and their impact on various populations."[11]

TECHNICAL STANDARDS FOR VALIDITY STUDIES

The bulk of the *Uniform Guidelines* consists of the federal government's interpretation of standards for conducting validation studies. According to the

Guidelines, there are certain minimum standards that should be met in performing a validity study. The standards established cover all three accepted procedures: criterion-related, content, and construct validity.[12]

Criterion-related Validity Studies

The following factors apply in conducting criterion-related validation studies.

Technical Feasibility. Employers electing to validate a test by criterion-related procedures should determine if it is technically feasible to do so. For a meaningful study to be conducted there should be: (1) a sample of individuals large enough to achieve findings of statistical significance, (2) a sufficient range of test scores and job performance measures to produce representative results, and (3) unbiased, reliable, and relevant measures of job performance or employee success.

Criterion Measures. The criteria used should represent important work outcomes or behaviors. Typical items that might be used are production rates, error rates, tardiness, absenteeism, and length of service. Other measures may be used where appropriate, including performance in a training program.

Representativeness of the Sample. Whether the validity study is a predictive or concurrent one, the sample should be as representative as possible of the candidates normally available in the relevant labor market for the job or jobs in question. To the extent feasible, the sample should approximate the mix of protected classes normally found in the relevant labor market.

Statistical Relationships. Professionally acceptable statistical procedures must be used to determine the degree of relationship between test scores and criterion measures. A statistically significant relationship is said to exist at the 0.05 level of significance; that is, the relationship is sufficiently high enough to have occurred by chance only once in 20 times.

Operational Use of Selection Procedures. Generally, the greater the correlation between performance on a test and one or more job performance factors, and the greater the number and importance of job performance factors covered by the criteria, the more likely it is that the test will be appropriate for use in selection. While there are no minimum correlation coefficients applicable in all employment situations, low correlations that result in adverse impact will be subject to close review by EEOC. Likewise, reliance on a single test that is related to only one of many job factors will be subject to close scrutiny.

Overstatement of Validity Findings. Reliance upon a few selection procedures or criteria of acceptable job performance when many selection procedures or criteria have been studied may tend to inflate validity findings that result from chance error. To safeguard against this possibility, large samples should be used and cross validation studies should be conducted.

Fairness. When members of a protected class score lower on a test than members of another group, and the difference in scores is not reflected in job performance, use of the instrument is questionable, since protected class members are denied job opportunities. When a test results in adverse impact and the group affected is significantly represented in the relevant labor market, the employer should investigate the situation further if it is technically feasible to do so. If unfairness is demonstrated through showing that members of a particular group perform better or poorer on the job than their scores on the selection test would indicate through comparisons with members of other groups, the employer may either revise or replace the test or continue to use it with appropriate revisions in its use to ensure greater compatibility between the probability of successful job performance and the probability of being selected.

Content Validity Studies

The eight factors that should be applied in conducting content validity studies are described below.

Appropriateness. A test can be supported by a content validity procedure to the extent that the test is a representative sample of job content. The content validity approach is not appropriate for validating tests that measure traits or constructs such as personality, intelligence, aptitude, etc. Nor is it a proper procedure when the test involves skills, abilities, or knowledge that the employee will be expected to acquire on the job.

Job Analysis. A job analysis should always be conducted to identify important work behaviors and their relative importance to the job. If the behavior results in a work product, the analysis should include this product. Any behaviors selected for measurement should be critical behaviors that constitute the bulk of the job.

Development of Selection Procedures. A test designed to measure work behavior may be developed from job analysis or may have previously been developed by the employer, by other users, or by a test publisher.

Standards for Demonstrating Content Validity. To establish the content validity of a test, the employer should show that the behaviors of the job in question or the test itself provide a representative sample of actual job behaviors or work products. When a test measures knowledge, skill, or ability, the item being measured should be operationally defined. Knowledge is that body of learned information that is used in and is a necessary prerequisite for job performance. Skill or ability relates to observable aspects of work behavior or job performance. Any test that measures knowledge, skill, or ability should be a representative sample of what is used in the job and is a necessary prerequisite to performance of the work entailed in the job.

Reliability. Wherever possible, statistical estimates of the reliability of the job content test should be made.

Prior Training or Experience. Requirements for prior training or experience should be justified on the basis of the relationship between the content of the training and experience and the actual content of the job for which such training or experience is required.

Operational Use. A selection test that is supported on the basis of content validity may be used if it represents critical work behaviors that constitute most of the important parts of a job.

Ranking Based on Content Validity Studies. If an employer can show that a higher score on a content-valid test is likely to result in better job performance, the results of the test may be used to rank individuals who score above minimally acceptable levels. Where a test supported solely or primarily by content validity is used to rank job applicants, the test should measure those aspects of performance that differentiate among the various levels of job performance.

Construct Validity Studies

When a test is validated by construct validity procedures the following factors should apply.

Appropriateness. Construct validity is a more complex method than the other two forms of validation. Moreover, it is a relatively new procedure in the employment field. Efforts to obtain sufficient empirical support for such studies are extensive and arduous tasks involving a series of research studies that may utilize both criterion-related and content validity studies. Particular care should be taken in utilizing this method because of the lack of research supporting its use in the selection process.

Job Analysis. Job analysis is absolutely essential when construct validity is used. The analysis should show the work behavior required for successful job performance, the critical or important work behaviors in the job, and an identification of the construct or constructs believed to underlie these critical or important work behaviors. Each construct should be named and clearly defined.

Relationship to the Job. A selection test should be identified or developed that measures the construct believed to be crucial to successful performance of the job. The relationship between the construct and job performance should be supported by empirical evidence.

Use of Construct Validity Study without New Criterion-Related Evidence. Federal agencies will accept a claim of construct validity without a criterion-related study only when the selection test has been used elsewhere in a situation where a criterion-related study has been conducted and its use lends itself to the test and situation at hand. If construct validity is to be generalized to other jobs or groups of jobs not included in the original criterion-related study, additional empirical research evidence is expected.

As the preceding standards for test validation indicate, the *Uniform Guidelines* require rather stringent, methodical procedures for validating tests. While these requirements may seem burdensome, time-consuming, and expensive, they are necessary to ensure the fair, nondiscriminatory usage of selection instruments.

TYPES OF PSYCHOLOGICAL TESTS

Psychological testing is basically concerned with identifying and measuring differences among individuals. Five differences that are important in the employment setting, because they relate to success or failure on the job, are cognitive abilities, psychomotor abilities, job knowledge, interests, and personality. Over the years, various tests have been developed to measure these differences.[13]

Cognitive Aptitude Tests

Cognitive aptitude or ability is a person's capacity to learn or to perform a job that has been previously learned. Tests that measure this characteristic are most often used in the selection of employees who have had little or no job experience. Aptitudes or abilities may be broken down into many factors, but the ones that are most often job-related are verbal, numerical, perceptual, spatial, and reasoning.

Verbal Ability. Verbal aptitude refers to an individual's ability to use words in thinking and communication. Managerial, technical, and sales positions are jobs for which verbal ability is crucial. Conversely, it is relatively unimportant for manual or operative level production jobs. Measurement of a person's ability in this area is usually accomplished by a vocabulary test.

Numerical Ability. Numerical aptitude is the ability to perform the basic arithmetic functions of adding, subtracting, multiplying, and dividing. These abilities are essential in engineering, accounting, and similar jobs.

Perceptual Speed. This is the ability to identify rapidly, accurately, and in detail similarities and differences. Tests that measure this aptitude typically utilize pairs of numbers and names. The test taker must make a quick comparison and indicate if a pair is identical or not. Perceptual speed is most likely to be used to ascertain clerical aptitude.

Spatial Ability. This ability is concerned with visualizing objects in space and determining their relationship to each other. Jobs that may require this aptitude include design engineer, tool and die maker, aviation mechanic, and assembler.

Reasoning Ability. Reasoning is the ability to analyze items or facts and make correct judgments based on the logical implications of the items or facts given. Reasoning ability may be measured relative to very concrete things or it may be measured relative to abstract concepts. Because of its relationship to decision-making and conceptualization, this aptitude is critical for executive, managerial, or sales jobs.

General Intelligence. Intelligence refers to an individual's overall mental abilities. Tests used in this area attempt to arrive at some global estimate of a person's intellectual performance or aptitude. Normally, they provide a single score such as an IQ (Intelligence Quotient). Although general intelligence tests have been in existence for many years and have been widely used in selection in the past, their use as employment devices is highly questionable today for several reasons. First, intelligence consists of a number of separate abilities that do not lend themselves to the development of a single composite score. Second,

EEOC regards intelligence tests with great disfavor since they tend to adversely impact certain protected classes. Third, intelligence tests often contain items that are unrelated to successful job performance. Consequently, if an organization chooses to use an intelligence test, it should proceed with great caution, making absolutely certain that the test has been validated in terms of job relatedness and job performance.

Psychomotor Abilities

Psychomotor abilities refer to strength, dexterity, coordination, and other aspects of physical performance. Tests that measure these abilities are very important for selecting the most appropriate employees for some jobs. In the electronics industry, for example, workers may assemble components so small that the operation has to be performed under a high-powered magnifying glass using very delicate instruments. Particular psychomotor abilities are crucial to performance of this kind of work.

There are a number of abilities that may be measured in the psychomotor area. Finger dexterity is the ability to make precise, skillful, coordinated manipulations of small objects by using one's fingers. Manual dexterity refers to the ability to make skillful, coordinated, well-directed movements of the hands and arms. Wrist-finger speed is the ability to make rapid movements such as the ones involved in tapping. Aiming is the ability to move the hands and fingers rapidly, accurately, and successfully from one location to another. Arm-hand steadiness is the ability to make precise positioning movements where strength and speed are minimized. Reaction time is the speed with which an individual can respond to a stimulus when it appears.

Job Knowledge Tests

Job knowledge tests measure an applicant's level of understanding of the duties and responsibilities of the position for which he or she is applying. While there are commercially available tests, a test for any specific organizational job can be designed based on the data gathered from an in-depth job analysis. These tests may require written responses or they may be administered orally. Normally, these tests are short, consisting of a limited number of key questions that readily distinguish experienced applicants from less experienced ones. A primary advantage of the job knowledge test is that it is by definition job related inasmuch as it is based on a specific job.

Work Sample Tests

A work sample test is one in which the applicant completes a task or series of tasks that are representative of or actually a part of the job for which the person is applying. Mentioned earlier in this chapter was the example of a keyboarding test. This is probably the most commonly used of all work samples.

Evidence suggests that work sample tests can produce high predictive validities and reduce adverse impact. Moreover, they tend to be more acceptable to applicants than other forms of testing. There are, however, problems associated with work samples. First, it may not be feasible, if operation of a large piece of equipment is involved, to have the machine available in the human resource department so that the applicant can demonstrate proficiency in operating it. Second, assuming that the person is taken to the shop floor to demonstrate ability to operate a machine, there is the potential risk of damage to the equipment or injury to the individual if the applicant, in fact, does not know how to operate the equipment. Third, work sample tests do not lend themselves readily to group administration. Rather, they have to be given individually and are thus more expensive than tests that can be given to a group.

Vocational Interest Tests

Interest tests are designed to measure the degree of interest a person has in various occupations. Theoretically, the higher the level of interest, the more likely the individual would be to succeed in that field of endeavor. Most of these tests determine occupational interest by comparing the test taker's scores with those of a representative sample of people already in particular jobs.

Interests should not be confused with aptitudes or abilities. It is very possible that a person may have a high interest in a given career field yet lack the basic abilities to perform will in that field. Consequently, interest measures should always be used in conjunction with aptitude and ability tests.

Test dishonesty can be a major problem in using interest tests because answers can be faked to display a high degree of affinity for whatever position is under consideration. While it is possible that interest tests may have some application in employee selection, their primary use is in career counseling and vocational guidance.

Personality Tests

Personality tests have extremely limited use as selection devices. These tests are often low in both reliability and validity. Inasmuch as some personality instruments require a subjective interpretation, when they are used the services of a trained psychologist or psychometrician are needed. There are questions, too, about the job relatedness of personality tests. Considerably more research on these instruments is needed before they can be used with confidence as selection criteria. For now, their use in selection should be avoided.

ESTABLISHING A TESTING PROGRAM

The first step in establishing a selection testing program is, of course, job analysis. Through analyzing, examining, and carefully studying the jobs in an organization, data can be developed that indicate the behaviors and abilities needed for successful performance on a specific job or a group of similar jobs. After this has been accomplished, the proper test or tests can be either developed by the organization or selected from those already commercially available.

There are advantages and disadvantages to developing organization-specific tests as well as to using tests that have already been developed. Perhaps the biggest advantage of using an available test is cost. Test development is expensive; thus, from a cost standpoint, an organization may find it more economical to buy a test than to attempt to develop one. Also, if a firm has an immediate need to begin testing applicants, there may simply be insufficient time to develop a test because development is usually a lengthy process. On the other hand, it is possible that an existing test that has been demonstrated to be valid for one organization may not be valid for another. Several factors may account for this phenomenon: the jobs in one company may be subtly different from those in another firm; jobs that have the same title in two organizations may be entirely different; or applicants from different regions of the country may possess different characteristics and motivations.

While historically it has been held that test validity must be established on a situation-specific basis and that a test validated for one location may not be valid in another, a new concept is emerging. This development stems from the *Uniform Guidelines,* wherein methods necessary to generalize validity results from one set of jobs to the similar jobs are explained. Court decisions have further embraced the concept of validity transportability. For example, in *Pegues v. Mississippi State Employment Service* (31 FEP 257), the plaintiff questioned the use of aptitude tests that had not been validated for the particular set of tasks, location, and applicant population involved. The court found in favor of the organization and held that generalized validity evidence was acceptable.

Developing Selection Tests

In preparing a new selection test, a human resource specialist—normally a psychologist trained in tests and measurements—must develop appropriate items (questions) from job analysis data. Once the test has been prepared, its validity for a specific purpose must be determined. In validating the instrument, the designer conducts an item-by-item analysis to determine how well each item distinguishes between those individuals who scored high on the overall test and those who scored low. A test question that is perfectly valid is one that was answered correctly by all those scoring high on the total test and was incorrectly answered by all those scoring low. Only items that have a high validity correlation coefficient would be included in the final version of the test.

Another question that must be addressed by the test designer is the difficulty level of each question. If test questions are too easy, most individuals taking the test will score high; if the questions are too difficult, most test takers will score low. In either case, it would be hard to distinguish between extreme and moderate ability levels on the basis of the test results. Thus, establishing the appropriate level of difficulty is a major challenge for the designer.

In continuing the validation study, the previously discussed procedures for ascertaining reliability and validity would be used.

Selecting an Existing Test

Thousands of tests are commercially available for use in selecting employees. In fact, about 300 publishers in the United States distribute printed tests of various kinds. Needless to say, not all of the tests offered for sale have been properly developed or validated. Some are worthless at best.

In searching for appropriate selection tests, one of the most important sources of information is the series of *Mental Measurements Yearbooks* edited by Oscar Buros. Each of the periodically published *Yearbooks* describes tests published during a specific span of time, thus supplementing each of the earlier volumes. Almost all of the commercially available psychological, educational, and vocational tests printed in English are included in this series. Information on publisher, price, usage, as well as critical reviews by test specialists are included for each test. Any tests not discussed in the *Yearbooks* should be approached with a good deal of skepticism.

Because all tests are not reliable or valid, caution must be exercised in choosing proper instruments. Staffing specialists play an important role in this area by assisting organizations in identifying tests that provide a sound basis for making selection decisions.

THE REEMERGENCE OF PERSONALITY TESTING IN EMPLOYEE SELECTION

In today's world where online dating services promise to locate the perfect mate through the use of personality tests, it is reasonable for employers to expect that they too could locate the perfect employee through personality testing. According to one survey, 30 percent of all companies, including some large and well-known ones, subject their applicants to some sort of personality test.[14] According to another survey, 41 of the *Fortune* 100 companies use some form of psychological testing. In short, personality testing has made a comeback in the contemporary American workplace despite admonitions by EEOC and legal concerns voiced by others.

Why has personality testing reemerged so strongly in the employee selection process? There seem to be four reasons behind the increased use of personality testing today: (1) companies want to improve their selection of appropriate candidates, (2) employers want to prevent negligent hiring, (3) companies seek to avoid economic loss resulting from hiring of employees who engage in theft and fraudulent activities, and (4) companies view personality testing as a means of team development.

Unless EEOC takes a stronger position on the use of personality tests in employee selection and backs this position with stronger enforcement efforts, the increasingly widespread use of personality testing will undoubtedly continue to be a trend in human resource selection.

NOTES

1. "Ability Tests: They Can Provide Useful Information About the Probability of an Applicant's Performing Successfully on the Job," *Across the Board* (July/August 1982): 27.

2. Anne Anastasi, *Psychological Testing,* 5th ed. (New York: Macmillan Publishing Co., 1982), 32–36.

3. Ibid.

4. Robert M. Guion and Scott Highhouse, *Essentials of Personnel Assessment and Selctions* (Mahwah, NJ: Lawrence Erlbaum Associates, 2006), 133–134.

5. Ibid., 142–143.

6. Richard D. Arvey, *Fairness in Selecting Employees* (Reading, MA: Addison-Wesley Publishing Company, 1979), 31.

7. Ibid., 34.

8. R. Wayne Mondy and Robert M. Noe III, *Human Resource Management,* 5th ed. (Boston: Allyn and Bacon, 1993), 223.

9. Guion and Highhouse, *Essentials of Personnel Assessment and Selection,* 251–254.

10. Dawn D. Bennett-Alexander and Laura B. Pincus, *Employment Law for Business* (Chicago: Richard D. Irwin, Inc., 1995), 393.

11. Ibid.

12. *Uniform Guidelines on Employee Selection Procedures,* sections 1607.5–1607.14.

13. George Bohlander and Scott Snell, *Managing Human Resources,* 14th ed. (Mason, OH: Thomson South-Western, 2007), 263–266.

14. Morrison & Foerster, *Personality Tests: Proceed with Caution,* http://www.mofo.com/news/updates/bulletins/bulletin02182.html, 2006.

10

Employment Interviewing

The most basic selection tool, used by virtually every organization for filling every job opening, is the employment interview. The interview is a significant step in the selection process because it is the point at which a decision will be made concerning an applicant's suitability for a particular position. Applicants who reach this stage are obviously viable candidates; they have survived the screening interview, scored satisfactorily on selection tests, and fared well on reference or background checks. Consequently, candidates reaching the employment interview appear to be qualified, at least on paper. Every experienced manager knows, however, that appearances can be deceiving. It is by means of the interview that additional information is gathered to determine if the candidate can actually perform the work of the job, is willing to exert the effort necessary for successful performance, and can adapt to the environment of the job and the company.

THE EMPLOYMENT INTERVIEW DEFINED

The employment interview is a directed, goal-oriented discussion in which the interviewer and the applicant exchange relevant information so that both parties can make an intelligent decision about a job opening. The interviewer's purpose in this interactive process is to determine if the applicant is right for the position and the company. The applicant's purpose is essentially the same except that it is highly personal.

The employment interview has three general objectives. The first is to obtain additional, specific information from applicants so that their suitability for a particular position can be meaningfully evaluated. Resumés, employment applications, test results, and other similar devices provide, at best, only a sketchy profile of an applicant. The interview extracts more detailed information, clarifies particular points, and educes additional facts about the applicant.

The second general objective of the interview is to give the applicant information about the job, the company, coworkers, benefits, and other relevant matters. This information should be conveyed in a truthful manner wherein both positive and negative aspects are shared with the candidate.

The third objective of the interview is to create a positive feeling toward the prospective employer, regardless of the outcome of the interview. If the applicant leaves the interview with a negative impression of the organization, he or she is unlikely to consider the company for any future employment opportunities. Moreover, the individual may be adversely influenced as a consumer of the firm's products or services or may be totally unwilling to refer other applicants to the organization.

Clearly, the interview must be carefully planned and conducted if it is to fulfill its objectives effectively.

RESPONSIBILITY FOR THE EMPLOYMENT INTERVIEW

The employment interview is typically conducted by the supervisor or manager for whom the applicant will be working. Other managers may also participate depending upon the level of the position to be filled. For some types of clerical or entry-level production jobs, it is not unusual for the human resource manager or a staffing specialist to handle the interview and actually make the hiring decision.

For professional and managerial positions, multiple interviews are generally the rule. These interviews may include the immediate supervisor, the next higher manager, and possibly other managers as well. Because professionals and managers frequently interface across departmental or organizational lines, the viewpoints of several managers may be desired to ensure a more objective decision about the candidate. While the opinions of all interviewers involved are important, the judgment of the manager for whom the applicant is to work will likely carry the greatest weight in the final selection decision.

Although the immediate supervisor may have primary responsibility for the employment interview, the human resource department is typically responsible for developing and monitoring the interview process. A key concern is that interviews be conducted in a consistent manner throughout the organization and adhere to the legal requirements imposed on interviewing.

LEGAL IMPLICATIONS OF INTERVIEWING

As mentioned in the preceding chapter, following the Supreme Court decision in *Griggs v. Duke Power Company,* many employers abandoned the use of selection tests altogether and relied almost exclusively upon employment interviews. This abrupt switch in personnel practices occurred primarily because of the false assumption that the court decision requiring validation of tests applied only to paper-and-pencil tests and not to other selection devises. But, as pointed out in Chapter 4, under the *Uniform Guidelines on Employee Selection Procedures,* a test encompasses "any measure, combination of measures, or procedure used as a basis for any employment decision." [1]

Today an increasing number of employers are utilizing employment testing once again in order to improve the selection process and select the right employees who will make positive contributions to the business. "In a recent survey by the American Management Association forty-four percent of the respondents reported the use of testing to select employees." [2] Cognitive ability tests are the most frequently used form of testing in the workplace. However, personality tests, as previously discussed, are being used more often to determine during the interview if the individual possesses the right characteristics, behavior, and personal traits that is necessary to succeed in the position.

Although Title VII does not prohibit employers from using employment or personality tests in the workplace, legal problems can arise when an employment test discriminates against one or more protected classes and when tests are not job related and have an adverse impact on protected classes. There have not been any cases to date that have found an employer's use of a personality test to cause disparate treatment to protected classes. However, if the employer utilizes employment tests to intentionally exclude members of a protected class, then legal implications would apply. In order for legal action to occur, evidence would have to substantiate that "members of a protected class were treated differently than the majority." [3] For example, for a telephone operator position, it would be illegal for an employer to test minority applicants on how well they can articulate words or phrases (being that they have an accent), but not the majority applicants.

There is no question that the interview is definitely a test. It is subject to the same validation requirements as any other test or step in the selection process should adverse impact on a protected class be shown. For the interview, the matter of validation presents special difficulties. Few firms are willing to pay the cost or put forth the effort necessary for validating their interviews. Interviews can only be validated by a follow-up method that requires collecting data over a fairly long period of time. For any test to withstand legal challenge, it must also be reliable; that is, it must measure what it purports to measure. This is also a problem area for employment interviews inasmuch as significant evidence exists to indicate that if two managers in a firm interview the same applicant at different times, the outcomes will differ.

Human resource professionals also play a very important role in analyzing the selection procedures of the company. They must constantly ensure that all procedures are reliable, valid, legal, and cost-effective due to the fact that there is potential for a discriminatory suit to occur regarding a selection decision. In order for selection criteria to be reliable and turn out effective nondiscriminatory results, it must be consistent.

Perfect reliability is difficult to achieve due to interviewer biases, unrelated interview questions, etc. One way to improve reliability among those involved in the selection decision is through training. Training will provide each decision maker with the tools he or she needs to be consistent with properly seeing the selection process through. The interview and selection process must also be valid in order to ensure effective nondiscriminatory results. "Validity measures the degree to which the conclusions drawn from an interview or a test are accurate." [4] If the interview accurately measures job-related factors identified that are needed for successful job performance, then the interview is most likely valid.

The interview is perhaps more open to potential charges of direct discrimination than any other tool used in selection, although few court cases have been concerned solely with the employment interview. In the majority of instances, there is little or no documentation of the questions asked or the answers received. There is, since most interviews take place in a private one-on-one setting, little or no organizational control over the type of questions the interviewer may pose to an applicant. Some interviewers may ask totally irrelevant questions; others may ask blatantly discriminatory ones. Some interviewers are inclined to ask questions that are not job related but that reflect their personal biases, believing that this practice will remain free of criticism or challenge since there is no documentation of what occurred in the interview.

The legal risks associated with employment interviewing are real; consequently, it is imperative that anyone conducting interviews knows what can and cannot be asked in an interview. Table 10.1 at the end of this chapter shows the types of questions that should be avoided in conducting a nondiscriminatory employment interview.

Although some organizations have tried, the give-and-take nature of the interview does not realistically permit the formulation of a completely standardized list of questions that can be asked of each prospective employee. No effective interview can be subjected to such rigidity, nor does any existing federal equal employment opportunity legislation or guidelines require it. Observance of the spirit of the law in interviewing is more important than imposition of a mechanistic list of questions from which an interviewer cannot deviate.

PLANNING FOR THE INTERVIEW

Planning is absolutely essential for conducting effective employment interviews. As a prerequisite to planning the interview, the interviewer must have a basic understanding of the job for which an applicant is applying, knowledge of the company and the environment in which the candidate may be working, and an insight into human behavior.

Assuming the interviewer has the necessary background information, the first step in planning is to develop a set of specific objectives to be accomplished during the interview. These objectives involve the information that must be obtained from the applicant and the information that must be provided to the applicant.

Because of the time constraints typically imposed on an interview, the interviewer must have a specific idea of what questions to ask and what information to furnish. By clarifying in his or her own mind the objectives of the interview, the interviewer is more likely to conduct an effective interview and make efficient use of the time available.

During the interview process the interviewer plays a major role in the candidate's impression of the company.[5] The interviewer's presence, attitude, and character play a major role in the likelihood of a candidate accepting or declining a job offer.

In order to produce a candidate's favorable impression on a company, the company and every employee involved in the interview process must genuinely care about attracting highly skilled and talented employees. The challenge then is to display this care throughout the interview itself. The first impression a candidate will receive of a company is the very first point of contact made, which in many cases is a telephone call when the candidate is being invited to come in for an interview. When a candidate knows what to expect of the interview before setting foot in the facility, he or she will feel more prepared, relaxed, and comfortable about the entire process because he or she knows what to expect. Each candidate should be furnished an itinerary in advance, detailing what will occur during the interview process. At the start of each interview the interviewer should build rapport and ask "warm-up" questions to put the candidate at ease. By doing these things the candidate will most likely develop a favorable impression of the company from the start.

In order to make sure a favorable impression lasts throughout the interview process, the interviewer must have a solid understanding of the major duties of the job and the human qualifications necessary for successful job performance. The interviewer must explain how this position will play an important role in the success of the company. The interviewer should obtain a copy of the job description and the accompanying job specifications and familiarize himself or herself with both duties and qualifications. The interviewer should understand thoroughly such items as job content, education, experience requirements, and personal characteristics required. Each interview should also be structured to some extent and tailored to the specific job to be filled.

Additionally, the interviewer must review the applicant's resume (if one has been provided), employment application, test scores, reference checks, and so on in order to have a general indication of the individual's qualifications and background. This review frequently provides an indication of the candidate's potential interest in the position as well as areas to be probed in determining the person's potential for performing the job satisfactorily.

Another planning concern is the physical location in which the interview will take place. Ideally, the interview should be conducted in a place that ensures privacy, is relatively quiet, and is free from disruptions of any kind. (The primary disrupting factor in many interviews is the telephone; thus, interviewers must make certain that they will not be required to answer any telephone calls during the interview.) While the physical environment need not be plush—an impossibility in many organizations—it should at least be comfortable enough to alleviate as much anxiety as possible on the part of the interviewee.

The importance of sound planning cannot be overemphasized. The interview must be a well-planned event, not just a casual happening. The candidates themselves will always have expectations and questions prepared prior to the interview. These questions should always be answered, and if for some reason the interviewer does not know the answer to the question he or she should find out before the candidate leaves. You should never let the candidate leave with unanswered questions.

INTERVIEW TYPES

Interviews may be classified by the degree to which they are structured. At one end of the spectrum are those that are highly structured, with practically every question and the precise order in which it is to be asked specified in advance. At the other end of the spectrum is the completely nonstructured interview where questions are posed as they occur to the interviewer. In actual practice, most interviews fall somewhere between these two extremes, but with tendencies toward one side or the other. Regardless of which approach is used, the interview must always gather three basic types of information from the applicant: ability to perform the job, motivation to stay on the job, and adaptability to the job situation and organizational environment. Obviously, the structured interview is much more likely to secure this information than the nonstructured interview.

Some interviewers may oppose the structured interview because they feel it restricts their freedom to ask questions or explore areas that might be of personal, although not job-related, interest. The nonstructured interview, on the other hand, poses a risk for the organization: where there is no structure the wrong questions may be asked, including those that expose the organization to discrimination charges. Consequently, a total lack of structure in the interview is not recommended. There is, however, a middle ground between structure and nonstructure that allows the interviewer some freedom as to the types of questions that may be asked and the order in which they may be posed: the nondirective interview. In the following paragraphs this type of interview will be described as will the structured interview.

The Nondirective Interview

This interview is comprehensive in nature and may cover a broad range of topics. Probing, open-ended questions are one of its main features. The responsibility of the interviewer is to keep the applicant talking as much as possible. The assumption is that as the applicant responds to open-ended questions, he or she is likely to reveal information that might not otherwise be elicited. Typical questions used in this interview format include:

- Tell me something about yourself.
- Why do you want to leave your present job?
- What do you consider to be some of your most important accomplishments?
- What are your primary strengths?
- What are your primary weaknesses?
- What contribution do you feel you can make to this organization?
- Describe the best boss you ever had. What do you think made this person a good boss?
- Describe the worst boss you ever had. What do you think made this person a bad boss?
- What do you consider to be your most significant contribution to your last employer?
- Where do you see yourself five years from now?
- What are some other things I should know about you?

As these questions suggest, the intent of the nondirective interview is to get applicants to reveal as much about themselves as possible. Often, the answers to the questions are not as important as the way in which the questions are answered and the thought processes utilized in formulating responses.

Because of the nature of the questions used, the nondirective interview is generally much more time-consuming than a more structured approach. Yet, some interviewers believe it is extremely effective in obtaining significant information. For this type of interview to be really effective, however, a highly trained and skilled interviewer is required.

The results of the nondirective interview may be difficult to summarize objectively. Different candidates respond in different ways to the questions asked. The appraisal of candidates may, therefore, be highly subjective in nature. The verbally facile candidate is likely to receive a higher evaluation than the candidate who has trouble expressing himself well, even though the latter may be more qualified for the job than the former.

Research conducted on traditional selection interviews, such as the nondirective, indicates that they have low reliability and little or no validity.

The Structured Interview

Generally, most interviews are somewhere between being unstructured and structured. An unstructured interview has no structure and no outline of questions, is conversational, and typically leads to non-job-related conversation. For example, the interviewer might create conversation by asking the applicant if she has children. Though the interviewer might not mean to discriminate, if the female interview candidate has children, it could be construed that the company did discriminate on the basis of sex if she is not selected for the position. Also, unstructured interviews are essentially unplanned and never follow the same format for each candidate. They generally differ greatly due to the types of questions asked. This produces unreliable results that decisions will be based on.

Structured interviews are preplanned and typically follow a set outline. The outline always includes only questions that are job-related.[6] A structured interview consistently asks each candidate the same questions. Then candidate responses are scored in order to compare to other interview candidates who are asked the same questions. Consistent findings regarding employment interview research over the past 30 years prove that structuring the interview increases both validity, reliability, practicality, and usefulness. Structured interviews also eliminate bias because all applicants are asked the same job-related questions. This type of interview style can help defend the company should the company encounter a discrimination charge.[7]

Though structured interviews seem to be the most beneficial in order to get the most out of an interview, there has to be some degree of ambiguity to the interview. This unstructured aspect of the interview should include probing questions to answers the interviewee provides. This will allow the interviewer to clearly understand the candidate's answers and elude more information regarding his or her past work experience and behaviors exuded within work-related situations.

The structured interview consists of a series of job-related questions—with predetermined acceptable answers—that are consistently asked of each applicant for a particular job. It is believed that this kind of interview increases reliability and accuracy by reducing the subjectivity and inconsistency present in more traditional interview approaches. The advantages of structure are diminished, however, if the interviewer asks each of the questions in a perfunctory manner. The structured interview, too, may easily result in an overly formal or cold atmosphere that severely impedes the candidate's ability or desire to respond.

A structured interview typically contains four types of questions: situational, job knowledge, job simulation, and worker requirements.

Situational questions pose a hypothetical job situation to determine what the applicant would do in a particular situation. For example, "If the main valve on the hydro-impulse regulator malfunctioned, what action would you take to correct the problem?" Theoretically, questions of this kind provide information on the applicant's ability to recognize and deal with problems that might actually occur on the job.

Job knowledge questions assess the applicant's grasp of requisite background knowledge for performing a job. These questions may be related to basic educational skills or complex scientific or managerial skills. For instance, "How do you determine the radius of a circle?"

Job simulation questions may require the applicant to actually perform a sample task from the job such as demonstrating how to operate a machine or typing samples of letters. When physical performance of activities is not feasible, some other kind of simulation of critical job aspects may be used.

Worker requirements questions seek to determine the applicant's willingness to conform to the requirements of the job. The applicant may be asked, for example, about his or her willingness to perform repetitive work, travel extensively, relocate, work weekends, and so forth. These questions, centering as they often do on the negative aspects of the job, are attempts to ascertain some idea of the applicant's motivational level and tolerance for adverse job aspects. They also serve as realistic previews of the job and afford the candidate the opportunity to evaluate whether he or she really wants the job.

A properly designed structured interview contains only those questions that are job-related. Each question is asked for a specific purpose.

INTERVIEW METHODS

Several different methods may be used for conducting employment interviews. These range from the traditional one-on-one method to the controversial stress method, each of which has certain advantages and disadvantages. The choice of method is usually contingent upon the specific job to be filled, its level in the organization, and the preferences of those conducting the interviews.

One-on-One Interviews

By far the most widely used interview method is the one-on-one approach where applicant and interviewer meet in private. Since the interview itself is often a highly emotional experience for the job applicant, this interview method is probably the least threatening one that can be used. The disadvantage of this method, unless a series of interviews is incorporated into the selection procedure, is that evaluation of the candidate is the responsibility of a single interviewer.

Behavior-Based Interviews

Behavior-based interviewing, a recent approach to interviewing, has been defined as, "A thorough, planned, systematic way to gather and evaluate information about what candidates have done in the past to show how they would handle future situations." [8] The key assumption is that past behavior is the best predictor of future behavior. One can assume that a person who has previously behaved a particular way to resolve a problem or to address some type of work-related situation will repeat that same type of behavior when a similar situation occurs. The role of the interviewer is to identify which specific behaviors are necessary or critical to successful job performance based on an analysis of the job. Then the interviewer should develop questions from the key competencies that ask for examples of how the candidate has exuded these behaviors. For example, if the job required the ability to multitask, then the interviewer would want to ask a question relating to a time that the candidate has had to multitask in a previous job. Interviewers should listen carefully to candidate responses and evaluate which candidate exhibited behaviors previously identified during the job analysis as being the most critical to successfully performing the job.

Behavioral-based questions might be phrased as follows:

• Think of an occasion when you. . .

- Can you give me an example of. . . ?
  - What needed to be done about that situation?
  - What was the outcome?
- Tell me about a time when you. . . ?
- What did you do when. . . ?

For the most part behavioral-based interviews are effective, accurate, easy to use, consistent, fair, job related, legal, and, if used correctly, they decrease the likelihood for discrimination charges. On the other hand, because each job is unique, management must determine what specific behaviors are associated with each position's success, which can be time-consuming. Therefore the behavioral-based interview is best used when many people are needed to fill the same position.

Group Interviews

Unlike one-on-one interviews, a group interview consists of several applicants interacting in the presence of one or more company representatives. This method may provide useful insights into the candidates' interpersonal competence as they engage in group discussion. An advantage of this approach is that it saves time for the interviewer since several applicants can be evaluated at once. Two major disadvantages are as follows: (1) the interview is hard to control (the candidates may, in fact, take charge of the interview and prevent the interviewer from getting to really pertinent questions and issues) and (2) the situation may be highly threatening to the candidates since they know they are competing with each other for a job opening. The group interview is best used in conjunction with, and not to the exclusion of, other methods. Also, it is normally suited only for those jobs where a great deal of interpersonal actions are involved.

Panel Interviews

In a panel interview, one candidate is questioned by several interviewers sitting as a board. This approach allows for a thorough examination of the applicant in that several interviewers are more likely to cover all significant areas than is a single interviewer. On the other hand, the panel may be very intimidating or threatening to the interviewee. Also, this type of interview may be time-consuming and costly since several company representatives are tied up at the same time. In actual practice, the panel method is usually reserved for higher level positions or for positions where the applicant would have to interact frequently on the job with members of the panel.

Stress Interviews

While most interviews attempt to alleviate discomfort and threat for the applicant, the stress interview intentionally creates a relatively stressful—sometimes hostile—environment for the candidate. The main purpose of a stress interview is to determine how well the candidate can handle and respond to a stressful situation encountered on the job. This type of interview typically operates opposite of the traditional one-on-one interviews because they may include criticism of the candidate, unclear instructions, intentional silence, and confrontations. Some examples include:

- "Your experience level cannot possibly enable you to perform well in this job."
- "Your personality doesn't seem to be a fit for this type of position."
- "Your response doesn't make any sense."
- "Why would we even want to choose you?"

Advocates of this method point to the fact that many jobs involve dealing with stressful situations and that it is better to discover how a person will react to an unfavorable environment before that person is placed in the job. For example, some companies subject applicants for sales positions to stress interviews that attempt to simulate actual job conditions. In the first interview the exchange of information may progress very smoothly. The candidate is led to believe that practically all he or she has to do is come back for the second interview and a job offer will be made. However, on the second interview the candidate might be kept waiting in an outer office for a considerable period of time before the interview begins—a tactic that may cause the individual's anxiety level to increase. Once the interview begins, the interviewer may open the conversation by very curtly stating, "Mr. Hargett, I appreciate your time and interest, but I don't feel there is any need for further discussion. It's obvious that your qualifications just don't match our current needs." The purpose of this approach is to test the applicant's reaction to a totally unexpected situation. Some interviewers believe that candidates who are able to turn such a situation around are likely to become good sales representatives inasmuch as this is a common situation in sales work.

Does the stress interview actually achieve what it is supposed to achieve? Research suggests that it does not. The information exchanged in a stress situation can be distorted and misinterpreted—hardly the type of information upon which to base a selection decision. Moreover, the stress interview is apt to create ill will on the part of job applicants, even those who may be hired. Bad feelings about the company and the way it treats applicants may impede recruiting efforts as candidates share this information with outsiders. Consequently, it seems clear that the stress interview is completely inappropriate for the vast majority of situations.

CONTENT OF THE INTERVIEW

Specific content of an employment interview varies greatly by organization and level of the job concerned. However, the following general topics are the ones most commonly covered: work experience, educational background, interpersonal skills, career orientation, and personal qualities. Because of the potentiality of discrimination, the interviewer should deal only with information in these categories that is job related.

Work Experience

Exploring an individual's previous work experience provides an indication of the applicant's skills, abilities, and willingness to handle the duties and responsibilities of the position for which the person is applying. Although good performance in one job does not guarantee good performance in the next job, it is an indication of the applicant's capabilities.

Areas of work experience that should be explored in the interview in the form of open-ended questions include:

- The degree to which previous work experiences are similar to the requirements of the open position.
- Any qualifications or skills acquired in previous jobs that will be important to successful performance in the new job.
- Level of performance and significant accomplishments in previous positions.
- The situation and organizational context in which experience was gained and the relevance of this background to the organization and work climate of the prospective employer.
- Ability of the candidate to transfer, generalize, and capitalize on earlier work experiences as the individual has progressed through his or her career.

Questions relative to previous work experience are the most important ones to ask in an interview. In hiring a person an organization is, in reality, buying skills, abilities, talents, and knowledge; consequently, a complete, probing investigation of previous experience is essential to determine if the applicant possesses what the organization actually needs. Moreover, questions relating to work experience are the safest questions (that is, nondiscriminatory) that can be asked.

Educational Background

Although an applicant's educational record is usually shown on the employment application or resume, a mere listing of schools attended or courses taken does not provide much assistance in making effective hiring decisions. It is the interviewer's responsibility to pursue a line of questioning that will uncover the relevance of the candidate's educational background for the position under consideration. Some useful questions to ask would include the following:

- Summarize your educational background for me.
- How has this background prepared you for the position for which you are applying?

- In college, what were your favorite courses? Why did you like these courses best?
- In college, what courses did you dislike? Why did you dislike these courses?
- What was your major field of study? Why did you choose that field?
- How would you compare your academic performance with other students at your school?
- Since graduating from college, what other education or training have you been involved in? How does this education or training relate to the job you are seeking?
- What are your future educational or training plans?

Note that the general thrust of the preceding questions is toward obtaining the applicant's assessment of the relevance of his or her education and training to the position under consideration. A secondary thrust is toward identifying the applicant's interests and motivation. Having a degree in business, engineering, or computer science does not mean that that is the area of the applicant's real interests. Nor does a degree in a particular field mean that the applicant has acquired the skills and knowledge necessary for successful job performance.

Interpersonal Skills

The main reason for job failure is not technical skill failure; it is the lack of appropriately utilizing one's interpersonal skills. Interpersonal skills support our ability to create, maintain, and manage relationships as well as communicate appropriately in a variety of situations.

Within the workplace today there is a large need for effective and adaptable communication skills. However, questions regarding communication competence during candidate interviews are often not asked. In order to avoid the high cost of turnover, an employer must hire the candidate with the right set of communication skills for the particular job. The majority of jobs these days require some sort of relationship building, which in order to do so requires strong communication and interpersonal skills. Relationships with other coworkers, customers, and whomever else applicable are very important in how effective the employee will be at carrying out his or her professional responsibilities. In order to determine how well the applicant can relate to and work with others, questions should be asked in regards to interpersonal skills such as stated below.

- What would your last manager/supervisor say about you?
- What would your previous/current coworkers say about you?
- Tell me about how you like to be managed.
- Tell me about the most effective manager you have had and why.
- Describe the strengths you possess that could be applied to this job/position. Describe the weaknesses you possess that might affect this job/position.
- Describe your work ethic. Explain what "work ethic" means to you.

- What kind of people do you find it most difficult to work with? Why?
- How do you handle a situation where you have to deal with a person very different from yourself and it becomes difficult?
- Describe a difficult time you have had dealing with an employee, customer, or coworker. Why was it difficult? How did you handle it? What was the outcome?
- What do you do when others criticize, resist, or reject your ideas or actions?
- Give me an example of how you have reacted in a stressful situation.
- When you have entered a new workplace in the past, describe how you have gone about meeting and developing relationships with your new coworkers, supervisors, and reporting staff?
- What are some of the major factors that influence your ability to get along with others?
- Describe the kinds of people you get along with most effectively.
- Describe the kinds of people who irritate you the most.
- Do you feel that you work best in group or one-on-one situations? Why?

This line of questioning should be pursued carefully, however, because it may lead into areas where charges of discrimination could arise.

Career Orientation

Questions about a candidate's career objectives may aid the interviewer in determining the degree to which an applicant's aspirations are realistic. Hiring an applicant with unrealistic expectations usually results in fairly rapid dissatisfaction with the organization and increases employee turnover. Some useful questions in this area are the following:

- Where do you see yourself in this company in the next two years? Five years?
- What do you consider to be your ultimate career objective?
- What kinds of things might you like to do in future jobs?
- What kinds of things might you like to avoid in future jobs?
- What are you doing now to prepare yourself for future positions?
- Assuming that your progress in this organization is not as rapid as you might desire, what would you be most likely to do?

In addition to determining that applicant's career goals, the interviewer should present an honest, accurate description of advancement and career prospects in the organization. Complete honesty is essential on this point. The candidate should not be led to believe that opportunities exist where they, in fact, do not. Deception is counterproductive in that when the truth unfolds the applicant is certain to become dissatisfied with the organization and is more likely to leave. If so, the firm has lost a substantial investment in the individual's recruitment, selection, and training.

CONDUCTING THE INTERVIEW

Job interviews can be a very stressful experience for the candidate. In order to alleviate the tension, the interviewer can apply the following tips, which can help make the interview as successful as possible:

- Make the applicant feel at ease. The interviewer should always introduce himself or herself at the start of the interview. The interviewer should make sure to use the candidate's name often. Forgetting the candidate's name can make a bad impression and give the candidate the impression that the interviewer is really not listening to the interview.
- Establish rapport. Take a few moments to establish rapport or "break the ice" by asking the applicant how his or her trip to the company was, etc.
- Make the applicant aware of what you do and how your job relates to the position for which he or she is interviewing. After the "ice breaker" conversation, the interviewer should explain his or her position and how it relates to the job in question.
- Give the applicant some key facts about the organization. The interviewer should give the candidate information about the company, but should not spend an inordinate amount of time doing so. Most companies have a Web site loaded with company information that can be given to the applicant.

After doing these things, the interviewer should attempt to learn as much job-related information as possible about the candidate. Since much surface data on the candidate are already available on the employment application or resumé, the interviewer's task is to seek additional information, gather explanations of experience and background, and fill in gaps. A critical mistake that some interviewers make is to ask questions that have already been answered on the application or resumé. For example, "I see you attended Elon College" or "Your last job was with Henson and Bedges, wasn't it?" or "You have a degree in horticulture, don't you?" Spending time on such matters does not generate any new information helpful to the interviewer in making an assessment of the candidate and should be avoided. Moreover, it may be annoying to the interviewee.[9]

During the interview, questions should initially be general in nature. Then, as the interview progresses, the questions should become more specific. Using the previously suggested interview content as a basis, it is appropriate for an interview to proceed along the following lines:

1. Discussion of work experience
2. Exploration of educational background
3. Examination of interpersonal skills
4. Discussion of career orientation
5. Examination of personal qualities
6. Description of the job and the company
7. Answering of questions from applicant

While it is not absolutely essential that strict adherence to this sequence be observed, all of these topics should be covered in the interview. Observing the suggested progression will introduce structure into the interview and keep it from going off on tangents.

When the necessary information has been obtained and the applicant's questions have been answered, the interview should be brought to a conclusion. At this point, the applicant should be told when and how he or she will receive notification of the company's decision. An inconclusive response such as, "We will be contacting you at a later date," should definitely be avoided. It is far more preferable to say, "We are interviewing two other candidates for this position. We will call you next Tuesday to let you know of our decision." The organization should not keep the candidate hanging nor should it run the risk of hurting its reputation by being ambiguous about when an employment decision will be made.

After each interview, the interviewer should prepare a written assessment of the candidate. This assessment need not be elaborate but should reflect the interviewer's evaluation of the applicant's work experience, educational background, interpersonal skills, career orientation, personal qualities, and overall impression. Many organizations use an evaluation form similar to the one shown in Figure 10.1. Use of an appraisal form helps ensure that all interviewers are evaluating on the same criteria. Furthermore, it documents the reasons for making employment decisions—a practice that is important should claims of discrimination arise.

POTENTIAL PROBLEMS IN INTERVIEWING

As possibly the most imperfect process in human resource management, employment interviewing contains a number of potential problems or pitfalls, especially for the untrained interviewer. It is critically important, therefore, for any interviewer to be fully aware of these potential problems so that they can be handled satisfactorily.

Lack of Goals

An axiom in management says that clearly stated goals are essential if meaningful activity is to take place. The requirement for goals or objectives is no less essential for the interviewing process. Goals for the selection interview are tied to both the job to be filled and the qualifications of the applicants being considered. It is unfortunate, but often true, that individuals are selected on the basis of whim, with less consideration for specifications (skills, abilities, and knowledge) than is typically given for the acquisition of a personal computer or other type of nonhuman asset.

To conduct an interview effectively, the interviewer must have a good understanding of the duties and responsibilities of the job to be filled and the human qualifications necessary for satisfactory job performance. The goal of the

Figure 10.1
Applicant Evaluation Form

APPLICANT _____   INTERVIEWER _____

POSITION _____   DATE _____

FACTOR	COMMENTS		RATING
	FAVORABLE	UNFAVORABLE	
EXPERIENCE			1 2 3 4 5
EDUCATION			1 2 3 4 5
INTERPERSONAL SKILLS			1 2 3 4 5
CAREER ORIENTATION			1 2 3 4 5
PERSONAL QUALITIES			1 2 3 4 5
OVERALL EVALUATION			1 2 3 4 5

interview is, quite simply, to find the best qualified person to perform the job. But unless the interviewer understands the job and the qualifications needed, it is unlikely that an effective match between job and individual will be made. The information needed to establish clear-cut goals for the interview can be obtained from the job description and the job specifications for the position to be filled.

Premature Judgments

When interviewing job applicants, first impressions and bias can take over a person's feelings and attitudes towards a candidate. "As many as four out of five hiring decisions are made within the first 10 minutes of an interview, according to some studies." [10] These quickly made decisions are typically based on the applicant's look, stereotype, or a preconceived notion about a particular candidate or type of candidate. The first impressions of interviews have the ability to delineate the entire interview. In the case of a good impression the interviewer may anticipate high-quality answers from the candidate. Similarly, in the case of a bad first impression a candidate's responses may be deemed on a much less favorable basis, which can ultimately drive the final selection decision away from them. The interviewer must remember to focus on job-related criteria and that first impressions are simply that: a first impression. Thus, a more appropriate approach is to deliberately suppress one's first impression, objectively collect the needed information, analyze this information, and then make a final evaluation.

Interviewer Domination

When interviewers dominate the conversation, the collection of job-related information about the candidate is severely hindered. In an effective employment interview, the applicant should be permitted to talk about 75 percent of the time. This probably does not happen in the vast majority of interviews. Since the objective of the employment interview is to acquire sufficient information for making an informed selection decision, when the interviewer dominates the conversation this objective cannot be met. The interviewer's primary responsibilities are to pose questions and gather information from the applicant, not to do all of the talking.

Inconsequential or Trivial Questions

Without a somewhat structured approach or specific goals for an interview, the interviewer is likely to succumb to asking questions that have little or no bearing on the position to be filled. These questions may be asked because the interviewer does not know what to ask or they may be asked simply to kill time. Inconsequential or trivial questions are risky because they frequently lead into discussions of areas where the potential for discrimination exists. For example, "Tell me about your family," is inconsequential because it is not job related; it is potentially discriminatory because it may lead to a discussion of national origin, religious preference, or a subset of sex such as number of children or marital status.

Halo/Horns Error

This is a type of bias that is manifested when an interviewer is overly impressed (halo effect) or overly repulsed (horns effect) by one or more personal characteristics of the applicant and allows this bias to unduly affect his or her opinion of the candidate. An interviewer who places a high value on neatness and conservatism in dress, for example, may automatically favor candidates who rate high in this area and just as automatically underrate those who do not meet his or her standards of dress—regardless of skills, abilities, or other job-related factors. As with other forms of bias, the interviewer must recognize its existence and make a conscious effort to withhold judgment about the applicant until sufficient information has been collected.

Contrast Effects

A contrast effect is an error in judgment that occurs when an interviewer meets with one or more poor or marginally qualified candidates and then interviews a candidate who, without benefit of comparison with the previous applicants, would be considered only fair in skills and abilities. By comparison, however, the last applicant may appear to the interviewer as a "superstar" because previous applicants have been so poorly qualified. Realistic, objective, written evaluations of candidates are crucial for combating this kind of error.

Stereotyping

Stereotyping is another form of interviewer bias. It usually occurs when the interviewer has a preconceived notion of the ideal candidate. Some interviewers may believe, for example, that women or minorities are not qualified to handle executive or professional positions because they do not fit the interviewer's preconceived idea of the ideal candidate—a white male. Some interviewers still think of women or minorities as being more suited for secretarial, clerical, or menial jobs. While actions taken on stereotyped views are illogical and clearly illegal, they do occur, and as a result interfere with the selection of qualified candidates.

Lack of Interviewer Training

Lack of interview training can and most likely will constitute for wasted time and money because the right information is not secured. Bias and personal judgments become decision-making factors, reliability and validity of the interview process are merely nonexistent, and poor decisions are made. Lack of interview training also puts the company at risk for asking illegal questions unintentionally. Typically, without interview training goals are not set for the interview. Lack of interview training also reflects negatively on the candidate. He will be able to detect that the person who is interviewing him is unprepared and unknowledgeable of the interview process. When poor decisions are made due to the lack of proper interview training, the following can occur:

- Lawsuits from negligent hiring
- Turnover (created by hiring employees with the wrong skill set or those whom the overall fit with the company did not exist)
- Poor morale on the part of good employees because they have to work with an unqualified person
- Time and energy taken away from managers required to handle performance problems, which also distracts the department and/or team.

Also, the lack of interview training hurts the accept rate due to the fact that the interviewer is not trained on how to appropriately "sell" the candidate on the job, company culture, location, and benefits.

Behavior Sample

At best, an employment interview is a very small sample of an applicant's behavior. Moreover, the candidate's behavior during the interview is seldom typical or natural due to the stress or anxiety of the situation. Unfortunately, this problem will always exist in interviews. It is incumbent upon interviewers to recognize that they are dealing with behavior samples. Emphasis should be placed on gathering factual information; even then the sample may be too small to make a totally accurate evaluation.

Interpretation of Behavior

An extension of the previous problem is that of assessing the behavior that is observed in the interview. If an applicant fidgets constantly or continually shifts his position in the chair during the interview, how should this behavior be interpreted? As a sign of anxiety? As tension? Or as an indication that the applicant is afraid that something will slip out that he does not want known? If the applicant slouches in a chair and casually answers questions without much elaboration, should this be viewed as a sign of disinterest? No one, including the experts in interviewing, has satisfactorily solved the problem of interpretation. Because the interview is an unnatural situation for the applicant, it is probably best for the interviewer to withhold judgment on these kinds of behaviors and concentrate on evaluating the candidate's qualifications.

Inappropriate and Illegal Questions

Before the passage of Title VII, there were essentially no restrictions on employment interviewing. Employers could legally request any kind of information on an applicant. Today, as a result of Title VII of the Civil Rights Act and in an effort to reduce the potential for discrimination in hiring there are many legal restrictions interviewers must be aware of when interviewing.

Inappropriate and illegal questions are quite easy to stumble upon asking in an interview setting, but with proper preparation and knowledge the interviewer can effectively obtain the necessary information from the candidate without crossing legal boundaries. In order to accomplish an effective interview, one must start with a job description, which includes specifics about the job requirements and expectations. During the interview, interviewers should avoid all personal information and the protected characteristics such as race, color, national origin, religion, or sex and just focus on job-related questions, which should relate to the job description. Specifically questions that should not be asked are those that are not job related or not directly related to whether or not the applicant can do the job. Basically all information requested should be job related. This is as true for the interview as it is for any other selection device or procedure.

Table 10.1 shows the kinds of questions that should be avoided. Careful examination of the table will show that each of these questions is not job related.

Table 10.1
Selected Questions to Avoid in Interviewing

Question	Discriminatory Potential
Have you ever been arrested?	Race; National Origin
Did you receive an honorable discharge from the armed services?	Race; National Origin
Have your wages ever been garnished?	Race; National Origin
What is your credit rating?	Race; National Origin
Do you own a car?	Race; National Origin
Do you have a telephone?	Race; National Origin
Do you have a high school diploma?	Race; National Origin
Do you have a current driver's license?	Race; National Origin
Do you own your home?	Race; National Origin
Have you ever been refused a surety bond?	Race; National Origin
To what social organizations, clubs, or societies do you belong?	Race; National Origin; Religion
Do you have relatives from a foreign country?	National Origin
How did you learn to speak Spanish, Polish, etc.?	National Origin
Where were you born?	National Origin
What is your native language?	National Origin
What is the nationality of your parents?	National Origin
Do you attend religious services on Saturday or Sunday?	Religion
Do you attend church regularly?	Religion
Are you married?	Sex
How many children do you have?	Sex
What are the ages of your children?	Sex
Do you plan to have any more children?	Sex
How reliable are your arrangements for child care?	Sex
Are you pregnant?	Sex
Do you prefer to be addressed as Ms. or Mrs.?	Sex
Where does your spouse work?	Sex
What is your maiden name?	Sex
How does your husband or wife feel about you being away from home overnight?	Sex
How old are you?	Age
What is your date of birth?	Age
When did you graduate from high school? From college?	Age
Are you disabled in any way?	Disability
Do you have any physical defects?	Disability
What is the general status of your health?	Disability
What is your corrected vision?	Disability
Would you need a reasonable accommodation to perform this job?	Disability
How many days were you ill last year?	Disability
Have you ever filed for worker's compensation?	Disability
What medications are you currently taking?	Disability
Does stress affect your ability to be productive?	Disability

THE IMPORTANCE OF LISTENING

The main goal of an interview is to learn as much as possible about the candidate in order to have an adequate amount of reliable information to make an effective hiring decision. In order to retrieve this information, the interviewer must engage in careful listening.

During the interview, every moment the interviewer spends talking is lost evaluation time. Other than providing the necessary information about the job, the department, and the organization, the interviewer must limit talking to answering the applicant's questions. An effective interview should follow the eighty-twenty rule, which says the interviewer should spend 20 percent of the time asking questions or talking and 80 percent of the time listening to the candidate's responses. In order to effectively listen, the interviewer must plan the questions he or she will ask in advance of the interview. This allows the interviewer to dedicate the majority of his or her time to listening rather than to thinking about what questions he or she is going to ask next.[11]

The interviewer must learn to listen empathically and attempt to put himself or herself in the applicant's place so that what is being said can be more readily understood. Empathic listening requires that the listener put aside his or her own biases and frames of reference. While all transmissions from the applicant must ultimately be evaluated, the evaluation should not be made prematurely but should be delayed until the entire message has been received and a sincere effort has been made to fully comprehend what the applicant has said. Some helpful guidelines for the interviewer are the following:

- *Allow sufficient time.* The specific amount of time allotted to an interview will vary depending upon, primarily, the level of the position to be filled. Lower level positions may require only a half-hour or less while executive level positions may require several hours or more. The point to remember is that an interview should never be rushed because the quality and quantity of information gathered will suffer if the interviewer hurries through the interview.

- *Remove distractions.* Noise, interruptions, or physical discomfort create difficulties for both interviewee and interviewer and interfere with the effective two-way exchange of information. Take steps to ensure privacy and a distraction-free environment. By all means make certain that the interview is not interrupted by the telephone or drop-in visitors.

- *Be patient.* People do not always answer questions as directly as we might like. Do not attempt to finish the other person's sentence; allow the person to express himself or herself in his or her own way; do not try to fill in those moments of dead silence that may occur in an interview (in fact, it is often in these moments of silence that significant information is discovered as the interviewee rushes to eliminate the silence and the accompanying awkwardness).

- *Listen with the proper attitude.* Show the person that you are interested in listening to what is being said. Look at the person. Concentrate on what you are hearing. Keep an open mind and do not overreact to what is being said. Reassure the person through positive body language such as the use of head nods. Restate what has been said to make sure that it has been completely understood.

- *Empathize with the interviewee.* Try to put yourself in the interviewee's position. Recognize that the person may be tense or anxious. Empathizing helps the interviewer understand more clearly what is being said; proper understanding is definitely crucial to effective interviewing.

- *Avoid argument and criticism.* Arguing and criticizing puts the candidate on the defensive and often leads to a complete cessation in the flow of information. Let the person talk, even if it is obvious that what is being said is incorrect. Evaluation comes after the interview, not during.

- *Guard against your biases.* Even the most experienced interviewers have biases. The way an interviewer feels about certain individuals, groups of people, attire, physical appearance, grooming, etc., can affect what happens in the interview. It is important to recognize biases and take steps to prevent them from prejudicing the results of the interview.

- *Question effectively.* Use the types of questions previously mentioned in this chapter as effective ones. Avoid questions such as those listed in Table 10.1. Do not "grill" the candidate with question after question in staccato fashion. Always allow time for sufficient responses between questions.

Also, during the interview few notes should be taken. Taking notes while interviewing can make the applicant feel uneasy and distracted because he or she will become concerned with what is being written down. Taking notes while a candidate is speaking also reduces the listening capacity of the interviewer. While it may be difficult to remember everything that was said during the interview without taking a lot of notes, "capturing single key words to recall what was said" will help the interviewer remember important conversations after the conclusion of the interview. After the interview is the time when the interviewer can take more elaborate notes that might be helpful to him in the future.

MAKING THE HIRING DECISION

Once the candidates for a position have all been interviewed, a hiring decision must be made as to which candidate is the best for the job and the organization. Hiring decisions are critical to an organization's success because they are among the most important business decisions employers will ever make. A bad hiring decision can lead to damaging consequences. Managers must determine whether the candidate is able to do the job effectively and whether he or she possesses the experience, education, and other factors that fit the needs of the position.

Things to take into consideration when making the hiring decision are the following:

1. Work history and experience
2. Skills and knowledge

3. Education record
4. Logical problem solving capability
5. Communication skills
6. Commitment to level and motivation to perform the job at the organization

Hiring the right person is a difficult task. The one cardinal rule in making a hiring decision is this: if there is *any* doubt about the candidate's ability to perform or if there is *any* doubt about the candidate's motivation to perform, do not hire that person.[12] Doubts about a candidate too often become self-fulfilling prophesies.

THE NEED FOR INTERVIEWER TRAINING

Because of the importance of interviewing in the selection process as well as the potential legal ramifications involved, it is imperative that organizations provide sufficient training in interviewing for managers who must perform this vital task. For small organizations, training can be provided through various public seminars that are available. Large organizations may wish to consider offering their own in-house programs due to the numbers of people who need to be trained. The following list shows the kinds of topics that should be included in an employment interviewing training program:

- Overview of the Interviewing Process
- Definition and Purpose of the Employment Interview
- Preparing for the Interview: Establishing Objectives
- Establishing and Maintaining Rapport
- Structuring and Controlling the Interview
- Methods for Obtaining Information: Questioning Techniques
- Methods for Obtaining Information: Listening Techniques
- Note Taking
- Closing the Interview
- Interpretation of Interview Data
- Problems to Avoid in Interviewing
- Practice Exercises in Interviewing
- Legal Issues in Interviewing

NOTES

1. James G. Goodale, "The Neglected Art of Interviewing," *Supervisory Management* (July 1981): 27.
2. David J. Shaffer and Ronald A. Schmidt, "Personality Testing in Employment," *SHRM LEGAL REPORT* (September-October 1999), last reviewed June 2006.

3. Ibid.

4. Leslie A. Weatherly, "Reliability and Validity of Selection Tests," SHRM Employee Testing Series Part I, June 2005.

5. Elliot D. Pursell, Michael A. Campion, and Sarah R. Gaylord, "Structured Interviewing: Avoiding Selection Problems," *Personnel Journal* (November 1980): 908.

6. Noël Smith, "Using Structured Interviews to Increase your Organizations Hiring Requirements," *SHRM* (October 2006).

7. Ryan Olson and Chris Wright, "Structured Interviews: Step-by-Step Guide to Getting a Return on Your Investment in the Selection Process," *SHRM* (October 2006).

8. Roger D. Sommer, "Behavioral Interviewing," *SHRM* (January 1998), reviewed May 2002.

9. Douglas B. Richardson, "A Simple Guide to Help You Gain a More Effective Style," *Career Journal,* 2003.

10. Laura Gassner Otting, "Put Substance Before Style during Hiring Interviews," *SHRM* (Spring 2004).

11. "Don't Overlook Communication Competence," *Nursing Management* (March 2007): 12.

12. T. L. Stanley, "Hire the Right Person," *SuperVision* (July 2007): 10.

11

Performance Appraisal

Individuals working in an organization perform at varying levels of proficiency. Some use their skills, energy, and time effectively and efficiently. Others do not. Some display an abundance of initiative and seek opportunities for additional responsibilities. Others do not. Decision making in many areas of human resource management depends upon management's ability not only to recognize such differences in individual performance, but also to measure them accurately. This is the task of performance appraisal.

Performance appraisal is by no means a simple task, yet it is a crucial one. Decisions made in this area affect other parts of the human resource management system, as well as the organization itself. Compensation, promotion, career development, job design, selection criteria, and training are some of the areas directly influenced by the appraisal process. Consequently, a sound, effective approach to determining how well employees are performing their jobs is essential to organizations of all types and sizes.

PERFORMANCE APPRAISAL DEFINED

Performance appraisal may be defined as "an on-going, systematic evaluation of how well an individual is carrying out the duties and responsibilities of his or her current job. Additionally, it typically includes an assessment of the individual's need or potential for further development." [1]

Four key terms in this definition merit further consideration because they indicate the nature of an effective approach to assessing employee performance. These terms are the following: (1) ongoing, (2) systematic, (3) evaluation, and (4) development.

Performance appraisal has traditionally been viewed as a task that is done once a year when a supervisor or manager completes an employee evaluation form. This practice of annual evaluation is a strong norm in many organizations.[2] However, in order to be a more effective practice in organizations, performance appraisal should be an *ongoing* activity, spanning the entire year. Several organizations are starting to use "more frequent, streamlined performance reviews" in order to help improve the performance of their employees.[3] Monitoring and assessing the efforts expended and the results produced by employees should be done on a daily, weekly, and monthly basis, if it is to be accomplished effectively. The culmination of this continuous process is the completion of a written report or form. The completion of the formal document, however, is not performance appraisal. Rather, it is a recapitulation of the many individual evaluations of how an employee has carried out the duties and responsibilities of his or her job over the entire period covered by the report. In fact, if it were not for the continuous evaluations made of performance, the formal report could not be completed accurately.

Performance appraisal is, or should be, *systematic* in nature. It should be a logical, objective assessment of how well an employee has performed a job. Several researchers have proposed a variety of models to help practitioners conduct performance appraisals in a more systematic fashion.[4] Effective performance appraisal depends upon well-defined standards of accomplishment that are measured in accordance with a systematic approach that eliminates—or severely reduces—subjectivity. Job standards are the yardsticks by which job accomplishments are measured; a consistent methodology for comparing accomplishments with standards establishes the system necessary for accurate, effective performance appraisal.

Performance appraisal is an *evaluation.* In the case of performance appraisal, the amount and quality of work actually accomplished by an employee is evaluated. Measurements are critical to evaluation. Without measurements and standards, accurate evaluation cannot take place; there can only be guesses, subjective opinions, and estimations.

Finally, performance appraisal, if it is to be fully effective as an internal staffing tool, must include a *development* aspect. The focus of development is twofold: (1) identifying current needs for employee growth and improvement on the present job and (2) identifying employee potential for promotion to positions of higher responsibility. The developmental aspect of performance appraisal looks at what the employee has done and seeks to determine what he or she needs to be able to do to perform the job better. It also seeks to determine how the employee could be better utilized to his or her own personal advantage, as well as to the organization's benefit. When used as a developmental tool, performance appraisal can help an organization successfully achieve its strategic objectives. Performance planning and evaluation systems are growing in popularity and are used to create a link between formal appraisal and the company's strategies.[5]

Performance appraisal, in essence, has a bidirectional focus. It objectively evaluates what has been accomplished by the employee in the past and then looks to the future by describing individual developmental needs.

USES OF PERFORMANCE APPRAISAL

Unfortunately, most managers—and employees—have a very restricted view of performance appraisal, visualizing it as merely the means whereby increases in compensation are awarded. However, performance appraisal, used to its fullest extent, is much more than a wage and salary administration device. One study identified 20 uses of performance appraisals. In addition to wage and salary administration, the researchers examined some of these other uses:

- Promotion Decisions
- Retention/Termination Decisions
- Identifying Individual Training Needs
- Providing Performance Feedback
- Determining Transfers and Assignments
- Identifying Individual Strengths and Weaknesses
- Assisting in Goal Identification
- Evaluation of the Personnel Systems
- Identifying Organizational Development Needs
- Criteria for Validation Research
- Meeting of Legal Requirements[6]

Relating these uses of performance appraisal to the staffing process, it is apparent that performance appraisal yields data valuable for decision making in such staffing activities as human resources planning, recruiting, selecting, career planning and development, and human resource administration.

Human Resource Planning

To accurately assess an organization's internal supply of human resources for planning purposes, data must be available that describe the profitability and potential of all employees, especially high-level professionals and managers. An effective performance appraisal system is one means by which these data are derived. A well-designed appraisal system provides a profile of an organization in terms of the strengths, weaknesses, and potentialities of its current work force. Studies have shown that the information derived from a performance appraisal has a large impact on the identification of employee strengths and weaknesses.[7] Knowing the strengths and weaknesses of your current work force can help you to more strategically fill your future personnel needs.[8]

Recruiting

Performance evaluations can provide information that may be used to improve an organization's recruiting efforts. For example, an analysis of high performing employees or managers may reveal that the majority of these high performers tended to receive their training at particular schools and major in certain disciplines, and were recruited from the same sources. Such tendencies and patterns identified in the appraisal information could certainly influence a firm's approach to recruiting. The firm could concentrate more of its efforts on the sources and approaches that have proven to yield higher performing employees in the past.

Selecting

Performance appraisal is crucial to validating the use of certain selection standards. Validation requires the identification of successful and unsuccessful performers and a correlation between success on the job and the selection standard or test used. An accurate performance appraisal system is essential not only for identifying successful and unsuccessful performance but also for establishing a reliable database to make the required correlations. If the performance appraisal system is inaccurate, attempts to validate selection devices will fail.

Career Planning and Development

Whether viewed from an individual or an organizational perspective, effective career planning and development is heavily dependent upon performance appraisal information. Managers need information concerning the strengths, weaknesses, and potentialities of their subordinates in order to counsel and assist them in developing and implementing their career plans. Likewise, employees need the information provided by performance appraisal to make personal decisions about their own career aspirations.

Human Resource Administration

Performance appraisal data are used as the basis for making a number of administrative decisions in an organization. Decisions concerning promotions, transfers, demotions, terminations, and layoffs are frequently based on performance appraisals.[9]

Promotions. While an individual's performance in one position is not necessarily an accurate predictor of success in a position of greater responsibility, it is a useful indicator that is widely used. Through performance appraisal, an employee's ability to successfully handle particular types of tasks is identified, as are other kinds of skills. This *track record* gives an organization a reasonable basis for making promotion decisions.

Transfers. As with promotion decisions, an employee's performance record in one job may be useful in determining his or her ability to perform in another job of equal importance. While this may not be a prime factor when transfers are used solely for the purpose of employee development, it is important when making lateral moves to fill job vacancies.

Demotions. Unfortunately, an employee is sometimes placed in a position that requires greater skill than the employee possesses, a fact that is revealed through performance appraisal. Demotion to a job more commensurate with the employee's level of skills and abilities may be in order when this happens. Inability to perform one particular job well does not mean that an employee is incapable of successfully performing other jobs. Demotion can be a viable means of salvaging the organization's investment in a person.

Terminations. Performance appraisal data are frequently used to make termination decisions. When an employee cannot perform and there are no lower-level jobs to which he or she can be demoted, when work is completely unsatisfactory, or when an employee commits serious or repeated violations of company rules, he or she may have to be terminated. Because of the increasingly complex legalities involved in discharging employees, an accurate performance appraisal system is rapidly becoming necessary as a source of documentation to support a termination action.

Layoffs. When it becomes necessary for an organization to reduce the size of its work force because of economic factors, performance appraisals provide a rational basis for determining which employees will be laid off. Obviously, the marginal performers should be laid off, and more productive workers should be retained. However, when employees are working under a labor agreement, layoffs are determined on the basis of seniority, not performance, and management is deprived of its flexibility in deciding which people to lay off.

PERFORMANCE APPRAISAL METHODS

Over the years, several different methods of formally appraising performance have been developed. Some of the most commonly used approaches found in organizations today include: (1) graphic rating scales, (2) ranking, (3) rank and yank, (4) checklists, (5) behaviorally anchored rating scales, (6) behavioral observation scales, (7) work standards, (8) essays, (9) management by objectives, and (10) 360-degree performance appraisal.

Rating Scales

The single most widely used method of appraising the performance of nonexempt employees is some form of rating scale. One of the most common forms is the graphic rating scale. Approximately half of all organizations with performance evaluation systems use some type of rating approach.[10] This method is popular because it is simple and quick.

With rating scales, employees are evaluated according to a set of predetermined factors such as quantity of work, quality of work, and absenteeism. Each evaluation factor is ranked from the lowest level of performance to the highest level of performance. The ranking can be divided into as many as 15 categories, but most rating scales use five categories. In some instances, definitions of the evaluation factors are printed on the evaluation form itself; in other instances, only the name of the factor is shown.

To complete a performance appraisal using a rating scale, the evaluator simply checks the degree of each factor that is most descriptive of the employee's performance during the period covered by the appraisal. Figure 11.1 shows a fairly typical rating scale. Often, numerical values are assigned to each factor degree so that the evaluator can quickly compute a mathematical average performance rating.

Many rating scale forms also include a comments section below each factor so that the appraiser can provide written justification for the factor degree assigned. Other rating scale forms provide a comments section at the end of the form, allowing the evaluator to make general comments supporting the overall appraisal.

Advantages. There are several advantages to rating scales as a method of performance appraisal: (1) they are easy to use, (2) they do not take much time to complete, (3) a set of standardized factors can be developed to cover all jobs in an organization, and (4) when numerical values are assigned to factor degrees, an average performance rating can be quickly calculated.[11]

Disadvantages. Although rating scales are probably the oldest and most popular approach to performance appraisal in existence, they do have significant disadvantages: (1) factors and degrees are often vaguely defined, if they are defined at all; (2) lack of factor and degree definitions may produce highly subjective evaluations by supervisors; (3) there is usually no factual basis for the evaluation; (4) factors used frequently contain items that are, at best, tangentially related to the job; (5) central tendency errors are likely to occur because it may be difficult for the appraiser to factually justify a rating above or below acceptable performance; and (6) the courts have usually taken a jaundiced view of rating scales because the factors used often include personality traits.[12]

Ranking

The simplest approach to performance appraisal is the ranking method. In its most elementary form, ranking entails placing all employees into a specific order based on their overall performance, from the highest or best performer to the lowest or worst performer. In a group of seven employees, for example, the best performer would be designated as a one, the next best performer a two, and so on. To determine the rankings, evaluators frequently use an alternation ranking procedure: the evaluator first selects the best performer and then identifies the worst performer; next, the second best performer is selected and the second worst

Figure 11.1
Typical Rating Scale

PERFORMANCE FACTORS	Below Minimum (unacceptable)	Below Expectations (marginal)	Meets Expectations (normal)	Exceeds Expectations (good)	Clearly Outstanding (excellent)
JUDGMENT	☐	☐	☐	☐	☐
INITIATIVE	☐	☐	☐	☐	☐
CREATIVENESS	☐	☐	☐	☐	☐
PROBLEM SOLVING	☐	☐	☐	☐	☐
THOROUGHNESS	☐	☐	☐	☐	☐
ACCURACY	☐	☐	☐	☐	☐
QUANTITY	☐	☐	☐	☐	☐
COMMUNICATION	☐	☐	☐	☐	☐
JOB KNOWLEDGE	☐	☐	☐	☐	☐
SKILL IMPROVEMENT	☐	☐	☐	☐	☐
WORKING WITH OTHERS	☐	☐	☐	☐	☐
LEADERSHIP ABILITY	☐	☐	☐	☐	☐
ADVANCEMENT POTENTIAL	☐	☐	☐	☐	☐
ABSENTEEISM	☐	☐	☐	☐	☐
ATTITUDE	☐	☐	☐	☐	☐

performer is identified. This alternation is continued until all employees have been put into rank order.

As typically used, ranking involves no specific criteria or performance guidelines. It relies entirely upon the appraiser's (or evaluator's) judgment for determining the order of employee performance.

Advantages. Ranking, it is claimed, has several advantages as a performance appraisal method: (1) it is inexpensive, (2) it is easy to use, (3) it eliminates the problem of central tendency error because it forces the appraiser to place employees into a ranking based on overall performance, (4) it does not require extensive evaluator training, and (5) since employees and supervisors naturally tend to rank individuals in some order of performance anyway, it legitimizes an already existing informal procedure.[13]

Disadvantages. Unfortunately, no simple approach to dealing with a complex process is without limitations or shortcomings. The disadvantages to ranking are the following: (1) there are usually no objective criteria for determining an employee's position in the rank order, (2) it may be difficult to explain to an employee his or her ranking since most employees consider themselves to be above average in performance, (3) ranking may produce morale problems among employees who are not rated at or near the top of the list, (4) performance comparisons across departmental lines are impossible since a lower ranking employee in one unit may actually be superior in performance to a higher ranked employee in another work group, (5) ranking forces a distribution of performance that may not fit a work group because it is possible that all employees may be superior or all may be inferior, and (6) ranking does not provide the evaluator with useful information for counseling employees about their performance.[14]

Rank and Yank

The rank and yank performance appraisal method, also known as a forced distribution rating system, is a combination of ranking employees based on their performance and then terminating those employees who are ranked the lowest. At General Electric Company, employees are ranked each year and the employee rankings fall into three categories. The top 20 percent are considered star performers, the middle 70 percent are acceptable performers, and the bottom 10 percent are labeled nonperformers. These nonperformers are generally terminated.[15] While this method may appear cruel to those ranked at the bottom and would seem to induce some fear and paranoia among the employees that remain, rank and yank systems have been shown to benefit organizations, at least in the short run.[16]

Advantages. The main advantage to using a rank and yank system is that an organization is able to identify and terminate underperforming employees. The organization can then replace these underperforming individuals with more capable individuals. By replacing poor performers with higher performing individuals, organizations can be continuously raising the bar for all of their employees and improving the quality of their total work force.[17]

Disadvantages. There are several potential disadvantages to using rank and yank systems. The positive effects that rank and yank have on the work force are usually not long term and reach a point of diminished return within a few years. In addition, such systems will most likely have negative effects on employee morale, recruitment, retention, and productivity.[18]

Checklists

Performance appraisal checklists provide the evaluator with a series of statements, phrases, or adjectives that describe employee performance. These statements may be subdivided into specific factors such as quantity of work or quality of work, with the descriptors listed under each category. Occasionally, the phrases or adjectives are simply listed without categorization. The appraiser marks the statement or adjective considered to be most descriptive of the employee's performance during the period covered by the appraisal. Figure 11.2 shows a typical checklist.

There are two variations to the straight checklist method. One variation is the forced choice technique. In this approach, the appraiser reviews a series of statements about an employee's performance and indicates which statement is most descriptive or least descriptive of that individual's performance. Figure 11.3 is an example of a forced choice checklist. After the checklist is completed, the evaluator reviews all of the behaviors checked and composes a written description of the employee's performance. A second variation of the checklist is the weighted checklist. It is very similar to the forced choice method except that weights have been assigned to each possible response. Normally the weights, developed by the human resource management group, are not known to the evaluator. This approach, it is believed, tends to reduce bias on the part of the person conducting the appraisal.

Advantages. Proponents of checklists claim that this method offers the following advantages: (1) the evaluation is not as vague as in the rating approach because actual job behaviors are described in the checklists, (2) evaluator objectivity is greater than with rating scales or ranking because appraisers have to evaluate specific job performance behaviors, (3) the evaluator tends to act more as a recorder of observed behaviors than as a judge, and (4) checklists are typically developed for groups of similar jobs so that evaluation factors are more job-specific than the general ones used in rating scales.[19]

Disadvantages. The shortcomings of checklists include: (1) it takes time and money to develop statements for job groups that truly reflect job performance; (2) appraisers often have difficulty interpreting the statements because some items appear to be virtually identical; (3) when the weighted checklist is used, the appraiser has no knowledge of the assigned weights and may give an employee a different evaluation than intended; (4) factual data to support the assigned evaluation is usually lacking; (5) lacking knowledge of which items are the most heavily weighted, the appraiser may be at a disadvantage in

Figure 11.2
Typical Checklist

QUALITY OF WORK (Disregard Quantity)

___Extremely neat and accurate.
___Good accurate worker. Makes few mistakes.
___Adequate but some improvement would be desirable.
___Barely up to minimum standards. Often inaccurate.
___Below minimum standards. Complete checking required.

QUANTITY OF WORK (Disregard Quality)

___Outstanding volume.
___Well above average volume.
___Adequate volume.
___Barely up to minimum standards.
___Below minimum standards. Needs much improvement.

JOB KNOWLEDGE (Technical)

___Expert. Has superior knowledge.
___Well-rounded knowledge. Seldom needs assistance.
___Possesses acceptable knowledge.
___Knowledge is adequate to perform minimum job requirements.
___Very limited knowledge. Needs frequent assistance.

RESPONSIBILITY (Ability to Plan and Direct Work)

___Plans and carries out own work in superior manner. Self Sustaining.
___Plans and carries out work well. Requires little supervision.
___Requires occasional work direction.
___Carries out only the most tasks without follow-up.
___Always waits to be directed.

---

counseling the employee about his or her job performance; and (6) there is little evidence to indicate that checklists are an improvement over other appraisal methods.[20]

Behaviorally Anchored Rating Scales

Behaviorally anchored rating scales (BARS) are basically a more detailed and refined version of the traditional rating scale. The implementation of BARS begins with a detailed analysis of a job and a precise identification of effective

Figure 11.3
Forced Choice Checklist

Most Descriptive	Least Descriptive	
☐	☐	Seldom makes mistakes.
☐	☐	Fails to follow through on assignments completely.
☐	☐	Always meets deadlines.
☐	☐	Constantly seeks help on routine assignments.
☐	☐	Does not plan ahead.
☐	☐	Grasps instructions quickly.
☐	☐	Seldom wastes time.
☐	☐	Communicates well.
☐	☐	Leader in group activities.
☐	☐	Spends too much time on trivial matters.
☐	☐	Patient with others.
☐	☐	Industrious worker.

and ineffective job behaviors. Once each performance factor has been identified, descriptive statements for each level of performance are created for each job factor. Each factor's set of descriptive statements is then arranged on a scale in rank order. Typically, the scale provides for seven descriptive statements for each performance factor, although sometimes points along the scale will not have a behaviorally descriptive statement attached to them. Figure 11.4 provides an example of a behaviorally anchored rating scale for the performance factor "Customer Relations" in a payments cashier's job.

The BARS method was developed to overcome weaknesses in other performance appraisal methods by addressing specific job behaviors and performance expectations. While research has been conducted on the effectiveness of BARS as compared to other methods, such as rating, the results appear to be mixed, leading several researchers and practitioners to question its usefulness.[21]

Advantages. Proponents of BARS claim several advantages for this method: (1) it is job-based inasmuch as each job must be carefully studied to identify

Figure 11.4
Behaviorally Anchored Rating Scale (BARS)

Job: Payments Cashier

Factor: Customer Relations - Includes all those behaviors the cashier demonstrates when dealing
          with the customers.

☐ 7 Clearly Outstanding Performance	Carefully explains company services to customers and attempts to cross-sell services whenever possible.
☐ 6 Excellent Performance	Answers all questions knowledgeably and occasionally attempts to cross-sell one or two services.
☐ 5 Good Performance	Answers most customer inquiries knowledgeably and courteously.
☐ 4 Neither Good Nor Bad Performance	Is friendly toward customers and answers some questions correctly.
☐ 3 Slightly Poor Performance	Answers questions by referring customers to another department.
☐ 2 Poor Performance	Responds to customers' inquiries grudgingly and lacks adequate knowledge of company services.
☐ 1 Very Poor Performance	Indifferent to customers' needs.

specific behaviors that will be used to assess performance, (2) it is more objective than other methods because specific behavioral statements rather than vague descriptions of performance are used, (3) its validity is superior to methods that rely on worker traits or personality factors that may not be job-related, and (4) it provides for an easier communication of job expectations to employees since these expectations are specifically identified in advance.[22]

Disadvantages. As a performance appraisal device, BARS have the following disadvantages: (1) they are expensive and time-consuming to develop since each job must be studied in detail; (2) their development normally requires professional expertise because of the extensive job analysis entailed; (3) there are usually little or no backup data to support the evaluator's assessment of performance; (4) problems of evaluator bias are not eliminated because judgment still plays a significant part in the evaluation; and (5) there is no clear-cut evidence that this method, although more detailed and expensive, is superior to other commonly used approaches.[23]

Behavioral Observation Scales

With the behavioral observation scale (BOS), raters are asked to describe how frequently the employee engaged in specific behaviors over the course of time covered by the appraisal. Supporters of this method claim that the BOS eliminates much of the subjectivity involved with evaluative judgments, but skeptics argue that reporting frequency information can be just as subjective since raters are using cognitive processes to try to recall how many times an employee engaged in a certain behavior in the past.[24] If an organization conducts appraisals on an annual basis, the likelihood of a rater accurately remembering the exact frequency of a variety of behaviors over the span of a year is rather low. However, research comparing graphic rating scales, BARS, and BOS suggest that the BOS is the preferred method.[25]

Advantages. Researchers suggest that the BOS method appears to yield the following advantages: (1) it improves communication between the rater and ratee; (2) it leads to clearer and more observable goals for the ratee; (3) it contributes to higher ratee commitment to carry out these goals; and (4) raters tend to feel more comfortable using this method because they feel as if they are focusing on less subjective criteria.[26] Other researchers have also found that (5) ratees report higher satisfaction with the BOS over other appraisal systems.[27]

Disadvantages. The main disadvantage of the BOS method is that all of the advantages listed above may not hold true across all organizations and situations. Researchers question the actual objectivity of the BOS, suggesting that reporting frequency information can be just as subjective as evaluating the quality of the employee's performance. While on the surface, it appears to be the preferred method in terms of reducing subjectivity, the BOS can still contain the same rating errors and biases that reduce the effectiveness of other methods.[28]

Work Standards

In the work standards approach to performance appraisal, each employee's output is compared to a predetermined level of output of acceptable quality. Standards, established through work measurement techniques such as time study, work sampling, or predetermined time systems, reflect the amount of work that a qualified employee working at a normal rate of speed under normal conditions could produce within a specified period of time.[29] This method is most commonly used in manufacturing where output is readily quantifiable, but is also found in clerical and other nonmanufacturing environments.

Advantages. Where work standards can be used, they offer distinct advantages: (1) they are objective, quantifiable criteria for determining performance; (2) they provide for the easy identification of high as well as low performers; (3) they establish a definitive basis for relating merit pay increases to performance; and (4) they set expectations that can be communicated to employees.[30]

Disadvantages. Some of the drawbacks of work standards include the following: (1) the standards used to measure output must be very accurate,[31]

(2) standards cannot be applied to jobs where there is no readily quantifiable output, (3) this approach typically does not provide developmental data that can be used by a supervisor for counseling employees, (4) workers must perceive that the standards are fair, and (5) any changes made in the standards may have an adverse impact on employee morale.

Essays

Free-form essays are another performance appraisal method. In their simplest form, the evaluator merely writes a brief narrative describing the employee's performance, usually elaborating on strengths as well as areas where the individual needs to make improvements. This method tends to focus on extremes in an employee's behavior rather than routine day-to-day performance because extremes are more easily remembered by the appraiser. Evaluations of this nature obviously depend quite heavily upon the writing ability of the evaluator. However, some managers believe that this method is the best approach to performance appraisal because there are no constraints on the subjects that can be covered in the evaluation. Essays are most often used in conjunction with other appraisal methods rather than as the sole method. They are also more common for managerial positions than for operative-level jobs.

Advantages. The advantages claimed for the essay approach include: (1) the thoughtful attention an appraiser must give to writing a report that is truly reflective of an employee's performance, (2) the wide latitude given to the evaluator to cover items that may not be included in a set of predetermined evaluation factors, (3) the attention that must be given to citing specific examples of demonstrated performance in order to compose an accurate narrative, and (4) the kind of information provided to the employee that may help the individual improve his or her performance.[32]

Disadvantages. Essays have several inherent drawbacks when used as the only means of performance appraisal. Among these are the following: (1) the quality of the evaluation is more often than not a function of the appraiser's ability to write well than it is of the employee's ability to perform a job successfully; (2) the method can be very time-consuming if it is given the attention it deserves; (3) inasmuch as essays require time, supervisors may be inclined to perform them perfunctorily if several employees are being appraised at once; (4) the evaluator tends to concentrate more on behavioral extremes than examples of day-to-day performance; and (5) comparisons of employee performance across departmental lines is difficult because appraisers do not all cover the same aspects of performance, nor possess the same writing skills.[33]

Management by Objectives

Management by objectives (MBO) is both a management philosophy and an approach to performance appraisal. As a management philosophy, it utilizes employee participation in setting meaningful, attainable goals for each individual. These individual goals are directed toward departmental goals and ultimately toward the overall goals of the organization.

As an approach to performance appraisal, MBO is a results-centered technique that does not attempt to evaluate traits or personality characteristics; its focus is entirely on actual accomplishments measured in terms of expected achievements set by the employees themselves. With MBO, the focus of the appraisal process shifts from evaluation of the worker's personal attributes or tangentially related job factors to actual job accomplishments. The appraiser's role changes from that of performance judge to one of counselor, mentor, and performance facilitator. The employee's involvement in the appraisal function becomes one of active participator rather than one of passive bystander.

In an MBO appraisal system, the employee and his or her supervisor mutually set goals that the employee will achieve during the next evaluation period. These goals then become the standards by which the employee's performance will be measured. While goals are normally set in quantitative terms that lend themselves to clear-cut measurement, qualitative goals that are not as easily measurable are often used too. At the conclusion of the appraisal period, the employee and the supervisor meet to discuss the extent to which stated goals have been achieved and review further actions that may be necessary to accomplish goals that were not met in the current appraisal period. In this review session, goals for the next period are also usually established. With MBO, the supervisor keeps communication channels open and attempts to assist in any way possible to see that the employee actually achieves the goals that have been set.

Advantages. MBO has been touted as a performance appraisal system for over 50 years. Among the advantages claimed for it are the following: (1) it increases the employee's involvement in setting performance objectives and concomitantly increases the motivation required to reach those objectives; (2) it offers an objective, factual basis for measuring accomplishments; (3) it emphasizes results, not traits or personality characteristics; (4) it is entirely job-centered; (5) it establishes the appraiser as a facilitator of performance rather than as a critic of performance; (6) it assures the organization that all employees are working toward a common purpose; and (7) it supports the psychological concept that people will exercise self-direction and self-control in the accomplishment of organizational objectives that they have participated in setting.[34]

Disadvantages. While the advantages of management by objectives as a performance appraisal system are real, it also has disadvantages that are just as real. For example: (1) MBO is incompatible with certain managerial styles: it will not work under authoritarian conditions; (2) it is an organizational philosophy: it cannot operate at one organizational level without operating at all levels; (3) installing a truly effective MBO approach is time-consuming: it requires an installation period of at least five years before it can permeate the entire organization; (4) MBO cannot be implemented at all organizational levels simultaneously, nor can it be implemented from the bottom up: it must begin at the very top of the organization and work its way down; (5) it requires a total and sizable commitment of management support, interest, and time if it is to succeed; (6) it does not lend itself to all types of jobs: individuals performing routine, repetitive, or machine-paced jobs are better appraised by another method; and (7) employees require extensive training before they normally will respond in a positive fashion to MBO.[35]

360-Degree Performance Appraisal

A performance appraisal method that has grown in popularity over the years is the 360-degree performance appraisal, also known as multirater feedback. One survey indicated that approximately one-third of U.S. organizations utilize this method.[36] With this approach, ratings may be made by supervisors, peers, subordinates, customers, and by the ratees themselves. The logic behind this method is that collecting information from a variety of individuals who observe the ratee's performance from different viewpoints and in different situations should lead to a more complete and accurate appraisal.

Advantages. The 360-degree performance appraisal can be beneficial for the following reasons: (1) including observations from different perspectives should lead to a more comprehensive assessment of job performance; (2) the comprehensive assessment should help to more accurately identify strengths and weaknesses, and the ratee can use this information for developmental purposes;[37] (3) asking for peer and subordinate ratings can give these employees a sense of empowerment;[38] and (4) ratings from multiple sources can reduce the impact of an inaccurate individual rating.[39]

Disadvantages. The research findings regarding the reliability and validity of this method are mixed. Some studies reveal positive findings while other studies suggest the following disadvantages: (1) the reliability among different types of raters can be quite low, with the correlation between subordinate and self-ratings being the lowest;[40] and (2) there tends to be greater error when the ratings are used for administrative purposes.[41]

This brief discussion of performance appraisal methods demonstrates that there is no perfect approach to assessing employee job performance. Some approaches are decidedly better than others; some are clearly deficient. Specific approaches employed by an origination must take into consideration several factors: the uses that will be made of the results, the organization's philosophy and climate, the types of jobs being evaluated, and the time and expense that will be required to furnish the organization with an effective system.

PROBLEMS IN PERFORMANCE APPRAISAL

As pointed out in previous chapters, many human resource practices and procedures, unfortunately, are imperfect at best. Performance appraisal is no exception. Many of the problems in performance appraisal occur, not so much from the method used (although some methods are more susceptible to problems than other), but from the way that it is used. Often, problems occur because supervisors and managers are largely untrained in how to appraise employee performance. Even when appraisers are trained, they frequently find it difficult to accurately and effectively assess the accomplishments of their subordinates. Some of the most commonly encountered problems are described below.

Perfunctoriness

For many supervisors, performance appraisal is a task they find difficult and unpleasant. Some view it as too time-consuming; some see it as an unnecessary administrative function the human resource department requires; others dread the thought of having to explain or discuss an evaluation with an employee. Therefore, it is not unusual to find the appraisal handled very superficially. The form is completed without much thought and any discussion with the employee is cursory. While it is important to both employee and employer, performance appraisal is often handled in a fashion that suggests it is not important.

One of the authors once witnessed an annual performance review discussion with a relatively high-level professional employee that took place in a hallway and was concluded in no more than 30 seconds. Granted, this is an extreme example, yet it is indicative of the superficiality with which many appraisals are handled. The fact that it transpired at one of the largest defense contractors in the country is astonishing.

Lack of Objectivity

An obvious weakness in many performance appraisal systems is their lack of objectivity. Rating scales, for example, commonly use personality traits or characteristics such as attitude, loyalty, appearance, resourcefulness, and personal conduct, which are not only difficult to measure, but are also open to completely subjective interpretation. In addition, these and similar factors may have little or nothing to do with actual job performance. As discussed in Chapter 3, the courts have a negative view of subjective appraisal systems.

While some element of subjectivity probably exists in even the best of systems, a definite attempt must always be made to ensure that objective factors—quantifiable, measurable, and job-related—are stressed in the appraisal method. Lack of objective criteria place the evaluator and the employer in an untenable position if an employee challenges the performance appraisal system.

Central Tendency

One of the most common errors in appraising performance is central tendency: rating all employees as average or at the middle value of a numerical scale. This problem may occur for three reasons. First, it is the most expedient way for supervisors to do appraisals, especially when many employees have to be evaluated at the same time. Second, rating scales have a built-in tendency that forces ratings toward the center rather than toward the outer limits. Third, evaluating an employee as average relieves the appraiser of having to explain or justify high or low evaluations. Appraisers committing central tendency errors are seeking to avoid controversy, criticism, or lengthy discussions.

Halo or Horns Effect

A halo effect refers to the tendency to rate an employee high on all aspects of performance, even though actual performance across all aspects has not been uniformly high. This happens because the evaluator places an extraordinary importance on just one factor where performance has been high. For example, if an evaluator places great importance on quantity of work produced, the employee who turns out the most items will tend to receive a higher rating on quality of work than is justified by the actual quality level. Likewise, other factors (i.e., attitude, communication, punctuality) will receive a higher rating than can be factually supported, just because the individual performed at a high level with respect to quantity of work.

The horns effect is the direct opposite of the halo effect. Poor performance on one highly valued aspect of performance leads to lower than deserved ratings on all other performance factors.

Leniency and Strictness

Leniency, sometimes referred to as *evaluation inflation,* is the giving of undeserved high ratings. Research on performance appraisal suggests that when evaluators are required to discuss evaluations with employees face-to-face, there is a tendency to overrate actual performance.[42] In many instances, the evaluator simply gives the employee the benefit of the doubt about performance. Leniency obviously eliminates the necessity to discuss any unpleasant aspects of performance with the employee. The problem of overrating is more apt to occur when subjective appraisal factors are used.

Strictness refers to the problem of being unduly critical of an employee's work performance. Supervisors sometimes use performance reviews to enumerate all of an individual's deficiencies, weaknesses, and developmental needs— ostensible, of course, for the employee's own good. When performance appraisal is used in this manner, the result is likely to be a much lower than warranted evaluation.

Personal Biases

An evaluator's personal feelings about the person being appraised can significantly affect the result of a performance appraisal. Appearance, mode of dress, hair styles, mannerisms, and a host of other factors may cause an evaluator to like or dislike particular employees and produce positively or negatively skewed appraisals, respectively. Individuals of particular religious affiliations, ethnic groups, sex, age, or disability status, although protected by law, do not always receive fair evaluations because of personal biases of the supervisor conducting the appraisal. Personal biases are often subconscious prejudices that are difficult to eliminate or control.

Recent Behavior Bias

This type of bias occurs when the appraiser takes into account only the latest performance of the employee and fails to consider the performance over the entire evaluation period. Since the normal appraisal period is one year, it is difficult, in the absence of detailed documentation, to remember what has happened in the earlier part of the period; thus, the appraiser tends to focus on the most recent and easiest to remember aspects of performance.

Employees also contribute to this problem. Most employees are very aware of when they are scheduled for a performance review, and while their actions may not be intentional, their behavior and productivity tend to improve right before the scheduled evaluation. Consequently, the supervisor's memory of recent behavior is even more positively reinforced.

Guessing

In the absence of quantitative, objective performance measures, evaluators may resort to guessing about what an employee has or has not done during the appraisal period. Lacking sufficient documentation relative to accomplishments, appraisers may simply make assumptions about an individual's performance. Usually, these guesses are incorrect.

Use Bias

The way in which performance appraisal is used in an organization may also introduce bias into the process. If the primary purpose of the evaluation is for awarding merit pay increases, appraisers may display a tendency to rate poor performers as average so as not to deny them raises. In times of high inflation, supervisors also tend to overrate performance so employees receive raises that are more commensurate with inflation rates.[43]

Conversely, where the emphasis of performance appraisal is on helping the employee to develop and improve his or her job skills, evaluators may tend to be more stringent in their performance assessments because they are concerned with assisting employees to develop their talents more fully. Much of the research supports these claims that the purpose of the performance appraisal, administrative versus developmental, has such influences on rater evaluations.[44]

Lack of Documentation

A major problem with most appraisal systems is that they do not require any form of continuous documentation of employee performance. When documentation does exist, it is often inadequate to support an accurate assessment of employee accomplishments. Nonexistent or inadequate documentation leads supervisors to commit many of the performance appraisal errors described above.

Lack of Evaluator Training

Many organizations offer little or no training in how to evaluate performance and conduct performance appraisals. It often seems that the firms believe promotion to a supervisory or management position automatically gives an individual the ability to perform all managerial functions without the benefit of formalized training. Most of the aforementioned performance appraisal problems could be eliminated, or at least reduced, through proper rater training.[45]

CHARACTERISTICS OF AN EFFECTIVE APPRAISAL SYSTEM

It is highly unlikely that any performance appraisal system will be completely free from criticism or immune to legal challenge. However, systems that possess certain characteristics are more likely to be legally defensible and produce useful results for an organization, its managers, and its employees. Described below are 12 characteristics that an effective performance appraisal system should possess.

Consideration of these characteristics will make another significant point abundantly clear: development of an effective appraisal system is not an easy task nor does it happen overnight. An effective performance appraisal system is the result of hard work and careful planning.

Formalization

The first requirement for any effective performance appraisal system is that it be formalized in writing. There should be definite policies, procedures, and instructions for its use. Written guidance on how to conduct the appraisal should be furnished to all appraisers. General information about the system should be given to all employees via an employee handbook or in a separate document if there is no handbook.

Formalizing the system forces an organization to think through all facets of performance appraisal and to clarify what it wants the system to achieve and how it will achieve it. Many potential problems can be eliminated by documenting the system in writing.

Job-Related Characteristics

All factors used to evaluate performance must stem from the jobs that are being appraised. Inasmuch as performance appraisal is an employment test according to the definition of "test" given in the *Uniform Guidelines on Employee Selection Procedures,* general traits, personality characteristics, and tenuously related job factors should be scrupulously avoided. Only appraisal factors that account for success or lack of success in performing a job should be used. These factors must be susceptible to standardized definition and uniform interpretation.

Developing job-related performance factors may necessitate creating different sets of factors for different groups of jobs. Since most jobs are dissimilar in their content and expected results, it is difficult to develop a single set of performance appraisal factors that will adequately cover every job in an organization.

Performance Factors Based on Standards and Measurements

Standards are expectations, norms, desired results, or anticipated levels of job accomplishment that express the organization's concept of acceptable performance. To set standards, an organization must carefully examine each of its jobs and determine reasonable expectations that are acceptable to both the institution and the employees performing the jobs. Although it is a difficult task, it must be accomplished if performance is to be meaningfully evaluated.

Once standards have been set, some method of measuring actual results has to be developed. In many cases, measurements are difficult to establish because the jobs do not lend themselves to easy or meaningful quantification. However, comparisons with an established standard must be based on measurements. Even an imperfect measurement will be better than no measurement at all. As with standards, establishing measurements is a difficult but necessary task in accurate performance evaluation.

Validity

Any test is valid if it measures what it purports to measure. In performance appraisal, the system employed or the method used is valid if it measures what it is designed to measure—which is actual job performance. Unfortunately, few performance appraisal systems have been subjected to statistical validity studies as required by the *Uniform Guidelines.*

Establishing the validity of performance appraisal actually begins with job analysis, the process wherein job performance factors are clearly identified. A thorough job analysis will reveal several performance factors such as quantity of work, quality of work, meeting deadlines, and adhering to prescribed procedures. The factors must be quantifiable and specifically defined so as to reflect expected outcomes.

In the performance appraisal itself, there should be a reasonably high relationship between the evaluation an employee has received on a particular performance factor and the actual results the individual has achieved as measured by that factor. For example, employees who consistently produce high volumes of output should consistently receive a higher rating on this performance factor than employees whose output is lower.

Reliability

Reliability, statistically speaking, refers to the ability of any test to yield consistent results across multiple measurements. A performance appraisal system that does not consistently measure work performance accurately cannot be considered effective. Assume, for example, that an employee's work performance on a particular job factor was measured three times with the same test. The first time, the performance was rated high, the second time it was rated low, and the third time it was rated average. Based on these ratings, it is impossible to accurately determine whether the employee is a high, low, or average performer with respect to this factor because the ratings are inconsistent. A performance appraisal system producing such results could not be considered reliable because of the absence of consistency. In a reliable performance appraisal system, high performance consistently receives a high rating, and low performance consistently receives a low rating.

Using definitive standards and measurements helps reduce reliability problems in performance appraisal because supervisors have objective criteria for evaluating performance. Without objective criteria, they may commit performance evaluation errors that produce inconsistent, unreliable results.

Open Communication

All employees have a strong psychological need to know how well they are performing. An effective performance appraisal system ensures that feedback is provided continuously—not in an annual written evaluation, but in daily, weekly, and monthly comments from a supervisor. The annual evaluation and its accompanying performance discussion should be devoid of surprises. While the interview presents an excellent opportunity for both parties to exchange ideas in depth, it is not a substitute for day-to-day communications about performance.

Trained Appraisers

Essential to the effectiveness of performance appraisal is thorough training—as well as updating and retraining—of all individuals who conduct evaluations. Classroom training is especially important when a new or revised system is being installed; it is also essential for all new managers and supervisors. An organization must not assume that, because performance appraisal information is contained in a supervisory handbook or is included in the company personnel policy manual, supervisors will automatically be able to conduct effective appraisals.

An organization should also incorporate opportunities for coaching and counseling, by the appraisers' immediate supervisors, into the performance appraisal procedures. Such personal sessions often permit the discussion and resolution of appraisal problems in their incipiency. Moreover, by actively involving each level of management in teaching performance appraisal, the system becomes more strongly imbedded in the organization as a vital function of human resource management.

Ease of Use

A performance appraisal system does not have to be complex to be effective. In fact, the simpler and easier a system is to use, the more readily it can be understood by evaluators, and the more likely it is to be used in the manner intended. If the system is firmly based on standards and measurements, it will not only be easier to use, but also more valid and reliable than many other performance appraisal methods.

Employee Access to Results

As a result of the Federal Privacy Act of 1973, employees of the federal government and of federal contractors must be given access to their personnel records, including all files or other data pertaining to their performance appraisals. While this legislation is not extended to the private sector, there are good reasons for allowing employees to examine their job performance records. First, secrecy breeds suspicion about the fairness of the system. Second, concern about the fairness of the system could possibly lead to lawsuits. Third, fairness in dealing with employees suggests that they have an implicit right to certain kinds of information that directly affects them on their jobs. Fourth, permitting employees to review their performance records builds a safeguard into the system because employees then have the opportunity to detect errors. Finally, since one of the purported goals of performance appraisal is employee development, employees must have access to performance records so they can try to improve their job performance.

Confidentiality

The results of performance appraisals must always be kept confidential. A supervisor or manager should never share one employee's performance appraisal with another employee. Nor should a supervisor discuss the results of his or her employees' performance with other supervisors—except in a joint appraisal process. While the appraiser may be required to discuss individual results with his or her immediate supervisor, performance appraisal is best viewed as a strictly private matter in which access to individual results is closely controlled.

Review Mechanism

To eliminate any problems of bias, discrimination, or favoritism, a performance appraisal system should include a review mechanism. Each evaluation of an employee should be automatically reviewed by the next higher level of management—usually the evaluator's immediate supervisor so that confidentiality is maintained. The purpose of this review is not to have the superior perform a second appraisal. Rather, it is to audit the evaluation for fairness, consistency, accuracy, as well as to make certain that the evaluator has objectively carried out the appraisal tasks. While review by the immediate superior increases the time that must be devoted to the performance appraisal process, it protects both the employee and the organization by ensuring fairness and consistency in employee evaluations. Allowing the employees to review their own appraisals can also help with accuracy and fairness issues.

Appeal Process

An accepted principle of American jurisprudence is the right of due process. Unfortunately, in a number of organizations there is no procedure whereby an employee can appeal what he or she considers an unfair or inaccurate performance appraisal. The employee is simply stuck with the immediate supervisor's evaluation. In such situations, the employee has few options other than living with the unfavorable review or leaving the organization. There have even been instances when employees whose performance was acceptable for years were summarily discharged on the basis of one bad performance appraisal. Now that an employer's right to fire at will is being challenged more and more in the courts—often successfully—the need for a clearly delineated appeal procedure in the performance appraisal system seems imperative. (It should be noted that organizations having to deal with unions have long had well-established appeal mechanisms in the form of grievance procedures.)

The number of steps that should be contained in an appeal procedure depends on the size of the organization. At a minimum, there should be two steps: (1) an appeal to the next higher level of management and (2) an appeal to the level above that. In larger organizations, the human resource department would be included at some point in the process—possibly the third or fourth step. The procedures by which an employee can appeal an unfavorable review should be clearly spelled out in the formalized policies and procedures of the performance appraisal system and in the employee handbook.

An appeal process serves three purposes: (1) it protects the employee, (2) it protects the organization, and (3) it helps ensure that supervisors do a more conscientious job of evaluation since they know that their appraisals are subject to scrutiny and interpretation by others in the organization. Also, applying the concept of due process to the performance appraisal process increases an employee's perception of fair treatment.[46]

THE PERFORMANCE APPRAISAL DISCUSSION

Once the appraisal forms have been completed and the necessary documentation prepared, the evaluator faces what is often the most difficult of all performance appraisal tasks—the appraisal discussion.[47] Many evaluators consider the performance discussion or interview an unpleasant task,[48] particularly if the employee has not performed up to standard. Others view the discussion as simply an organizational requirement that should be disposed of as quickly as possible. A more realistic perspective of the discussion, however, would suggest that it is an opportunity for *both* evaluator and evaluatee: an opportunity for the evaluator to coach, counsel, and assist the employee to improve his or her performance; an opportunity for the evaluatee to recognize his or her areas of strength and potential growth and development opportunities. Conducted properly, the performance appraisal interview can increase organizational effectiveness.

Preparing for the Discussion

An effective performance appraisal interview is not something that just happens; it must be carefully planned. To prepare for the interview, the evaluator must clarify in his or her own mind and outline the following:

- The favorable aspects of performance that will be discussed.
- The deficient areas of performance where improvement is needed.
- The anticipated reaction of the employee to both areas of strength and areas of improvement.
- The employee's likely emotional or personal reaction to the discussion.
- The specific facts to present during the discussion and the order in which to present them.
- The specific suggestions and assistance to be offered to the employee.
- The follow-up action that will be taken to ensure that improvements in performance occur.[49]

Types of Performance Appraisal Discussions

There are two basic approaches to conducting the performance appraisal discussion. The appraiser can use either a direct or an indirect method.[50]

The direct method is more structured, deals primarily with facts, and is closely controlled by the supervisor through the use of direct questions or statements. The tone of the interview is set by the evaluator, and the employee has little opportunity to do more than answer questions or respond to statements. Specific areas of interest to the employee are covered only to the extent that the supervisor's structured questions permit. Frequently, this type of performance interview places the employee in a defensive position and the interviewer in a judgmental role. However, the direct method is commonly used because supervisors find it easier to discuss performance when they are in control of the direction of the discussion. The biggest drawback to the direct interview is that little is learned of the employee's ideas about areas of desired personal growth, development, and improvement.

The indirect method, on the other hand, is an interactive approach that encourages the employee to talk as much as possible. It is an attempt to explore performance areas with the employee, to uncover reasons for good as well as poor performance, and to discover the employee's ambitions and perceived developmental needs.

Comparing the two types of discussions, it is obvious that improvements in performance are more likely to come from the indirect approach than from the direct approach. Since the employee is an active participant in the indirect interview, he or she is more apt to accept suggestions for improvement and recognize developmental needs. Additionally, a sense of joint responsibility for performance may develop from the discussion. The indirect discussion will, however, require much more time than the direct discussion, but this time will have been well spent if performance actually improves as a result.

Guidelines for Conducting the Discussion

Performance appraisal discussions are not easy. They have to be planned and carefully thought out. If handled improperly, they can create poor morale, misunderstandings, or even outright hostility on the part of the employee. Some suggestions for conducting an effective performance interview include the following:

- *Prepare the employee.* Notify the individual far enough in advance so that he or she can come to the meeting prepared to meaningfully discuss performance.
- *Establish the proper climate.* Create an atmosphere that suggests that the discussion is important.
- *Compare actual performance to standards or expectations.* Use specific examples. Avoid vague generalities about performance.
- *Bite the bullet.* If performance has not been satisfactory, address the subject directly. Do not try to evade the issued by attempting to cover up poor performance with insignificant items of good performance.
- *Comment on improvement.* Recognize areas where the individual has improved and express appreciation for the improvement.
- *Avoid sitting in judgment.* The rightful role of the evaluator is coach, counselor, mentor, and facilitator—not judge.
- *Listen and ask questions.* Give the employee sufficient opportunity to discuss areas that he or she thinks are important.
- *Ask what you can do to help the person improve.* Offer assistance to facilitate performance and growth.
- *Work with the person to establish new performance goals.* Make this a joint effort so that the employee becomes more committed to actually achieving the goals.

• *Allow sufficient time.* Never rush the interview. Make certain that the discussion will not be interrupted.[51]

Keeping these points in mind when discussing a performance appraisal will help ensure that the discussion achieves its objectives.

OTHER PERFORMANCE APPRAISAL CONSIDERATIONS

Three final considerations that must be taken into account in designing and operating an effective performance appraisal system are the following: (1) assigning the responsibility for conducting the appraisal, (2) determining the length of time to be covered by the appraisal period, and (3) establishing the point in time at which the appraisal will occur.

Responsibility for Appraisal

Typically, the human resource department is responsible for designing and administering the performance appraisal program. Responsibility for actually conducting the appraisals, however, is assigned to others within the organization. There are several possibilities for fulfilling this responsibility.

Immediate Supervisor. The most logical choice for conducting a performance appraisal is the employee's immediate supervisor because this individual is in the best position to know the most about the employee's performance level. The immediate supervisor is also the most common choice in organizations. One study disclosed that 96 percent of the firms surveyed assign the responsibility for appraisal to the immediate supervisor.[52] Three reasons favor the supervisor's handling of the appraisal: (1) he or she normally observes the employee's performance on a day-to-day basis, (2) assigning the responsibility to someone else seriously erodes the supervisor's authority as manager of a work unit, and (3) one of the primary functions of any supervisor is training and development of his or her people—a function that is inextricably tied to performance appraisal.

Subordinates. Skeptics question whether a supervisor or manager can be effectively evaluated by his or her subordinates. The conclusion reached by a limited number of firms is that they can. Subordinates are in a unique position to view the overall effectiveness of their managers; they can sometimes recognize strengths or weaknesses not seen by others. Managers who advocate this approach suggest that evaluations by subordinates will make supervisors more conscientious in carrying out their responsibilities. On the negative side, ratings by subordinates may cause a supervisor to become excessively concerned with popularity rather than effective performance of the work unit.

Peers. Evaluation by one's peers may be feasible in limited instances. Where employees must work closely together as a team, it is possible that coworkers would know more about an individual's work performance than the unit supervisor.

Team Appraisal. This form of evaluation occurs when two or more supervisors who are familiar with an employee's performance jointly appraise his or her performance. In many instances, an employee actually works for two or more supervisors; in other cases, the employee works for one supervisor, but interfaces across organizational lines with several supervisors or managers. Under these conditions, a collective appraisal would probably be more accurate and objective than one by a supervisor who has not had sufficient opportunity to observe the employee's work in all areas. Perhaps the biggest disadvantage to this approach is that it undermines supervisory authority and responsibility.

Self-Appraisal. Another appraisal possibility is to have each employee evaluate his or her own performance. If individuals truly understand the objectives they are expected to reach and the standards by which their accomplishments will be measured, they may well be in the best position of all to appraise their performance.[53] Moreover, since all development is essentially self-development, appraisal by employees themselves may lead to greater levels of motivation. However, research indicates that self-ratings tend to be fraught with inflation.[54]

Combinations. Often some combination of the approaches mentioned above is used. The combination used most frequently is some form of self-appraisal and appraisal by the supervisor. With this approach, the employee is asked to complete an evaluation form and the supervisor does likewise. Then the two parties meet to discuss their separate appraisals, resolve any discrepancies, and complete a mutually agreed upon evaluation. This approach works well because it involves the employee in the process and reemphasizes the joint responsibility for effective performance.

Another combination approach that has grown in popularity in recent years is the 360-degree appraisal. As discussed earlier in the chapter, this approach combines ratings from all possible sources that could provide information about some aspect of an employee's performance.

The Appraisal Period

"Annual" is usually a word that is attached to formalized performance appraisal and is probably a fairly good indicator of how often appraisals are conducted. However, many researchers question whether annual appraisal is enough. There are two schools of thought on this matter. One maintains that performance feedback should be provided more frequently, especially if the primary purpose of the appraisal is employee development. The other school of thought maintains that if the system is operating effectively, feedback will be provided on a daily, weekly, and monthly basis, and that there is no need for a formal appraisal more than once a year.[55]

In the case of new employees, exceptions should be made to the annual review process. Good human resource practice suggests that a new employee should be given a formal evaluation at the end of his or her probationary period—the juncture at which the organization makes the decision as to whether the individual will be retained. A review at this point can also relieve anxiety for employees who pass the probationary period because they know that they are performing at an acceptable level.

When to Appraise

Assuming that formal evaluations will occur annually, there is still the question of precisely when the evaluations will take place. There are two approaches to solving this problem: (1) evaluate all employees on a fixed date or (2) evaluate each employee on the anniversary date of his or her employment. The latter approach appears to be the most feasible. Conducting a performance appraisal properly and discussing it thoroughly with an employee is time-consuming. When a supervisor is forced to evaluate all employees on a fixed date, he or she tends to rush through the process, not accomplishing it effectively. Consequently, the recommended approach is to conduct appraisals on the employment anniversary date since the supervisor will have fewer evaluations to conduct at any specific time and can give each one the thorough attention it deserves.

NOTES

1. Donald L. Caruth, *Compensation Management for Banks* (Boston: Bankers Publishing Company, 1986), 206.

2. Kevin R. Murphy and Jeanette N. Cleveland, *Understanding Performance Appraisal: Social, Organizational, and Goal-Based Perspectives* (Thousand Oaks, CA: Sage Publications, Inc., 1995), 39.

3. Raymond A. Noe, John R. Hollenbeck, Barry Gerhart, and Patrick M. Wright, *Human Resource Management: Gaining a Competitive Advantage,* 6th ed. (New York: McGraw-Hill Irwin, 2008), 344.

4. Murphy and Cleveland, *Understanding Performance Appraisal,* 15–19.

5. Noe, Hollenbeck, Gerhart, and Wright, *Human Resource Management,* 346.

6. Jeanette N. Cleveland, Kevin R. Murphy, and Richard E. Williams, "Multiple Uses of Performance Appraisal: Prevalence and Correlates," *Journal of Applied Psychology* 74, no. 1 (1989): 130–135.

7. Ibid., 132.

8. Noe, Hollenbeck, Gerhart, and Wright, *Human Resource Management,* 347.

9. Cleveland, Murphy, and Williams, "Multiple Uses of Performance Appraisal," 130–135.

10. Caruth, *Compensation Management for Banks,* 212.

11. Ibid.

12. Ibid.

13. Ibid., 216.

14. Ibid.

15. Scott Sedam, "Rank and Yank," *Professional Builder* 70, no. 6 (June 2005): 33–34.

16. "Rank and Yank Benefits Work Force," *Industrial Engineer* 37, no. 4 (April 2005): 23.

17. Steven E. Scullen, Paul K. Bergey, and Lynda Aiman-Smith, "Forced Distribution Rating Systems and the Improvement of Workforce Potential: A Baseline Simulation," *Personnel Psychology* 58 (2005): 1–32.

18. "Rank and Yank Benefits Work Force," 23.

19. Caruth, *Compensation Management for Banks,* 214.

20. Ibid., 215.

21. Murphy and Cleveland, *Understanding Performance Appraisal,* 435.

22. Gary P. Latham and Kenneth N. Wexley, *Increasing Productivity through Performance Appraisal,* 2nd ed. (Reading, MA: Addison-Wesley Publishing Company, 1994), 81–82.

23. Caruth, *Compensation Management for Banks,* 215.

24. Murphy and Cleveland, *Understanding Performance Appraisal,* 437.

25. Aharon Tziner and Richard E. Kopelman, "Is There a Preferred Performance Rating Format? A Non-Psychometric Perspective," *Applied Psychology: An International Review* 51, no. 3 (2002): 479–503.

26. Tziner and Kopelman, "Is There a Preferred Performance Rating Format?" 495.

27. Aharon Tziner, Christine Joanis, and Kevin R. Murphy, "A Comparison of Three Methods of Performance Appraisal with Regard to Goal Properties, Goal Perceptions, and Ratee Satisfaction," *Group and Organization Management* 25 (2000), 175–190.

28. Murphy and Cleveland, *Understanding Performance Appraisal,* 437.

29. Donald L. Caruth, *Work Measurement in Banking,* 2nd ed. (Boston: Bankers Publishing Company, 1984), 206.

30. Ibid., 28.

31. Ibid., 73.

32. Caruth, *Compensation Management,* 218.

33. Ibid., 218–219.

34. Ibid., 219.

35. Ibid., 220.

36. *Performance Management Survey* (Alexandria, VA: Society for Human Resource Management, 2000).

37. S. Bartholomew Craig and Kelly Hannum, "Research Update: 360-Degree Performance Assessment," *Consulting Psychology Journal: Practice and Research* 58, no. 2 (2006): 117–122.

38. David W. Bracken, Carol Timmreck, John Fleenor, and Lynn Summers, "360 Feedback from Another Angle," *Human Resource Management* 40 (2001): 3–20.

39. Ginka Toegel and Jay A. Conger, "360-Degree Assessment: Time for Reinvention," *Academy of Management Learning and Education* 2 (2003): 297–311.

40. James M. Conway and Allen I. Huffcutt, "Psychometric Properties of Multisource Performance Ratings: A Meta-Analysis of Subordinate, Peer, and Self-Ratings," *Human Performance* 10, no. 4 (1997): 331–360.

41. Anthony T. Dalessio, "Using Multisource Feedback for Employee Development and Personnel Decisions," in *Performance Appraisal: State of the Art in Practice,* ed. J. W. Smither (San Francisco: Jossey-Bass Publishers, 1998), 278–330.

42. Gunna J. Yun, Lisa M. Donahue, Nicole M. Dudley, and Lynn A. McFarland, "Rater Personality, Rating Format, and Social Context: Implications for Performance Appraisal Ratings," *International Journal of Selection and Assessment* 13, no. 2 (June 2005): 97–107.

43. Don Caruth, Bill Middlebrook, and Frank Rachel, "Performance Appraisals: Much More Than a Once-a-Year-Task," *Supervisory Management* (September 1982): 28–36.

44. Aharon Tziner, Kevin R. Murphy, and Jeanette N. Cleveland, "Performance Appraisal: Evolution and Change," *Group and Organization Management* 30, no. 1 (2005): 4–5.

45. David J. Woehr and Allen I. Huffcutt, "Rater Training for Performance Appraisal: A Quantitative Review," *Journal of Occupational and Organizational Psychology* 67 (1994): 189–205.

46. M. Susan Taylor, Kay B. Tracy, Monika K. Renard, J. Kline Harrison, and Stephen J. Carroll, "Due Process in Performance Appraisal: A Quasi-Experiment in Procedural Justice," *Administrative Science Quarterly* 40, no. 3 (September 1995): 495–523.

47. Caruth, Middlebrook, and Rachel, "Performance Appraisals," 32.

48. Joann S. Lublin, "It's Shape-up Time for Performance Reviews," *The Wall Street Journal,* October 3, 1994, B1.

49. Donald L. Caruth and Gail D. Handlogten, *Management 2000* (Rockwall, TX: Spinnaker Publications, 1996), 76.

50. Ibid., 77.

51. Ibid., 78–79.

52. Charles J. Fombrun and Robert J. Laud, "Strategic Issues in Performance Appraisal: Theory and Practice," *Personnel* (November–December 1983): 27.

53. Margaret A. Bogerty, "How to Prepare Your Performance Reviews," *S.A.M. Journal* (Autumn 1982): 12.

54. Jiing-Lih Farh and Gregory H. Dobbins, "Effects of Comparative Performance Information on the Accuracy of Self-Ratings and Agreement Between Self- and Supervisor Ratings," *Journal of Applied Psychology* 74, no. 2 (1989): 606–610.

55. Caruth, *Compensation Management,* 235.

12

Career Planning and Development

Today most employers need formalized career planning and development activities. The work force is becoming more highly educated and has greater occupational expectations. With slower economic growth and reduced promotion opportunities in contemporary organizations, there is a recognition that "job security died with the 1980s." [1] Additionally, compliance with equal employment opportunity and affirmative action requirements necessitates that positive steps be taken to ensure adequate career progression for minorities, women, and other protected classes. Once considered a luxury useful for only a limited number of large organizations, career planning and development is now becoming an essential activity for companies of all sizes and types.

CAREER PLANNING AND DEVELOPMENT DEFINED

Several definitions are in order before examining this process in detail. The term *career* can be defined in a few different ways. It is often defined as "a sequence of positions occupied by a person over the course of a lifetime," but is also referred to as "a sense of where a person is going in his or her work life." [2] *Career planning* is the support mechanism that helps individuals set and plan out their career goals. [3] The organization's role in career planning is one of helping individuals achieve a better match between personal aspirations and opportunities that are available in the organization. One way of doing this is by developing *career paths*. Career paths are possible sequences of positions that employees could logically progress through, based on an analysis of what the employees actually do in that organization. [4] *Career development* is the continuous, formalized effort by an organization to develop and enrich its employees in order to satisfy both the employees' and the organization's needs. [5] This ongoing and formalized effort should help employees successfully follow their career paths.

As the preceding definitions suggest, effective career planning and development is, ideally, a joint effort. While the primary responsibility for career planning rests with the individual inasmuch as work choices and occupational pursuits are personal matters, organizations can help employees make better decisions by acquainting them with various options and providing avenues through which their choices can be pursued. Although each individual has a personal responsibility for undergoing the preparation required for a particular line of work, career development can be facilitated by the organization as it offers formal and informal means of acquiring needed skills and experiences. Organizations that assist their employees in career planning and development benefit themselves as well as their employees.

PURPOSES OF CAREER PLANNING AND DEVELOPMENT

Organizations typically have several purposes for implementing career planning and development programs—purposes that serve institutional needs as well as the needs of employees. These basic purposes are described below.

Organizational

There are nine specific organizational purposes that are served through career planning and development programs. In general, these purposes center around having sufficient numbers of qualified people available so that the company can fulfill its mission and goals.

Improve Utilization of Personnel. Talent is not always obvious. Often, developmental activities are necessary to bring out the latent abilities in people. The first purpose of career planning and development, therefore, is to ensure that an organization is effectively utilizing the human resources already employed by the firm.

Reduce Turnover. Companies that display an active interest in fostering career development have a much greater chance of retaining skilled personnel. Employees are more likely to remain with a firm that is genuinely interested in providing opportunities for career advancement. Thus, the organization benefits in two ways: (1) turnover expenses are reduced and (2) qualified employees are available for advancement to positions of greater responsibility when vacancies occur.

Increase Motivation and Commitment. By providing opportunities to gain new skills and experiences, companies enhance employee motivation and loyalty. Knowing that their efforts will be recognized and rewarded with chances to further their careers, earn promotions, and obtain higher salaries, employees are apt to perform at higher levels and remain committed to an organization. The organizational payoff is increased productivity and job tenure.

Reduce Employee Obsolescence. Because of technological and scientific advancements, many careers for which people spend years in training become obsolete in a relatively short time. Unless an organization takes positive developmental actions to counter this possibility, it may find itself with a number of employees whose skills are no longer appropriate for essential tasks. In effect, a company may find itself burdened with employees who can no longer make a contribution to achieving the objectives of the enterprise. Career planning and development is one solution to this problem. For example, Motorola requires its employees to complete 40 hours of training each year in order to help the company maintain a high-performing work force and a competitive advantage.[6]

Increase Organizational Effectiveness. The effectiveness of any institution is increased by having thoroughly trained individuals continuously available to perform necessary activities. Career enhancement is a means of accomplishing this. Developmental activities improve the utilization of employees, reduce turnover, increase motivation and commitment, alleviate obsolescence, and substantially improve the company's effectiveness in achieving desired results.

Aid in Recruiting Highly Talented People. Given a choice, talented individuals will seek employment with a firm that offers opportunities for advancement and growth. Career planning and development is, therefore, a recruiting tool that aids a company in attracting skilled applicants.

Aid in Equal Employment Opportunity and Affirmative Action. Goals in these areas include more than merely hiring sufficient numbers of protected class applicants. They also include upward mobility for minorities, women, and others. Career planning and development is one means an organization can help protected classes progress within the company. In fact, programs may be designed to address specific training and experience needs of protected class individuals.

Eliminate Barriers to Upward Mobility. In many organizations, there are often subtle, or sometimes not so subtle, barriers to progression. One purpose of career planning and development is to identify and eliminate these obstacles.

Be Socially Responsible. In an era of downsizing, restructuring, layoffs, and offshoring there is growing concern that it is the responsibility of organizations to make investments in the employability of their workers.[7] With uncertain organizational futures, many employees will undoubtedly need career assistance to ensure their mobility between organizations. From society's point of view, it is incumbent upon organizations that they view career development not only from a perspective of corporate self-interest, but also from the standpoint of what is in the best interests of society at large. In the long run, neither corporations nor society benefits from having a large number of individuals who cannot be gainfully employed.

Individual

An organization usually implements career planning and development because it desires to achieve the purposes described above. At the same time, it generally has in mind some other purposes that directly relate to employee satisfaction. As far as individual employees are concerned, career planning and development programs serve five essential purposes.

Encourage Growth. Developmental activities cause employees to grow, to acquire new abilities, and to become more capable. Career-focused activities help bring out the full potential in employees.

Develop New Skills. Systematic career planning and development, in conjunction with human resource planning, seeks to identify the skills that employees will need in the future and provide opportunities to acquire these skills.

Alleviate Plateauing. In any organization, there are always employees who seem to progress well up to a certain point and then remain at that plateau. There is a point beyond which many people are not able to advance; however, these individuals can often be utilized more effectively in other lateral positions. With individualized training and development, some might even be capable of further advancement. Career planning and development addresses this problem and attempts to ensure that employees are not victims of artificial plateauing.

Satisfy Employment Expectations. Every employee entering a firm has certain expectations about his or her employment opportunities. These expectations may include advancement, learning and growing in the job, or opportunities for new experiences. Career planning and development can assist in satisfying these desires.

Increase Employability. Proper career planning and its accompanying developmental activities increase the employability of individuals. Indeed, this should be of paramount concern to all employees. If sufficient opportunities are not available with his or her current employer, an employee may be able to get a job with another employer based on the skills and knowledge acquired at the current job.

A well-planned, carefully designed career planning and development program can produce substantial benefits for an organization as well as its employees. It can increase organizational effectiveness while satisfying basic psychological needs of the firm's employees.

BARRIERS TO UPWARD MOBILITY

In the absence of career planning and development, there are usually a number of barriers that impede upward mobility in an organization. In order for employees to have the potential to "move up" in an organization, the following barriers need to be overcome.[8]

Lack of Career Paths

Career path information is vital to effective career planning. One of the major factors limiting employee progression in a company is lack of career paths. When organizations have not thought about how jobs relate to each other and the sequence in which employees should move from one job to another to gain experience, progression opportunities are severely limited. Promotions or transfers, consequently, are likely to be made haphazardly. Higher-level positions tend to be filled externally because current employees have not been sufficiently trained to move into jobs of greater responsibility.

Inflated Job Descriptions and Specifications

The necessity for developing realistic job descriptions and specifications that set forth the minimum human qualifications for satisfactory job performance is important in career planning. Unfortunately, descriptions and specifications are sometimes inflated. If this occurs, it can seriously inhibit promotional opportunities for employees within the organization and result in positions of higher responsibility being continuously filled from outside of the organization, since insiders do not meet the overstated specifications. Thorough job analyses can help improve the accuracy of job descriptions and specifications.

Lack of Internal Recruiting Programs

In the absence of career planning and development programs, organizations are unlikely to have definitive procedures for recruiting current employees to fill job vacancies. Skills and management inventories, two basic tools for internal recruiting, may not be utilized at all. If so, systematic identification of internal talent is impossible and the organization will have to look outside for the skilled human resources it needs when new jobs are created or vacancies occur.

Lack of Job Posting

A common complaint of many employees is that they did not know that a higher-level position for which they considered themselves qualified was vacant until someone was brought in from the outside to fill it. Organizations should post all job openings in a highly visible location and encourage employees to bid for these jobs. Present employees are the greatest potential source of candidates for higher-level jobs; but if they do not know about the jobs, they cannot apply for them.

Inadequate Performance Appraisal

Failure of the performance appraisal system to accurately evaluate performance on the present job or to identify areas where an employee needs to improve, or already possesses needed strengths, creates a mobility barrier. An inadequate system provides no usable basis for making promotion or transfer decisions. Excellent performers may be completely overlooked, and underperforming employees may miss out on the training they need to improve their skills so that they can eventually move up in the organization.

Lack of Training and Development Programs

Training programs impart skills for performing the present job or another job. Development programs, in essence, are attempts to bring out the full potential in individuals so that they can progress as far as possible within the organization. Where these kinds of efforts are lacking, another barrier to upward mobility exists.

Managerial Indifference

One of the most important tasks of a manager, but one that is often overlooked, is training and development of subordinates so that they can be fully productive in their present jobs and prepared to move up to other jobs when vacancies arise. When managers are indifferent to this training and development task, mobility is tremendously hampered. Employees are effectively "stuck" in their present positions.

Discrimination: The Glass Ceiling

Despite the advances that have been made in creating equal employment opportunities since the passage of Title VII, discrimination—subtle and insidious in many instances—still exists in today's organizations. Minorities, women, and other protected class members tend to rise only so high in organizations and then go no further. They encounter what has been described as a *glass ceiling*—an invisible but real barrier to upward mobility. According to recent estimates, females hold merely 10 percent of all line-corporate positions in *Fortune* 50 companies,[9] suggesting that women are facing a barrier in advancing to higher-level positions in organizations.[10] Organizational culture, managerial attitudes, stereotypical thinking, lack of training, and similar factors contribute to the construction of the glass ceiling. Obviously, when an institution precludes individuals from advancing as far as their talents could take them, both the organization and the individuals lose. Companies must take extra care to ensure that a glass ceiling that curbs career advancement does not exist.

Career planning and development is an effective way of eliminating the foregoing mobility barriers. Indeed, they must be eliminated if the program is to be successful.

CONSEQUENCES OF NOT PLANNING AND DEVELOPING CAREERS

Organizations that do not take responsibility for the career development of their employees will experience a decrease in their overall effectiveness.[11] A lack of career planning can also seriously impair the staffing process, especially through increased turnover.[12] In addition to excessive turnover, increased recruiting costs, underutilization of talent, employee dissatisfaction, performance problems, stymied progression, poor promotion decisions, and potential discrimination also have significant effects on the staffing process.

Excessive Turnover

Employees who find themselves in dead-end jobs, or who discover that promotional or lateral movement opportunities are severely limited, are prone to leave an organization fairly early in their employment experience, usually within the first six months or so. In one organization that did not have a career planning and development program, turnover of hourly personnel ran as high as 250 percent annually.[13] Certainly, not all of this turnover was the direct result of the lack of a career development program, but undeniably the existence of a number of dead-end jobs and lack of promotional opportunities was a contributing factor to the conservatively estimated $6 million in annual turnover costs incurred by the company.

Increased Recruiting Costs

Excessive turnover increases recruiting costs: constant and sometimes intensive recruiting efforts are required just to keep positions filled. Moreover, if a company gains a reputation for lack of interest in the careers of its employees, the recruiting task becomes even more arduous and more expensive.

Underutilization of Talent

In the absence of career-centered developmental activities, available talent is highly susceptible to underutilization. Employees may be hired to do a particular job, with little or no thought given to other jobs for which they could be trained and developed. Under these conditions, overall organizational effectiveness suffers, and the human resource department bears the burden of excessive turnover and increased recruiting expenses.

Employee Dissatisfaction

When employment expectations are not adequately fulfilled, employees become dissatisfied, motivation decreases, and productivity typically declines. Dissatisfied employees often quit. Those employees who stay may become organizational deadwood.

Stymied Progression

For every employee whose upward mobility is precluded, one or more other employees cannot progress because the employee whose progress is stymied blocks the promotion channel. Organizations sometimes hold an employee in a particular position because of the claim that no one else could take their place. This usually means that an organization has not taken steps to develop or identify replacements. By holding one individual in place, promotional opportunities are being denied to other employees—a situation that may cause dissatisfaction and increased turnover.

Poor Promotion Decisions

Lack of career planning and development may result in poor promotion decisions that are based on favoritism, politics, and inconsequential factors, rather than on performance, preparation, and organizational needs. When the wrong people are promoted—for the wrong reasons—there is a negative impact on institutional effectiveness. Morale, motivation, and commitment are likely to decrease.

Potential Discrimination

In the absence of formalized career planning and development, promotion decisions may tend to be made on the basis of nonrelevant job factors—stereotypes, friendships, or "the good old boy network." Qualified individuals in protected classes may be overlooked. This situation could result in charges of discrimination.

This brief review of the consequences of not engaging in career planning and development has underscored the need for a formalized program. Career management should not be left to chance; the organizational risks of doing so are too great. By demonstrating an interest in employees' careers through a career planning and development program, the benefits of improved morale, increased productivity, and organizational efficiency can be reaped.[14]

RESPONSIBILITY FOR CAREER PLANNING AND DEVELOPMENT

As mentioned earlier, career planning and development is a joint responsibility involving the individual employee and the organization. The following sections cover the roles each party must fulfill for this activity to be accomplished effectively.

Organizational

The organization's principal responsibilities are to develop and implement the career planning and development program, ensure that it produces results, and assist employees through formal as well as informal means. Top management, human resource management, and the firm's immediate supervisors each play an important part in seeing that the program is successful.

Top Management. Although not involved in the day-to-day operation of the program, top management's role in career planning and development is crucial. Management must support the program by emphasizing its importance to all staff, committing adequate resources to its operation, and evaluating the overall results. The program will not work without strong backing from the top echelon of the organization.

Human Resource Management. Human resource administrators have a number of responsibilities in career planning and development. These include: (1) designing the overall system, (2) developing policies and procedures, (3) formulating career paths in conjunction with other managers, (4) selecting the developmental methods, (5) training managers and supervisors for their responsibilities in career management, (6) designing and maintaining replacement tables (see the upcoming section on replacement tables), (7) designing and maintaining skills and management inventories, (8) designing the performance appraisal system and instrument, (9) designing and offering training and development programs, (10) counseling employees, (11) coordinating the program, and (12) evaluating program effectiveness.

Immediate Supervisors. Much of the success of a career planning and development program rests with an organization's supervisors. Without the support and active participation of supervisors, these programs will not work. Supervisors must be able to counsel their staff about career opportunities and developmental needs. They must also be committed to providing needed training, even if this means that the work unit loses some employees to promotions and transfers. A career planning and development program places an additional training responsibility on first-line management. Upper-level management should find ways to reward supervisors who do an outstanding job of developing employees for progression through the organization.

Individual

The one individual who has the primary responsibility for career development is the employee.[15] As Peter Drucker succinctly states, "Development is always self-development." [16] This is not to say that the organization cannot assist development through work experiences, courses, seminars, or other actions. It does suggest, however, that whether developmental opportunities are successful or not depends upon the individual and his or her willingness to take advantage of these opportunities by recognizing the personal responsibility to learn and grow. All workers must become lifelong learners, continually seeking to maintain their job skills. The organization can provide guidance and assistance, but the employee must recognize the responsibility for undertaking the training and development necessary to progress along a chosen career path.

An effective career planning and development program can help stimulate employee interest in development by emphasizing the necessity for learning and growing in a particular job. Training opportunities can also stimulate interest in career management. Reward systems that recognize developmental efforts of employees can, additionally, encourage employees to prepare themselves for current and future opportunities. Ultimately, however, the burden of development rests with the employee.

CAREER PLANNING AND DEVELOPMENT TOOLS

Many tools and methods are used in the career planning and development process. These devices run the gamut from very structured, formal approaches, such as career paths and replacement tables, to unstructured, informal approaches, such as coaching, counseling, and mentoring.

Career Paths

The most basic career management tool for organizations is the career path—the line of job progression along which an employee typically moves during his or her tenure with a company. Depending upon the organization and the nature of the jobs involved, one of three types of career paths may be used: traditional, network, or dual. Examples of these types of paths are illustrated in Figure 12.1.

Traditional. In a traditional career path, an employee moves along a vertical line of progression from one specific job to the next specific job. Figure 12.1 depicts the route a person might take from an entry-level position of teller trainee to an ultimate position of manager of teller services. The traditional career path assumes that each preceding job is essential preparation for the next higher-level job. Consequently, an employee must move step by step from one job to the next to gain needed experience and preparation. This career path is most likely to be found in clerical or production operations functions. However, it may not be as viable as it once was. Traditional career paths no longer consist of employees steadily ascending the organizational ladder. Instead, career paths are now more cyclical or spiral in nature, with employees exploring a variety of directions and working for many different bosses and employers over the span of their careers.[17] The traditional career path is being replaced with the concept of a protean career, a career that is driven by the individual and continuously changes over time.[18] Consequently, the alternative career paths discussed below will probably continue to increase in use.

One of the biggest advantages of the traditional career path is its straightforwardness: the path is clearly laid out and the employee knows the specific sequence of jobs through which he or she must progress. However, this progression ladder fails to recognize that other organizational jobs may provide equivalent or even more substantial experience that could enable an employee to advance without having performed certain jobs in the specified linear sequence. Another potentially serious disadvantage of the traditional career path is that of blockage; that is, a long-tenured employee at one level who is not capable of

Figure 12.1
The Three Types of Career Paths

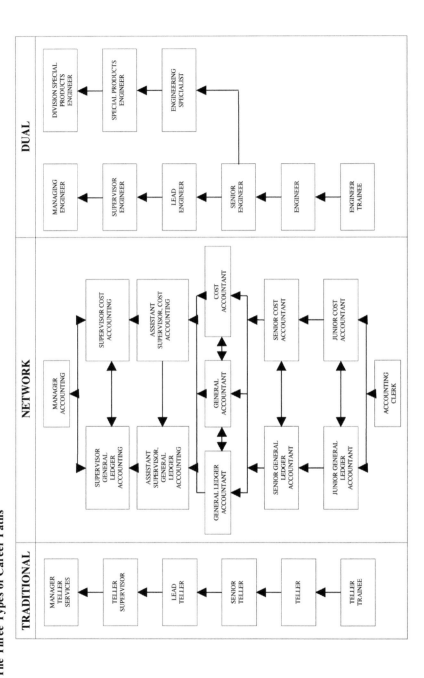

being promoted to the next level may retard the progress of other employees in lower positions.

Network. The network career path is sometimes referred to as a lattice career path, a result of continuous collaboration between an organization and an employee to customize a career path that will help to satisfy the changing needs of the business and the changing life of the employee.[19] This type of career path contains not only a vertical sequence of jobs, but a series of horizontal options as well. Figure 12.1 shows a fairly typical network career path for jobs in an accounting department. Vertically, there are seven levels of jobs through which an employee progresses before becoming manager of the accounting department. At five of these levels, there may be lateral movement between two or more jobs before moving upward to the next level, or there may be no lateral movement before progressing vertically. The network career path recognizes two things: (1) the interchangeability of experience at certain levels and (2) the need to broaden experience at one level before promotion to a higher level.

The network path is a more realistic representation of jobs in an organization than the traditional career path. Moreover, it provides more opportunities for employee development. The network's vertical and horizontal options make it less likely that one employee will block the progression of other employees. A minor disadvantage of this type of career path is that it becomes more difficult to explain to employees the specific route their careers may take within a given line of work.

Dual. The dual career ladder was originally developed to deal with the problem of technically trained employees who had no desire to move into management— the normal procedure for upward mobility in an organization. The dual career path recognizes that technical specialists can and should be allowed to continue to contribute their expertise to a company without having to become managers. Consequently, it provides an alternative progression route whereby an employee such as a scientist or engineer can increase his or her knowledge of a specialized field and make contributions to an organization that are just as valuable as those made by managers. This type of path is also shown in Figure 12.1. Note that after an individual reaches the position of senior engineer, his or her career can be pursued vertically along either a management path or a technical path. Whether on the management or technical side of the path, compensation is the same at each level.

The dual career path is becoming increasingly popular today. In a high-tech world, specialized knowledge is as important as managerial skill. Rather than creating poor managers out of competent technical specialists, the dual career path permits an organization to have both skilled managers and highly competent technical people.

Career paths are very important to successful career planning and development. Not only do they identify typical lines of progression, but they also suggest the developmental experiences and activities that are needed for employees. They are essential for preparing today's employees for tomorrow's jobs.

Replacement Tables

Another career management tool—one that is often valuable in human resource planning—is the replacement table. Because of the time and expense of preparation, replacement tables are usually used only for management or high-level professional positions. Replacement tables generally resemble an organizational chart in that they identify positions and reporting relationships. However, the resemblance ends there because the replacement table contains substantial evaluative information that is used to identify potential successors, assess their current performance, estimate when they may be ready for promotion, and specify developmental needs. Figure 12.2 presents such a table for the position of division manager. The sensitive and confidential nature of the information displayed practically dictates the use of a coding system.

Information for developing a replacement table may come from several sources: the performance appraisal system, reports from a manager's superior, or assessments made by the human resource department. To be used effectively in career planning and development, the information must be updated at least annually.

Replacement tables require an organization to analyze its previous employee developmental efforts and evaluate the extent to which specific individuals have responded to those efforts. In addition, they help an organization discover other experiences and training that individuals may need to prepare them for upward progression.

Skills Inventories

Skills inventories were discussed in Chapter 6 as a human resource planning tool. They are also useful devices for career planning and development. Where skills inventories are maintained on a regular basis, they can be used as a means of internal recruiting, thereby ensuring that current employees are not overlooked when promotional opportunities arise. Analysis of the data maintained in the inventories can also be useful for determining what kinds of training or developmental experiences should be provided to specific employees or groups of employees.

Management Inventories

Management inventories were also discussed previously as a human resource planning tool. They, too, are extremely beneficial in career planning and development. In fact, they are essential in developing replacement tables inasmuch as some of the information needed for table construction is derived directly from the inventory. Additionally, they serve the same basic career management

Figure 12.2
Typical Replacement Table

Position   ⇐ Date Prepared

⇐ Developmental Needs

		Division Manager				6-21-20XX	
Incumbent	B. P. Willis	2-101	5	5	N	58	0
	J. C. Peckins	2-101	5	5	N	47	1,3
	L. O. Stone	2-101	5	5	1	59	1,2,5
Potential Replacements	G. D. Gladden	1-101	4	4	1	49	1,2,3
	S. S. Wycowsky	1-101	4	4	2	35	1,2,3,4
	A. J. Martinez	1-102	4	3	3	42	1,2,5,6,7

Current Position Code   Performance In Current Position   Advancement Potential   When Ready For Advancement   Current Age

EXPLANATION OF CODES

Current Position	Performance in Current Position	Advancement Potential	When Ready for Advancement	Developmental Needs
2-101 Division Manager	5 Excellent	5 Unlimited	N Now	0 None
2-102 Assistant Division Manager	4 Outstanding	4 Excellent	1 Within 1 Year	1 Contract Administration
1-101 Department Manager	3 Acceptable	3 Good	2 Within 2 Years	2 Contract Negotiation
1-102 Assistant Department Manager	2 Needs Improvement	2 Limited	3 Within 3 Years	3 Cost Control
	1 Unsatisfactory	1 None	4 Within 4 Years	4 Delegation
				5 Motivation
				6 Communication
				7 Planning

functions as skills inventories, except at a higher level where development may be extremely crucial to organizational success.

Job Rotation

If carefully planned, job rotation is an excellent way to develop both employees and managers. Through rotation of job assignments, individuals can gain experience in other areas or fields, broaden their backgrounds, and gain a better perspective of company operations. For example, an engineer who knows little about sales or marketing may be given an assignment in the marketing department so that he or she can gain insight into how products are sold, how customers use the products, and what problems customers encounter in using them.

For job rotation to be used successfully as a development tool, several principles must be observed. First, each assignment must be planned so that it adds to, or fills gaps in, the person's background. Therefore, the individual's previous education and experience must be carefully analyzed so that the rotational assignment increases the employee's capabilities. Job rotation that adds little in the way of new skills and experiences is of dubious value. Second, assignments must entail responsibility and the requirement for performance on the job. Rotation that is merely an observational tour, while interesting to the persons involved, is not developmental. Meaningful development comes only through responsibility for performance. Third, each assignment must be long enough to provide the employee with in-depth knowledge of the job and the department. While short assignments may be helpful in understanding what goes on in a particular area, and their use for this purpose should not be precluded, longer assignments are required if significant development is to take place.

Coaching and Mentoring

Coaching is an on-the-job development approach in which a supervisor teaches, trains, counsels, and explains how things are done and why they are done that way. It differs from the typical job instruction approach in that it is highly interactive in nature; the supervisor shares his or her experiences with the employee and the employee asks questions and shares viewpoints with the supervisor.

Since effective coaching is time-consuming, it is not used with all employees in a work group. It is normally reserved for those who show the greatest potential for career development and advancement.

At the managerial level, coaching is frequently referred to as mentoring. An experienced manager takes a subordinate manager under his or her wing and attempts to impart insights and techniques that will make the subordinate a better manager.

A problem that frequently confronts women and minorities in the workplace is that there are few managers who are willing, or able, to serve as mentors for them. Although conscious efforts on the part of organizations are beginning to address this situation, it still remains a problem that must be solved if mentoring is to be an effective career development tool for protected classes. Mentors are more likely to be willing to work with individuals who are similar to themselves. Since the majority of managers are male, white, conservative, etc., females and individuals of nonwhite races have difficulty finding a mentor who will work with them. This preference may or may not reflect prejudice. In many instances, mentors may simply feel that they cannot relate to or understand the career development problems of protected class members. Obviously, increased training and sensitization of mentors is needed.

Counseling

Closely allied to coaching is counseling. Counseling differs from coaching in that it is specifically related to career opportunities or discussion of areas in which an employee needs to make improvement. Much of the responsibility for counseling falls on the first-line supervisor or immediate manager. These individuals are usually best suited for the job because they have the practical experience, possess knowledge of the company, and are in a position to make an accurate appraisal of the organizational opportunities for an employee.[20] However, the human resource department should also be involved in the process, especially as it relates to career progression or development.

Training and Development Programs

Another essential career development tool is training and development. Programs offered in this area may be related directly to employees' jobs or they may be oriented to career-related topics. Obviously, job-related programs could cover almost every aspect of a person's duties and responsibilities. Career programs are usually directed to increasing a person's knowledge of self, aptitudes, interests, and similar attributes. The purpose of job-related programs is to improve present or future work performance; the purpose of career programs is to make the employee more aware of his or her potential so that appropriate career fields within the organization can be pursued.

Performance Appraisal

A performance appraisal system that encourages employees to work toward specific goals, identifies strengths and weaknesses, and accurately measures current performance is important to career development. Feedback from the system may lead to a great deal of self-development or it may require the organization to initiate specific training activities to assist in developing employees.

Special Projects or Work Teams

In recent years, work teams have become popular and have been used to help develop employees, professionals, and even managers. Undoubtedly, the widespread use of "Total Quality Management" in organizations has focused interest on the organizational, as well as the individual, benefits to be gained from participating in teams. Teams, or special projects, expose employees to different situations and different people while providing them the opportunity to solve problems, make decisions, and participate in important organizational activities. By working on different teams, an individual can increase his or her understanding of the organization, its processes, its problems, and its people, thereby adding to the individual's career mobility opportunities.

Ideally, any organization truly interested in furthering the careers of its employees would use all of the career planning and development tools available. This would ensure that the organization is fulfilling its role, and that managers and supervisors are prepared to carry out their roles in support of the career management endeavor.

REQUIREMENTS FOR A SUCCESSFUL PROGRAM

Most of the requirements for a successful career planning and development program can be deduced from the material that has already been presented in this chapter. However, for the sake of emphasis, the essential ingredients for an effective program will now be specifically delineated.

- *Top management commitment.* No major organizational program can be successful without the full support and commitment of top management. This commitment is more than just allocating resources to implement and operate the program. It entails a belief in the value of human resources and the recognition of the organization's responsibility to itself and its people to take positive steps to help employees reach their full potential.
- *Formulation.* Career planning and development is too important and too complex to be handled informally. The program must be carefully thought out, policies and procedures developed, and responsibilities assigned. Needless to say, it must be written down and communicated to all concerned parties.
- *Promotion from within policy.* Such a policy is one of the cornerstones of effective career planning and development. This policy must be adhered to as assiduously as possible. Failure to follow the policy will cast serious doubts on the organization's interest in the careers of its employees.
- *Job posting and bidding system.* Concomitantly with promotion from within, the organization must have an effectively functioning job posting and bidding system that clearly provides current employees the right and the opportunity to apply for job vacancies (promotional or lateral) before efforts are initiated to fill positions from external sources. The right to bid for job openings signifies the organization's interest in the progression of its employees.

- *Training and development programs.* Training and development opportunities of all kinds are requisites for effective career planning and development. Workshops, seminars, skills training sessions, educational assistance, and many similar endeavors are necessary to develop employees to their fullest potential. These programs are also tangible evidence of the organization's commitment to its human resources.

- *Training of managers and supervisors.* Support for a career planning and development program must not only come from the top of the firm, it must also come from the operating managers and supervisors who coach, counsel, and assist employees in their development. All managers must be thoroughly trained to fully and effectively carry out their responsibilities in the program.

- *Communication.* Communication of the program must be accomplished through any and all means possible—personnel policy manuals, supervisory handbooks, employee handbooks, bulletin boards, and periodic announcements. Free and open communication is another indication of the company's interest in and commitment to the program.

NOTES

1. Keith H. Hammonds, Wendy Zellner, and Richard Melcher, "Writing a New Social Contract," *Business Week* 3466 (March 11, 1996): 60.

2. Wayne F. Cascio, *Managing Human Resources: Productivity, Quality of Work Life, Profits,* 7th ed. (New York: McGraw-Hill Irwin, 2006), 375.

3. Ibid., 673.

4. Ibid., 391.

5. Lloyd L. Byars and Leslie W. Rue, *Human Resource Management,* 9th ed. (New York: McGraw-Hill Irwin, 2008), 194.

6. Cascio, *Managing Human Resources: Productivity, Quality of Work Life, Profits,* 28.

7. Charles R. Greer, *Strategic Human Resource Management: A General Managerial Approach,* 2nd ed. (Upper Saddle River, NJ: Prentice-Hall, 2001), 6–8.

8. Byars and Rue, *Human Resource Management,* 193–207.

9. *Women in U.S. Corporate Leadership: 2003* (New York: Catalyst, 2003).

10. Raymond A. Noe, John R. Hollenbeck, Barry Gerhart, and Patrick M. Wright, *Human Resource Management: Gaining a Competitive Advantage,* 6th ed. (New York: McGraw-Hill Irwin, 2008), 434.

11. Cascio, *Managing Human Resources: Productivity, Quality of Work Life, Profits,* 373.

12. Byars and Rue, *Human Resource Management,* 194.

13. Based on one of the author's experiences as a manager with this organization.

14. Deborah A. F. Koehle, "Study Looks at How Exemplary-Practice Companies Use Training and Development Efforts to Attract and Retain Employees," *Training & Development* 54, no. 7 (July 2000): 78–79.

15. H. Fred Walker and Justin Levesque, "Climbing the Career Ladder: It's Up to You," *Quality Progress* 39, no. 10 (October 2006): 28–32.

16. Peter F. Drucker, *Management: Tasks, Responsibilities, Practices* (New York: Harper & Row, 1974), 427.

17. Jean M. Kummerow, *New Directions in Career Planning and the Workplace,* 2nd ed. (Palo Alto, CA: Davies-Black Publishing, 2000), 51–52.

18. Douglas T. Hall, "Protean Careers of the 21st Century," *The Academy of Management Executive* 10, no. 4 (November 1996): 8–16.

19. Cathleen Benko and Anne Weisberg, "Implementing a Corporate Career Lattice: The Mass Career Customization Model," *Strategy & Leadership* 35, no. 5 (2007): 29–36.

20. Byars and Rue, *Human Resource Management,* 199.

13

Staffing System Administration

Human resource administration begins when an employee is hired and continues throughout the person's tenure with the organization and even beyond. Human resource administration encompasses a multitude of activities: issuing payroll checks, processing insurance claims, maintaining time and attendance records, updating employee files, revising compensation rates, and so forth. Every functional area in an organization's personnel system affects, and is affected by, human resource administration. This chapter, however, deals only with those administrative activities directly related in a major way to the staffing system. These activities are the following: (1) employee orientation; (2) promotions; (3) transfers; (4) demotions; (5) resignations; (6) downsizing, layoffs, and reductions in force; (7) terminations; (8) retirements; and (9) providing references to other employers. While line management has the responsibility for carrying out most of these activities, the human resource department develops the policies, procedures, and guidelines for ensuring that these activities are accomplished in a logical, consistent, equitable, and legally defensible fashion. The human resource department, of course, has the responsibility for maintaining adequate records relative to these activities.

EMPLOYEE ORIENTATION

Orientation is the process whereby a new employee is familiarized with the organization, the job, the work group, and other terms and conditions of employment. Orientation is both a formal and an informal process. On the formal side, the human resource department may conduct classes that introduce the worker to company history, policies, codes of conduct, health and insurance benefits, and other items of importance; or the new worker's supervisor, following a prescribed format, may introduce the employee to the requirements of the job, departmental operations, and other employees. On the informal side, there may be no formal classes. There may, on a new worker's first day, simply be oral explanations, delivered in one-on-one fashion, covering major items of importance, or the new worker may receive an employee handbook to read. In other cases the supervisor may, without adhering to any formalized procedure, explain the job and introduce the new worker to other employees in the work group and identify starting and quitting times, and inform the new employee of the lunch hour.

Purposes of Orientation

Whether it is accomplished formally or informally, employee orientation has five general purposes: (1) to introduce the new employee to the organization, its history, traditions, and culture; (2) to create a favorable impression of the organization; (3) to help the new employee adjust to the organization; (4) to provide information about the job and performance expectations; and (5) to furnish information on policies, rules, employee services, benefits, and similar items. For orientation to be effective, it must accomplish each of these purposes.

Introduction to the Organization. Every organization has its history, traditions, and culture—its own way of doing things. An essential purpose of orientation is to give new employees this sense of what the institution is about, what it values, where it has come from, where it is now, and where it is going. Whether it is the "HP Way" (Hewlett-Packard) or McDonald's restaurant's four key values,[1] new employees need to understand organizational culture and how they will fit into it.

Favorable Impression. A second purpose of orientation is to create a favorable impression of the organization and the job. It is not unusual for a new employee to have doubts about the new organization and the new job even after learning of its history, traditions, and culture. Consequently, the orientation process must attempt to demonstrate that the organization is a good place to work and that each job is vital to successful operation of the firm. A word of caution is in order, however. It is very easy, and perhaps too tempting, to go overboard in this area. The impression conveyed to the new worker should be an honest one. If it is not, employees will soon discover the truth for themselves and become disillusioned

Adjustment to the Organization. For many people, the first few days on a new job can be a frightening, tension producing, or anxiety-laden experience.[2] There is much to be learned—new procedures, new methods, new requirements. There are new people to be met. There are new customs and traditions to be absorbed. The new employee may well feel at a loss unless the organization makes a deliberate attempt to ease the transition into the job and surroundings.

The immediate supervisor plays a large role in helping the employee make the initial adjustment to the organization. Explanations concerning the job, introductions to members of the work group, familiarization with the physical surroundings, and information regarding break times, lunch times, and so forth are a few of the basic things a supervisor needs to do to make the new worker feel more comfortable with the job and organization.

Integration of the new employee into the formal work group is also important. Often, this can be accomplished best by assigning the new person to work with a senior employee who not only trains the new hire but also introduces him or her to the other workers and generally sees that the new person is made to feel part of the total work group.

Of special concern may be the problem of easing the adjustment of women or minorities to the work group, particularly where the group previously has been predominantly white males. Without proper introduction to the work group, employee turnover may be higher for members of protected classes than those in the more traditional work group.[3] A supervisor has the additional responsibility in this case of preparing the work group in advance for the arrival of the protected class employee. The supervisor should reiterate the organization's policy on equal employment and state his or her expectations of behavior from current employees.

Information about the Job and Performance Expectations. Another purpose of orientation is to give the new employee specific information about how the job is to be performed, the quantity of work expected, and quality levels that must be maintained. It is axiomatic that people cannot be fully productive unless they completely understand what is expected of them. Not knowing what is expected, they may set their own bogus performance standards either too high or too low. Or they may grow frustrated with the job and become another number in the organization's turnover statistics. It is clearly the responsibility of the immediate work group supervisor to ensure that each new employee has a thorough understanding of what is to be done on the job, how it is to be done, why it is to be done, when it is to be done, and where it is to be done. Proper explanation of these matters not only reduces turnover but also assists employees to become productive workers as rapidly as possible.

Information on Rules, Policies, and Benefits. The final purpose of employee orientation is to furnish the worker with information concerning a host of items that are important not only to the employee but to the organization as well. Among these are the following: (1) policies relative to promotion, vacation eligibility, outside employment, ethics, and the like; (2) work rules concerning time clock procedures, labor hour reporting, absence reporting, and so forth; (3) employee services such as discounts on merchandise, tuition refund programs, recreational opportunities, child care or elder care centers, and (4) benefits related to health insurance, life insurance, profit sharing, retirement plans, and other forms of indirect compensation. Some of this information will come from the supervisor, while other parts will come from the human resource department, often in the form of an employee handbook or an online site.

It is estimated that between 60 and 80 percent of the current work force in an organization is not only new to the organization but to the job market as well. The new work force with which many companies have to deal includes either late entries or reentries of women, people who were formerly self-employed, recent high school and college graduates, and individuals who have made career changes.[4] Undoubtedly, many of these individuals have anxieties about entering an organization—anxieties that can be alleviated through an effective new employee orientation program.

Stages in Effective Orientation

An effective employee orientation program has four stages. These are described below in the order in which they typically occur.

Human Resource Department Overview. For the vast majority of employees, the first day on a new job begins in the human resource department. There are forms to be completed, insurance options to be exercised, beneficiaries to be designated, and other administrative details to be attended to just to get a person on the payroll and enrolled in an organization's benefits programs. At this time, the new employee is usually given some general information about the company, its policies, procedures, compensation, etc. An employee handbook or Web site may also be provided to the new hire. Some companies use new employee checklists such as the one shown in Figure 13.1 to ensure that human resource representatives cover all basic information with the worker. Additionally, information may be provided about the company's products, services, locations, subsidiaries, and other matters pertaining to the overall organization.

Supervisory Indoctrination. The new employee's supervisor is responsible for the second stage of the orientation program. Items covered include an overview of the department, job requirements, safety procedures, break and lunch times, specific work rules, location of restrooms and cafeterias, a tour of the department, and personal introductions to other employees. It is beneficial to use a checklist here, too, so that the supervisor does not neglect to mention any item of importance. A supervisory orientation checklist is shown in Figure 13.2. Comparing this figure with the previous one reveals that the immediate supervisor must explain a number of job-related details, whereas the human resource department is basically concerned with benefits, services, and company overview. It cannot be emphasized too strongly that the key role in successful orientation is performed by the work group supervisor.

Formal Orientation. Formal orientation typically takes place in a classroom and is conducted by a member of the human resource staff. These sessions may be as short as one or two hours or as long as a full day, depending upon the importance the organization attaches to new-hire orientation. Shorter sessions generally focus on benefits and employee services; longer sessions tend to include company history, products, processes, and even presentations by high-ranking company representatives. Orientation classes fulfill two general purposes: they provide in-depth explanation and discussion of matters that are important to new employees, and they introduce new employees to each other so that the new

Figure 13.1
New Employee Orientation Checklist

EMPLOYEE _____   EMPLOYMENT DATE _____
JOB TITLE _____   DEPARTMENT _____
PAY GRADE _____   SUPERVISOR _____

I. INFORMATION PROVIDED

☐ 1.   COMPANY ORGANIZATION
☐ 2.   BASIC INSURANCE BENEFITS
    ☐ Medical   ☐ Dental   ☐ Life
    ☐ Disability   ☐ Travel
☐ 3.   OPTIONAL INSURANCE BENEFITS
    ☐ Additional Life Insurance
    ☐ Comprehensive Medical
☐ 4.   PAYMENTS FOR TIME NOT WORKED
    ☐ Holidays   ☐ Vacations
    ☐ Sick Leave   ☐ Miscellaneous Time Off
☐ 5.   EMPLOYEE SERVICES
    ☐ Training Programs   ☐ Tuition Reimbursements
    ☐ Recreational Facilities ☐ In-House Medical Services
    ☐ Products Discounts   ☐ Retirement Programs
☐ 6.   COMPENSATION
    ☐ Salary Range   ☐ Performance Reviews
    ☐ Pay Periods
☐ 7.   OTHER
    ☐ Equal Employment Opportunity
    ☐ Promotion Policy
    ☐ Suggestion System

II. MATERIALS PROVIDED

☐ 1.   ORIENTATION PACKET
☐ 2.   I.D. CARD
☐ 3.   EMPLOYEE HANDBOOK
☐ 4.   LABOR AGREEMENT
☐ 5.   INSURANCE HANDBOOK

The employee has been given the information and materials indicated above.

_____   _____
Human Resource Representative   Date

I have received the information and materials indicated above.

_____   _____
Employee   Date

person's acquaintances are not limited solely to his or her department or sphere
of operations.

Employee orientation classes usually occur after a person has been on the job
for a while—at least a few days and sometimes several weeks. Some experience
on the job and with the organization affords the new worker time to formulate
questions that might not otherwise surface if formal orientation was held the first

Figure 13.2
Supervisor's Orientation Checklist

Employee	_____	Employment Date	_____
Job Title	_____	Department	_____
Pay Grade	_____	Supervisor	_____

I. **General Information**
- o **Departmental Organization**
- o **Products or Services**
- o **Relationship to Other Departments**

II. **Employer's Job**
- o **Job Description**
- o **Relationship to Other Jobs**
- o **Performance Expectation**

III. **Working Conditions**
o	**Hours of Work**	o	**Time Cards**
o	**Employee Entrances**	o	**Lunch Hours**
o	**Break Periods**	o	**Restroom Locations**
o	**Cafeteria Location**	o	**Overtime Requirements**

IV. **Work Rules**
o	**Absences**	o	**Tardiness**
o	**Personal Phone Calls**	o	**Safety Procedures**
o	**Probationary Period**		

V. **Introductions**
- o **Co-Workers**
- o **Trainer**
- o **Union Representative**

_____

Employee's Signature   **Date**

_____

Supervisor's Signature   **Date**

day of employment. While it is critical that an employee be given adequate information about the company and job on the first day, information overload may occur if too much is provided at that time.

Follow-up. For orientation to be completely effective, there must be some form of follow-up and evaluation. During the first few weeks on the job, the immediate supervisor should work very closely with the employee to clarify any misunderstandings and see that the employee is properly integrated into the work group. The human resource department also plays a part in follow-up, either by working with the supervisor or by directly contacting the employee.

Training Supervisors for Their Role in Orientation. Of critical importance to any successful orientation program is training for supervisors so that they can carry out their key role. The human resource department can provide the new employee with a great deal of organizational information, but only the supervisor can fulfill the function of integrating the employee into the work group.

In training supervisors, the following points about orientation should be emphasized:

- Orientation is an investment in people since it prepares new employees for organizational entry and successful job performance.
- Effective orientation reduces employee turnover, thereby saving money for the organization.
- Proper orientation enables employees to become productive more quickly.
- Both positive and negative features of the job should be explained to the employee.
- Orientation is not limited to the employee's first day on the job—nurturing and support may be needed for several weeks.
- The supervisor should explain his or her likes and dislikes relative to job performance.
- All questions, comments, and concerns on the part of the employee should be considered important and addressed appropriately.
- Introductions to other employees are crucial and should not be handled perfunctorily.
- Details—location of restrooms, lunch periods, time clock procedures, and so forth—should not be overlooked because little things can make a big difference to the new employee and his or her adjustment to the organization.

PROMOTIONS

Promotion, the upward movement of an employee to a position of greater responsibility and compensation, is another crucial human resource administration or staffing system activity. Promotions have a direct impact on staffing because they are signals to employees that growth and advancement are realities within an organization. Decisions as to promotion criteria and who will be promoted are made by line management, but usually with assistance from human resource staffing specialists. In a unionized environment, seniority is normally the ruling criterion; in a nonunionized organization, work performance—or some combination of performance and seniority—is generally the basis for making such decisions.

One major problem associated with promotions—one that may necessitate counseling with employees or other efforts to retain productive workers—is that not everyone can or will receive a promotion. It has been estimated that once beyond entry-level positions, only one out of every seven employees will receive a promotion.[5] Thus, for every elated employee who is promoted, there may be six other disappointed employees for line management and the human resource department to deal with. Promotion decisions can be made more palatable to those who are not promoted by having clear promotion policies and criteria. It is here that staffing specialists can be of invaluable assistance to supervisors and managers who must make promotion decisions.

In the future, promotions may be even harder to obtain than they are today. Changes in work force demographics, removal of the mandatory retirement age, organizational downsizing to reduce costs, and global competition that retards the growth of firms are factors that will restrict the number of higher-level positions to which employees can be promoted. Outsourcing of company functions will further curb advancement possibilities as firms continue to subcontract the execution of their noncore functions to outside institutions. Additionally, greater numbers of women and minorities vying for positions denied them in the past will place limitations on promotional opportunities for white males.[6] This is becoming a problem that will have to be dealt with in the near future.

Considering the changes that are likely to occur in promotional opportunities, human resource specialists may be well advised to consider two alternatives to traditional promotions. First, place a greater emphasis on learning, growth, and development in the present job through various types of training and development efforts. Second, develop "dual promotion" ladders that reward creative, technical, or professional personnel with financial rewards similar to those people who advance into management positions. The dual promotion ladder supports the first alternative by allowing individuals to grow in their own fields without having to make a switch into management positions—the typical promotion route for many employees. The individual can advance in his or her own area of expertise and reap the normal rewards of promotion, but continue doing the same type of work. Currently, this concept of dual ladder promotion is being used in high-tech companies to keep engineers and scientists in areas where they are vitally needed, but it is also being increasingly used in other industries such as education, publishing, and banking.[7]

TRANSFERS

A transfer is a lateral movement of an employee from one job to another job of essentially equal responsibility and compensation. Transfers may be initiated by the organization or by the employee. Transfers, by definition, are neither promotions or demotions; they are shifts in jobs.

Transfers serve several useful purposes in organizations. First, they are a means of developing employees by giving them experience in different functional areas of a firm. An employee's knowledge of the organization can be broadened or an employee's skills can be sharpened by lateral movement through meaningful organizational job assignments. In essence, transfers can serve training as well as career development purposes.

Second, transfers are often necessitated by reorganizations. As offices and departments are created, it may be imperative to transfer employees to fill positions. By the same token, when work units or positions are eliminated, management may find transfers a viable way to retain valued employees who might otherwise be terminated.

A third reason for transfers is to satisfy needs or desires of employees. Personal reasons for wanting to transfer are numerous: to reduce commuting time, to learn a new job, to use different skills, to work with new people, to experience a new working environment, etc. By accommodating the employee's wishes, the organization can retain productive workers who might quit if the transfer is not forthcoming.

Another reason for using transfers is to open up promotional opportunities. Productive, but nonpromotable, employees may retard the upward mobility of lower-level workers who are qualified for advancement. In order not to lose qualified workers, it may be necessary for organizations to resort to transfers to create promotion vacancies for up-and-coming employees.

Finally, transfers may be utilized to eliminate personality clashes. An employee may not be able to work effectively for a particular supervisor or with other members of a work group. By shifting the person to another position, this problem may be eliminated.

Transfers can serve the best interests of both employee and organization. However, definite policies that clearly spell out the conditions under which transfers will be used or granted must be developed. Development of these policies is, obviously, one of the functions of human resource administration.

DEMOTIONS

A demotion is the movement of an employee to a job of lesser responsibility or lower-level duties than the one the employee currents occupies. Typically, a reduction in compensation accompanies a demotion. There are basically three conditions that may require the use of demotion as a staffing tool: promotion of an individual beyond his or her level of capabilities, reduction of the organization's work force, or an alternative to discharge.

Promotions are normally made on the basis of performance or seniority in one's current job—neither of which are necessarily valid indicators of how a person will perform in a higher-level position. It may turn out that the employee cannot perform satisfactorily at a higher level of responsibility. In this case poor performance is not the worker's fault; it is management's fault. To terminate an employee who was productive in his or her previous job would be unjust to the employee and could even result in other employees becoming reluctant to take promotions. Consequently, it is better to move the poorly performing employee back to the level at which his or her performance was satisfactory.

Work force reductions or downsizing may also involve demotions. For example, where two similar units are combined into one to reduce the total number of workers, one supervisory position will be eliminated. Instead of terminating the unneeded supervisor, the organization may elect to demote that person to retain his or her skills and abilities so that if expansion occurs in the future a qualified person is already available for a higher-level job.

Where long-tenured employees are involved, demotion may be used successfully as an alternative to termination. An employee may have performed well in a position for a number of years but due to physical or other reasons is no longer capable of performing at the same level. Demotion can be used to deal with this problem.

In a unionized environment, demotion policies and procedures are delineated clearly in the labor-management agreement. In a nonunionized organization, they may or may not be, depending upon the consideration that has gone into formulating comprehensive human resource policies. Demotion, however, is too much of an emotionally charged process to be handled on a case-by-case basis; there should be definitive policies defining its usage.

RESIGNATIONS

Even in the best of organizations, it is inevitable that employees will resign. A certain amount of turnover is beneficial for a company because it provides an opportunity to bring in new people with fresh ideas and approaches, creates promotional opportunities for current workers, rectifies poor selection or placement decisions, and helps prevent organizational stagnation. But too much turnover can be disruptive and expensive for a firm. Unfortunately, no one has yet established how much turnover is good and how much is bad. The Bureau of National Affairs (BNA), however, does publish a quarterly report on job absence and turnover that provides baseline information organizations can use to compare their turnover rates with other institutions. BNA's report shows turnover by organizational size, industry, and region. While these figures encompass both voluntary and involuntary turnover, the report offers data that a company can use to establish what it considers to be a reasonable resignation rate.

Why Employees Leave

Employees may choose to leave an organization for a variety of reasons. Table 13.1 shows the major causes of resignations and suggests actions that can be taken to deal with each potential cause of turnover.

Table 13.1
Why Employees Leave and What to Do About It

1. Poor Selection or Mismatching • Develop job descriptions and job specifications. • Train interviewers. • Use appropriate selection tests. • Check references carefully. • Use employment agencies for screening.	**6. Monotonous Work** • Use realistic job previews. • Redesign jobs to enrich content. • Use a job rotation system. • Pay premium compensation.
2. Lack of Opportunity for Advancement • Use realistic job previews. • Develop career progress ladders. • Use a job posting and bidding system. • Provide training and development opportunities.	**7. Inadequate Grievance Procedures** • Implement a formal system for handling complaints. • Maintain open communications. • Develop an open door policy. • Use an ombudsman.
3. Poor Supervision • Provide interpersonal skills training. • Reward supervisors for turnover reduction. • Replace ineffective supervisors.	**8. Personal Problems** • Train supervisors to be listeners and counselors. • Train supervisors to watch for warning signs. • Implement an employee assistance program.
4. Inadequate Compensation • Implement a compensation plan. • Conduct compensation surveys to assure competitiveness. • Review compensation and benefits on regular basis. • Use a performance appraisal system.	**9. Low Work Group Morale** • Provide interpersonal skills training for supervisors. • Train supervisors to be listeners. • Train supervisors to watch for warning signs. • Conduct attitude surveys on a regular basis. • Maintain good physical surroundings.
5. Insufficient Training • Provide thorough orientation. • Implement formal training programs. • Train supervisors to be trainers and coaches.	**10. Labor Market Conditions** • Stay attuned to changes in supply and demand for various skills. • Implement a compensation plan. • Conduct compensation surveys to assure competitiveness. • Review compensation and benefits on a regular basis.

Source: Don Caruth and Frank Rachel, "Why Employees Leave and What to Do About It," unpublished working paper, 2008.

While understanding the general causes of resignations is an excellent starting point, an organization should conduct its own analyses to isolate specific causes so that the organization can initiate specific corrective actions to eliminate excessive resignations.

Analyzing Resignations

Two techniques for determining the reasons behind voluntary resignations are exit interviews and post-exit questionnaires. Often, both methods are used in combination with each other.

Exit Interview. An exit interview is conducted while the employee is still on the firm's payroll. It is normally the last formal contact the employee has with the organization. The responsibility for conducting the interview usually rests with the human resource department inasmuch as the employee is more likely to respond in a free and open fashion to a human resource representative than he or she would to an immediate supervisor or other manager. In conducting the exit interview, the interviewer typically adheres to the following pattern:

- Establishes rapport with the employee.
- Explains the purpose of the interview.
- Assures the employee of confidentiality.
- Solicits attitudes relative to the old job.
- Solicits attitudes relative to the company.
- Explores the employee's reasons for leaving.
- Asks the employee to compare the old job with the new job he or she is taking.
- Asks the employee to suggest any changes he or she would recommend for the job, the department, or the organization.
- Concludes the interview on a positive note.[8]

An effective exit interview focuses on job-related factors and probes in depth for the real reasons the employee is leaving the company. While one specific interview may not provide much eye-opening information, a series of interviews conducted over time can identify patterns that indicate weaknesses in the human resource management system or the organization's methods of operating. On the basis of this kind of information, appropriate corrective actions can be taken.

Post-exit Questionnaire. The second method for uncovering causes of resignations is the post-exit questionnaire. When this approach is used, former employees are sent a questionnaire to complete and mail back to the company. The instrument is usually sent to the former employee's home two to three weeks after the employee has terminated. The advantage of this method is that, since the person is no longer with the organization, he or she may respond more candidly, thereby revealing the real reasons for leaving. When a questionnaire is used, it should be carefully constructed so that it provides sufficient information and is designed so that it can be completed fairly quickly. Ample blank space should also be included to allow the former employee to express his or her feelings about the job, supervisor, or company.

To obtain the most complete resignation information possible, both the interview and the questionnaire should be used.

Resignation Policies

Two human resource policy areas that merit attention are advance notification of intent to resign and whether or not the terminating employee will be allowed to remain on the job until the resignation is effective. Organizational practices in these areas vary considerably.

Normally, organizations request that employees give two weeks notice when resigning. It is not unusual to find firms that request a month's notice from professional or managerial employees. Advance notice gives the organization time to seek a replacement. When advance notice is requested, the organization typically pays the individual for the stipulated period even if it does not allow the person to remain on the job. Of course, an employee is always free to quit without any notification whatsoever in which case the company is not obligated to compensate the employee further.

Should the departing employee be allowed to remain on the job for the length of the notification period? There are two sides to this question. On the one hand, the employee may be needed to perform important work or to help train a replacement. On the other hand, a terminating worker can create problems by becoming nonproductive; or the worker, if resentful of the company or the supervisor, can be a disruptive force that causes morale problems among other employees. As a general policy, it is preferable to keep the worker in the job, but exceptions will have to be made if problems arise.

LAYOFFS, DOWNSIZING, AND REDUCTIONS IN FORCE

Strictly speaking a layoff is a temporary or indefinite termination of an employee because of economic reasons usually with the stipulation that the employee will be recalled to work as soon as business picks up. Today it is common for organizations to refer to downsizing, reductions in force, or any other large-scale termination of employees as a layoff; however, there is now no implied return to work at a later date. Currently corporate layoffs in the United States involve as many as one million workers per year.

Although being laid off does not carry the same stigma as being fired, the short-term effect is the same: the person is unemployed. In a sense, a layoff may be more devastating to an individual than a termination. When a person is terminated, the relationship with the organization is permanently severed and the former employee is completely free to seek other employment. In the case of a layoff, the individual still has ties to the company and there is the lingering hope that the future may hold, however slim the odds, the possibility of recall. Moreover, the person may find job search opportunities hampered because other organizations may be unwilling to hire someone who may leave at some point to return to his or her former job.

In a union contract layoff and recall procedures are clearly spelled out. Employees are laid off in inverse order of seniority and recalled on the basis of seniority. Typical contract procedures provide for "bumping rights" or job regression privileges; that is, when a senior level position is eliminated, the person occupying the position has the right to bump an employee with less seniority from a lower-level position. The worker who is bumped may, in turn, bump another worker. Thus, in a unionized company, a layoff may drastically alter the composite of the work force as employees bump other employees throughout the organizational hierarchy.

In a nonunion environment, layoff policies and procedures are more likely to be ill-defined, with factors other than seniority deciding the question of which workers go and which workers stay. Productivity or performance may be the biggest consideration. To avoid charges of favoritism or discrimination, union-free organizations should establish definitive policies and procedures regarding downsizing, layoffs, or reductions in force and formulate a downsizing plan in order to protect themselves and ensure compliance with both federal and state statutes. This plan should answer the following questions:[9]

- What cuts in the workforce are actually required?
- Which jobs or functions are involved?
- How will employees be selected for termination?
- Will the reduction be accomplished all at once or in stages?
- When will the reduction occur?
- How will the company communicate its downsizing plans to employees, the community, and other stakeholders?
- What assistance will be available to displaced employees?
- What will be included in the severance package?
- What will be done to ensure that operations run smoothly during the downsizing period?
- What policies will be adopted, if any, for rehiring terminated employees?
- What consequences must be dealt with to ensure normal operational functioning after the reduction in employees has been completed?

Spurred by the success of Japanese companies in providing what is tantamount to lifetime employment, a few American companies have adopted a "no layoff" policy as a means of maintaining a stable work force. Considering the number of layoffs and the size of work force reductions announced each year, however, it seems doubtful that an employment guarantee policy will develop into a trend among U. S. companies.

Theoretically, a reduction in force differs from a layoff in that it is a permanent separation from the company. Today reductions in force are euphuistically referred to as "downsizing," "rightsizing," or "reengineering." Permanent reductions in staff may be necessitated as follows: (1) by elimination of certain company operations or departments, (2) by subcontracting functions to other companies, (3) by increased automation, (4) by the need to cut costs to remain competitive, (5) by relocation of a plant from one geographical area to another, (6) by changes in customer demand for products or services, (7) by corporate reorganizations, or (8) by mergers and acquisitions.

Under the Worker Adjustment and Retraining Act of 1989, employers with 100 or more full-time employees are required to notify workers 60 days in advance of any intended plant closing or mass layoff. This notice must be in writing and must be given to state officials and each representative of the employees affected or, if there is no employee representative, directly to the employees themselves.[10]

Many of the questions that must be answered in layoffs, as listed above, must also be addressed when a reduction in force occurs.

TERMINATION

Termination, the permanent severing of the relationship between organization and employee, is the most severe penalty a company can impose on an individual. It is usually a drastic step for the organization and a traumatic experience for the employee. The employee is likely to feel angry, hurt, depressed, shocked, or concerned about the future. The supervisor or manager making the termination is apt to be tense or anxious as well.

While there are a number of similarities in the termination of employees at any level in the organization, there are also distinct differences that exist between the discharging of operative level employees, managers and professionals, and executives.

Termination of Operative Employees

Generally, the policies and procedures for terminating operative employees are well defined and outlined in human resource policy manuals or employee handbooks. Most organizations are careful to delineate the types of offenses or behavior that will result in immediate discharge of an employee. These offenses typically include:

- Theft of company or another employee's property.
- Appropriation or misappropriation of company funds.
- Possession, use, or being under the influence of alcohol or drugs on the organization's premises.
- Possession of a firearm on company property.
- Deliberate falsification of personnel records such as employment applications or time cards.
- Willful abuse or deliberate damage of company property.
- Immoral conduct or indecency.

- Insubordination or willful failure to perform assigned tasks.
- Fighting on company premises.
- Job abandonment—absence without notice or approval for three consecutive working days.
- Revealing proprietary information to a competitor.

Repeated violations of other work rules may also constitute grounds for immediate termination; for example, sleeping on the job, soliciting political contributions, or leaving the premises without permission during working hours.

Termination of Managers and Professionals

Perhaps the most vulnerable group of organizational members subject to termination are managers and professionals. These individuals may be discharged for any number of reasons—the ones that apply to operative level employees or the ones that apply to executives. Managers and professionals lack the political clout that executives have; they are not protected by labor agreements; the reasons for their terminations are not clearly defined; they often are not inclined to seek protection under antidiscriminatory statutes. Undoubtedly, individuals in this group are the organizational workers most likely to be fired on the basis of whim or caprice.[11] It would appear that definitive policies are needed for the termination of managers and professionals.

Termination of Executives

Discharging an executive is quite different from terminating other types of employees. In most instances, there are no identified policies, procedures, or grounds for termination of executives, nor is there an appeal mechanism the executive can use. The primary reasons for firing an executive are the following:

- Lack of "fit"—the executive has a personality conflict with another executive, is not considered a "team player," or has philosophical differences with other officials relative to operation of the company. In other words the executive just "does not fit in with the rest of the executives.
- Reorganization—mergers, acquisitions, realignments, or leveraged buyouts may result in elimination of the position.
- Economics—adverse business conditions, recession, global competition, and the like may force the elimination of high level jobs.
- Decline in performance—inability to produce the results desired by the organization, inability to generate new business, failure to meet deadlines, and the like may necessitate the removal of an individual.

Of all of the above cited reasons for executive terminations, the major one is usually "lack of fit."[12] At other levels in the organization, people are usually terminated because of poor performance or job elimination, whereas at the executive level personality, politics, and personal factors are the predominant causes of discharge.

Increasingly, contemporary organizations are taking a more socially responsible attitude concerning executives—and other personnel, for that matter—who are terminated by assisting them in finding further employment. This effort, known as outplacement, will be discussed in a subsequent section.

General Guidelines for Termination

There is no question that terminating an employee, regardless of the individual's level in the organization, is a necessity at times—a necessity that is in the best interest of the organization as well as the employee. The basic problem is how to go about it in a manner that preserves the dignity of the person and the reputation of the organization. The starting point is the development of termination policies that clearly state the organization's position on termination. Next is the establishment of procedures on how the actual termination will be handled. The biggest difficulty in terminating anyone is the face-to-face meeting in which the person is informed that his or her services are no longer needed by the organization. Here are some guidelines for handling a termination effectively:

1. Document the reasons for the termination. Include accounts of all previous performance or disciplinary discussions.

2. Do not terminate in haste or while under emotional stress. Discharging workers on the spot may result in serious legal repercussions.

3. Do not terminate an employee on Friday afternoon (the most typical termination time) because the individual cannot initiate efforts to secure new employment over the weekend and may even resort to forms of nonproductive behavior—excessive consumption of alcohol, for example—to relieve his or her frustrations. The individual's family may also have to suffer through a weekend of anxiety, depression, dread, anger, and tension.

4. Terminate early in the week, preferably on Monday or Tuesday, and do it early in the morning. This gives the individual the opportunity to begin a job search immediately.

5. Always terminate an employee in the superior's office, not at the person's workstation or at a neutral site. This practice ensures more privacy in handling a delicate matter.

6. Once the discussion begins, terminate the employee quickly—in the first five minutes or so—and leave the remainder of the time for the employee to talk.

7. Do not become emotional; be businesslike and to the point.

8. Explain the termination decision, but do not attempt to justify it or defend it since such action is likely to result in argument.

9. Be prepared and organized; know in advance what you are going to say.

10. Keep the discussion short. Thirty minutes should be the absolute maximum time allotted. In most cases, no more than 15 minutes will be needed.

11. If assistance is to be provided for securing further employment, outline what the organization is prepared to offer.[13]

12. At the conclusion of the session, write an accurate record of the termination discussion.

As these guidelines suggest, termination should be planned in advance, documented thoroughly, given thoughtful consideration, and concluded as quickly as possible. In addition to what is recommended above, the terminated employee should be escorted from the premises as soon as the meeting is over to avoid any problems that might be caused by the discharged worker talking with other workers or damaging company property.

Outplacement Services

When terminations occur because of management decisions and not because of violations of work rules (theft, drunk on the job, fighting, etc.), many organizations elect to assist the terminated employee, especially at the executive or managerial level, in his or her search for new employment. Outplacement, the term used to describe such assistance, is a systematic process designed to help the discharged employee find suitable employment with another organization within a reasonable length of time and with a minimum of psychological trauma.[14] This process normally utilizes an outside consultant who counsels the former employee, assists in determining job interests, helps prepare resumés, offers training in how to be interviewed, assists in identifying potential employers, and is available to assist the individual in other ways.[15]

Outplacement services typically are provided on an individual basis to executives, managers, and professionals. If these services are offered to operative level employees, the services are usually provided on a group basis. Outplacement services tend to take some of the sting out of termination, while creating a favorable reputation for the company. The benefit for the individual is that professional assistance and support is available to reduce the trauma of termination and aid the person in locating a new job. The benefit for the organization is that it is acting in a socially responsible manner that enhances its image as an employer who cares about its employees.

Employment at Will

Under common law the courts have traditionally held that an employer could discharge an employee for any one of three reasons: good cause, bad cause, or no cause. This, in essence, is the concept of employment at will. The U.S. legal system has long held that the employment relationship is a tenuous one subject to severance at any time by either party with or without reason.[16] Consequently, employment has been viewed as an agreement rather than a contract; the employee agrees to work for an employer for a stipulated amount of compensation, but neither party makes a commitment as to how long the agreement is expected to remain in force.

With the exception of the state of Montana, which in 1987 passed legislation requiring employers to show "just reason" when terminating workers, the employment at will concept is still the standard interpretation of the employment relationship in this country.[17] Ten states allow no exception to this doctrine. However, there is an emerging trend that is redefining what is meant by employment at will. In the majority of states judicial interpretation or legislative intervention has affected the application of the employment at will concept.[18] So far, four exceptions to the rule have been identified. These involve terminations that are contrary to public policy, abusive discharge, the implied guarantee of employment unless there is just cause for discharge, and the theory that there is an implied covenant of good faith and fair dealing contained in the employment relationship.[19] Additionally, of course, if a discriminatory motive is involved in discharge, exceptions to employment at will can be made under federal statutes.

Public Policy. In many instances, state courts have ruled that when an employee is discharged under conditions that are contrary to established public policy, the concept of employment at will does not apply. The most frequent application of this exception has been in cases where an employee has been terminated for filing a worker's compensation claim.[20] The exception has also been applied where so-called whistle-blowing has been involved, that is, reporting violations of state or federal statutes by the organization or by fellow employees or refusing to perform an illegal act when requested to do so by one's supervisor or manager.

The public policy exception is generally interpreted very narrowly and is applied only where the discharged worker can establish that his or her termination was contrary to some well-established public policy and that no other remedy is available to protect either the individual involved or society.[21]

Abusive Discharge. Retaliatory discharges have also been the basis for exceptions to employment at will. If, for example, an employee is terminated for refusing to do personal favors for a supervisor that are outside the scope of normal job duties, the courts may rule that wrongful discharge has occurred.[22] If an employee is transferred to an untenable job situation and subsequently quits, the courts may rule that "constructive discharge" has occurred because the company intentionally forced the employee into a situation where it had good reason to believe the employee would terminate his or her employment. In this instance, a tort law exception to employment at will has been created.

Implied Guarantee of Employment. Heretofore the employment relationship has been viewed as an agreement, but the courts are increasingly interpreting it as a form of contract requiring just cause for termination. In some cases, statements made by the hiring manager or contained in company human resource policy manuals and employee handbooks have been cited as evidence that discharge can occur only for just cause and not at the whim or caprice of the employer. Essentially, either oral or written statements to the effect that the employee has a job as long as he or she performs satisfactorily have been viewed, in some instances, as implying a continuation of employment that can only be broken for good cause.[23] Likewise, classifying a worker as a "permanent employee" can be construed as a guarantee of employment.

Good Faith and Fair Dealing. In the employment relationship, it is assumed that each party will deal fairly and in good faith with the other party. Where organizations have acted conversely, state courts have held that an exception to employment at will has occurred. In *Fortune v. National Cash Register Co.,* the firm allegedly terminated a salesman in order to deny him bonuses and other benefits that were due him. A Massachusetts court ruled that the company had acted in bad faith and solely for its own benefit in discharging the employee.[24] Consequently, an exception to the employment at will concept was allowed.

Federal Statutes. As discussed in earlier chapters, there are numerous statutes that protect employees from termination on a variety of discriminatory bases. Thus, federal law provides a firm, identifiable foundation for exceptions to the employment at will doctrine if protected classes are involved.

In summary, employment at will has long been considered legally sacrosanct. This is no longer the case. It is not an inviolable concept in today's employment environment. To withstand legal challenges, organizations must develop policies that specifically state their position on job security or permanent employment. If the organization chooses to follow an employment at will policy, it must clearly identify its intentions and avoid any implications suggesting job security or employment permanency. A statement to this effect on the application form, signed and dated by every job applicant, is a starting point. Training of those involved in the hiring process is another step.

RETIREMENT

Since employee turnover rates tend to decrease as length of service with the organization increases,[25] the majority of long-term employees will leave a company through retirement. Although under the 1986 amendments to the Age Discrimination in Employment Act most employees cannot be forced to retire at any age, organizations usually stipulate that an employee may elect to retire at a certain age or after a certain number of years with the company, or at some combination of age and years of service. Upon retirement, former employees, provided the firm has a pension or retirement system, receive retirement payments for the remainder of their lives.

It is still too early to speculate just what impact removal of the mandatory retirement age will have on organizations and the composition of their work forces. Certainly it will have an effect. Conceivably it could clog promotion channels, making it more difficult for younger workers to advance; or it could increase insurance costs. This issue is one that staffing specialists must watch very closely because it will affect the manner in which traditional staffing activities are conducted.

Two other issues that must be addressed in the retirement area are early retirement and retirement planning.

Early Retirement

A policy that permits workers to retire before reaching the customary age or length of service requirements serves five purposes. First, early retirement can be used as an alternative to layoffs. When a product line is discontinued, a plant is closed, or economic conditions cause a business downturn, an organization may, of necessity, have to discharge employees. Allowing eligible workers to retire early benefits both employees and the organization. The employee is ensured some continuity of income or a lump sum financial payment, and the organization enhances its reputation as a socially responsible institution that cares about its workers—a positive image that may affect future staffing efforts in a positive manner.

Second, early retirement may be used to cut an organization's operating expenses. Firms with many long-tenured employees may find that their compensation costs are higher than other companies in the same line of business, thereby placing the firm at a competitive disadvantage in pricing its goods or services or eroding profit margins if competitive pricing is maintained. A solution to this problem is often one of encouraging early retirement so that the compensation cost structure can be adjusted.

Third, early retirement is an alternative to termination. When a long-term employee's performance falls below an acceptable level, an organization may find itself in a dilemma. Termination of the individual might result in discrimination charges, seriously affect work group moral, or tarnish the company's reputation in the human resource area. Rather than discharge such an individual, the person may be encouraged to retire early.

Fourth, too many long-service employees in an organization may seriously hamper promotional opportunities for highly qualified employees—a blockage that can be alleviated through an early retirement option.

Finally, early retirement benefits the employee by providing him or her with a means of making a career change without having to undergo severe financial strain. Second careers are becoming more common and popular—a trend that early retirement has certainly contributed to and one that human resource planning must take into consideration.

Retirement Planning

Although a worker may have happily looked forward to retirement for many years, the actual experience of retiring can be an emotion-laden event. Leaving one's career, on-the-job friends, and familiar organizational environment behind can be a frightening experience. Questions concerning money, how time will be spent, and whether the adjustment to retired life can be made successfully may be of concern to the employee as the retirement date approaches. Just as a well-planned and executed orientation program eases the transition of a new hire into the organization, organizations are finding that company-sponsored retirement planning programs help ease the transition of the employee from work to leisure.[26]

Retirement planning programs provide information on finances, housing, relocation, family relations, adjustment to a nonorganizational setting, legal affairs, and similar matters. In large organizations where groups of employees may be retiring at essentially the same time, formal classroom sessions may be conducted. In small organizations, retirement planning is more likely to be a one-on-one situation handled by a member of the human resource department or an outside specialist who handles the company's retirement plans.

Retirement is a major event in a person's life. Organizations can help the individual make the transition more smoothly by offering the assistance needed to make the change successfully.

REFERENCES: PROVIDING INFORMATION TO OTHER EMPLOYERS

Even after an employee leaves an organization, the employment relationship has not totally ended. Employers will be called upon from time to time to furnish reference information about former workers. Many employers are reluctant or even unwilling to give information to other employers, fearing that former workers who receive a negative reference may sue for defamation. On the other hand, some courts have found previous employers guilty of negligent referral when injury results from the former employer's failure to disclose information about an ex-employee. Many employers, unfortunately, have failed to note that the majority of states in the United States now have referencing legislation that allows an employer, without fear of litigation, to provide truthful reference information to other prospective employers.[27] This legislation was enabled through the efforts of the Society for Human Resource Management (SHRM), which pushed state legislatures to pass statutes that would result in useful reference information for both the hiring employer and the referring employer.

To deal with reference situations, with or without state enabling legislation, organizations may take either of two approaches: a no reference policy or a consent to release reference information policy. Either approach protects a firm from charges of negligent referencing.

No Reference Policy

Many organizations consider a no reference policy to be the safest course of action to pursue when confronted with requests for information about former employees. Under such a policy the only information released is limited to the following: (1) dates of employment, (2) job title, (3) salary, and (4) job location. Providing any other information could be construed as an invasion of the former employee's privacy.

To enforce this policy, all supervisors and managers must be instructed to refer every reference request to the human resource department. Organizations checking references often attempt to speak directly to the applicant's former supervisor because a supervisor may be more candid and more willing to provide information. Human resource administrators must emphasize to supervisors and managers that they personally, as well as the organization collectively, can be sued for defamation if the wrong kind of reference information is divulged.

Consent to Release Reference Information Policy

A second approach to handling references is to have each employee sign a consent form authorizing the employer to release additional information (other than dates of employment, job title, etc.), as specified by the employee in the consent document. However, it would appear that few companies allow employees this degree of participation in determining what reference information will be released to prospective employers.[28]

Where a consent to release information policy is adopted, it is essential that certain guidelines be adhered to rigidly:

1. To assure consistency in the information provided to other employers, only designated human resource representatives should be permitted to give references. Supervisors and managers must be instructed to refer other employers to the human resource department.
2. All documentation should be complete and thorough.
3. Limit any information provided to factual information. Do not offer opinions.
4. Never give oral references. Employers requesting information should be told to do so in writing. This practice ensures confidentiality as well as release of the information to proper parties only.
5. Be truthful in providing information. Do not describe a former employee as "good" when, in fact ,the person was an unsatisfactory performer.
6. Disseminate only current information—typically what happened in the last three to five years of the employee's tenure.
7. Do not volunteer negative information.
8. Be balanced in all remarks; identify strengths as well as weaknesses.

Because reference checking has become a major problem for hiring institutions as well as referencing companies, state legislators are increasingly providing legal protection to employers who release information in good faith. As of August 1996, 26 states have enacted reference protection legislation.

OUTSOURCING HUMAN RESOURCE AND STAFFING ADMINISTRATION FUNCTIONS

Outsourcing of human resource and staffing administration functions is a growing trend today.[29] Long used as an effective business model in manufacturing operations, outsourcing in human resource management is currently estimated to be a $15 billion industry.[30] What is outsourcing? Defined at its most basic level, outsourcing is the process of contracting with a third party to perform company functions that were previously performed in-house. Outsourcing arrangements may run the gamut from subcontracting one or a few administrative functions to a third-party provider (traditional outsourcing) to relinquishing all employees to a professional employer organization that then leases the employees back to the original employer (total outsourcing). With either outsourcing arrangement, companies are seeking to reduce administrative costs, free themselves of activities that others can do more effectively, and create additional time to devote to core company activities and competencies.

Traditional Outsourcing

Over the years the number of organizations skilled in performing specific human resource or staffing administrative functions has grown to the point where there is now a provider or specialist organization that can perform any type of human resources or staffing administrative tasks. Among the administrative functions that can be effectively outsourced are the following:

* Payroll processing
* Benefits administration
* Pension and retirement plan administration
* Incentive compensation management
* Wage and salary administration
* Employee relocation
* Policy manual development
* Employee assistance counseling
* Recruitment
* Reference and background checks
* Retirement planning
* Human Resource Information System development, implementation, and operation
* Temporary staffing
* Training and management development programs
* Executive recruiting and staffing
* Executive compensation administration
* Risk management

Examination of this list will reveal a commonality among functions that can be outsourced effectively—they are activities that lend themselves to routine and standardization.[31] Areas of human resource and staffing management that do not lend themselves to outsourcing are strategic functions such as human resource planning, succession planning, and downsizing as well as confidential activities such as promotions, performance management, and plant closings.

Advantages of Outsourcing

Outsourcing may offer several benefits to a company. Among the most common are the following: (1) the utilization of experienced professional talent to handle human resources issues and concerns—a level of talent that a company may not have internally; (2) a freeing of management time and effort that can be devoted to core business competencies or strategic concerns; (3) reduced management stress resulting from having fewer human resource management issues with which to deal; and (4) an overall saving of monetary and other costs.

Outsourcing human resource management administrative activities permits a company to focus on developing its core competencies and other strategic aspects of the business. Outsourcing allows managers to be strategists rather than administrators. Moreover, outsourcing changes the role of human resource managers from "jacks-of-all trades" to management advisors.[32]

Disadvantages of Outsourcing

Among the disadvantages of outsourcing are the following: (1) the perception by employees that in-house managers have little or no control over human resource functions; (2) the costs of outsourcing may seem quite expensive—to some extent human resource management costs are often hidden costs spread among several functional unit budgets; seeing them posed as a single budget item can be disturbing to managers who may have no real idea of what organizational human resource costs actually are; (3) perceived loss of control over functions that were previously performed in-house; and (4) when multiple vendors are used, there may be some confusion in delineation of responsibility and reporting relationships.

Professional Employer Organization Outsourcing

Formerly referred to as employee leasing or co-employment, Professional Employer Organizations (PEO) offer the most radical approach to human resource outsourcing. Under this arrangement a firm transfers all of its employees to a third party, the Professional Employer Organization or employee leasing company, which in turn then leases the employees back to the first company. Employees still perform their same jobs in the same physical settings but are now employees of record for the Professional Employer Organization. For accounting, tax, and human resources the PEO is now the official employer. Some 2–3 million U.S. employees are now employed by PEOs.

The most obvious advantage of the PEO approach to outsourcing is that the outsourcing company relieves itself of all human resource management administrative functions, which are now performed by the Professional Employer Organization. Another advantage may be a reduction in costs associated with group benefits. Because the PEO has a larger number of employees in its benefits pool than a single employer does, cost savings may be passed along to the company doing the outsourcing.[33]

Whatever the particular approach used, outsourcing of human resource and staffing administrative activities offers the promise of cost reduction as well as an increase in the professionalism with which some important but often mundane staffing activities are performed.

NOTES

1. Thomas J. Peters and Robert H. Waterman Jr., *In Search of Excellence* (New York: Harper & Row Publishers, 1982).

2. One of the authors vividly recalls, over 30 years later, his first day on the job with a major electronics manufacturer. The normal tension and anxiety were further heightened by the fact that no one explained how to find the restrooms, which were situated in a nonconspicuous location.

3. John B. Miner and Donald P. Crane, *Human Resource Management* (New York: Harper Collins College Publishers, 1995), 394.

4. Mark S. Tauber, "New Employee Orientation: A Comprehensive Systems Approach," *Personnel Administrator* (January 1985): 65.

5. Peter F. Drucker, film series, *The Manager and the Organization: How to Make the Organization Work for You* (Washington, DC: BNA Communications, 1977).

6. Jonathan Kaufman, "How Workplaces May Look Without Affirmative Action," *The Wall Street Journal,* March 20, 1995, B2.

7. Susan Dillingham, "Rewarding Expertise," *Insight,* January 19, 1987, 49.

8. Adapted from Wanda R. Embrey, R. Wayne Mondy, and Robert M. Noe, "Exit Interview: A Tool for Personnel Development," *Personnel Administrator* (May 1979): 46.

9. *Employment Coordinator* (Deerfield, IL: Clark, Boardman Callaghan, 1996), 146, 302–304.

10. Stephen P. Pepe and Scott H. Dunham, *Avoiding and Defending Wrongful Discharge Claims* (Deerfield, IL: Clark Boardman Callaghan, 1995), chap. 10, 1–2.

11. R. Wayne Mondy and Robert M. Noe III, *Personnel: The Management of Human Resources,* 3rd ed. (Boston: Allyn and Bacon, 1987), 645.

12. William J. Morin, *Successful Termination* (New York: Drake Beam Morin, 1981), 22.

13. Adapted from James Walsh, *Rightful Termination* (Santa Monica, CA: Merritt Publishing, 1994), 266–268; and Morin, *Successful Termination,* 7–27.

14. Morin, *Successful Termination,* iv.

15. William J. Morin, "Outplacement Counseling: What Is It?" *The Personnel and Guidance Journal* (May 1977): 555.

16. Lorance Z. Lorber, J. Robert Kirk, Kenneth H. Kirschner, and Charlene R. Handorf, *Fear of Firing: A Legal and Personnel Analysis of Employment at Will* (Alexandria, VA: ASPA Foundation, 1984), 1.

17. Walsh, *Rightful Termination,* 2.

18. Ibid., 16.

19. Ibid., 96–97.

20. Ibid., 99.

21. Ibid.

22. *Monge v. Beebe Rubber Co.,* 114 N.H. 130. 316A. 2d 549, 1974.

23. David P. Twomey, *A Concise Guide to Employment Law, EEO & OSHA* (Cincinnati: Sourth-Western Co., 1986), 99.

24. *Fortune v. National Cash Register Co.,* 373 Mass. 96, 364 NE 2nd 1251, 1977.

25. Guvenc G. Alpander, *Human Resources Management Planning* (New York: AMACOM, 1982), 115.

26. Marilyn Merikangas, "Retirement Planning with a Difference," *Personnel Journal* (May 1983): 420.

27. *Especially for Texas Employers* (Austin, TX: Texas Workforce Commission, 2007), 26.

28. Ibid., 26–27.

29. http://www.wkforce.com/k-human-resource-outsourcing.html

30. EquaTerra, "Taking the Pulse of Today's Human Resources Outsourcing Market," April 2007, *PDF.*

31. "Outsourcing, One Step at a Time," *HR Magazine* (July 2005).

32. http://www.shrm.org/outsourcing/library_published/nonIC/CMS_017175.asp

33. http://napeo.org/peoindustry/faq.cfm

14

Evaluating the Staffing Function

The success of any organization depends not only on the formulation and execution of well-thought-out plans but also on the continuous evaluation of progress toward accomplishment of specified goals and objectives. For individual functional units within the organization, such as the human resource department in general or the staffing function specifically, evaluation may be more difficult because absolute measures that indicate whether the unit is fulfilling its mission successfully are absent. Yet the need for evaluation is just as important in these areas as it is in other areas of company operation.

It is increasingly important today to examine the human resource management function, especially staffing, on a periodic basis to ensure that all activities in this area are being carried out completely, effectively, efficiently, and professionally, as well as in a manner that reflects the spirit and the letter of the law. Feedback from periodic assessments of staffing will enable adjustments and corrective actions to be taken before any seemingly minor deficiencies become serious problems.

How often should the staffing component be evaluated or audited? Ideally, just as in the accounting and financial areas of an organization, it should be examined formally on an annual basis. While it may not be practicable to audit completely every aspect of staffing with such frequency, the major activities within staffing—legal compliance, job analysis, recruiting, and selecting, for example—should be subjected to an annual review. The other functional activities could be audited less frequently, perhaps every 18 to 24 months. In no case, however, should the evaluation of staffing, because of its critical nature, exceed the 24-month time period.

METHODS OF EVALUATION

How should an organization go about evaluating its staffing function? Are there particular measures or indicators that reveal how well this function is carrying out its responsibilities and supporting the overall efforts of the organization to reach planned objectives? These are salient questions this chapter will attempt to answer.

There are three basic methods that may be used to evaluate how well staffing activities are accomplished in an organization: internal checklists, internal quantitative indicators, and benchmarking internal activities against those of external organizations. The checklist approach, the simplest of the three approaches, poses a number of questions that can be answered either "yes" or "no." This method is concerned with whether important activities have been recognized and, if so, whether they are being performed properly. Essentially, the checklist method is an internal evaluation in terms of what should be done and the extent to which it is being done. The more "yes" answers the better the evaluation; "no" answers indicate areas or activities where follow-up or additional work is needed to increase the effectiveness of staffing. The checklists presented below should be viewed as representative, not inclusive. Organizations opting to use this evaluation approach will, undoubtedly, discover many questions of their own that can be added. The checklist method is solely an internal evaluation device; it is not a vehicle for comparing one company with other companies.

The second method for evaluating the performance of staffing activities is a quantitative one that relies on the use of various numerical data that can be accumulated internally and ratios that can be computed from these data. Numerical data are mainly useful as an internal indicator of activity levels. From these numbers important trends can be identified. Ratios show the results of activities or volumes—numbers that in themselves are important, but also reveal, when maintained over a period of time, trends that may be extremely critical. Quantitative indicators, as described below, are an internal means of evaluating staffing activities.

The third method of evaluating the performance of an organization's staffing component, and the newest, is benchmarking a firm's internal performance with that of external institutions. In essence, benchmarking involves identifying the best performing company or companies within an industry and then comparing an individual organization's performance against the performance of those organizations serving as benchmarks. Two obvious areas for benchmarking internal activities against best performers in the industry are turnover and absenteeism. Benchmarking enables a company to use its internal data to make external comparisons.

In the following sections checklists, quantitative indicators, and benchmarking will be examined as methods or tools for evaluating how well an organization is performing its staffing activities.

CHECKLIST EVALUATIONS

Checklists can be used to evaluate each activity performed in the staffing function. The checklists that follow cover legal compliance, job analysis, human resource planning, recruiting, selecting, performance appraisal, career planning and development, and staffing administration—the same topics and the same order as presented in this text. A total of 163 evaluation questions are presented. An organization may, quite easily, develop additional questions of its own to evaluate staffing in greater depth.

Legal Compliance

The risks associated with noncompliance to various federal (as well as state) statutes dealing with employment practically dictate that this area be the first one evaluated for effectiveness. Any deficiencies that show up here should be addressed immediately.

The following questions indicate the areas and activities to be addressed in evaluating the legal compliance portion of the staffing function.

1. Have all managers and supervisors been informed of their responsibilities under federal and state equal employment opportunity and antidiscrimination statutes?
2. Have all managers and supervisors been informed of their responsibilities under employment law torts?
3. Are all legally mandated reports submitted to requiring agencies on time?
4. Are all jobs properly classified as to exempt and nonexempt status?
5. Are data necessary for filing EEO-1 reports, if required, maintained on a current basis?
6. Is an applicant flow analysis conducted on a periodic basis?
7. If required, does the organization have an up-to-date affirmative action plan?
8. Is progress toward accomplishing affirmative action goals evaluated on a regular basis?
9. If progress toward accomplishing affirmative action goals is deficient, has corrective action been taken to ensure the necessary degree of progress?
10. Does recruitment advertising conform to applicable legal and affirmative action standards?
11. Is a four-fifths rule analysis performed on a regular basis?
12. Is the organization's policy concerning equal employment opportunity posted in conspicuous places?
13. Are adequate safeguards taken to ensure nondiscrimination against protected classes?
14. Is executive level management committed to and fully supportive of equal employment opportunity?

15. Has a policy on sexual harassment and other forms of harassment (age, religion, disability, etc.) been developed?

16. Have managers and supervisors received training concerning their responsibilities relative to enforcing sexual and other harassment policies?

17. Have policies and procedures been developed to ensure reasonable accommodation of the religious practices of employees?

18. Has the organization's affirmative action program information been disseminated to all appropriate parties?

19. Is a utilization analysis of minorities and females conducted on a regular basis?

20. Have the causes of underutilization of minorities, females, and other protected classes been identified?

21. Have appropriate corrective actions been taken to remedy any underutilization problems?

22. Have all selection tests and procedures been validated as required by the *Uniform Guidelines?*

Job Analysis

The criticality of job analysis has been emphasized many times throughout this book. As the cornerstone on which many other human resource activities depend, it is important that the effectiveness of this process be carefully evaluated.

Here are some questions that may be used to assess the effectiveness of job analysis.

1. Have formalized procedures and methods been developed for conducting job analysis?

2. Is the most appropriate method or combination of methods being used to conduct job analyses?

3. Have all jobs in the organization been analyzed?

4. Are standardized job titles from the *Dictionary of Occupational Titles* used to identify all jobs?

5. Have job descriptions been prepared for every job in the organization?

6. Are all job descriptions current?

7. Do all job descriptions clearly identify essential functions?

8. Have job specifications been prepared for every job in the organization?

9. Are all job specifications current?

10. Do all job specifications reflect minimum rather than ideal human qualifications necessary for satisfactory job performance?

11. Do all employees have copies of their job descriptions?

12. Are all job descriptions reviewed periodically to determine if they are accurate and up to date?

13. Are all job specifications reviewed periodically to determine if they are accurate and up to date?

14. Have procedures been developed whereby managers and supervisors can request reanalysis of a job when changes occur in that job?

15. Are job descriptions and specifications written in readable, easy-to-use formats?

16. Is the job analysis process effectively integrated with other human resource management processes?

Human Resource Planning

Perhaps one of the most difficult areas of staffing to evaluate is human resource planning. Even though planners customarily deal with statistical data in forecasting requirements and availability, a great amount of subjectivity is involved. Moreover, the best-laid plans may be negated by unanticipated changes in the economy, technology, or other external or internal forces.

The following are some essential questions that must be asked about human resource planning.

1. Is human resource planning interactively involved with the strategic business planning process?

2. Are human resource requirements forecasts made periodically?

3. Are appropriate quantitative and subjective techniques used in conjunction with each other to forecast human resource requirements?

4. Do operating managers participate in the development of requirements forecasts?

5. Are requirements forecasts used to develop a pro forma organization structure?

6. Are requirements forecasts used to develop staffing tables that reflect human resource needs at various levels of organizational activity?

7. Are human resource availability forecasts made periodically?

8. Are skills inventories maintained on all employees?

9. Are management inventories maintained on all managerial personnel?

10. Are skills and management inventories updated periodically?

11. Are skills and management inventories used in the human resource planning process to assist in determining the internal availability of personnel?

12. Are sufficient demographic, economic, and other data maintained in current fashion for forecasting the availability of personnel from external sources?

13. Does the organization have standing plans, policies, and procedures for dealing with anticipated shortages or surpluses of personnel?

Recruiting

Recruiting is the most publicly visible of all staffing activities. By its very nature it is concerned with making known the availability of open positions to many individuals and agencies. Recruiting, in a sense, is much like advertising and public relations in that it creates both an image and an awareness of an organization in the external environment. Obviously, the high visibility of this function warrants a careful evaluation of its effectiveness.

In evaluating recruiting it is necessary to examine its internal as well as external effectiveness. The following questions may be helpful.

1. Does the organization have policies and procedures governing the use of alternatives to recruiting?

2. Is the recruiting process effectively integrated with human resource planning?

3. Does the organization have a promotion from within policy?

4. Does the organization typically adhere to the promotion from within policy before looking to external sources to fill vacancies?

5. Is a job posting and bidding system used to fill vacancies from internal sources?

6. Have all recruiters been thoroughly trained?

7. Have the most likely external sources from which candidates may be recruited been properly identified?

8. Have each of the most likely external sources of candidates been evaluated to determine their effectiveness in furnishing qualified candidates?

9. Is there a formal procedure whereby managers and supervisors may request authorization to hire an employee?

10. Have appropriate recruiting methods been identified and analyzed?

11. Have each of the various recruiting methods been evaluated to determine their effectiveness in generating sufficient quantities of qualified candidates?

12. Are recruiting methods effectively matched to sources of qualified candidates?

13. Have sources of minority, female, and other protected class candidates been properly identified?

14. Have sources of minority, female, and other protected class candidates been evaluated to determine their effectiveness in providing qualified candidates?

15. Are special recruiting methods used to reach minority, female, and other protected class applicants?

16. Does the recruiting program utilize affirmative action approaches to attract minority, female, and other protected class applicants?

17. Are minorities and females used as recruiters?

18. Does recruitment advertising conform to applicable legal and affirmative action standards?

19. Is recruitment advertising done in a fashion that creates a favorable image for the organization?

20. Are different advertising media used in conjunction with each other?

Selecting

One of the most sensitive areas of staffing is selection. It is here that an organization frequently opens itself to charges of discrimination. In fact, the majority of the court cases examined in Chapter 3 center on charges of discrimination that occurred during the selection process. Consequently, this area of staffing should be subjected to rigorous evaluation concerning not only its effectiveness but also its adherence to statutory and regulatory requirements.

A great many questions can be asked about selection, beginning with the employment application and proceeding all the way through the organization's ability to retain the employees it hires. Here are a few of the questions that could be posed.

1. Does the application form conform to applicable legal and affirmative action standards?
2. Has the feasibility of using a weighted application blank been investigated?
3. Does the employment application, if applicable, contain an employment at will clause?
4. Are references systematically checked before an employment offer is extended?
5. Where appropriate, are background investigations conducted?
6. Where appropriate, are physical examinations of potential new hires required after an employment offer is extended?
7. Have policies and procedures for conducting employment interviews been developed?
8. Have all managers and supervisors received training in interviewing?
9. Do all managers and supervisors understand the legal ramifications of employment interviewing?
10. Do all managers and supervisors understand the types of questions that can, cannot, or should not be asked in an employment interview?
11. Is an applicant evaluation form used in the interviewing process?
12. Are realistic job previews given during employment interviews?
13. Are job descriptions and specifications used during interviewing to assist in determining an applicant's qualifications?
14. Are rejected candidates notified promptly of the organization's decision not to extend an employment offer?
15. Are candidates who are rejected for one job encouraged to apply for other organizational jobs for which they may be qualified?
16. Are selection ratios calculated on a regular basis?
17. When necessary, is selection ratio information used to evaluate and revise selection criteria?
18. Are all selection criteria used realistic and job related?

19. Are all selection criteria reviewed on a regular basis to ensure that they are nondiscriminatory?

20. Are appropriate selection tests used to evaluate candidates?

21. Where tests are used, are the results utilized as one of several selection criteria and not as the sole basis for selection?

22. Have all employment tests used been validated in accordance with the requirements of the *Uniform Guidelines?*

23. For all employment tests used, have reasonable cutoff scores been established?

24. Is a four-fifths rule analysis performed on a regular basis to determine how protected classes succeed in the selection process?

25. Are turnover statistics used to evaluate or revise selection criteria?

Performance Appraisal

Possibly one of the most neglected areas of staffing evaluation is performance appraisal. It is not unusual for organizations to develop and implement formal appraisal systems and subsequently do little or no follow-up to determine if these systems are working as planned or producing the results anticipated. Moreover, few organizations recognize performance appraisal as a type of employment test that should be validated in terms of job content. Effective evaluation of this staffing area is, it would seem, long overdue.

Valuable insight into performance appraisal effectiveness can be gained by asking pertinent questions about the system and the instrument used. Some relevant questions are as follows:

1. Are all employees and managerial personnel appraised at least annually?

2. Are all new employees appraised at the end of their probationary period?

3. Are performance appraisal results integrated with the human resource planning process?

4. Are performance appraisal results used in the career planning and development process?

5. Is performance appraisal information used to assist in evaluating the recruiting and selecting processes?

6. Have formalized policies and procedures been developed for using performance appraisal?

7. Have all appraisers received training in performance appraisal?

8. Has the performance appraisal instrument used been validated in terms of actual job content?

9. Are different appraisal instruments used for different levels of jobs such as operative employees, professionals, and managers?

10. Does the performance appraisal instrument rely on standards and measures rather than subjective factors such as worker traits or personality characteristics?

11. Does the performance appraisal system and the instrument produce reliable results?

12. Is a periodic audit of performance appraisal results performed to determine if evaluation inflation or deflation is occurring?

13. Is the performance appraisal instrument easy to understand and use?

14. Are promotion, transfer, demotion, termination, and layoff decisions based on performance appraisal information?

15. Does the performance appraisal system contain an appeal procedure whereby an employee may challenge an unfavorable appraisal?

16. Does the system contain a review procedure wherein the next higher level of management is required to review the results of each employee's performance appraisal?

17. Are managers and supervisors required to discuss appraisal results with employees?

18. Do managers and supervisors spend sufficient time discussing appraisal results with employees?

19. Do employees have access to their performance records?

20. Are appraisals conducted in accordance with a predetermined schedule?

Career Planning and Development

Assessing the effectiveness of career planning and development is sometimes difficult. This is particularly true of the developmental portion of the process. Since all development is essentially self-development, results are not always obvious in the short run. Years may elapse before it becomes apparent that development is actually occurring. If an organization is going to invest time and money in efforts to assist employees in their careers, this activity must be examined carefully to determine whether it is producing the desired results.

The following questions are representative ones that can be used to evaluate career planning and development.

1. Have career paths or ladders of job progression been identified?

2. Where appropriate, have dual career ladders been developed?

3. Is career planning and development integrated with human resource planning as a means of identifying personnel available in the organization for promotion or transfer?

4. Are skills inventories maintained on all employees?

5. Are management inventories maintained on all managerial personnel?

6. Are skills and management inventories used to assist employees and managers in developing their careers within the organization?

7. Are career opportunities communicated clearly to all employees and managers?

8. Is a promotion from within policy used to foster career development within the organization?

9. Does the organization typically adhere to a promotion from within policy?

10. Does the organization offer formal career planning and development assistance to employees?

11. Do managers and supervisors understand their roles in career planning and development?

12. Are replacement tables used to assist in career planning and development?

13. Is job rotation used as a means of developing employees and managers?

14. Are employees and managers encouraged to participate in internal and external workshops, seminars, or other programs to enhance their career potential?

Staffing Administration

As discussed in the preceding chapter, human resource administration encompasses a broad range of activities. While the performance of each of these activities is important, this evaluation section will focus only on those functions related to staffing.

Human resource administration is very susceptible to evaluation by checklist. A performance audit of this area would involve asking the questions listed below.

1. Does the organization have a formal employee orientation program?

2. Are orientation checklists used by the human resource department to provide new employees with an overview of the organization?

3. Are orientation checklists used by the new employee's immediate supervisor to ensure that the employee is familiarized with the job, the work unit, and other items of importance?

4. Have supervisors received training in how to carry out their role in orientation?

5. Does the human resource department have policies and procedures for orientation follow-ups after new employees have been on the job for a stipulated period of time?

6. Have policies and procedures on promotions been developed?

7. Have policies and procedures on transfers been developed?

8. Have policies and procedures on demotions been developed?

9. Have policies and procedures on layoffs or reductions in force been developed?

10. Have policies and procedures on involuntary terminations been developed?

11. Have policies and procedures on promotions, transfers, demotions, layoffs, reductions in force, and terminations been communicated clearly to all employees?

12. Are these policies on promotions, transfers, demotions, layoffs, reductions in force, and terminations followed consistently?

13. Have the reasons for termination of employees been identified and stipulated?

14. Have the reasons for voluntary separations from the organization been identified and analyzed?

15. Are exit interviews used to identify causes of resignations?

16. Are post-exit questionnaires used to identify causes of resignations?

17. Have appropriate corrective actions been taken on the basis of information gathered from exit interviews and post-exit questionnaires?

18. Are outplacement services provided for employees?

19. Are outplacement services provided for managers and professionals?

20. Are outplacement services provided for executives?

21. Have policies, programs, and procedures on retirement been developed?

22. Have policies, procedures, and programs for early retirement been developed?

23. Are retirement planning programs and services provided for employees and managers?

24. Are organizational climate surveys conducted on a regular basis?

25. Is the information from organizational climate surveys used to take appropriate corrective actions?

26. Are employees, supervisors, and managers informed of the results obtained from organizational climate surveys?

27. Is employee turnover data maintained on job, work unit, departmental, functional, and organizational bases?

28. Is employee turnover analyzed on a regular basis?

29. Is appropriate corrective action taken on the basis of analysis of employee turnover data?

30. Is employee absenteeism data maintained on job, work unit, departmental, functional, and organizational bases?

31. Is employee absenteeism analyzed on a regular basis?

32. Is appropriate corrective action taken on the basis of analysis of employee absenteeism data?

33. Are all personnel records maintained in accordance with a prescribed records retention schedule?

QUANTITATIVE INDICATORS

Quantitative indicators reflect the amounts, ratios, and trends associated with performance of staffing activities; they are the numbers and the interpretations that can be constructed from volumes of activity; they are the data that most organizations already have available or can readily construct. The direction in which staffing activities are trending can often be deduced from a study of these statistical measures. Again, the same topics are presented in the same order as they were presented earlier in this text. Some 76 different quantitative measures are cited below.

Legal Compliance

Compliance with federal and state statutes and regulations necessitates the accumulation of various kinds of data; consequently, organizations may have a good deal of quantitative information readily available for evaluating this area of staffing. Some of the data useful in evaluation of the legal area include the following:

1. Total Number of Applicants
2. Number of Applicants Classified by Protected Group Status
3. Total Number of Employees Hired
4. Number of Employees Hired Classified by Protected Group Status
5. Total Number of Employees Promoted
6. Number of Employees Promoted Classified by Protected Group Status
7. Total Number of Employees Involuntarily Terminated
8. Number of Employees Involuntarily Terminated Classified by Protected Group Status
9. Number of Discrimination Charges Filed
10. Number of Wage and Hour Complaints Filed
11. Number of Employment Law Tort Cases Filed

The preceding kinds of data provide an organization with the raw material it needs to analyze trends and perform other analyses in the compliance area. The following ratios provide additional means of evaluation:

$$12. \quad \frac{\text{Protected Group Selection Rate}}{\text{Best Achieving Group Selection Rate}} = \text{Protected Group Selection Ratio}$$

$$13. \quad \frac{\text{Protected Group Promotion Rate}}{\text{Best Achieving Group Promotion Rate}} = \text{Protected Group Promotion Ratio}$$

$$14. \quad \frac{\text{Protected Group Termination Rate}}{\text{Majority Group Termination Rate}} = \text{Protected Group Termination Ratio}$$

$$15. \quad \frac{\text{Number of Minorities and Women Hired}}{\text{Total Number of Employees Hired}} \times 100 = \text{Minority and Female Hiring Percentage}$$

$$16. \quad \frac{\text{Number of Minority and Female Employees}}{\text{Total Number of Employees}} \times 100 = \text{Minority and Female Work Force Percentage}$$

$$17. \quad \frac{\text{Number of Minority and Female Employees Protected}}{\text{Total Number of Employees Protected}} \times 100 = \text{Minority and Female Work Force Promotion Percentage}$$

Job Analysis

Suggested quantitative indicators for job analysis evaluation include:

1. Total Number of Jobs Analyzed

2. Number of New Jobs Created

3. Number of Job Analysis Requests by Managers and Supervisors

4. $\dfrac{\text{Number of New Jobs Analyzed}}{\text{Number of New Jobs Created}} \times 100 = \text{Percentage of New Jobs Analyzed}$

5. $\dfrac{\text{Number of Job Analysis Requests Completed}}{\text{Number of Requests for Jobs Analysis}} \times 100 = \text{Percentage of Job Analysis Requests Completed}$

6. Number of Job Descriptions Audited

Human Resource Planning

The effectiveness of human resource planning, from a quantitative viewpoint, can best be judged by the accuracy of the requirements and availability forecasts made. The closer the forecasts approximate reality, the more effective the planning process is. Thus, two key measures are the following:

1. Requirements forecast compared to actual personnel needs
2. Availability forecast compared to actual availability of personnel

Recruiting

Because many organizations are required to maintain data on applicant flow, statistical information may already be available to assist in evaluating recruiting effectiveness. Additionally, identification of recruiting costs can also provide relevant analysis data. Items that may be used for evaluation purposes include:

1. Total Number of Job Applicants
2. Number of Applicants Classified by Protected Class Status
3. Employment Advertising Expenses
4. Employment Agency Fees
5. Executive Search Firm Fees
6. Number of Applicants Generated by Source
7. Number of Applicants Classified by Protected Class Status Generated by Source
8. Total Recruiting Function Costs
9. $\dfrac{\text{Total Recruiting Costs}}{\text{Number of Applicants}} = \text{Average Recruiting Cost per Applicant}$
10. $\dfrac{\text{Total Recruiting Costs}}{\text{Number of Employees Hired}} = \text{Average Recruiting Cost per Employee Hired}$
11. $\dfrac{\text{Total Employment Agency Fees}}{\text{Number of Employees Hired from Agencies}} = \text{Average Cost per Employee Hired from Agencies}$

12. $\dfrac{\text{Total Relocation Expenses for New Hires}}{\substack{\text{Number of Employees Hired}\\ \text{Receiving Relocation}}} = \substack{\text{Average Relocation Cost for New Employee Receiving}\\ \text{Relocation}}$

13. $\dfrac{\text{Number of Applicants Hired by Source}}{\text{Number of Applicants Generated by Source}} \times 100 = \text{Recruiting Source Hiring Percentage}$

Selecting

As in recruiting, the necessity of maintaining statistical records for EEO, OFCCP, or other reporting purposes means that quantitative data may be available already for analyzing and evaluating selection activities. Potential evaluative data encompass such items as follows:

1. Total Number of Employees Hired
2. Number of Employees Hired Classified by Protected Class Status
3. Number of Positions Filled Internally
4. Number of Positions Filled Externally
5. Number of Employment Offers Extended
6. Number of Employment Offers Accepted
7. Total Testing Costs

8. $\dfrac{\text{Protected Group Selection Rate}}{\substack{\text{Best Achieving Group Selection}\\ \text{Rate}}} = \text{Protected Group Selection Ratio}$

9. $\dfrac{\text{Number of Employees Hired}}{\text{Number of Applicants}} = \text{Selection Ratio}$

10. $\dfrac{\text{Number of Positions Filled Internally}}{\text{Number of Positions Filled}} \times 100 = \text{Percentage of Positions Filled Internally}$

11. $\dfrac{\text{Number of Positions Filled Externally}}{\text{Number of Positions Filled}} \times 100 = \text{Percentage of Positions Filled Externally}$

12. $\dfrac{\text{Total Testing Costs}}{\text{Number of Applicants Tested}} = \text{Average Testing Cost per Applicant}$

13. $\dfrac{\text{Total Testing Costs}}{\substack{\text{Number of Tested Employees}\\ \text{Hired}}} = \text{Average Testing Cost per Employee Hired}$

Performance Appraisal

While performance appraisal may not be as amenable to quantitative evaluation as other staffing areas, there are some indicators that can shed light on how well the system is working. Among these are the following:

1. Correlation of Performance Appraisal Results with Actual Job Performance Measures
2. Average Performance Ratings by Job, Work Unit, and Department

3. $\dfrac{\text{Number of Appraisals Performed}}{\text{Number of Appraisals Scheduled}} \times 100 = \text{Percentage of Required Appraisals Actually Completed}$

4. $\dfrac{\text{Number of Employees Rated at Below Standard}}{\text{Number of Employees Appraised}} \times 100 = \text{Percentage of Employees Rated Below Standard}$

5. $\dfrac{\text{Number of Employees Rated as Excellent}}{\text{Number of Employees Appraised}} \times 100 = \text{Percentage of Employees Rated in Highest Performance Category}$

6. $\dfrac{\text{Number of Appraisals Appealed}}{\text{Number of Appraisals Completed}} \times 100 = \text{Percentage of Appraisals Appealed}$

Career Planning and Development

Quantitatively, some indication of the effectiveness of career planning and development can be ascertained through measures of employee retention and upward mobility. These include:

1. Number of Positions Filled Internally
2. Number of Promotions Made
3. Number of Employees Promoted Classified by Protected Class Status
4. Number of Transfers Made for Developmental Purposes
5. Number of Employees Transferred for Developmental Purposes Classified as to Protected Class Status
6. Number of Voluntary Terminations
7. Number of Voluntary Terminations as a Percentage of Total Terminations
8. Number of Employees with One or More Years Service as a Percentage of Total Employees
9. Employee Turnover Rates by Job, Work Unit, Department, and Protected Class
10. Number of Employees and Managers Attending Workshops, Seminars, and Other Developmental Programs
11. Number of Positions Filled Internally as a Percentage of Total Positions Filled
12. Number of Positions Filled Externally as a Percentage of Total Positions Filled

Staffing Administration

Because of the all-inclusive nature of staffing administration, many measures can be used to evaluate the performance of this activity. In fact, most of the quantitative measures suggested for the evaluation of other staffing processes can be used, to some extent, to evaluate the effectiveness of the administrative function. Thus, rather than repeat previously enumerated measures, this section will present only a few critical indicators relative to employee turnover and retention.

1. $$\frac{\text{Number of Terminations from All Causes}}{\text{Average Number of Employees}} \times 100 = \text{Turnover Percentage}$$

2. $$\frac{\text{Number of Terminations from All Causes} - \text{Number of Voluntary Terminations}}{\text{Average Number of Employees}} \times 100 = \text{Unavoidable Turnover Percentage}$$

3. $$\frac{\text{Number of Voluntary Terminations}}{\text{Average Number of Employees}} \times 100 = \text{Avoidable Turnover Percentage}$$

4. $$\frac{\text{Number of Employees with One or More Years Service}}{\text{Total Number of Employees}} \times 100 = \text{New Hire Retention Percentage}$$

5. $$\frac{\text{Number of Employees Leaving within First Year}}{\text{Number of Employees Hired in One Year}} \times 100 = \text{Percent of New Hires Lost}$$

6. $$\frac{\text{Average Number of Employees Absent}}{\text{Average Number of Employees}} \times 100 = \text{Average Annualized Employee Percentage}$$

BENCHMARKING

Benchmarking is a method of comparing similar processes, activities, and functions across organizational lines. The goal of benchmarking, in addition to assisting in evaluating internal activities, is to identify practices used by well-performing organizations so that the evaluating firm can improve its ways of doing business. The characteristics and attributes of benchmarking include measuring performance, systematically identifying best practices, learning from other organizations, and adapting more effective practices as appropriate.[1] Benchmarking is a management tool that has been around for some time. It originally developed out of the total quality management school of thought as an approach to continuous improvement.

In general benchmarking is the process of determining standards for the performance of activities and functions, ascertaining which organizations set those standards, and then comparing one's organization's performance (i.e., benchmarking) against that standard.[2] The end result of benchmarking, hopefully, is improvement in the effectiveness of internal company operations. For human resource management more specifically, the purpose of benchmarking is to provide tools, models, skills, methods, and data to improve the effectiveness of human resource programs and activities, especially staffing.[3] Benchmarking information indicates what other organizations are doing effectively and enables an organization to learn from other organizations.

Human resources departments (and staffing specialists) are continuously challenged to demonstrate their value to the organization. Human resource managers must show how the internal information used to track and evaluate its function fits into the organization's overall strategic goals. This same challenge applies to the external benchmarking data used for comparison purposes. To compare one company with another company or with several other companies is one means of demonstrating the value of human resource management in general and staffing in particular.

Advantages of Benchmarking

As a purely evaluative tool for gauging staffing effectiveness, benchmarking offers several advantages:

- It focuses on numerical outcomes; results are expressed in terms of statistics or quantitative values.
- It creates an increased awareness of the costs of performing staffing activities.
- It creates a greater sense of competitiveness because one organization's performance is being measured against that of other organizations.
- It can be used in all types of organizations, private as well as public.
- It encourages an organization to strive to improve its performance by indicating the performance of other organizations.
- It focuses management's attention on quantifiable results.

Proponents of benchmarking claim that its reach extends far beyond its use as an evaluation devise. They claim it encourages innovation, fosters team building, emphasizes creativity, etc. An exploration of these alleged benefits of benchmarking is beyond the scope of this chapter.

A disadvantage of benchmarking is it can on occasion require a large investment in time, labor, and capital. These disadvantages can be minimized through careful, thoughtful, and deliberate planning. With careful planning benchmarking investments can be kept to a minimum.

Disadvantages of Benchmarking

As an evaluation tool for use in determining the effectiveness of human resource management or staffing activities in an organization, benchmarking has the following disadvantages or limitations:

- Reliable results may demand a fairly large-scale study of many organizations inasmuch as results from a small sample of organizations may prove inconclusive.
- Costs of a benchmarking study may place the study beyond the capability of any one organization; hence, it may be necessary for several organizations to pool their resources for a study.
- Because of sample size and cost considerations, benchmarking may be beyond the capabilities of small organizations.

- The required pooling of resources may make it difficult for directly competing organizations to engage in a study without raising some appearance of collusion.
- A considerable amount of time may be required of organizations engaged in a benchmarking study.

Typical Benchmarking Areas

Typical benchmarking studies in human resource management generally consider the following areas:

- Ratios of human resource personnel to other personnel and numbers of human resource specialists per capita in various categories of organizational personnel.
- Costs of performing activities, expenditures on various activities, and human resource budget comparisons.
- Trends in human resource activities such as employee benefits provided and activities outsourced.
- Organizational services provided by the human resource department and information concerning which specific unit provides which specific services.
- Human resource activity volumes and which human resource unit performs which activities.

As the foregoing indicates, a human resource management benchmarking study tends to provide a great deal of information concerning the performance of various human resource functions and activities. To evaluate staffing activities as described in this book, it is usually necessary to extract particular bits of information that are applicable. In some cases, while the benchmarking report does an excellent job of providing important information on overall human resource activities, it may be difficult to easily obtain data on only staffing functions. Nevertheless, benchmarking offers an evaluation approach each organization should consider for itself.[4]

One of the best benchmarking studies available commercially is *HR Departments Benchmarks and Analysis 2007,* published by BNA, Inc. of Washington, D.C. This volume offers a great deal of information on all aspects of human resource department management.

SUMMARY

Effective staffing is critical to the success of contemporary organizations. It promises to become even more so as global competition continues to heighten and American enterprises struggle to remain leaders in effectiveness, efficiency, and productivity. Having the right people in the right places at the right time—the basic objective of staffing—is imperative in today's rapidly increasing competitive environment.

For staffing to be effective totally, it must be viewed as a system that is fully integrated within itself and also fully integrated within the entire human resource management system of an organization. Each staffing activity must be performed as effectively as possible; each staffing activity must be continuously evaluated to eliminate deficiencies and enhance strengths. This is the challenge of today as well as tomorrow. It is a challenge that can and will be met as the criticality of staffing as a component of organizational viability becomes more fully recognized.

NOTES

1. *Benchmarking & Best Practices* (Alexandria, VA: International Public Management Association for Human Resources, 2008), http://www.ipma-hr.org/content.cfm?pageid=42

2. *Management Analysis & Development* (St. Paul, MN: Minnesota Department of Administration, 2008), http://www.admin.state.mn.us/mad/benchmarking.htm

3. *HR Department Benchmarks and Analysis 2007* (Washington, DC: The Bureau of National Affairs, Inc.).

4. Joseph Blakeman, Center for Urban Transportation Studies (Milwaukee: University of Wisconsin–Milwaukee, June 2002), http://www.uwm.edu/Dept/CUTS/bench/bm-desc.htm

Bibliography

The following bibliography has been compiled for the individual who desires to delve into staffing further. The references cited will help the reader acquire more detailed and technical information as well as gain a better understanding of staffing issues, problems, and their potential solutions. Included in this bibliography are classic reference works in the field and contemporary texts. The bibliography is representative rather than exhaustive. Journal articles have been omitted in order to reduce the length of the reference list and make it more manageable for the working human resource management professional.

Alpander, Guvenc G. *Human Resources Management Planning*. New York: AMACOM, 1982.

Bennett-Alexander, Dawn D., and Laura P. Hartman. *Employment Law*. 5th ed. Boston: McGraw-Hill Irwin, 2007.

Bohlander, George, and Scott Snell. *Managing Human Resources*. 15th ed. Mason, OH: Thomson South-Western, 2009.

Byars, Lloyd L., and Leslie W. Rue. *Human Resource Management*. 9th ed. New York: McGraw-Hill Irwin, 2008.

Caruth, Donald L. *Compensation Management for Banks*. Boston: Bankers Publishing Company, 1986.

Caruth, Donald L., and Gail D. Handlogten. *Managing Compensation (and Understanding It Too)*. Westport, CT: Quorum Books, 2001.

Caruth, Donald L., and Steven Austin Stovall. *NTC's American Business Terms Dictionary*. Lincolnwood, IL: National Textbook Company, 1994.

Cascio, Wayne F. *Costing Human Resources.* 4th ed. Cincinnati, OH: South-Western College Publishing, 2000.

Cascio, Wayne F. *Managing Human Resources: Productivity, Quality of Work Life, Profits*. 7th ed. New York: McGraw-Hill Irwin, 2006.

Challenger, James E. *Outplacement.* Chicago: Challenger, Gray & Christmas, Inc., 1994.

Cihon, Patrick J., and James Ottavio Castagnera. *Employment and Labor Law.* Cincinnati, OH: West Educational Publishing Company, 1999.

Dessler, Gary. *A Framework for Human Resource Management.* 4th ed. Upper Saddle River, NJ: Pearson Prentice Hall, 2006.

Drucker, Peter F. *Management: Tasks, Responsibilities, Practices.* New York: Harper & Row, 1974.

Fear, Richard A. *The Evaluation Interview.* 3rd ed. New York: McGraw-Hill Book Company, 1973.

Greer, Charles R. *Strategic Human Resource Management: A General Managerial Approach.* 2nd ed. Upper Saddle River, NJ: Prentice-Hall, 2001.

Guion, Robert M., and Scott Highhouse. *Essentials of Personnel Assessment and Selection.* Mahwah, NJ: Lawerence Erlbaum Associates Publishers, 2006.

Heneman, Herbert G., III, and Timothy A. Judge. *Staffing Organizations.* 5th ed. Middleton, WI: Mendota House, 2006.

Howard, Phillip K. *The Death of Common Sense: How Law Is Suffocating America.* New York: Random House, 1994.

HR Department Benchmarks and Analysis 2007. Washington, DC: BNA, Inc., 2007.

Jarrell, Donald W. *Human Resource Planning.* Englewood Cliffs, NJ: Prentice-Hall, 1993.

Kummerow, Jean M. *New Directions in Career Planning and the Workplace.* 2nd ed. Palo Alto, CA: Davies-Black Publishing, 2000.

Latham, Gary P., and Kenneth N. Wexley. *Increasing Productivity through Performance Appraisal.* 2nd ed. Reading, MA: Addison-Wesley Publishing Company, 1994.

Lindemann, Barbara, Paul Grossman, and C. Geoffrey Weirich. *Employment Discrimination Law.* 4th ed., vols. I and II. Washington, DC: BNA Books, 2007.

Mondy, R. Wayne, and Robert M. Noe III. *Human Resource Management.* 5th ed. Boston: Allyn and Bacon, 1993.

Murphy, Kevin R., and Jeanette N. Cleveland. *Understanding Performance Appraisal: Social, Organizational, and Goal-Based Perspectives.* Thousand Oaks, CA: Sage Publications, Inc., 1995.

Neter, John, Michael H. Kutner, Christopher J. Nachtscheim, and William Wasserman. *Applied Linear Regression Models.* 3rd ed. Chicago, IL: Irwin, 1996.

Noe, Raymond A., John R. Hollenbeck, Barry Gerhart, and Patrick M. Wright. *Human Resource Management: Gaining a Competitive Advantage.* 6th ed. New York: McGraw-Hill Irwin, 2008.

Robbins, Stephen P., and Timothy A. Judge. *Organizational Behavior.* 12th ed. Upper Saddle River, NJ: Pearson Education, Inc., 2007.

Rutherglen, George. *Employment Discrimination Law.* New York: Foundation Press, 2001.

Schlei, Barbara Lindemann, and Paul Grossman. *Employment Discrimination Law.* Washington, DC: Bureau of National Affairs, 1983.

Smither, J. W. (Ed.), *Performance Appraisal: State of the Art in Practice.* San Francisco: Jossey-Bass Publishers, 1998.

Twomey, David P. *Labor and Employment Law.* 3rd ed. Cincinnati, OH: West Educational Publishing Company, 2001.

U.S. Department of Labor. *Federal Contract Compliance Manual.* Washington, DC: U.S. Government Printing Office, 1998.

U.S. Department of Labor. *The Revised Handbook for Analyzing Jobs*. Washington, DC: U.S. Government Printing Office, 1991.

Walker, James W. *Human Resource Planning*. New York: McGraw-Hill Book Company, 1980.

Walsh, James. *Rightful Termination*. Santa Monica, CA: Merritt Publishing, 1994.

Table of Cases

Index

About the Authors

Donald L. Caruth is Professor of Management at Texas A&M/Commerce. He spent thirty years in the private sector as an HR consultant, both with his own company and with Drake Beam Morin, among others. He is the author of numerous books and articles, including *Managing Compensation* (Praeger, 2001).

Gail D. Caruth is principal of Human Resource Management Systems, a Texas-based HR consultancy. She is a certified mediator and arbitrator and author or coauthor of more than thirty articles and books, including *Managing Compensation* (Praeger, 2001).

Stephanie S. Pane is Assistant Professor of Management at Texas A&M/Commerce. She received her Ph.D. from Rensselaer Polytechnic Institute in 2006.